BY PETER GOLDMAN

Civil Rights: The Challenge of the Fourteenth Amendment

Report from Black America

The Death and Life of Malcolm X

NEWSWEEK BOOKS BY PETER GOLDMAN
WITH VARIOUS CO-AUTHORS

Charlie Company: What Vietnam Did to Us

(with Tony Fuller, Vern E. Smith and others)

The Quest for the Presidency 1984

(with Tony Fuller, Lucille Beachy, Thomas M. DeFrank, Vern E.

Smith and others)

The End of the World That Was

(with Lucille Beachy and others)

Brothers

(with Sylvester Monroe, Vern E. Smith and others)

BY VERN E. SMITH

The Jones Men

BY ROY WILKINS WITH TOM MATHEWS

Standing Fast: The Autobiography of Roy Wilkins

THE QUEST FOR THE PRESIDENCY 1988

Peter Goldman
Tom Mathews

and the **Newsweek** *Special Election Team*

A TOUCHSTONE BOOK
Published by Simon & Schuster Inc.
New York London Toronto Sydney Tokyo

Simon and Schuster/Touchstone
Simon & Schuster Building
Rockefeller Center
1230 Avenue of the Americas
New York, New York 10020

1   3   5   7   9   10   8   6   4   2
1   3   5   7   9   10   8   6   4   2 pbk.

Library of Congress Cataloging in Publication Data

Goldman, Peter Louis, date.
The quest for the presidency, 1988 / Peter Goldman, Tom Mathews,
and the Newsweek special election team.
p.   cm.
"A Touchstone book."
1. Presidents—United States—Election—1988.   2. United States—
Politics and government—1981–1989.   I. Mathews, Tom.
II. Newsweek.   III. Title.
E880.G65   1989
324.973′0927—dc20   89-19710
                                                                                      CIP

ISBN 0-671-69079-5
0-671-69080-9 pbk.

THE QUEST FOR THE PRESIDENCY 1988

by Peter Goldman and Tom Mathews
with
Lucille Beachy
Thomas M. DeFrank
Shawn Doherty
Vern E. Smith
Bill Turque
Anne Underwood
Lauren Picker

For John J. Lindsay, again,
in fond memory
and for those players in politics
who care not only about who wins
but why

No man is a hero to his valet.

—Madame de Cornuel, c. 1670

Handlers and consultants and managers always tend to view the candidate as a necessary pain in the ass.

—David Keene, a Republican campaign consultant, 1988

Contents

CONTENTS

Foreword

□═════════════════□

EXCEPT IN THEIR MOST PARTISAN HUMORS, Americans approaching a presidential election like to think, or hope, that the best man wins. A defensible case could be made that that was the outcome in 1988; the real as against the campaign-model George Bush was a man of intelligent mind, good manners, peaceful temperament and cautious politics, and was vastly more experienced in national and world affairs than the novice running against him. But he never quite closed the case for himself on those terms, not during the course of his campaign or, for that matter, in his quarter century in public life. His unfavorable rating in the polls on Election Day was at a level thought by his own campaign manager to make a candidate unelectable. Bush became our forty-first president not so much because he had proven himself the best man as because he—or, more accurately, his promoters— persuaded his fellow citizens that Michael Dukakis was even worse.

This book is the eyewitness record of how that outcome was engineered and an introduction to the men and women who engineered it—not only the candidates but those tradespeople of modern politics who have come to be known as handlers. We began following them full time as early as the winter of 1986–87, nearly two years before Election Day, on assignment for *Newsweek;* a much shorter first draft of this work appeared as the centerpiece of a special issue of the magazine, published a day and a half after the polls closed. But our reporting did not end even then. Members of our team stayed in the field for weeks or months thereafter, reinterviewing old sources and developing new ones; the last dispatch from the last correspondent at work on the project came in the day before the finished manuscript was delivered to the publisher.

Over those two years, we achieved a rare and intimate degree of access to the inner workings of presidential politics while the campaign was still in progress. Our team operated separately from reporters, writers and editors involved in *Newsweek*'s week-to-week political coverage; the project's director and principal writer was in fact not a *Newsweek* staff member but a contributing editor, and his office off the premises was the central repository for our reporting and our substantial file of confidential memos, papers and polls. Our understanding with our sources was that our findings would remain confidential within the project team and would not be published until after the returns were in. We did not encounter anything so shattering as to alter the outcome of the election, nor did we expect to. If any such information had come into our hands, we would have recommended to our editors that we abort the project and publish it. But secrets of the sort that bend history are usually leaked to daily and weekly journalists precisely in the hope of producing such an effect. Our interest instead was in the way we choose our presidents, a process regularly described by participants in it as lunatic. Our agreement to hold our findings confidential for the duration was our passkey—and our readers'—into the places and the minds where politics happens.

We believe that the time, intensity and person power we devoted to the effort was unique in the quarter-century history of these campaign chronicles. Thomas M. DeFrank, *Newsweek*'s veteran chief White House correspondent, and Bill Turque, then a Detroit correspondent, covered the Republican contenders from the seedling days of their respective campaigns to the election of George Bush and beyond; their entrée was facilitated by DeFrank's acquaintance of more than fifteen years with the vice president and with his most senior associates. Lucille Beachy, a special-projects correspondent based in New York, and Shawn Doherty, then assigned to the Boston bureau, reported the Democrats; they were joined for long passages by Vern E. Smith, the magazine's Atlanta bureau chief, who followed Jesse Jackson's extraordinary second run for the presidency. Anne Underwood and Lauren Picker, both researchers in the New York office, joined in the reporting effort and made valuable contributions to it.

Our relations with most of the candidates and their managers were smooth and made smoother by the fact that we had done a similar project and produced a similar book in 1984. The rules of the game and several of the faces on our reporting team—Beachy, DeFrank and Smith—were familiar to a sizable number of the permanent corps of campaign professionals. We encountered passages of static with the vice president, who bore *Newsweek* a grudge for a cover story that had displeased him, and with some of the governor's senior people, who held the press generally in some contempt; one prominent Boston journalist was counted "part of the family" for his friendship and occasional assistance to the campaign, but epithets like "nincompoops" and "bimbos" were common currency at Dukakis headquarters for reporters as a class. These problems, happily, were resolved during our years in the field, and silence, in any case, is not easily enforced in politics. The rewards of participating in the quest for the presidency, beyond money, influence and notoriety, include the sense that one is living and shaping history. It is a verbal trade almost by definition, and people high on so heady a wine almost always like to talk about it.

It tends to be a cynical trade as well. Some of its practitioners have ideals, or had them when they got into the business of winning elections; some can even be described as political romantics, doing what needs to be done to turn ideals into agendas for action. What was disturbing about the 1988 election, both for itself and as a harbinger of our future, was that ideals were never really in play. It was instead a contest between two men who could not say with any precision why they wanted to be president, or why they ought to be. In the circumstances, there was no agenda to fight for, only victory for its own sake. The result was a contest at manipulation, a war between high-tech button-pushers unburdened by contending visions or issues, and, whatever else one made of the outcome, the better button men surely won.

Our debts are numerous, to our colleagues at *Newsweek* and to many others. They begin with the men and women who covered the campaign for the weekly magazine; our own million or so words of reporting were reinforced and enriched by their remarkably skilled work in the trenches and on the campaign planes. We are especially grateful to our 1984 co-author, Tony Fuller, who directed the magazine's weekly political coverage as national-affairs editor, and to Evan Thomas, the Washington bureau chief, who oversaw much of the reporting and who helped bring us together with Simon and Schuster. We are indebted as well to the correspondents who chronicled the campaign as it unfolded, among them Howard Fineman,

Margaret Garrard Warner, Eleanor Clift, Ann McDaniel and Sylvester Monroe, all of the Washington bureau; Ginny Carroll, then Detroit (and now Houston) bureau chief, who covered the Robertson campaign for the magazine and, in those small windows of time when she could be spared, for this project; to numerous correspondents in *Newsweek*'s domestic network, especially John McCormick in Chicago, Mark Starr in Boston, Erik Calonius in Miami, Michael Reese in Los Angeles, Peter McKillop in New York, and others who reported the campaign on the ground; and to an all-pro team of photographers, principally Arthur Grace, Larry Downing, Jacques Chenet and Ira Wyman, for their war stories as well as their pictures.

Our own team was blessed with a relay of researchers drawn from among *Newsweek*'s very best, starting with Melanie Cooper in the earliest days of the project, then Anne Underwood, and finally Lauren Picker, joined by Constance Wiley in the closing rush at the magazine. Picker stayed on to work on the book, both as the guardian of its accuracy and as a member of the reporting team. She and her colleagues were our first vigilant line of defense against errors of fact and interpretation, a task they discharged with wit and grace under trying and, toward the end, impossible conditions. They were aided throughout by *Newsweek*'s library director, Ted Slate, and his staff, especially his assistant director, Peter J. Salber, a reference librarian of invincible patience and magical skill. If this is not an error-free work, that is the authors' fault, not theirs.

Our further thanks are due to Richard M. Smith, the magazine's editor-in-chief, who made the necessary commitments of resources and of encouragement to the project; to Maynard Parker, *Newsweek*'s editor, who launched it, and especially to Kenneth Auchincloss, the managing editor, who shepherded the magazine version to print with his customary intelligence, engagement and care. Robert Rivard, chief of correspondents, shaped our reporting team, and Annabel Bentley, chief of research, chose our researchers; we hope this book does justice to the concern and insight they brought to the selection process. The magazine version was greatly enhanced by the work of *Newsweek*'s art director, Patricia Bradbury; its picture editor, Karen Mullarkey; and photo editor Guy Cooper. Lynn Povich, a senior editor, was a source of wisdom and counsel on this as on many past special projects. Rollene Saal led the search for the right home for the book version, and Alice Mayhew of Simon and Schuster saw possibilities in it; we are indebted to her and to George Hodgman for their large role in its publication.

Helen Dudar, the writer and critic, was once again First Reader, a task to which she brought a literate eye, a sensitive touch and a loving concern both for the work and for its principal writer.

Most of all, we are grateful to the more than four hundred men and women who, engaged in the highest-stakes game in American politics, found time for us when there was none—often many hours spread over multiple sittings—and responded to our questions with patience, intelligence and candor. If some of them appear minimally or not at all in these pages, it should not be taken as a reflection on their contributions to their respective campaigns. This book is not a scorecard for professionals, the worth of the players to be measured by the number of times they are mentioned. It is instead, or attempts to be, a common reader's guide to presidential politics as it is lived and practiced in the media age. It is the record of high hopes and steep falls, of grand strategies and desperate improvisations, of moments of genius and passages of foolishness, of dreams ground under by adversity or sacrificed to the higher end of winning.

It is the collective memoir of a presidential election, perhaps the first, in which the handlers so completely upstaged the candidates as to become the principal players. Every one of our sources was a contributor to it in some degree, whether visibly or not, and we would like to extend our thanks to them here—to Will Abbott, Tara Agen, Roger Ailes, Steven Akey, Madeleine Albright, Michael Alcamo, Art Athens, Harvey Atwater, Lee Atwater, Toddy Atwater, Gerald Austin, David Axelrod, Bruce Babbitt, Hattie Babbitt, Douglas Bailey, Sandra Bakalar, Charlie Baker, James A. Baker III, James David Barber, Bob Beckel, Dave Beckwith, Paul Begala, Jeff Bell, Sergio Bendixen, Terry Bergman, Berkley Bedell, Jeff Bingaman, Tony Bisignano, Charlie Black, John Blackshaw, Lucien Blackwell, Paul Bograd, Rich Bond, Robert Borosage, Katie Boyle, Bob Bradsell, Donna Brazile, William Broadhurst, Bill Brock, Pat Brock, Paul Brountas, Floyd Brown, Ralph Brown, Ron Brown, Sally Brown, Dan Buck, John Buckley, George Burger, George Bush, George W. Bush, Michael Calabrese, Sue Calegari, Debra Callahan, Andrea Camp, Carroll Campbell, Chuck Campion, Heather Campion, Joe Canzeri, Andrew Card, David Carle, Robert Carley, Dave Carney, Bill Carrick, Rita Carrillo, Barry Carter, Sue Casey, Carl Casselman, Alex Castellanos, Hale Champion.

And to Joe Chaplinski, Marvin Chernoff, Kip Cheroutes, Pat Choate, Jim Cicconi, Nancy Clark, Forrest Claypool, Bill Clinton, Del Marie Cobb, John Connorton Jr., Jack Corrigan, Tom Cosgrove, Roger Craver, Jerry Crawford, Steve Crawford, Page Crosland, Gerald Crotty, Rhonda

Culpepper, Andrew Cuomo, Mario Cuomo, David D'Alessandro, Leslie Dach, Allison Dalton, Bill Dalton, Mitch Daniels, Richard Darman, Michael Deaver, Michael Del Giudice, Kristin Demong, John DeVillars, Don Devine, Tad Devine, Bill Dixon, David Doak, Elizabeth Dole, Robert Dole, Tom Donilon, Jim Dorsey, David Dryer, Pete du Pont, Kenneth Duberstein, Eugene J. Duffy, Andrea Dukakis, John Dukakis, Kara Dukakis, Kitty Dukakis, Michael S. Dukakis, Dayton Duncan, Chris Dunn, Dick Durbin, Fred DuVal, Paul Eckstein, Bob Edgar, Chris Edley, Eric Elbot, Robert Ellsworth, John Emerson, Carter Eskew, Susan Estrich, Tony Fabrizio, Bob Farmer, Geraldine Ferraro, Vic Fingerhut, Floyd Fithian, Marlin Fitzwater, Don Foley, Pat Forciea, Dennis Frankenberry, Sigrud Freese, Sandy Frucher, Craig Fuller, Paul Furiga, Gary Galanis, Doug Gamble, Michael Ganley, Duane Garrett, David Garth, Mark Gearan, Bill Geary, Bart Gellman, Don Gephardt, Jane Gephardt, Loreen Gephardt, Richard Gephardt, Doug Gerhart, Mark Gersh, Dick Giesser, Sid Gillman, Larry Gilpin, Newt Gingrich.

And to Mark Gitenstein, Alixe Glen, Tom Glynn, Vic Gold, Michael Goldman, Robert Goodman, Bob Goodwin, Al Gore, Pauline Gore, Tipper Gore, Bob Grady, Chuck Grassley, Stanley Greenberg, Tom Griscom, Mandy Grunwald, Jon Haber, Hal Haddon, Alexander M. Haig Jr., Marcia Hale, Chris Hamel, William Hamilton, Judy Harbaugh, Larry Harrington, Brad Harris, Louis Harris, Tubby Harrison, Lee Hart, Peter Hart, Tom Herman, John Holum, Pamela Huey, Ira Jackson, Jesse Jackson, Peter Jacobs, Paul Jacobson, Kathleen Hall Jamieson, Paul Jensen, Deborah Johns, Mark Johnson, Nancy M. Jones, Lowell Junkins, Elaine Kamarck, Karan Kaplar, Hackie Kassler, Ron Kaufman, Ted Kaufman, Frank Keefe, David Keene, Jack Kemp, Joanne Kemp, Judith Kemp, Ned Kennan, Leslie Kerman, Ken Khachigian, Tom Kiley, Jim Kilpatrick, Josh King, Ethel Klein, Peter Knight, Perry Knop, Mike Kopp, Tom Korologos, John Kraushar, Nancy Kuhn, Ellen Kurz, Bill Lacy, Celinda Lake, Jim Lake, Bert Lance, Nate Landow, Tony Lane, Ed Lashman, John Law, Ed Lazarus, Denise Lee, Robert Lighthizer, Marty Linsky, Ronnie Lopez, Mindy Lubber, Mary Lukens, Brian Lunde, Dotty Lynch, Malcolm Mac-Dougall, Jon Macks, Paul Manafort, Vada Manager, Charles Manatt, Charles Marck, Mike Marshall, Thurgood Marshall Jr., Fred Martin, John Marttila.

And to Mari Maseng, Paul Maslin, Colin Mathews, Tom Mathews, John Maxwell, Laura May, Bob McAlister, Terry McAuliffe, Ed McCabe, Larry McCarthy, Mitch McConnell, Mike McCurry, John McDonald, Robert McElvaine, Mark Mellman, Ronda Menka, Terry Michael, Scott

Miller, Pat Mitchell, Nick Mitropoulos, Ron Mix, Richard Moe, Linda Moore, Hank Morris, Mike Muir, Janet Mullins, Mike Murphy, Steve Murphy, Paul Nace, Roy Neel, Jeff Nesbit, Sally Novetzke, Nancy Nusser, Francis O'Brien, Patricia O'Brien, Terry O'Connell, Kirk O'Donnell, Barbara Opacki, Fabian Palomino, Barbara Pape, Dan Payne, Dave Petts, Paul Pezzella, Jim Pinkerton, Tully Plesser, John Podesta, Tony Podesta, Nan Powell, Scott Probasco, David Prosperi, Dan Quayle, Jack Quinn, Steve Rabinowitz, Gerald Rafshoon, Larry Rasky, Tom Rath, Bruce Reed, John Reed, Scott Reed, Herb Regal, Ed Reilly, Joe Ricca, Vicki Rideout, Tim Ridley, Ethan Riegelhaupt, Walt Riker, Don Ringe, Steve Roberts, Will Robinson, Dennis Rochford, Ed Rogers, Ed Rollins, Bill Romjue, Richard Rosenbaum, Steve Rosenfeld, Warren Rudman, John Russonello, Ed Rutkowski, Larry J. Sabato, Fred Salvucci, John Sasso, Chris Sauter, Andy Savitz, Arlie Schardt, Robert Schiffer, Arthur M. Schlesinger Jr.

And to Harrison Schmitt, Greg Schneiders, Jim Schroeder, Pat Schroeder, Brent Scowcroft, John Sears, Buie Seawell, Eli Segal, Kim Shafer, Jeanne Shaheen, Bob Shaine, Mike Shea, Rod Shealy, Michael Sheehan, Craig Shirley, Bill Shore, Bob Shrum, Arthur Simon, Jeanne Simon, Paul Simon, Martin Simon, Sheila Simon, Joanne Simons, Jerry Sinclair, Lea Sinclair, Jean Sindad, Barney Skladany, Peter Smith, Vann Snyder, Pam Solo, Theodore Sorensen, David Sparks, Stu Spencer, Bud Spillane, John Spinola, Robert Squier, Martin Steadman, Deborah Steelman, Fred Steeper, Jim Steinberg, Mark Steitz, Terry Stephan, Greg Stevens, Roger Stone, Bob Strauss, Ray Strother, Katie Sullivan, Paul Sullivan, John Sununu, Barry Surman, Gary Susnjara, Kevin Sweeney, Ken Swope, Tom Synhorst, Sheila Tate, Pete Teeley, Bob Teeter, Lance Tarrance, Dixon Terry, Don Terry, Ginny Terzano, Warren Tompkins, Alice Travis, Joe Trippi, Paul Tully, Marco Turbovich, Margaret Tutwiler, David Van Note, Teresa Vilmain, Lorraine Voles, Jude Wanniski, Joe Warren, Frank Watkins, Norman Watts, Vin Weber, Jack Weeks, Stan Wellborn, Kim Wells, Ralph Whitehead, Bernie Windon, Richard Wirthlin, George Wittgraf, Bill Woodward, Richard Ybarra, Andrew Young, David Zamichow, Amy Zisook, Cliff Zukin. We are grateful as well for having been granted access to several privately circulated memos and papers by Richard M. Nixon.

PETER GOLDMAN

New York City
June 1989

PART ONE

THE REAGAN TWILIGHT

Pay no attention to that man behind the curtain.

—THE WIZARD, UNVEILED, IN *THE WIZARD OF OZ*, 1939

The Star and the Second Banana

THE MARINE HELICOPTER RODE LOW through the Washington night, bearing Ronald Reagan home to a capital already caught up in the wars of succession to the presidency. The election was a year away, but Reagan's mood was valedictory, and his view of the men contesting to be his heir was shadowed by doubt. It wasn't so much the Democrats who troubled his thoughts: Michael Dukakis was barely a blip on the screen in those days, one more indistinct face in that same old tax-and-spend gang he had been running against all his political life. No, it was the leading Republican candidates who gave Reagan pause. He had begun thinking ahead to his place in history—his wife and her friends were at him constantly on that subject—and he wasn't entirely sure that George Bush was the right executor for his estate.

Reagan had been on a bit of a losing streak at that juncture in his presidency; his Reagan Revolution was near stalemate in a hostile Congress, his sleight-of-hand approach to economics had weighed down his countrymen with debt, and his people kept getting entangled in scandals of policy and money. But he seemed personally immune to blame. His popularity was nearly as high in his last year as it had been in his first, and his blessing still seemed worth fighting for. Vice President Bush and his principal rival, Robert J. Dole, the Senate minority leader, jostled like schoolboys for some show of his favor; the smallest wink toward one would set the other rumbling at levels measurable on the Richter scale.

The View from the Helicopter Window

The president wasn't taking sides, not, at least, on the record. His public neutrality was in part a convenient mask; it concealed both his closet preference for Bush and his nagging reservations about both men. Take Senator Dole, he mused, gazing absently out the window of his helicopter at the city he had conquered seven years before. Washington was Dole's town, not his; Reagan had governed it for those seven years as if he were the head of a civil army of occupation. Dole *belonged* there. He was too much the legislative animal, Reagan said, too wholly the product of his quarter century on Capitol Hill and his two turns as Republican leader in the Senate.

The president had long suspected Dole of lukewarmth in his enthusiasm for the Reagan Creed; he seemed to do only what his duties as party leader required and not much more. He was most notorious for his sharp tongue, and, to Reagan's irritation, he had already turned it on Bush, accusing him of complicity in the attempt to ransom some American hostages by selling arms to Iran. Didn't Dole understand, Reagan wondered, that he wasn't only hurting George—he was hurting the president too? A piece was missing from Dole's makeup. Dole was tactics, an inside trader willing to barter away basic principles, Reagan said, in the interests of closing a deal. Dole needed more grounding, more *philosophy* if he were ever to be a good president.

The president's feelings about Congressman Jack F. Kemp of Buffalo, though unspoken, were plain to the men around him. There had been a time when Kemp had seemed his natural heir, a figure of youth, energy, optimism and boundless belief in the first principles of Reaganism. Kemp was in fact the chief author of the tax cut that, in two hundred days in 1981, elevated a fancy called "supply-side economics" into law; he could thus fairly claim to be a father of the Revolution.

But Kemp was a little abstract for a man of Reagan's commonsensical cast of mind, a bit *too* true a believer, and a lot too preachy besides. Get Kemp started on the Laffer curve or the gold standard at the president's regular Tuesday-morning meeting with the congressional leadership, people in the room said, and you couldn't turn him off. He was as ardent as

Savonarola in defense of the faith, and twice as talky; regulars at the table could see Reagan's jaw tightening in barely contained annoyance. Reagan owed Kemp a lot, for his ideas and for his zeal. Still, the inside betting was that, as a senior party official put it, the only way the president would look favorably on a Kemp candidacy would be if it lost.

Reagan's heart belonged instead to his old running mate, though with a curious lack of passion after all their years together. He praised Bush on television once as "the finest vice president in my memory," a plug that set Dole burning up the phone line to the White House in a fury. In fact, Reagan's manner had been that of an uncle speaking of a nephew of not very great attainments. The men around him understood that the emotion governing Reagan's regard for Bush was loyalty rather than love.

They had, in fact, had a hard time selling Bush to Reagan in the first place, seven years before. Reagan seemed to understand the political rationale for making the match, as a way of offsetting his own cowboy conservatism with the scent of old money and J. Press tweed; but getting him to say yes, one adviser remembered, had been as painful as pulling teeth.

"Why?" the adviser asked late one night before the 1980 convention. "What's your hesitancy about Bush?"

"It was the debate," Reagan answered.

"What do you mean, it was the debate?"

Reagan meant their celebrated debate in Nashua, New Hampshire, during the 1980 primary season, when the two of them had been the leading contenders for the Republican nomination. Bush had made a fuss about the ground rules, demanding, in concert with the local newspaper nominally sponsoring the show, that he and Reagan go at it one on one with no other contenders onstage. But Reagan, whose campaign was paying the bills for the debate, had wanted the rest included, and when the newspaper editor had tried to silence him he had reached into his attic of movie memories and retrieved the perfect line of dialogue from an otherwise forgotten film. "I'm paying for this microphone, Mr. Green," he had scolded the editor. Bush hadn't known how to respond. He had just sat there in tongue-tied silence, a beaten man; the debate had ended before it had properly begun.

"I'm wary of a man who freezes under pressure," Reagan said. "George Bush froze that night. That haunts me."

The match had been made anyway, and the intervening years had greatly softened Reagan's feelings about his vice president. A sound working relationship evolved between them, and with it a bond of trust; the president owed his partner *something* for his seven years of self-effacing service. Yet he watched Bush's rush to the top of the polls with mixed emotions. The old doubts lingered in his mind, questions, privately put, as to whether George was strong enough or leaderly enough for the job. Reagan liked Bush all right; everybody did. It was the question of his toughness that troubled people, and seven years on, the president still wasn't sure it was there.

Neither were there many cheerleaders around him urging Bush's cause. The widespread view in Washington and beyond was that there was something damp about Bush, or, anyway, in the way he came across as a public man—a taint of softness that had come to be known in the political trade as the Wimp Factor. The label enraged Bush, and people who knew him well considered it a case of badly mistaken identity; he was, in their view, a strong, bright, capable and profoundly decent man. But he was imprisoned in his stereotype like a man under house arrest, and relays of speech coaches and image doctors had been unable to deliver him from it. In a confidential early survey for Dole, the polltaker Richard Wirthlin had put the proposition in statement form: "There's just something about Bush that bothers me. Maybe he's a wimp." More than a third of the Republicans in Wirthlin's sample had agreed, a heavy load of baggage for the vice president to carry among the voters he needed first and most to please.

The suspicion was shared in the White House and did not stop with the end of the working day. Nancy Reagan found Bush a bit whiny, so she told friends, and wanting in backbone besides when she needed help persuading her husband to do what was good for him. There was, for one example, the passage early in 1987 when she and her court concluded that Donald T. Regan had become a liability as White House chief of staff and set about engineering his removal. The cabal tried through an intermediary, a confidant of Bush's, to enlist him in their cause; their plan was that the vice president call on Regan and tell him it was time to go. Bush refused. If the president wasn't inviting Regan to leave, he said, *he* certainly wasn't going to.

"Christ, he *is* a wimp," his friend muttered audibly, leaving Bush's office.

Bush finally did make the call, but only after the president himself had sent a public signal to Regan to start packing. The vice president's visit at that point amounted to little more than piling on, but he wanted credit for it and tried to get the White House staff to leak the story of his heroism. With barely concealed delight, they refused.

What Happened to George?

The doubters had an influential further voice in Richard M. Nixon; like Reagan himself, he was rigorously neutral for the record and seriously concerned in his private ruminations about whether Bush or anyone else in the Republican field was electable. Even in exile, the sage of Saddle River maintained a shrewd and active interest in politics; circumstance had made him largely a spectator, but his history and his connections guaranteed him a skybox seat, and as his own disgrace receded deeper into the past he found a widening audience for his counsel. Most of the party's contenders for president had made the pilgrimage to New Jersey for audiences with him—all of them, in fact, except George Bush. It did not suit the vice president's strategy of caution to risk being seen in Nixon's company, and his absence widened the divide between him and the former president.

As was his practice with an election year approaching, Nixon wrote a memo handicapping the race in the late spring of 1987 and circulated it privately among his friends in politics. His language on paper was circumspect. He worried the conventional worries about Bush's image—''he comes through as a weak individual on television''—and about Dole's waspish humor; voters, Nixon wrote, quoting Lord Blake, are suspicious of ''wits and cynics.'' The best thing the Republicans had going for them, indeed, was ''the weakness of the Democrats,'' he went on. ''There has never been such a motley collection of what former Ambassador William Bullitt used to call first-rate second-rate men.'' Only a timely downturn in the economy could save them from themselves; in a recession, Nixon ventured, ''the Democrats could nominate a jackass and probably win.''

He was almost as tough on the Republicans in informal talks with friends, and not nearly so sanguine about their chances. The former president visited Washington that summer, taking rooms, as usual, in a hotel away from the gawking crowds downtown, and, through an aide, he invited one of his favorites among the younger campaign consultants to come by and talk politics. ''He hasn't prepared,'' Nixon's man said. Spontaneity had never come naturally to Nixon; usually, he composed his conversation in advance and received his callers in a litter of yellow legal paper. This time, the tabletop before him was bare of notes. He was still organizing his thoughts on 1988.

His tour of the horizon was not a sunny one. He had always expected a close election, something like his own matchup with John F. Kennedy in 1960, and he seemed more pessimistic than optimistic about the outcome.

He remained unimpressed by the crowd chasing the Democratic nomination, dismissing them as mediocrities. Their strongest candidate would have been Mario Cuomo of New York, a politician, in Nixon's not unenvious view, with the gift of poetry; their problem was that Cuomo was not, or did not appear to be, running.

What troubled Nixon more was the drift of the Republican race. He plainly preferred Dole and had, in fact, become his frequent backstairs adviser. Dole was smart, experienced and tough—*very* tough, Nixon had written in his memo—and toughness was a quality he had always admired above all others. But the senator's organization was weak. He tended to be a one-man band, Nixon complained, and his headstrong ways worked to the detriment of his campaign.

It was Bush who held all the cards, in Nixon's practiced size-up; Bush had money, organization and position at Reagan's right hand, and no one else except Dole was even in the game. Nixon wasn't uncomfortable with Jack Kemp, but it was hard for him to see how anyone could manage the leap from the House to the presidency. He was fond of General Alexander M. Haig Jr., and owed him a large debt of gratitude for his service as White House chief of staff during the Watergate years; still, Haig's only shot at the prize depended on foreign policy's becoming the driving issue, and that didn't appear to be happening. Pete du Pont, the former governor of Delaware, would make an attractive candidate sometime, but not, Nixon guessed, in 1988. Pat Robertson, the evangelical Christian broadcaster, was a nonstarter—a man with as much chance of winning the Republican nomination as George C. Wallace had had on the Democratic side in 1968. No, Nixon's money instead was on Bush, which was, by his lights, precisely the problem. Bush, he feared, was a loser.

There were traces of regret in his judgment; he could, in fact, be said to have created Bush as a national figure. It was Nixon who had coaxed him out of a safe congressional seat into a losing race for the Senate in Texas in 1970; when that didn't work out, he had named Bush ambassador to the United Nations as a consolation prize. Other blue-chip assignments had followed under Nixon and his successor, Gerald R. Ford; Bush had chaired the Republican National Committee during the Watergate siege and afterward did turns as the United States envoy to China and as director of the Central Intelligence Agency.

Bush's value to Nixon had been at least partly ornamental, a touch of borrowed class; as the then president once put it in a memo, George would do anything for the cause, and his eagerness to serve was put to excellent decorative use. Bush made rather more of his assignments in his résumé than his patron had given them in practice. Nixon was amused, for example, at hearing a campaign claim on TV that Bush had played a major backstage role in the diplomatic opening to China. *Ridiculous,* the former president snorted; George not only had nothing to do with the venture, he didn't know a goddam thing about it at the time.

Bush, to be sure, had carried out his duties with the same fidelity and discretion he would later bring to the Reagan presidency. "He takes our line beautifully," a senior White House staff man enthused at the time, and he would repeat it publicly on command. But Nixon found something wanting in Bush, some lack of strength and conviction. Bush had taken Barry Goldwater's line just as beautifully in 1964, when Nixon had first encountered him in politics; he seemed not to have beliefs of his own. Nixon had served in the Senate long ago with Prescott S. Bush, the vice president's father, and the comparison, in his eyes, was not flattering. Pres Bush was smart and tough, tough as nails, Nixon recalled, almost sadly; I don't know what happened to George.

It puzzled him further that, in twenty years on a national and even global stage, Bush had never blazed his own path, never created a loyal following of his own. Nixon had had that when he was vice president; maybe 35 percent of the electorate would have died for him, he reckoned, as the premier anti-Communist of his day. Bush had no such hard core, no true believers. All Nixon's friends said they were for Bush, the ex-president told his visitor in the summer of 1987, but in the next breath they said he couldn't win. They had said that about Robert A. Taft in 1952, he recalled—they had said it so often that it got to be a slogan, and finally a self-fulfilling prophecy when Eisenhower won the Republican nomination.

At the Eve of Battle

It had become nearly a mantra about Bush at the eve of battle; no one seemed to believe in him as a presidential politician, not even his friends, and Ronald Reagan was neither deaf nor immune to their doubts. It had been years since the tastemakers of politics and journalism had been pleased with the available choice of candidates; disdain for all of them had become the vogue in Washington and in the national press, and no one in the class of '88 seemed able to fight off the virus, not Bush or anyone else. Not even the men charged with selling the vice president in the marketplace believed in their merchandise. Most of them had served in the Reagan wars of 1980 and 1984 and had been spoiled by his talent for the game. Reagan was a superstar, Bush a second banana; he had played Best Friend so naturally for so long that his own handlers doubted his readiness for top billing.

Reagan wished it were otherwise. Whatever his qualms, his vice president was the nearest thing he had to a surrogate, the heir who would carry on his name and his ideas after he was gone. But protocol forbade his taking sides, and in the late evening of his presidency he no longer had the power to make things happen.

He had had that magic once, but his authority had been battered by events and diminished by time and encroaching old age. There were days when even his most loyal retainers thought he looked smaller and frailer, days when they asked themselves whether, in his seventy-seventh year, the old man wasn't losing it at last. Reagan would be playing to posterity in his final months in office. He would campaign for the Republican nominee, of course, but the few chips he had left were otherwise largely reserved for his arms-control negotiations with Mikhail Gorbachev. His claim to a place in the pantheon, a quest that concerned him and consumed his wife, came down to doing deals with the rulers of the formerly Evil Empire.

Nothing else mattered at the end, not, anyway, to Nancy Reagan. She had spent thirty-five years as the guardian of her husband's well-being, and all that mattered to her in his last year was his safe passage out of Washington into history. "Get him home!" she commanded a member of his senior staff one day in the winter of 1987–88. The conclusion that most of his men had reached by then was that Reagan, in his heart and mind, was already halfway there.

The Wizard of Us

A PRESIDENTIAL ELECTION IS A RITE of renewal in America, a leap of faith from past to future and from old leaders to new. But a gray autumnal mood hung over the early days of the 1988 campaign, as if a long Indian summer were drawing to a close. A deep vein of anxiety ran just beneath the surface contentment in the polls, a sense of impermanence about the peace and prosperity of the Reagan years. The boom years were near burnout. Wall Street was shaken by the Panic of '87. The world order was changing; the book of the season in Washington was Paul Kennedy's *The Rise and Fall of the Great Powers,* a dour work placing the United States on the back slope of history, headed down. The seven-year Reagan high was ending. Morning in America had given way to the morning after, and the bills for the party remained to be paid.

The President of Grover's Corners

Reagan's passage across the stage of history had been a brilliant one nearly to the end, a flag-waving, chest-thumping time in which it had been possible for the nation to feel good about itself again. His was a hard act to follow, as the presidential class of '88 soon discovered; he had become his own monument, and even in his late lame-duck period the pretenders to his job seemed smaller and paler by comparison. Reagan had played president better than anyone since Kennedy—so well, indeed, that people liked him even when they disapproved of what he was doing. He restored the authority of the office as well, after twenty years of corrosion. One of the crowning ironies of his reign was that, having run against the Federal establishment, he restored the public's faith in it; whatever one made of his policies, Reagan had shown that the presidency could still be made to work.

He had been in some measure the Wizard of Us, a fabulist presiding over a wondrous Emerald City of the mind. Its white-clapboard look and its hearth-and-homey folkways were drawn less from fact than from popular fiction. Reagan himself had never really inhabited it. It was a nearer match for Grover's Corners than for the real Illinois towns he had grown up in, and, while he preached its values, he had not always followed them in his strained family life, say, or his modest charities, or his slack church attendance. Still, people wanted to believe in it, and for most of his run in Washington they did.

By his last years in office, his presidency had been soiled by scandal and stained with red ink; his Shining City on a Hill was then $2.4 trillion in debt and heavily mortgaged to bankers in Tokyo, Frankfurt and Riyadh. It could be fairly said that he had presided over a second Gilded Age, a time, like the latter nineteenth century, of great personal wealth and public neglect. The grandchildren of Jay Gatsby made paper fortunes on Wall Street—greed is OK, one of them said before the law caught up—and the god-children of Elmer Gantry got rich saving souls. The poor, meanwhile, got poorer, or at least more numerous. More than one hundred administration officials had been charged with various offenses against the criminal and ethical codes, a census that might have made Grant or Harding blush. Ends, however debatable, justified means, however questionable; a secretary named Fawn Hall instructed the Congress that it was sometimes necessary in government to "go above the written law."

For a time, the president's storied luck appeared finally to have run out. In November 1986, the Senate fell to the Democrats, and with it Reagan's sway over Capitol Hill; it would take him three tries thereafter just to fill a single opening on the Supreme Court. In short order, the president's men were caught having done their arms-for-hostages deal with the Ayatollah Khomeini and diverted part of the profits into what was then an outlaw war in Nicaragua—all, so they believed, in Reagan's name and with his blessing. And then, one terrifying Monday in October 1987, the bottom fell out of the stock market, vaporizing a half-trillion dollars in paper wealth in a single day. The emerald towers swayed. The Wizard, out of magic, was revealed to be an aged, inattentive and very mortal man.

Yet Reagan remained the largest single figure in the sad recent history of our politics, the first president since Dwight D. Eisenhower to have lasted out two full terms and arguably the most proficient since Franklin D. Roosevelt at making the office work in the service of his goals. He had seemed, at the peak of his powers, to be able to smile away problems that had brought his predecessors to grief. Inflation had cooled. Interest rates had dropped. Unemployment had flirted briefly with double digits in the bitter winter of '82–'83, then fallen back to levels considered, by all but the jobless, to be acceptable.

The so-called Reagan Revolution had been larger in rhetoric than reality. The welfare state raised by Democrats beginning in the 1930s survived it, largely, though not completely, intact. But Reagan's tax cuts and his military buildup put a choke hold on its funding; hardly anyone was proposing new social programs anymore. Selfishness was no longer a source of embarrassment, altruism no longer a now feeling. The business of America was business again, and the president's policies bought five unbroken years of good times and fast bucks. The benefits were unevenly shared, and Reagan had to pawn tomorrow's treasure to pay for today's. The United States, once lender to the world, had suddenly become its leading borrower. Still, as long as the cash flow ran strong, no one except doom-criers and Democrats seemed alarmed.

Much of what Reagan wrought had been done with mirrors, or, more accurately, TelePrompTers and minicams. His presidency was a master-piece of the politics of telemarketing—the art, in the late Adlai E. Stevenson's prophetic phrase, of selling candidates like breakfast cereal. It had seemed an ill omen, in Stevenson's day, when Dwight Eisenhower sought pointers in screencraft from the film star Robert Montgomery; the general saw television, accurately, as his enemy, and he wanted advice from a pro on how to survive it without, say, nuking the networks.

By the 1980s, an actor had *become* president, and the people behind the cameras were professionals of a different breed—a growing tribe of con-sultants, or, in the vernacular, handlers, whose sole business was winning elections and whose medium of choice and necessity was TV. Their studios by then had contrived to make Jack Kennedy look Arthurian, Lyndon B. Johnson peaceable, Richard Nixon new and Jimmy Carter capable; putting a client in office was more important in their line of work than the accuracy of his packaging or the uses to which he might actually put power once having attained it. But it was not till Reagan that they found the perfect president for the video age: a man trained over an adult lifetime to act the part.

Ronald Reagan was not wholly their creation, given that he had come into their hands with a set of stubbornly held core beliefs and could not easily be budged from them. He was to the new artisans of politics what a block of marble, as against a lump of clay, was to a sculptor; he could be shaped, smoothed and polished, so long as the chisel respected the basic contours of the stone. Within those bounds, and his wife's restrictive gaze, he was mostly compliant with the wishes of the fellas—the imagists who chose his props and settings, the writers who provided his lines, the schedulers who managed his road tours, the polltakers who instructed him in what was or wasn't playing in Peoria. His habits were formed on the back lot at Warner Brothers; he took direction well, added his own pleasing bits of business—the cocked head, the damp eyes, the crinkly smile—and became the hot political property of the age.

The packaging process did not end with his election. He was accompanied to the White House by his handler-in-chief, Michael K. Deaver, an authentic genius at the new court portraiture; Deaver became a hero of the Revolution not so much by contributing to its store of ideas as by making it look nice on TV. Television, in the Reagan years, became an instrument of leadership. The star commanded the screen with his presence and his plain speech; the stage manager saw that he was well lit, properly scripted and flatteringly framed.

It was governance as docudrama, the Great Communicator appearing nightly on the evening news, and for most of its eight-season, all-network run it played to extraordinarily high ratings. Only in its last years did it begin its slide into that spent state called entropy, and even then "Ronald Reagan: The Series" remained popular for its leading man. His magic endured, its glow backlighting the field of battle like a rosy autumn sunset. His popularity was the highest in the history of polling for a president leaving office; one of the major points of contention between Bush and Dole was which of them had been stronger, braver and more reverent in Reagan's service.

What Problem?

Reagan seemed bemused and then depressed by the downturn in his fortunes in his late period as president; it was as if he had come to believe he *was* his screen persona, the Gipper on an eight-year touchdown run. His spirits sagged as the evidence of his mortality mounted. His presidency was pinned down for a year and more by the proliferating inquiries into the Iran-Contra affair. His *best* defense was that he hadn't known or couldn't remember what was going on; the worst suspicion, widely held, was that he was lying. His approval rating went into a twenty-five-point overnight free fall, so steep that Dick Wirthlin found it painful bringing around the numbers; he knew the president was seeing himself in an unaccustomed new mirror, and the image looking back at him was not a flattering one. At low ebb, Reagan's natural optimism gave way to self-pity, a melancholic concern about what history would think of him now. The scandal had ruined his presidency, he told a Cabinet officer one day. No one would ever remember all the good things he had done.

His eulogy for himself was premature. His popularity stabilized and even boomed again, in the wake of his agreement with Gorbachev on a treaty to clear Europe of medium-range nuclear missiles. People didn't *want* him hurt, an old Reagan hand guessed; it was as if he were playing *Rocky V* or *X* or *L,* and they were pulling for that last big miracle turnaround, the bloodied champ landing that last big haymaker and putting everything right again. Wirthlin had told him that his favorable rating would get back into the sixties again, and after the Washington summit it did, topping out at 65 percent. Reagan's mood lightened. His smile returned, and his smoking-car bonhomie.

"Say," he told his inner circle at their first meeting on the first working day of 1988, "do you know one of the benefits of having Alzheimer's disease?"

Eyebrows twitched upward.

"You get to meet new friends every day," Reagan said, grinning broadly.

His men chuckled, though they might have preferred a less sensitive subject for his humor; at least he was telling jokes again.

Still, an air of stalemate lingered at the White House, a nearly palpable feeling of spent energy and exhausted vision. Second-term presidencies in this century had generally been downers, Richard Nixon wrote early on in a buck-up memo to some of his friends in the Reagan circle. It didn't have to be that way, in Nixon's view, and he ventured some ideas to break the pattern—ideas, he said, that he himself had formulated for his second term before Watergate aborted his plans. For starters, you had to clean house ruthlessly, shucking off not just the demonstrable incompetents but the good men who were worn out. You couldn't just carry on old policies with the same old straitjacketing crowd; you had to advance new ideas with new drive.

But in the slow fadeout of the Age of Reagan, the only idea of Nixon's with much resonance at 1600 Pennsylvania Avenue was the least new and the most obvious: a rapprochement with the Russians on nuclear arms. The Reagans had figured that out themselves; it suited the president's vision of national greatness, a White House alumnus said, and, he added dryly, Nancy's dreams of Ronnie rising up into the ether with her at his side. Defusing the Bomb was the stuff of history, and nothing else mattered.

Much of the old crowd lingered, pushing what one senior official called their old men's agendas; their gatherings, he thought, had the geriatric look of the Politburo in the Brezhnev era, and their major work product was rhetoric, not fresh policies or programs. Caution was the order of the day, the president spending what remained of his capital a penny at a time. When a memo crossed his desk proposing a new housing initiative, his scribbled response was that it might make a good radiocast; he had neither the drive nor the money to press it as legislation. The atmosphere wasn't good for blazing trails, Stu Spencer, the Reagans' old California *consigliere*, guessed unhappily. The Senate was gone, the clock was running, and all Reagan could hope to do in the last days of his Revolution was tinker at the margins.

His will to do more seemed depleted anyway, a casualty of time and waning energy. The actor in him had always liked a big finish, something to bring the crowd to its feet cheering. He couldn't even walk out of a staff meeting or a press conference with his back to the people in the room, and manners had little to do with it. He seemed to need to *see* some sign of approval, and if it wasn't there he would rummage around in his mind for a joke to leave everyone laughing.

But he was no longer looking much past his spring date with Gorbachev in Moscow for a grand finale. His age was creeping up on him at last, and with it a hankering for his ranch in the Santa Ynez Mountains. There had been operations for cancers of the skin and the bowel and for a rebellious prostate, and Nancy had had a mastectomy. The day the market crashed, it was *her* health that worried him, not Wall Street's; the frightened eminences of finance and politics were demanding some show of presidential leadership, and Reagan's first response was, What problem?

His people argued, with much asperity and some justice, that he wasn't really getting *old* old—he had always been that way. His gift was leadership, not management or hard intellectual labor; he could go gangbusters at a problem of state for a half hour, one of his people said, but stretch it to forty-five minutes or an hour and you lost him. The problem, in their view, was less his years than the slack work habits and the short attention span he had brought to the White House with him. The supposed symptoms of his decline—the disjointed speech, the lapses of memory, the errors of fact and understanding—had been part of the package from the beginning. If he was in fact losing it, a White House defector said with an irreverent smile, the process probably began nearer age fifty than seventy or seventy-five; it was only when things were going badly that people seemed to mind, or even notice.

It was true that, after seven years, the president did not know his way around the White House, beyond such dependable landmarks as the chief of staff's office down the hall or the barbershop in the basement. It didn't matter; people, and problems, found their way to him. It was likewise so that he tended to drowse off over the remains of the ice cream at his regular Monday issues lunch, and that a sitting with Secretary of State George P. Shultz—Mr. Potato Head, to the White House staff—almost unfailingly set him dozing. But he had always been that way too. Once, during the winter interregnum of 1980, his people assembled a group of twenty experts to brief him on the fundamental issues awaiting him in Washington. In midsession, one of them, a newcomer to the Reagan circle, stole a glance at the president-elect. He was fast asleep.

Reagan's "management style," in the delicate phrase of a blue-ribbon commission report on the Iran-Contra affair, was hands-off to the point of indifference to what his people were up to. His approach to work was formed in his first career, as a rip-and-read sportscaster and then a movie star; he still needed a script, and a director to tell him what to do. The new team that came in with chief of staff Howard H. Baker Jr., in the postlude to the scandal were astonished at his passivity. "If you tell him he should have a press conference, he'll say, 'Fine,' " one of them reported, "and if you tell him he should go to Detroit, he'll say, 'Fine.' " He lived by the schedule prepared for him by the fellas. Without it, he would shrug helplessly and say, "They haven't told me what I'm doing yet."

He could be magical at communicating policy, but was easily bored by the detail work involved in making it, once the basic directions had been set to his liking. The shrewdest of his people developed little rules for engaging his interest in an issue. It was sometimes helpful to open with a joke; otherwise, the best strategy was to state the problem up front, crisply, in short sentences and a loudish voice. Your chances of holding his attention improved if you could relate the matter to something concrete in his experience or his known store of notions, crotchets and anecdotes; he was stronger at narrative than at abstract thought. Playing to his prejudices often worked; everything he thought about budgets and taxes was wrong, a principal in the Reagan Revolution said, but he *believed* in his myths and could not easily be broken of them. The best tactic of all, if you wanted to sell him on a proposition, was to give it a happy ending—one he could actually see.

His aides were happiest of all when he had a pencil in his hand and a piece of paper in front of him, blocking out the questions to be decided; he always appeared to think better with a pencil, and it was an especially good sign if it was moving. Even then, they were not sure what was or wasn't registering. The phrase "with the knowledge of the president" seemed to one of them to have taken on a new layer of ambiguity in the Reagan years; it meant only that the president had been told or shown something, not that he had comprehended it.

He had been that way from his first year in office, but by his last some of his people did speculate privately that he had slowed a step or two, for all their public protestations to the contrary. When they prepared his talking points for the most routine visits to the White House, they felt it prudent to include reminders to greet his callers and thank them for whatever good works had brought them. An untaxing agenda was drawn for the winding-down of his presidency, layered with vanilla-pudding themes of the month—January was "looking ahead," May "the role of the peacemaker," August for "recognizing our American institutions."

His schedule was otherwise filled with extensive travels abroad. The weightiest single stop was his mission to Moscow. Otherwise, his itinerary had the look of a Dr. J. farewell tour, a showcase for a faded star. Reagan was unenthusiastic about it, weary as he was of long flights and strange beds. "I don't want to be the one to tell him," Frank C. Carlucci, then his national-security adviser, said, shuddering, when the State Department proposed adding Australia to the schedule. No one else did, either, and the idea went away.

The First Handler

Nancy Reagan was more than ever the president's protector against the demands of his staff and his own too-willing compliance with them. His people came to fear her voice on the phone from the East Wing; it was, they imagined, the way Woodrow Wilson's men must have felt when he lay ill in the White House and his wife, Edith, became his surrogate president.

Mrs. Reagan was more concerned about the Reagan legacy than Reagan was, a family friend mused; that was what made him so charming and her so—well, something else. She did not deal in the substance of public affairs, but she had become the custodian of the presidential person. She was the decision-maker, a staffer said, on questions of what Reagan would do, when he would do it and how it would be done.

Her wish was that he do as little as possible. She wanted the ripening relationship with Gorbachev to go forward and had in fact helped break Reagan of the habit of referring to the Soviets as the Evil Empire. But anything else ambitious involved risk, and risk, a White House official said, ran crossgrain with her agenda for the last year: to parachute Reagan to safety in January 1989. She reviewed his schedule for speeches, trips or television appearances that seemed to her questionable. Some, it developed, were rescheduled on the advice of her astrologer, to capture some favorable configuration of the planets. Others were scrubbed as unduly burdensome. "I don't think he needs to do these," Mrs. Reagan would say, and, usually, he wouldn't.

Her first imperative was that he be made to look good. Prime-time news conferences did not suit her design, not unless Reagan was given something pleasing to say, and they all but disappeared from his calendar. She fumed and fretted over his last State of the Union address to Congress; it had to be the best ever, she decreed, and she worried through a series of drafts and draftsmen till they got it to her liking. She was cross with Wirthlin when he was slow publicizing an uptick in Reagan's popularity rating. "For God's sake," she told a staffer, "can't we get good news out?" She fussed over her husband's personal appearance, particularly his slicked-down hair; her long lobbying campaign to get him to just say no to Brylcreem and yes to a younger, drier look was one of the few she ever lost.

She made known her desire for a last year without further change or turmoil in the Cabinet or the White House staff. "No more controversy," she told a senior adviser; if there were problems, she and her allies in the Reagan circle had quieter ways of dealing with them.

At her wish, most of the president's political friends and retainers had got the silent treatment at one time or another for acts of what she considered less than perfect fealty to her husband. A few miscreants on her list were terminated with extreme prejudice, from Al Haig to Don Regan, and with the turn of the year she made known her displeasure with Edwin Meese III, the much-investigated attorney general. Meese, as it happened, was one of Reagan's oldest and trustiest friends in politics, and Mrs. Reagan ultimately beat a strategic retreat; when Meese finally did quit, it was on his schedule, not hers. More often, she had her way; it was said backstairs at the White House that she could tell the president, "Ronnie, your *mother's* got to go," and if Nelle Reagan had still been alive he probably would have replied, "OK—she's gone."

Friendship, in Nancy Reagan's definition, was not so much a matter of sentiment as an unending series of loyalty tests. She was particularly wounded when Mike Deaver, sinking in scandal and legal bills, published a kiss-and-tell memoir unflattering to her and the president. There had been other such books, a small library of them, portraying her husband as an amiable underachiever and her as his controller. For a time, everyone seemed to be airing their linen in print, from a budget director to his press spokesman; even their daughter, Patti Davis, and Reagan's son Michael spit-broiled their parents in books.

But Deaver had been family, closer in daily proximity than Reagan's four children. Some of them showed up, sometimes, for holidays; otherwise, the Reagans almost never were under the same roof. Deaver, by contrast, had been a presence in their lives since California; he was always there, almost a son to the president and an ally to the First Lady in her court intrigues. His intimacy alone gave his book verisimilitude and thus made it all the more cutting. Reagan, in Deaver's portrayal, was a hopeless innocent, a political naif in constant need of handling. His wife, in partnership with his media man, provided it; the two were, in Deaver's telling, a kind of benign palace conspiracy "united by our shared belief that her husband needed to be protected, whether he wanted it or not."

"How could Mike do this to us?" Nancy demanded when his book came out.

He had a half-million reasons, a friend said. Deaver had by then retired to private life and had got embroiled in an influence-peddling case. He was fighting to keep from going to jail for perjury. His $500,000 advance on the book would only begin to cover his legal bills.

"That's a small price to pay for friendship," the First Lady answered curtly. "That's a small price to pay for affection." Mrs. Reagan had by then supplanted Deaver as First Handler; she was packaging her husband for history now, and no friend of hers would dare blot his page.

The Death of Peter Pan

The play, in Mrs. Reagan's eyes, was the thing, with Reagan downstage center where he belonged; a presidency begun with bold deeds would fade to dark in a series of heroic tableaus. Reagan's audiences applauded, but there was a retro quality in their affection, a kind of thank-you-and-goodbye to a man who had already passed into history. Peter Hart, the polltaker, had been doing focus groups on the president for six or eight years, asking people the first words that leaped to mind at the mention of his name. The responses had always been fond; Reagan had been our Peter Pan, Hart thought, and as long as he was flying high you had to believe. But suddenly even Reagan Republicans—his people—were throwing out words like "old" and "devious" and "senile," *raw* words unimaginable in the Gipper's glory days. Hart was a Democrat, but he found the sessions sad, even pathetic, to listen in on. It's run out, he thought. It's over. He's playing out the string. Peter Pan was dead.

With the president's slow passage into the shadows, a sense of drift spread outward from the White House across the nation, a feeling of rudderlessness on uncharted waters. An end-of-an-era mood lay over the capital as it had a quarter-century before, when another aged and comfortable president, Dwight Eisenhower, was winding down his tour and John F. Kennedy was still a back-bench senator of unserious reputation. It was as if a page were turning, and nothing was written on the other side. The polling wizards of both parties and a dozen presidential campaigns scanned their printouts for tactical guidance and found little to help them: no one dominant issue, no bumper-strip themes, no clear model as to what the next president ought to be like or what he ought to say.

Nothing, in fact, was certain on the flat plain of our politics after Reagan except uncertainty. Buried in the numbers was an almost Edwardian sense of decline, in wealth, morals and imperial power; for the first time since the early Reagan years, majorities in Dick Wirthlin's private polling felt that America had strayed back down the wrong track. The long Reagan spring had been more nearly an Indian summer, a holiday from leaders who talked about malaise and sacrifice and what the country couldn't do. But his hour was passing, and at the dawning of a new campaign Americans for the first time in years were apprehensive about tomorrow again.

Looking for Mr. Right

Early in 1987, a reporter friend asked Peter Hart who he thought would be the finalists in the crowded run for the Democratic nomination. Hart, as polltaker to the party among other clients, was paid not only for the accuracy of his numbers but for the confidence of his judgments, and he had a ready answer: the winner would emerge from a small, select circle consisting of Gary Hart, Joseph R. Biden Jr. and Mario Cuomo.

He smiled telling the story on himself a year later, and his dark eyes twinkled behind his horn-rims. There had been nothing in his readouts to suggest that Hart and Biden would bring themselves to grief, or that Cuomo would turn out to be no more than a tease, all tingle and no consummation. There had been no shape to the race at all—only shadings of gray where the identity of the winner and the soul of the party ought to have begun taking form.

The Democrats had become the spiritual displaced persons of our politics in the Reagan era, a lost and hungry tribe in search of a hero and a coherent body of belief. The campaign, in its early days, promised neither. There were, in fact, two parallel races for the nomination and for primacy in the party. One was heavily, though not wholly, black and was a solo star turn for the Reverend Jesse Jackson. The other was white, or rather, in the often-heard complaint, colorless. Four of its seven contenders were, or had been, senators: Hart of Colorado, Biden of Delaware, Albert Gore Jr. of Tennessee and Paul Simon of Illinois. A fifth, Richard A. Gephardt, was a congressman from St. Louis. The sixth, Michael S. Dukakis, was governor of Massachusetts; the seventh, Bruce Babbitt, a former governor of Arizona. Their pedigrees were conventional, their differences marginal, their demeanors earnest and unexciting. Even their number was unlucky: they came all too easily to be known as the Seven Dwarfs.

They were, in this, the victims of fashion, which has lately held that anyone seeking the presidency must ipso facto be unsuited for it. The suspicion is as old as American politics: Jefferson was reviled in his time as an atheist and an adulterer, Lincoln in his as a lunatic, Franklin Roosevelt and John Kennedy in theirs as spoiled popinjays. They are now in the pantheon, but not many of our forty presidents dwell there with them, not, anyway, by universal acclaim. The candidates of the class of '88 were no less experienced, or less wise, or less glamorous than most of their predecessors in the office they sought. What our opinion leaders saw as their ordinariness was not so much a break with our past as a homage to it.

At the Foot of the Matterhorn

The 1988 campaign coincided by chance with the centennial of *The American Commonwealth,* a clear-eyed and affectionate study by the British scholar-politician Lord Bryce; his book remains a minor classic and is best remembered now for a chapter called ''Why Great Men Are Not Chosen Presidents.'' Greatness in the office seemed indeed to Bryce to have died with the generation of the Founding Fathers. Only Lincoln since then had stood so tall, by Bryce's measure. ''Who now knows or cares to know anything about the personality of James K. Polk or Franklin Pierce?'' he wondered. ''The only thing remarkable about them is that being so commonplace they should have climbed so high.''

Lord Bryce found the selection process partly at fault, a lament still heard a century later. The chief difference is that the paid consultants of the 1980s have supplanted the party bosses of the 1880s as the objects of our blame. The results have arguably been the same, then and now. Neither class of managers favored risk; in a choice between a brilliant man and a safe man, as Bryce put it, ''the safe man is preferred.'' The fact did not seem so troubling in his simpler *fin-de-siècle* world, and Bryce's cheerful message to the former colonies was not to worry. Greatness is always rare in government, he said, and not usually necessary; in normal times, the American voter quite sensibly ''does not object to mediocrity'' in a president.

But the 1980s were not normal times, and the voices of the Victorian past
were cold comfort to the Democrats. For a fleeting passage in Reagan's
second term, 1988 had seemed to them as pink and gold with promise as
a sunrise by Tiepolo. The administration was waist-deep in scandals of
policy and money, some touching the president's innermost circle of
counselors and friends. The economy had the swollen look of a balloon
about to burst. An unpopular proxy war in Nicaragua was wakening the
ghosts of Vietnam, and the fact that members of the administration had
covertly financed it for a time with the Ayatollah's money, however
amusing to them, placed it outside the law.

The recapture of the Senate by the Democrats had been heartening, and
so was the tepid Republican love affair with George Bush. In the fall of
1987, Peter Hart had breakfasted with a bipartisan group of political
analysts, trading thoughts on what qualities America wanted in its next
president. They weren't naming names, but as the descriptives piled
up—experience, competence, leadership—it struck Hart suddenly that all
of them, Democrats and Republicans, were talking about Bob Dole. Dole
was the scary Republican; Bush by contrast seemed a beguilingly easy
target, and the Democrats said nightly prayers of thanksgiving for his
success.

And yet a party that had ruled our politics only a generation ago was full
of morbid doubts about itself and its future. Democrats found it hard
imagining Bush as president, but none of their available contestants quite
fit the picture, either, and the new math of presidential politics weighed
heavily against them. Long before the first shots were fired, a syndicate of
Democratic fund-raisers who called themselves Impac '88 commissioned
a monograph by the polltaker Patrick Caddell on the electoral lay of the
land. Caddell was a difficult man, a great, brooding bear who had banged
his way through the candidacies of George S. McGovern, Jimmy Carter,
Gary Hart and Walter F. Mondale and had always left bruises. But his
genius at reading polls and divining their hidden meanings was widely
conceded, and when he wrote that the Democrats were standing at the
bottom of ''an electoral Matterhorn,'' people who cared for the future of
the party listened.

Caddell's language, as usual, was apocalyptic; he was to political prose
what Hieronymus Bosch was to Flemish painting, an artist happiest and
best rendering a fiery doomsday landscape. His arithmetic, also as usual,
was hard to deny. In the five elections from 1968 through 1984, he noted,
the Republicans had won four times to Jimmy Carter's single aberrant
victory in 1976. They had outpolled the Democrats by eleven percentage
points in the aggregate popular vote—ten points is the common definition

of a landslide—and had swept 77 percent of the ballots that finally counted, in the Electoral College. The Democrats, indeed, had carried only the District of Columbia in all five elections and only Minnesota among the states in as many as four; otherwise, Caddell wrote, the party had no geographic base left at all. The Republicans, by contrast, were five-for-five in twenty-three states and four-for-five in thirteen more. That added up to a dependable pool of thirty-six states with 354 electoral votes—84 more than it took to win.

The Grand Old Party had, in sum, become the dominant force in our presidential politics; it was the Democrats who were an endangered minority, in peril of being realigned out of contention for the rest of the twentieth century. The first of their sins, in Caddell's reckoning, was "a decade of delusion" that they still were the majority; they seemed actually to believe that the old victory coalition forged by FDR was dormant, not dead, and would waken like Sleeping Beauty if only Prince Charming came around.

It was instead the heirs to Roosevelt's squandered estate who needed, in Caddell's fevered vision, to be shaken out of their slumber. The Democrats had come to be seen as the party of government and therefore of the status quo ante Reagan. The perception had served them nicely in hard times and world wars, when people *wanted* Washington to be up and doing. But that was then, in Caddell's analysis, and this was now. Support for the Democrats was hemorrhaging everywhere, most ominously among the young; voters under thirty, once the party's strongest age group, were deserting it in droves and taking its future with them. "Nationally," Caddell wrote, pulling out all the typographical stops in the full heat of his passion, "the Democratic Party is in its worst straits since the post–Civil War period. . . . *IT IS SUFFERING FROM AN INTERNAL STATISTICAL CANCER THAT SEEMS TO BE INEXORABLY SPREADING. ONLY A RADICAL CURE . . . ADMINISTERED WITH A RUTHLESS DISCIPLINE CAN SAVE THE PATIENT."*

The Quest for the Holy Grail

The remedy most commonly sought was Mr.—or perhaps, in the new order of things, Ms.—Right, that mythic lost godchild of FDR who would somehow return the party to its old glory. It was a rescue fantasy, of course, a search as dogged and as vain as the quest for the Holy Grail in Arthurian legend. Its failure was all but foreordained, starting as it did from the premise that anyone actually running must be Mr. or Ms. Wrong. Yet the

Democrats had been obsessed with the dream at least since the death and transfiguration of Jack Kennedy a generation ago. They were waiting for the redeemer and, in his absence, choosing sides among men of lesser clay. The result had been a series of debilitating fights for the nomination and for the dubious further honor of losing in November.

The search had finally become self-defeating; one nominee after another, from Hubert H. Humphrey to Walter Mondale, had come out of the primary season too bloodied and too spent to put up a credible fall campaign. A number of younger Democratic professionals and academics, mostly men with offices in or sentimental ties to Boston, talked during the winter of 1986–87 about sitting out the nominating season entirely and working up a strategy for winning a general election. The object, said one of them, Ed Reilly, a polltaker just breaking into the big time, was to come in the door when everyone else in the presidential election business was in a decompression chamber or a detox center somewhere and lay out a carefully drawn road map to victory. The group did some preliminary polling and lined up a financial angel, but their consortium barely lasted out the season. One after another signed up with the various pretenders—with Biden, or Gephardt, or Dukakis—and went back to the quest for the Grail.

No one had been in the hunt longer or more ardently than Tom Mathews, a political consultant who specialized in the alchemy of turning direct-mail begging letters into gold. Mathews was an idealist in a cynic's profession, a stumpy, iron-gray man who actually believed that the new technopolitics could be put to work toward ends larger than simply winning elections. He and his partner, Roger Craver, had dreamed for years of finding the perfect citizen-candidate, a man or woman of the center left with a feel for issues and politics, a history of independence, a winning television manner and, most important of all, a *center*—a core of beliefs more important to him or her than getting elected.

The search had begun in the early 1970s with John W. Gardner, then president of the citizens' lobby Common Cause; Mathews and Craver had, in fact, invented the group around him. But when Mathews tried to interest him in the presidency, Gardner told him brusquely, "You're crazy." Mathews moved on to other lost-cause campaigns—to Morris K. Udall's in 1976, John B. Anderson's in 1980 and Gary Hart's in 1984. Each candidacy had been fatally flawed and in the end had disappointed him. His dream survived, and in the late winter of 1984–85, with a new electoral cycle only just beginning, the identity of President Perfect shone forth as if in an apparition. His real name was Bill Moyers, and Mathews was sure he could put him in the White House.

They met one day that March in a small coffee shop across Fifty-seventh Street from the offices of CBS News in New York, where Moyers was serving out the last eighteen months of a contract as happily as if it were hard time at Sing Sing. He thought of himself as a serious broadcast journalist in an increasingly unserious business, at least as practiced at the networks; the pain had got so bad that, leaving home for the office, he regularly told his wife that this was the day he was going to go in and quit. So he was already thinking ahead to a new career, and when Mathews called proposing a lunch he was in a listening mood.

They ordered burgers and Cokes and traded pleasantries about their families for a few moments. Then Mathews leaned forward, so that they were nearly head to head, and said what he had to say in a low voice; there were some CBS people at the next table.

"Bill," Mathews said, "do you remember I once told you that television was too small for you? That what you should do is go back to East Texas and build yourself a political base, and then come up here and run for president?"

"I could never forget that, Tom," Moyers said.

"I'm here to tell you that you should be running for president now," Mathews said.

He watched Moyers's face for some further reaction. There was none; Mathews was surprised by his unsurprise.

"I've been thinking about it myself," Moyers confessed. He had strong credentials in and out of government, including a four-year tour at Lyndon Johnson's right hand, and his mastery at the principal medium of politics in the eighties was unquestioned; television, for him, was not just a knack but a *métier*. But he was stuck for the moment at CBS, and his own ruminations about the presidency were more restrained, in any case. There had been an interesting offer from a Texas newspaper, he said. He could go home, rebuild the paper and then maybe run for governor; it would be a more appropriate launch into politics.

"You don't have to do any of that," Mathews said; he had come with a do-it-*now* scenario. The money would be there, he said. Mathews and Craver would stake him to $40,000 in start-up capital to get a direct-mail effort up and running. They could put together $8 million in two years, enough, with Federal matching funds, to pay Moyers's way through the primaries.

Moyers wondered how the party establishment would react.

"Fuck 'em," Mathews said. Moyers wouldn't have to worry about them or about political-action-committee money or single-issue groups or vanity donors. He would be entirely free to speak his mind.

Moyers began to look interested. "I could create a team," he said; it was, Mathews thought, as if he were already forming a government in his mind. Moyers felt he was finding a voice as well. He had just done a speech to a group of corporate executives in Los Angeles, a call to the unselfish best in Americans, he said, and it had gone over well.

"I really had them going, Tom," he said.

Mathews suggested fielding a draft-Moyers campaign while Moyers was working out his contract at CBS. Moyers said no, that would be phony. He needed to work things out on his own. He looked misty-eyed just thinking about it.

"Bill," Mathews told him, "this is a tough, shrewd idea. You've gambled before. You've got guts. I think you can win."

They met three times more that spring, in Moyers's office, and their excitement grew at each sitting. The idea of the presidency had been no more than a fantasy for Moyers, an ambition without a blueprint, until Mathews brought one around.

The temptation, for a season, was powerful. One evening in June, the Moyerses took the Mathews family to dinner at a Chinese restaurant near Lincoln Center. The Subject came up only obliquely; Moyers asked each of his guests whether a person could have more influence as a journalist or in public office. When the topic had been exhausted and the dishes had been cleared, Moyers cracked open a fortune cookie, read the ribbon of paper inside and passed it wordlessly to Mathews.

"GET OFF TO A NEW START," it said. "COME OUT OF YOUR SHELL."

Moyers agonized deep into the summer, concluding, finally, that his time had not yet come. "I am not ready to be what you think I am," he wrote Mathews. "Perhaps I shall never be." He needed time, he said, time to explore the possibilities of television away from the networks; time to think through what he believed about where America had lately been and where it was going. "I am still on pilgrimage," he said, "still en route; I have not yet arrived to where I can move others."

Mathews argued on into the winter, knowing it was a rearguard action and was doomed. Moyers returned to public television, and Mathews found his way to Bruce Babbitt.

Others in the quest sought other heroes, looking, usually, in places other than the roll of announced candidates. It had become a commonplace of our time that the selection process itself had become a deterrent—that no one first-rate would willingly subject himself or herself to the required year or two or three of begging, borrowing, poking, prodding and plain running-on-empty exhaustion. The best and brightest seemed always to play hard to get, and nothing in contemporary politics was quite so aphrodisiac as reluctance.

Two senators, Bill Bradley of New Jersey and Sam Nunn of Georgia, stirred eddies of excitement for their serious minds and for their newness to national politics; they were figures of innocence and experience, men of Washington who seemed somehow untainted by it. Each, to be sure, was afflicted with a certain irremediable dryness of thought and speech. But their reputations inside the Capital Beltway were formidable, and their allure seemed only to grow in direct proportion to their unwillingness to run. They seemed the more salable because they were not on the market— not, in any case, in 1988.

There was a further flutter when Representative Patricia Schroeder of Colorado did an exploratory tour of the horizon in the summer of 1987. Schroeder had been hurt and angry when, three years earlier, Fritz Mondale had left her off his shortlist for vice president. She had been in Congress three terms longer than Geraldine Ferraro, the Other Woman in the affair; she was, moreover, endowed with a lancing wit—the phrase "Teflon president" for Reagan was her coinage—and a postmodern, whole-earth style of liberalism. She had wanted to be on the ticket, and her husband, Jim Schroeder, a prosperous international lawyer who managed her campaigns, had sent Mondale a memo promoting her for it. But Mondale hadn't given her a tumble, and the slight still rankled long afterward.

She got started on the subject, not for the first time, on a flight to Atlanta for a staffer's wedding.

"You'll never be taken seriously, because you can't keep your mouth shut," her aide and friend Don Terry told her. She was careless of the rules, including the one against pouting when the big guys left her out.

Schroeder wouldn't let go. Mondale hadn't treated her fairly, in her view, and she felt frustrated and hurt.

"Why don't you just run for president yourself?" Terry asked her abruptly, weary of her complaining.

"I've already committed to Hart," she said with a shrug. The answer was almost *too* ready, too rehearsed; it was plain she had considered the possibility on her own.

Her decision for Hart had been dictated less by admiration than by geography, the fact that she and the senator both represented Colorado and that he had got to the starting line first. Her feelings about him were otherwise mixed. She spoke privately about his flaws of character—Gary seemed to her to subsist on ego food—and about his reputation for sexual adventuring. Before she signed on, she told friends, she had demanded his assurance that all that was over. She accordingly felt betrayed when he was shamed out of the race in the spring of 1987, and she said so, for the record.

Still, a window had opened with his departure, and when Terry found Schroeder on the House floor one day soon thereafter, he asked her, "What's your excuse *now*?"

This time, she was silent for a moment.

"I can't do it," she said finally. "I'd get crucified. Look at these guys around here—they'd drop dead before they'd let me have it."

She was correct about the boys on the Hill, as Terry learned on the spot. The first two or three congressmen within buttonholing range suggested, with badly hidden hostility, that Schroeder couldn't win; all she would do was screw up someone else's chances. But Schroeder's rooters remained persuaded that there was a market out there on the far side of the Beltway, particularly among young people and women. The Ferraro campaign, for all its doleful ending, had knocked down the MEN ONLY sign in presidential politics. The notion of a woman aspiring to the presidency was no longer unthinkable, and when Schroeder remarked casually in June that she just might "look at" the idea of running, she found a large and newly wakening constituency in search of a champion.

She insisted from the first that she wasn't interested in symbolism; she wanted to run a real campaign, which meant, as she put it to her staff, "No dough, no go." The dough, as it turned out, was there—a low-budget 80,000-piece mailing brought in 20,000 checks and a million dollars—and so was the excitement. Schroeder took her show on the road, a fifty-city, 75,000-mile tour in a hundred days. Her style was unslick to the point of naiveté—she had the unfortunate habit of saying what was on her mind— and her scheduling was ragged, even amateurish. But raucously happy crowds greeted her everywhere, and her name rose quickly toward the top of the charts. In the waning summer, Louis Harris, the polltaker, was on the phone to her husband, guessing that she could be second only to Michael Dukakis by January.

The temblors rattled the china in the Democracy, and not just its ruling establishment; she had become a threat to everyone in the boys' club seeking the presidency, regulars and insurgents alike. Even Jesse Jackson seemed to see her less as a spiritual soul sister than as competition for the support of the disfranchised. You shouldn't be running, he told her when they crossed paths one day in Cleveland. You're splintering the vote and hurting my campaign.

It wasn't his opposition or anyone else's that finally led Schroeder to pull the plug on the enterprise. It was instead her late start and her discouragement with the Hi gloss and the Lite weight of politics in the 1980s. Schroeder was a free spirit in an uptight business, a people politician accustomed to saying whatever she pleased and sweeping up afterward. Presidential politics seemed to her to forbid that; you couldn't even put happy faces at the bottoms of your letters anymore. It was all too stylized, too confined by polls and photo ops. She had wanted it to be like a congressional race, up close and personal, and it wasn't; it was a scam, she thought, with the candidates and the voters as its common victims.

She didn't like the showbiz of it, the feeling, as she often complained, that she was the entertainment. She didn't like the new journalism of character; who *were* these people demanding to know what you were thinking when you looked out the window? She especially didn't like the hired-gun consultants and refused to hire any; her campaign instead was a low-tech motley of congressional staffers and cause people. She didn't want anyone telling her what to say or trying to make her into a movie star, which was what consultants did; they recorded these little cassettes and put them in you, she thought, and you were supposed to go out like a talking Disney World doll when what the electorate wanted was someone *real* to vote for. Give me a *break,* she thought, and when none was forthcoming, she opted to wait for a better moment.

Jim Schroeder had always been the ambitious one in the family; it was he who had volunteered his wife as a candidate for Congress fifteen years before, and he who led the cheers for her presidential candidacy long past the point where she had decided in her mind not to do it. He marshaled his arguments on paper one last time in late September. Everyone in the field, he said, was a long shot, which meant she had as fair a chance at the nomination as anyone else. He reminded her of a bit of advice he had given their teenage son on going to college: "If you apply to Princeton I certainly cannot say that you will get in. I can tell you one thing, though: if you do not apply, you will not be accepted." His moral was obvious: if you didn't run, you couldn't win.

He was waiting when she came in from a last nightmarish weekend on the road: a day trip from Washington to California and back for a single speech, home for a stolen two-hour nap in her own bed, then up and smiling again for a Congressional Black Caucus function the next day. She was red-eyed and nearly mute with exhaustion when her husband greeted her at the door.

"Look, I wrote two memos," he said, handing them over. "Here's a short one I wrote Thursday saying do what you think is right. Here's another one I wrote Friday saying do what you think is right, *but* I think you should run.''

She sighed heavily. She felt pleased by his faith in her, but there was too much to do in too little time. She had been out there alone for four months feeling like a high-wire performer working without a net; people kept wanting her to be Joan of Arc when all she wanted to be was Pat Schroeder. It was crazy, and she was tired.

''Well, look,'' she said, ''you know I—I just can't do it. It's not there.''

They flew back to Denver that night.

''Do you want to talk about this anymore?'' Jim asked, still hoping.

''No,'' she said. It was over.

A crowd of two thousand people gathered in an amphitheater in a Denver park a few days later, expecting her to announce her candidacy. The Paul Simon ballad ''Graceland'' rocked over the public-address system. Clusters of schoolchildren sat on the steps, buzzing about seeing the first lady president. Cheers went up when she appeared. Her husband stood near her, a teddy-bearish figure, staring glumly at his shoes.

''We love you, Pat!'' someone shouted.

It was the last hurrah. She announced her decision and had just begun explaining it when her voice cracked. Tears suddenly flooded her eyes. Jim produced a handkerchief. She nuzzled his chest, weeping for a few moments before she could go on.

Her show of emotion would be much analyzed by the new psychojournalists over the next several days; the rules of play, written by men, held that crying was for women and was a sign of weakness. Her exit, like her candidacy, was thus an affront to the codes of presidential politics. Her solace was her promise to herself that she would be back, and that the next time she would be ready.

The most tantalizing noncandidate of all was Cuomo, watching the show from the wings, by his own choice, with a Gioconda smile; whether it said come hither or was merely ironic lay in the eye of the beholder. Cuomo had insisted from the beginning that he had no plans to run, and no plans to make plans to do anything in 1988 except govern New York. But his keynote speech to the 1984 Democratic convention had so captivated the party and so eclipsed its luckless nominee that no one quite believed him. He remained a ghostly presence, the phantom in the opera of our politics, and the shadow he cast from the wings only lengthened as the real contenders began assembling onstage.

The interest seemed to tickle his ego and his irony, each well developed.

Congresspeople called him, urging him to run. Advisers sent him unsolicited memos, telling him how. Ordinary citizens wrote him moving letters, seeing in him their hopes and dreams for their children. Even Robert S. Strauss, the Washington power lawyer, told him it could be done. Strauss was a bit of a dinosaur, a deal-doer in an age when the run-amok democracy of the primaries had made deal-doing obsolete. But his mystique had survived, like the night scent of brandy and cigars at a men's club after the last call, and his attentions could not be ignored.

Strauss was a Texan, and when the two men chatted one day early in 1987 Cuomo cross-examined him about the prospects for a Northeastern ethnic in the South and the Southwest.

"They may not like Marios," Strauss told him, "and they may not like Cuomos. They may not like New Yorkers, and they may not even like liberals. But they do like balls, and you've got 'em. You've got balls that clank when you're walking down the hall."

"Balls that *clank*?" Cuomo puzzled afterward, telling friends the story. You couldn't exactly make a bumper sticker out of that, let alone a sound bite; you couldn't do much with it at all except maybe liven up your diary on an otherwise slow day.

The governor was not above encouraging the talk with a coquettish wink now and then—a stubborn shyness about endorsing anyone else in the field, a periodic hint that he would not resist a legitimate draft by the party convention. Sometimes, he teased himself for his hesitancy at the annual Gridiron dinner in Washington in the spring of 1988, he said that Satan had offered him the presidency in exchange for his soul, to which he had replied, "So what's the catch?" But mostly he professed bafflement about why anyone would question his reluctance. Politics, in his expressed view, didn't have to be a path leading inexorably upward toward the presidency. No, *heaven* was upward, he thought; going for president might take you in the other direction.

He was Mario the Unready, and even when he did give the possibility a winter's hard study in 1986–87, his lack of interest showed. He burrowed through a pile of forty memos from national party figures pushing him to run, but did not follow through on them. He sat through staff briefings on the steps required to a launch a candidacy, but took none of them. He held meetings with several front-rank Democratic consultants, jotting notes on a legal pad but signaling no real enthusiasm for the quest. One caller, Gerald Rafshoon, who had done Jimmy Carter's media, felt as if he were leading a seminar in political science rather than a serious discussion of strategy. Another, Bob Shrum, who had soldiered with George McGovern and Edward M. Kennedy, arrived for what he thought was a half hour to make the case for running. What he got instead was a leisurely two-hour stroll among the Jesuits, Augustinians, Vincentians, popes and presidents who peopled Cuomo's inner landscape. The politics of 1988 was almost a digression, and the governor's response, when they did touch on it, was that it didn't feel right to him.

Cuomo's mind was among the liveliest in public life, and the maziest; his interior monologue on 1988, to the extent he let outsiders tune in to it, was more nearly a Socratic dialogue with himself. Was he secretly running? No. Would he be open to possibilities? Of course; you had no right *not* to be. Was he eager to run? No—you *had* to feel it, and he didn't, not the way the others seemed to. Was he afraid of it? Of course he was. Was he so afraid he didn't think he could do it? Well, maybe he could. It was a relative matter, he thought; the question was not whether you could do it as well as Lincoln, say, or Roosevelt, or Kennedy, but whether you could do it as well as Candidate Smith.

It wasn't going to be enough just to sound good, he thought, not after people counted up the cost of the Reagan years. They would say Reagan was nice, he was sincere, he was beautiful, he spoke well, we loved him, he could stand on a beach in Normandy and make you feel like an American, but it obviously takes more than that to run the country. They would want competence first, and Cuomo, as a big-state governor, felt that his was a matter of record; his job was all bottom-line, all ideas that *had* to work. But could *anyone* deal with the problems Reagan was leaving behind—the deficits, the debt bomb, an economy in decline? Give me eight hours with the next president, Cuomo thought, and I'll make him crazy. I'll make him crazy in eight hours just proliferating the questions. You *had* to feel a terrible inadequacy. Lincoln had had to deal with that, and Roosevelt, and Truman. So would he.

He would have to fight his way as well through a tangle of stereotypes about him, as a man and as an Italian-American. You get up there, he thought, and you look like a great big guy with big hands and a heavy voice, one generation out of the Mezzogiorno, and people begin making the associations; you start hearing descriptives like passionate, volcanic, arrogant, vain, the Dark Side of Mario Cuomo. And worse: David Garth, the media consultant, had asked people in focus groups what they had against Cuomo, people who barely knew anything about him except that his name was Mario and he looked Italian, and a big percentage said he was obviously connected to organized crime. Reagan didn't frighten anybody. Cuomo did, he had to face up to that. He felt he wore well with sustained exposure—look at his 65 percent landslide reelection in 1986—but he knew he turned off a lot of people as soon as they saw him.

The process of seeking the presidency seemed to him resistible, even absurd. It was full-time work; Carter chased the prize for four years, Mondale for eight, Reagan for twelve, Nixon forever. You had to submit yourself and your family to heavy and sometimes savage scrutiny in the media. You weren't supposed to hit back, but Cuomo did regularly—what the hell were these guys in the media, Saint Francis of Assisi?—and it had cost him. And you had to go through the whole stupid business of spending 109 days begging votes in Iowa and New Hampshire to show you were a national candidate. Dumb as it was, the contenders were all up there, with booths and foreign policies and everything, chasing that Wednesday-morning headline—BABBITT WINS SENSATIONAL VICTORY. "Who's Babbitt?" "I don't know, but he won in New Hampshire." "How many votes?" "Eleven." So what? Who really cared?

You had to feel exactly right to put yourself through that, and Cuomo didn't. What none of the memos and the analyses had shown him was some urgent reason for his running, and the more extravagantly people pressed it on him, casting him as some kind of messiah, the more uncomfortable he got. If people wanted a hard worker, he could be that, he told Robert McElvaine, a writer at work on his biography, but he wasn't a savior; he believed, as a serious Catholic, that the worst sin of all was pride.

So he retired almost offhandedly to the sidelines one day in mid-February 1987. His setting was his monthly radio talk show, *Ask the Governor;* he came with a prepared statement that he would not be a candidate, but saved it nearly to the end, assuring that no one could ask the governor whether he meant it.

"What is the press going to do without us, Marty?" he wondered aloud to his press secretary, Martin Steadman. "What are they going to write about?"

They continued, in the event, to write about him, and he kept them well supplied with provocative ifs, ands and buts. Cuomo in politics, David Garth said, was like Bobby Fischer at a chess tournament: whether he was playing or merely kibitzing, he could not resist the game. So he hovered in the background, speaking regularly with the announced candidates, testing them, measuring them, encouraging them all, embracing none. Even his silences were taken to be as pregnant with meaning as Chekhov's or Pinter's; if he wasn't dancing with anyone else, the popular wisdom held, he must be planning to crash the party himself.

The lack of luster among the men who *were* available gave "Waiting for

Mario'' an extended run as theater. Larger numbers of voters in the early polls said they weren't happy with the announced candidates, and Cuomo was the absentee most commonly and warmly mentioned. But he remained, so far as anyone could see, unmoved. Rationale was everything in politics, he thought, and you couldn't let other people sell you on running without one. He had listened to them once in his life, when he undertook to run for mayor of New York City ten years earlier, and had lost. He had learned since then to trust his instincts, and they said no.

Missing Persons

All the candidates trooped to New York late in 1987 for a kind of command performance, a forum sponsored by the governor and the state party; the host was Cuomo, and the emcee, by wry chance, was Bill Moyers. In the early going, Congressman Gephardt, tongue in cheek, did a little paean to ''someone who is not up here on the stage tonight as one of the participants—someone who in the last months has been an eloquent spokesman . . . for family, for values, for community.'' It sounded like a tip of the hat to Cuomo, who sat beaming down front. But at the close Gephardt turned instead toward the moderator's table and said how relieved he was that *Moyers* wasn't running.

For one frozen moment, Moyers sat chin in hand and stared down at his notes, appearing to color deeply. Then he smiled. So did Cuomo. They were two more might-have-beens in their party's long quest for its beau ideal; the search once again had come down to the field of men brave, foolish or merely ambitious enough to have presented themselves for it. Each was worthy in his way, but they were mostly as bland and indistinguishable as their uniform blue suits, and their mere availability seemed to breed contempt; they all started out about five feet ten, Ed Reilly, the polltaker, mused, and ended up about three feet two. Just scanning the faces onstage told the Democrats in attendance that it was going to be another long election year—that Mr. Right was still among the missing and that what you saw was all you were likely to get.

PART TWO

THE MAKING OF
MICHAEL DUKAKIS

*Believe me, for certain men at least, not taking
what one doesn't want is the hardest thing in
the world.*
    —ALBERT CAMUS, *THE FALL*

The Marathon Man

It WAS A TRIP of the sort that makes ordinary candidates wonder whether their schedulers are lodged in insane-asylum basements: a 3,500-mile sprint from Los Angeles (money) to Chicago (Hispanics) and back to Los Angeles (Asian-Americans) in the space of a single day. Nick Mitropoulos, whose job it was to worry about such things, told his boss and friend Michael S. Dukakis that it was maybe just a little ridiculous; this was only 1987, and the election was more than a year away. But Dukakis went stubbornly on, flogging himself through time zones and crowd scenes in that bionic way of his, and as his jet streaked westward on the last leg of his tour, he insisted through set jaw that it was fun.

He was a bit of an odd duck, even measured against the mixed class of *papabili* who had presented themselves for the presidency in 1988. He could not match Dick Gephardt's inside moves, or Al Gore's grounding in geopolitics, or Paul Simon's aura of caring, or Bruce Babbitt's gawky candor, or Jesse Jackson's hot, visionary fire. He was neither very imposing—the only thing Napoleonic about Dukakis was his size—nor especially compelling in manner or speech. He was the prototypical inner-directed man, a marcher to his own music, in a business more suited to crowd pleasers; he listened badly, looked smug, spurned advice and radiated petulance and gloom when fortune did not bend to his will. He was hard to manage; hard, sometimes, just to be around. His own seconds, having endured his wide mood swings and his dismissive attitude, admired him but did not much like him.

It was Dukakis the property more than the man who drew them to his service, and even as merchandise he seemed somehow incomplete. His strengths were undeniable, though it often took people a second or even a third glance to discover them. He had a quick, analytical mind, trained for the law and unclouded by sentimentality or passion. His record as governor was solid—the best, by vote of his colleagues, in the business. He was good at television, having done his own talk show for a time between elective jobs; if he was not precisely warm and winning, he could at least handle himself and his adversaries on-screen. He approached the campaign, moreover, with a certain necessary relentlessness, the straight-ahead will of the marathon man driving himself up Heartbreak Hill, through the Wall and on to the finish line.

But he seemed not to know what he would do when he got there, or why he was going in the first place. Most men who seek the presidency feel driven to do so, by some mix of personal hunger and public concern. Dukakis showed no such fever symptoms; when people introduced him as the next president, he would think, Who, me? Geez Louise! His handlers wondered among themselves whether he really wanted the job at all and came ultimately to doubt that he did. It had been their idea, not his. His candidacy had been manufactured around him, along with his ambition; the main reason his managers could divine for his running was that they had told him he could win.

He had never been a fire-in-the-belly kind of guy, he said; people like that troubled him, they had no balance in their lives. He had never even thought about himself as president before 1986, never *ever*, he said firmly, and even then he had taken a long, slow time meditating on whether it was right for him. He had sought the counsel of men who had known and worked with presidents; of men who had run for the office; of Jimmy Carter, the single living Democrat who had actually held it. What was it like? Could he do the job? Look, they usually told him, You can do the job—the question is do you *want* to do the job?

Answering that one had given him pause. He was not the sort to admit self-doubt easily, but the presidency? It was, he confessed, rather formidable for a guy of his plain tastes and unburning belly to contemplate. He had never had that sense, running for governor; he had never questioned whether he was up to the task. He had sat in the Massachusetts legislature for eight years watching governors come and go and had realized that they were human beings like himself. But presidents were distant and mysterious figures, images on television, and when he pictured himself in their place, it was—well, kind of overwhelming.

The price of seeking the office, moreover, would be high. Dukakis was a creature of habit, a man of simple wants at the center of an ordered world. He didn't have an official mansion or want one; he lived in his own house, a two-family duplex in Brookline. Dinner was at six sharp every night, at home, and Sundays were family days with his wife, Kitty, and their kids; aides with state business requiring his attention would sneak up his drive and slip notes through the mail slot. He could go out power-walking in the neighborhood, or buy the family groceries at the Stop & Shop on Harbor Street, or check out the suits in the bargain basement at Filene's department store downtown, and it was no big deal. He was a man without majesty, and the trappings that drew some men to the office seemed oppressive, even suffocating, to him.

He didn't need the presidency as they seemed to. He loved his state and loved being its governor, the little king in his little kingdom; giving all that up, he said, had been the hardest part of his decision to run. And yet, knowing the cost, he had decided to play. He had committed himself, and once you crossed that bridge, he said, looking out at the purple glow of sunset over the Rockies, it was here we go. You hoped you'd enjoy it, have fun at it, and if you won it, great. If you didn't—well, how many people got to be serious candidates for president? Either way, he insisted, he was a happy guy.

If so, not much in his bearing confirmed it that autumn. His pace remained strong, but his team knew that his heart was not really in it, and it had begun to show in his private humors and his public performances; the governor was going through the motions. On his best days, Dukakis often wore the pleasureless look of the character in a Henry James novel who, finding himself in good spirits, worries guiltily whether he shouldn't cultivate discontent. On his bad days, and there had been a lot of them lately, his mood turned bleak and his manner mulish.

He needed structure in his life, he said, but events had conspired to tear him from his moorings. He missed his wife, his family, his homebody routines. He had lost the summer cucumbers in his backyard garden, because, he said, Kitty had forgotten to water them during his long absences; it was plain from the irritation in his tone months later that they remained a sore point with him, a metaphor for all he had given up to make the run. His surrender to ambition had even cost him his manager and alter ego, John Sasso, the nearest thing he had to a real friend outside his family circle. Sasso had cared more about winning than Dukakis did; he had been caught violating Dukakis's rules of order—priggish rules, his people thought—and had had to go. The wound to Dukakis's candidacy, and to his heart, had not healed. He did not have confidence in Sasso's successors, and yet could not bend enough to bring Sasso back to recharge his idling campaign. The inner-directed man was finally alone in the crowd; the only voice he appeared to hear was his own.

He had been in a snappish mood from the moment he boarded the plane for the return to Los Angeles, pestering Mitropoulos about when they were going to eat; he was as exigent as a stationmaster about keeping to his daily schedule, and as fussy as a *Guide Michelin* inspector about the quality of his food. Mealtime, to his annoyance, had had to wait until the jet was airborne. Mitropoulos had lumbered forward, squeezed his bulk into the galley and emerged with dinner—a plate of fresh shrimp and fruit for Dukakis, three helpings of some nameless, pulpy fish for his companions. Dukakis attacked his food as he did everything, crisply and efficiently, spearing shrimp with quick little stabs of his fork; it was as if the meal were one more necessary station on the journey to the presidency.

Was there ever a time, a traveler opposite him asked, when you thought to yourself—

"Why am I doing this?" he interrupted, guessing the question.

His seatmate nodded.

"No," Dukakis said, with a quick shake of his head. "I mean once you get into this, decide you're going to do it, obviously you do it because you decided you were going to do it."

Dukakis was running because he was running, and when his people nagged him for something more poetic, some rationale for his race, his regular reply to them was, "You tell me."

Enter Mike the Greek

John Sasso had known all along that there was a hole at the center of the campaign, where its soul was supposed to be. He had regularly defended Dukakis when the others at headquarters beat up on him—when they complained about his want of music, of poetry, of what one of them called the Big Idea that ought to drive a presidential candidacy. You're wrong, Sasso would chide them. He's better than that. He's really working at it.

You don't understand. You don't respect Michael enough. He does have a message—it's, Opportunity for all.

But during the campaign, and afterward, in sharper terms, Sasso would confess a private concern: that the governor really *didn't* have the language, the themes, the overarching vision it would take to win, and that he was lazy—there was no other word for it—about doing what had to be done to fill the void. In the beginning, Sasso himself underestimated the problem. We've got the best product to sell, he would tell the troops with the professional cheer of a sales manager launching a new line. He saw the vision gap as a management matter, something they would work around. In the meantime, the Product could be sold for its other virtues: its high performance and its clean design. Vision wasn't part of the package.

Vision wasn't Sasso's thing, either, and it wasn't what had drawn him to Dukakis in the first place. It was instead the governor's tensile strength, that spartan stubbornness that kept him moving forward even in adversity. They had met in 1978, on a whistle-stop train tour Sasso had organized in support of a statewide property-tax initiative. Sasso had been thirty-one then, a deceptively soft-looking young man with unruly hair, bloodhound eyes and a budding genius for the game of politics. Dukakis was forty-four, and his public life seemed perilously close to being over. He had served a single term as governor, a tour remembered less for its reformist successes than for its self-righteousness. The voters of Massachusetts, who had suffered rogues, roués and scoundrels gladly, could not forgive Dukakis his implacable goodness. A bare four days before Sasso's tax-reform tour, he had lost the Democratic primary and, ipso facto, the governorship to Edward J. King, a businessman and former football hero whose most visible advantage over Dukakis was his fallibility.

Sasso, watching his chartered train fill up at South Station, simply assumed that the governor wouldn't come. Losing had been a grievous blow to him—a public death, Kitty Dukakis would call it. He hadn't slept since primary night. Aides visiting his office would find him gazing out the window into some inner space; his family, on retreat in Nantucket, would discover him lying on a bed, like a mummy, his son said, with his eyes fixed blankly on the ceiling. He was bereft, a mourner at his own funeral, obsessed with what he had done wrong. And yet, as Sasso stood counting heads, there he came, short and dark-browed, churning along the platform toward the train in his steady, resolute stride. He looked like hell, Sasso thought, but you had to like his resilience. The guy kept his word. He had guts just showing up.

Sasso never forgot that image, and when the two next met, at the 1980

Democratic national convention, he went out of his way to say hello. Sasso, his sights rising, had worked in Ted Kennedy's failed campaign and had savored the taste of presidential politics. Dukakis had come out of his depression and had found refuge at Harvard, as a lecturer at the John F. Kennedy School of Government. But politics, or, rather, public service, remained in his blood, and so did the thirst for redemption.

The state was going cuckoo under King, Sasso told him. Was Dukakis coming back?

The answer then taking form was yes. Like a prince in exile, Dukakis had already begun assembling an army, as one of his foot soldiers put it, and needed the right field marshal to run it. The two men lunched in Boston that September, each auditioning the other. As autumn deepened, Sasso was invited back, this time to a tiny office Dukakis had kept near the statehouse for the remnants of his political apparatus. Dukakis was there, with his lawyer pal Paul Brountas and his own grim resolve. Otherwise, Sasso could see, looking around, there weren't many more resources to draw on—just some card files and a dated list of contributors. But Sasso had joined that fraternity of professional handlers known in the trade as the Jockey Club; he was a rider in search of a horse, a thoroughbred with the strength and heart to go all the way, and when Dukakis asked him to manage the resurrection, he said yes.

The partnership was struck, an extraordinary symbiotic relationship between wholly unlike men. Their bond was born of mutual need, Dukakis's for vindication, Sasso's for advancement from staff man to a congressman to maker of presidents. They would go through two winning elections together, and five productive years in the statehouse as governor and chief of staff, and as their successes piled up, Dukakis's dependence grew.

He did not like having handlers, finding most of them beneath him in intellect and wisdom. Even Sasso found it hard going at times, like trying, he told friends, to roll a boulder up a hill; you'd manage two steps, and it would roll you back one. But if you couldn't *push* Dukakis, Sasso learned with experience, you could *steer* him by more artful means. Handling him was an exercise in reductionism, the to-do list raised to the plane of strategy; the governor needed attainable short-term goals leading in an orderly march to some clear long-term objective.

Sasso thus succeeded where people of flashier mind and greater imagination failed. He and Dukakis were both incrementalists, with a common bent for process rather than message; the theme music of a campaign was something you commissioned from other, more creative people. Sasso was less architect than general contractor, the man who saw that the building got built. He was a broker in other people's big-picture ideas rather than his own; the talent he brought to Dukakis's service was not so much invention as diplomacy, an ability to synthesize the collective wisdom of his own privy councillors and get the governor to listen to it.

Sasso was, a mutual acquaintance thought, less a friend than a role model to Dukakis, a hero to be watched, learned from and maybe quietly envied. He was everything Dukakis was not. Dukakis was cool and armored, Sasso warm and open. Dukakis was broody, even depressive. Sasso smiled. Dukakis was dinner at six. Sasso was poker all night. Dukakis was cautious, a prisoner of habit. Sasso was a gambler, intense, ambitious and driven. Dukakis needed his road maps. Sasso supplied them, detailed quarterly memos setting forth what to do, why it needed doing and how to get it done.

He had a particular genius for marketing, which suited him well for the hour of the handler in American politics, and the repackaging of a man as undefined as Michael Dukakis gave his imagination ample running room. His artistry worked; it returned the exiled governor to the statehouse for a second term in 1982 and a third in 1986 and permitted him to be mentioned, seriously, for president. The means employed by Sasso and his circle amounted to microwave politics: cold image in, warm image out, all in the twinkling of an eye. Duke I's bumper strips had announced, imperiously, MICHAEL DUKAKIS SHOULD BE GOVERNOR. In "Duke II: The Sequel," he was mysteriously reborn as a natural, approachable, next-door kind of guy named Mike. No one close to him used the nickname, and Kitty warned new friends to call him Michael if they wanted to get his attention. He really didn't *like* "Mike," but he learned to endure it.

He became, in his new incarnation, not merely Mike but Mike the Greek, a tough little ethnic scrapper fighting for the American Dream because his family had been blessed by it. He was not in fact the immigrants' son of folklore, the child of tenements, sweatshops and hand-me-down clothes. His parents, both militant overachievers, had passed through Ellis Island as children and, with considerable struggle, had made affluent lives in the New World. By the time Michael was born, his father, Panos, was a doctor and his mother, Euterpe, a teacher. Their lifestyle, though frugal, was suburban, sheltered and wanting in nothing that mattered. When Pan Dukakis died, he left his surviving son a share in a million-dollar trust fund, along with a certain incapacity for enjoying the things money can buy. The legend of Mike the Greek made a point of his father's instruction to him: Much is given to you, and much you must give back.

Dukakis was thus nearer in spirit to the WASP traditions of good government and civic obligation than to the tribal politics of the Massachusetts past. Before his connection with Sasso, he had never made much of his origins; he had worked his way up from the Brookline town meeting at age twenty-five to the governorship at forty-one as a white-bread suburban reformer, running *against* the old ethnic barons and earls downtown. The statehouse crowd was mainly amused by his re-Hellenization in broadsides and TV commercials; I knew Dukakis before he became a Greek, the boys in the corridors kidded.

The cynics missed both the art and the power of Sasso's handicraft; a myth was growing around Dukakis, gathering force enough to put him in contention for the presidency. Sasso's First Law of Politics, as of poker, was that you were stuck with the hand you were dealt: you could play it smart or play it bad, but you couldn't change the color of the cards. The legend of Mike the Greek accordingly made a virtue of his plainness. It turned out, beginning in his comeback run in 1982, that the forbidding little techie of the first term wore cheap Filene's suits and a dime-store-quality watch; that he rode the Green Line streetcar to work, often carrying a brown-bag lunch; that he cropped his own lawn with a hand mower and cleared his own driveway with a period snowblower; that he was hopelessly and dependently in love with a married woman, who happened, fortuitously, to be his wife. It was even said that the taste of rejection had softened him, made him a more caring and less peremptory man.

The transformation was not total: Dukakis remained a difficult person, even in good times. Publicly, his people advertised his stubbornness as a virtue, an unwillingness, they said, to be handled. Privately, they called it arrogance or worse. Dukakis was domineering at meetings, unwilling to concede the smallest error of fact or understanding. It was, a friend said, as if he had studied binary logic at Harvard and never got over it; by the end of the campaign, aides had taken to calling him "Mr. I Know" for the way he regularly cut them off in midthought. He was sharp with staffers who worried about money, as if their futures, like his own, were guaranteed by large inheritances. "You sound just like Kitty," he told one employee who complained about his wages.

What defeat did teach him, a family acquaintance said, was that he needed friends. He had never made them easily or in great numbers, and was not a natural at it, as John Sasso was; the quarterly "strategic communications" memos he got from Sasso on matters of policy and strategy included pointers about where to go, whom to see, what to talk about and how to seem more sensitive, more concerned, more *human*.

His softened public manner helped him get things done, and Sasso, as his statehouse foreman, saw that he was kept well supplied with things to do—innovative programs with trendy names, moderate prices and wide popular appeal. The bright young men who produced them owed their allegiance first to Sasso; he sometimes had to remind them that it was Dukakis they were serving and that their single objective was to make him look successful—to manufacture a glow around a man who seemed to generate practically none of his own.

Sasso's boys, brash and brainy, competed at dreaming up good works; they were just like a bunch of kids, Eric Elbot, then a young statehouse personnel officer, remembered—each trying to bring home the neatest toy. Old-style welfare-statism was out; in the postliberal eighties, public-private partnerships had a more modern, cost-effective look. Acronyms were in, the letters spilling like Scrabble tiles and re-forming into new and sometimes catchy combinations. Sasso's personal favorites were ET, a job-training program aimed at delivering the poor from the dole, and REAP, a carrot-and-stick enforcement plan for collecting delinquent taxes; they were imaginative ventures with laudable results, but it was their logos that helped transmute them from programmatic gray into political gold.

Their sum, in Sasso's skilled promotional hands, came to be known as the Massachusetts Miracle—the return of a tapped-out Rust Belt ruin of a state to ruddy good health. The miracle, if it was one, was not Dukakis's alone; he had, in fact, resisted some of the programs that encouraged it until they had first been field-tested and shown to work. The Reagan boom in defense spending helped; so did the explosion of high-tech industry out of the brain banks of Cambridge; so did the generally rising fortunes of New England as a region. But the abecedarian tumble of programs in the Dukakis years helped new businesses get started, encouraged old ones to modernize and spread part of the wealth to some of the depressed mill towns beyond Route 128, the thriving ring road around Boston. Dukakis could thus claim a share of credit for the recovery, and Sasso saw that he did, to growing effect in the media and on public occasions. When he spoke in his early campaign speeches of how unemployment had fallen from nearly 12 percent in his first term to less than 3 percent in 1987, not even his flat delivery spoiled the effect; his audiences usually gasped.

Some of Dukakis's own people questioned whether he understood his Miracle well enough to communicate it in any but the prosiest terms. The poetry in it, in their view, was Sasso's; it was he who had shaped it and styled it for sale. He kept a sharp focus on issues of national concern, and saw that the governor's successes at dealing with them were well advertised. He put the Dukakis show on the road, two dozen sorties in 1986 alone, to bear the gospel to meetings, conventions and governors' conferences. He used his charm and his connections to attract the notice of the press to the Massachusetts story, and as its fame grew, so did Dukakis's; the payoff, in 1986, was a *Newsweek* poll of governors rating him the most effective among them.

All of it was part of Sasso's larger design, a plan he had been weaving as patiently as a medieval tapestry-maker since his earliest days with Dukakis. He had talked his reluctant boss into granting him a leave to manage Geraldine Ferraro's run at the vice-presidency. That it was yet another lost cause had not deterred him; there was a reason for everything with Sasso, and the prospect of a front-row seat in 1984 had meant more to him than the foregone conclusion of the race. He was not greatly impressed by either Mondale or Ferraro, or by their campaign; on the contrary, he came away thinking he and Dukakis could do better. He was working for Ferraro, a friend said, and dreaming about 1988. John was a long-range kind of guy.

He had come back to Boston that fall undaunted by the Reagan landslide. Sasso, being long-range, saw seedlings of opportunity in the scorched earth around him—a chance, just possibly, for a postliberal management man like Dukakis to lead a Democratic revival. The 1984 campaign, in his eyewitness view, had been kamikaze politics; the national party, he told his crowd back home, had no credibility with the voters. It didn't matter that the Democrats were on the right side of the issues people cared about— jobs, peace and social services. The voters felt they were incompetent as executives, he said. They think we're all heart and no hands, no head. But a new generation of governors was breaking those stereotypes. Governors *had* trust and credibility. They had to make ideas work. They did what presidents are supposed to do: they got things done.

There was an opening there, and Dukakis, in Sasso's view, was perfectly suited for it: he was just the right blend of innocence and experience, a proven manager who could not be blamed for the sins of the Democratic past. The only problem was selling the idea to him, or even getting him to consider it seriously. Dukakis was happy where he was, tending his budgets and his cucumbers; it was the world he knew, and he felt secure in it.

But Sasso swept doubt aside; he had already written his script and cast Dukakis in the lead role. Friends were convinced that the governor would never even have considered the idea if the one man he listened to hadn't forced it on his attention and persuaded him that he could be elected. Getting him to embrace it would be a long and difficult process, more like a siege than a courtship. I pushed him more than I'd care to admit, Sasso would tell friends ruefully long afterward, when the enterprise had come to its unhappy ending. Maybe it had been wrong of him to press his own ambitions so aggressively on so plainly ambivalent a man.

The Reluctant Dragon

For a suspensefully long time, Dukakis chose not even to *think* about running, and he turned cranky when Sasso or anyone else tried to interest him in the subject. His own gaze was fixed on a nearer horizon, his coming campaign for a second successive term as governor in 1986; he had not entirely got over the humiliation of his defeat, and a mandate for four more years would complete his vindication. Nothing else seemed to matter so much to him—not even the presidency of the United States.

His people trespassed on his obsession at their peril. Jack Corrigan, Sasso's deputy in the Ferraro campaign and at the statehouse, had tried early on to engage him. Corrigan was a mailman's son, young, shrewd, and tough as city pavement. People called him Sasso's designated sonofabitch, the ass-kicker on the team, but he knew how to count, and he liked the way the numbers added up for Dukakis.

He presented himself in the governor's office one day to say so, interrupting Dukakis at his paperwork.

"Look," Corrigan said, his Brillo eyebrows knotted in their permanent scowl, "a lot of people are talking to me about you in '88."

Dukakis peered up at him. *"Reelection,"* he answered curtly, and went back to his papers.

Sasso fared not much better. "Keep your eye on the ball," the governor would scold him whenever he got a little ahead of himself. But Sasso kept talking to anyone else who seemed interested and might help. He promoted his plan to Kitty Dukakis, who loved the sound of it. He pieced it out to his chums in the media, who were titillated by his confidences. He chewed over it endlessly with the members of his own kitchen cabinet, who met over pizza and beer on Thursday nights to dream, scheme and strategize; the unspoken consensus among them was that if they could get Dukakis reelected by a record margin, Sasso would somehow induce him to go.

Sasso did not wait for the returns. The gubernatorial race was child's play, too easy to require his full attention; he turned it over to Corrigan instead and spent the last month before Election Day holed up in his corner office at the statehouse, plotting the run for president. The hardest sell, as he knew, would be the governor. You couldn't tell Dukakis what he should do; you had to lay it all out for him as data, not argument or instruction, and let him feel he was making the decision on his own. So Sasso collected ideas from his boys and wove them into a memo, from "JS" to "MSD." Its tone was objective, almost clinical. Its subtext was that Dukakis had almost a duty to run, for the good of his party and his country. There would never be a better time; 1988 was his year.

Sasso gave due attention to the difficulties facing a little-known governor from the liberal Northeast with no foreign-policy experience and little personal flair. But the memo was subliminally weighted toward the plus entries on the ledger, the confidence-builders that would make the venture seem attractive. The political and financial base would be there, Sasso wrote; a sitting governor who happened also to be Greek and to have a Jewish wife would have access to rich sources of support. The positioning was good, though Gary Hart was the front-runner going in; voters shopping for a new president were likely to prefer someone who had values in common with them and who had actually done something, not just conjured New Ideas. The message, with work, would sell; people wanted optimism, and Dukakis embodied it. Finally, Sasso reasoned, Dukakis had the right temperament—the calm, the energy, the discipline and the balance to survive the rigors of the run.

Sasso delivered his white paper the day after Dukakis's reelection. Dukakis's mood was good, even, for him, buoyant; his people guessed that winning had been a kind of exorcism for him, a deliverance from his demons.

"Do you want to think about this thing at all?" Sasso asked.

"I really don't," Dukakis said. "I want to enjoy the holiday with my family."

Thanksgiving came and went. Sasso tried again.

Dukakis shook his head no. "I want to wait until after Christmas to decide this," he said.

Sasso started out the door. Dukakis called him back.

He might look at the idea after New Year's, he said. But as Sasso himself had been warning him, there were four questions that needed answers. Could he govern the state and run for president at the same time? If he did run, could he win? If he won, could he do the job? And what would it mean for him and his family—would anything in their lives be normal?

"You gotta think about the last one yourself," Sasso said.

"Yeah, I know," Dukakis said, "but I want you to think about the others."

Sasso's answers to the first three questions, unsurprisingly, were yes, yes and yes—Dukakis could run from the statehouse, he could win the presidency and he could handle it once he got there. Dukakis was less certain; he set out on his explorations, as he would confess later, assuming that his answer would be no. He knew he could manage Massachusetts, but the presidency was another, larger order. Could he win it? No sitting governor had done so since Franklin Roosevelt in 1932. Could he handle it? He had never worked in Washington and never served a president, and his canvass of people who had was only partly reassuring. He confessed his qualms over dinner in Washington one night with a group of political reporters assembled by Robert Healy of *The Boston Globe*. You had to ask yourself, he said, whether you really were up to the job.

Dukakis had never been notorious back home for his humility, and Healy looked at him skeptically. "We've had about fifty people in here in ten years talking about being president," he told the governor, "and not one of them has ever said that—'Can I do the job?' "

"Either they're kidding you," Dukakis replied, "or they're kidding themselves."

National-security issues in particular seemed as intimidating to him as astrophysics to a freshman English major. He attended a seminar on arms control at Harvard that December; he was never comfortable with a roomful of people more expert in a subject than he, and he came away visibly shaken at the sheer size of the decisions he might have to make as president. Afterward, Ted Kennedy invited him to an informal rap session with some of the conferees.

You really should go, Sasso told him; he needed all the help he could get on arms control.

Dukakis let Sasso lead him upstairs for the meeting, but he was withdrawn and grouchy in the elevator, and as they started down the hall toward the suite he turned back.

I can't go, he said.

Well, Sasso asked, why not? It would be good for you.

Tonight's my night to shop, Dukakis said.

He left, and Sasso feared for a time that they had lost him—that they would *never* get him to run.

The governor's people did what they could to ease him through his doubts—those, at least, having to do with the public questions of running and governing. Sasso and John DeVillars, the statehouse chief of operations, among others, organized a series of secret "discovery sessions" for their reluctant dragon, sittings at home or in Washington with past players in the big game. Mondale came by, and Senators John Glenn of Ohio, Alan Cranston of California and Ernest F. Hollings of South Carolina, all survivors of 1984; the governor was always more willing to listen to certified heavyweights, men of size, than to his own employees.

But the private cost of running had to be measured by Dukakis alone, and his people could only wait while he brooded through it. His family was far more enthusiastic than he, especially Kitty and their son, John, a staff man to Senator John Kerry of Massachusetts. They couldn't discuss it with him directly, not so long as he was concentrated on his reelection campaign. They spoke instead in a teasing code language when they were around him, little jokes about redecorating the White House, and John, in his regular phone calls home from Washington, would be sure to tell his father, "Weather's awful nice down here." Otherwise, they were reduced to caballing with the men designing the campaign-in-waiting. "Is it doable?" Kitty would demand in her off-the-record visits with Sasso at the statehouse. Sasso thought it *could* be done; he was losing faith that it would be.

A Family Affair

While his family waited for him, Dukakis worried about them; he dreaded what a campaign might do to all their lives, and particularly to Kitty's. She was a bright and lively woman, in many ways his opposite; she was impetuous where he was careful, extravagant where he was tight, warm-blooded where he was cool. But his need for her was palpable and strong, and his concern at how well she would endure the brutal pressures of a campaign was plain to their friends. Kitty was tense and volatile, quick to bleed if he or she was wounded. Once, when a Boston columnist called her "the Dragon Lady of Brookline," she had burst into tears. Could she handle the burning-glass scrutiny they both would come under if he were to run? Dukakis didn't know.

There was, moreover, a family secret to think about, one they had kept, successfully, for more than a dozen years. Kitty had been addicted to diet pills, the delicate name for prescription amphetamines, for practically all her adult life. Her habit had begun when she was nineteen years old, long before she and Michael had met. Her husband, like everyone else in the family, assumed that her flutters of hyperactivity and her gusts of anger were just Kitty being Kitty; it was, so far as they knew, the way she was. Michael had finally discovered her pills in 1974, in the eleventh year of their marriage, and had persuaded her to quit. She had for a time, then relapsed.

She had finally reached the point where her addiction was no longer worth its cost—where she didn't like herself or what her life had become. On Independence Day 1982, she had phoned a discreet clinic in the woods in Minnesota to make an appointment. Michael had been supportive, neither judging nor reproaching her. He had driven her to the airport two weeks later, in the midst of his comeback campaign. She had asked him not to make the journey with her; her traveling companion had been a single pill, carefully hoarded to get her through the day. It would be her last. She had spent four painful weeks looking inward, at the damage she had done her family and herself. At the end of it, she had come home drug-free.

The whole sad business had been sheltered by a certain respect for her privacy and her pain; she was said, for public consumption, to have been under treatment for hepatitis, and no one challenged the story. But privacy no longer existed in presidential campaigns, as the politics of 1988 would make brutally clear. Areas of life once thought off limits had been opened to public inspection and political attack; under the new rules, as Eric Elbot read them, it was best to break your own bad news, because if the press caught you first, you died. They all knew that. Michael understood it, and so did Kitty. If he ran, the story would have to be told, sooner rather than later.

So the governor worried his decision into the winter, more oppressed than his family by the issue of their well-being. They nagged him for weeks to sit down and talk it through with them. He kept stalling, until his son, John, finally cornered him at the kitchen table one day just after Christmas 1986 and forced a family council on him. John, then twenty-eight years old, was as enthusiastic as Kitty about making the run—more gung-ho, he worried long afterward, than perhaps he ought to have been. Maybe he had thought too little of what would be right for his father and too much about what would be fun for himself; maybe they had *all* put him off with their partisanship, made him feel as if he couldn't even discuss the matter with his own family.

But John's twinges came only with hindsight; his mood that morning, like most of the family's, was go, and Dukakis was obliged to listen. He began by polling the table, in a serious, almost formal way. Kitty was there, and John, with his fiancée, Lisa. So were the Dukakises' two daughters, Andrea, twenty-one at the time, and Kara, eighteen.

"What do you think?" Dukakis asked them. "What are your concerns?"

"Well, what's the White House like to live in?" one of the young women asked.

She was kidding, breaking the ice, but there were serious questions. John and Lisa were to be married that summer. Would they have private lives, separate identities? It was a worry. Andrea and Kara had been little girls when their father was elected governor, and the transition to public life had been tough on them, a childhood shared with reporters and cameramen; a presidential campaign could be ten times more intrusive.

"How'd you like to have Secret Service men along on your dates?" Dukakis asked them, playing devil's advocate.

The prospect was not a happy one.

If he did do it, he went on, an edge of warning in his tone, his commitment would have to be total. "If I'm going to run, I'm going to run to win. I'm not going to do this to make some kind of statement about something. This," he said, looking meaningfully around the table, "is going to involve everything that I have."

For Dukakis, assimilating new ideas had always been a bit like breaking in a pair of wingtips: he had to put them on and walk around in them awhile before they got comfortable. His approach to the race, as to all things, was methodical, a balance sheet of pluses and minuses, and the pluses were starting to add up. If he said no, his team would almost surely drift apart, putting his success as governor at risk; even Sasso had had feelers from Mario Cuomo. If he said yes—well, maybe John was right: he might actually win.

And so, with time, the four questions Sasso had posed for Dukakis at the outset of his deliberations were settled to his satisfaction. He found himself drawn inexorably into the race by the way he had framed the problem, as a checklist rather than a real self-examination. The sad and, in time, ruinous gap in the exercise was the fifth question he did not appear to have asked himself and did not like to be asked: whether he really wanted to be president, and if so, why. He was, one of his people said, afflicted by a serious lack of imagination, the gift for seeing expansively. "I am what I am," he would tell his people. What he was, in their view, was a task-oriented man who could put one foot in front of the other so long as someone could tell him where he was going.

"Who Are You?"

Night was falling on Boston Common. The scent of wood smoke hung over Beacon Hill. Most of the statehouse work force had gone home for the night, spilling out into the chill February evening. But the lights blazed late in Michael Dukakis's office. Three of his men had lingered after work, trying yet again to force his attention to the presidency. The meter was running; it was past time for him to decide whether he wanted the job and what he would do if he got it.

Dukakis frowned down at the three from the head of his conference table. Sasso sat at the far end. At Dukakis's left was John DeVillars, boyish and ambitious; to his right, his tax commissioner, Ira Jackson, handsome, brainy and vain. They had spent months tailoring a candidacy like a bespoke suit to Dukakis's odd measure, but the *why* of it remained to be stitched in, and they were running out of time.

Their minds were on a speaking date at an important party affair in New Hampshire a bare two weeks away, a chance for Dukakis to try out his style and his message in the first state on the primary calendar. It would, Jackson said, be tantamount to a bar mitzvah, the governor's rite of passage, politically speaking, into the company of men. The grandees of New Hampshire politics would be there, and of the national press. Dukakis would be judged on his performance. He couldn't just show up and expect to light up the room with his luminescence; he had to have themes, a coherent political philosophy. They had two weeks in which to think something up, and here they sat, still baffled.

"Why are you doing this, Michael?" someone asked in desperation.

"What is your vision?" someone else said.

"What is your ideology?" The questions were flying now.

"How do you separate yourself from the pack?"

"Why you?"

"Who *are* you?"

Dukakis sat silent and resistant in his eighteenth-century wingback chair. His shoes, innocent of style, dug into the blue rug under his feet.

The others waited for him to speak. He waited for them to supply the lines. Jackson, out of words, made an impatient gesture. If we can't get by this hurdle, he was thinking, there ain't gonna *be* a presidential race.

"Michael," DeVillars put in, trying to help, "when I was young, I got inspired to go into politics because of Jack Kennedy. Which politicians inspired you? What motivated you to get involved?"

"It's your job to advise me on what to say," Dukakis said.

His voice had a defensive edge. Sasso knew the danger signals, after six years' service. You couldn't force Dukakis to be visionary, and you couldn't make him read someone else's lines; the harder you pressed him, the more obstinate he could become. Usually, Sasso was patient. This time, the clock was against him, and he got blunt.

"Michael," he said, "It's your speech. What do you want to say in your speech?"

Dukakis thought a while longer.

"The first obligation of a president," he said finally, as if a new tablet had just come down Mount Sinai into his hands, "is to ensure that there's equal opportunity for every American."

There was a long, awkward silence.

There was something there, but it sounded a bit—um—thin. Wasn't there a different slant, a sexier way to say the same thing? Couldn't they flavor it with some of the language Sasso and Jackson had been playing with—the stuff about integrity and competence, and caring about plain people?

Dukakis cut them off with a wave of his hands.

"No, no, no," he said. "Don't you guys understand? That's who I am, that's what we've been doing, and that's why I want to be president."

He sat back, immobile as stone. His men were startled by his heat; it was as if what he had uttered was not a commonplace but an ideology, as whole and powerful as Ronald Reagan's. Glances darted across the table. Equal opportunity for every American—it wasn't exactly inspirational, but it had a certain now ring to it, and maybe, just maybe, they could find the music that could make it sing.

They made a game effort at it, and the New Hampshire speech, to their relief, was a great success; Dukakis was interrupted twenty-two times by applause, and a crowd of eight hundred party activists sent him off with a standing ovation. Doubt seemed to dissipate thereafter, giving place to something less like enthusiasm than dour civic resolve: *Michael Dukakis should be president*. On a Saturday morning not long after, three days before his self-appointed deadline, he poked his head out the kitchen door, picked up the morning paper and turned back inside to Kitty.

"Well," he told her, "I guess we're going to do it."

His demeanor in the days immediately thereafter was ill-tempered, even, in one aide's word, bitchy, as if he had been sentenced, not called, to the quest. The day he made his decision known, he rang up Senator Kerry's offices and had his son pulled out of a meeting.

"I hope you know what you've done," the governor said.

It was a family joke, of course, but not without its subtext of rebuke. He had become the candidate as artifact; his image, his rationale, even his ambition had been designed by others for him. It was only with the passage of time that the men and women who created the Michael Dukakis of 1988 wondered whether they should have—whether the real reason for his ineloquence about why he was seeking the presidency was that he had never wanted it.

Getting Started

One dank day in April, Dukakis stood on Boston Common in a slashing rain and made formal his entry into the race. A reader of signs and portents might have watched him, a small, unsmiling figure in the downpour, and foretold how things would come out. But a quiet confidence suffused the venture in those happier times, the faith of the tortoise plodding along behind the hare. So what if Gary Hart sat alone at the top of the polls and Dukakis was far behind? Hart could be taken if you framed the debate on your own terms, and Sasso smiled inwardly, watching Dukakis read the script they had given him. "As you look each of us over," the governor was saying into the sodden air, "ask more than what we are going to do. Ask what we have already done. . . . Ask whether we have already made new ideas *work*."

Sasso approached politics with a card-player's eye for an edge, and Dukakis's edge, in his view, was his record; apart from Bruce Babbitt, a horse of even darker hue, he was the only candidate who had one. Dukakis didn't just sit in Congress and cast votes. Dukakis had managed an economy, he had floated imaginative new programs, he had balanced eight budgets in eight years as governor.

In a word, he had competence, and absent anything more inspirational, Sasso's playbook sought to make competence the central—indeed, the only—issue in the campaign. Sasso was a believer in market research, and he had found support for his theory in Tubby Harrison's early surveys in Iowa, in New Hampshire and elsewhere. Harrison was a favorite of Sasso's, a slight, balding elf of a man whose nickname was a joke on himself. Some people in the trade quibbled with some of his more provocative polling techniques, but he was Sasso's kind of guy, a street fighter from the Bronx, tough, shrewd and fierce in his politics and his loyalties.

What his data told him that spring, he said one day, nursing a Polish vodka at a favorite bar in Cambridge, was that people longed for a new kind of president, more solid and less showbiz than they had lately experienced. The Reagan high was wearing off; the public, Harrison guessed, was coming to see that being good on television was not really enough. People wanted leadership, and it didn't necessarily have to come wrapped in the flash and dazzle of a Kennedy. It could as well be the quiet solidity they imagined they had seen in Jimmy Carter and might actually find in Michael Dukakis.

Ideology would be secondary, Harrison believed. The operative word for 1988 would be ''opportunity,'' the right of every man and woman to a fair chance on a level playing field, and it no longer carried a liberal or conservative label; voters cared only about what you were going to do to insure it. They wanted a *person,* not a message. Message candidates usually offered simple answers to hard questions, and people didn't think the answers were simple anymore. It was a manager they sought, not an ideologue or a prophet. They wanted someone competent, Harrison said, staring into the last of his vodka. They wanted someone they could trust to find the way.

Polltakers commonly find a popular thirst for someone just like their clients, and Harrison's profile of Mr. Right, unsurprisingly, was a fair match for Michael Dukakis. The problem, the governor's men knew, would be making the sale. Managerial skills were not the kind of product that would leap off the shelves, nor was Dukakis's hypothermic personality; the best his own team could find to say about his charm was that he grew on people, and the strategy Sasso and his men devised around him was accordingly designed for the long haul.

It was a poker player's game plan; its first premise was that winning would take time, guts, discipline and money—more of each than anyone else brought to the table. Dukakis did not have the star quality to blow the competition away in the early going. He was a gray man in a gray field, and the long game was more suited to his purposes—the campaign, as Dukakis himself would put it, seen as a marathon rather than as a series of sprints from primary to primary. He would grind it out, over time, going for delegates rather than headlines, and at the finish he would be alone, the tortoise laughing at the hares.

The design meant waging a fifty-state campaign; where Dick Gephardt and Paul Simon were going for broke in Iowa, and Al Gore was betting his stack on the South, Dukakis would be in play everywhere. He would fight the others for Iowa, to show he wasn't just another regional candidate. He would go for a big win in New Hampshire; that state, Sasso reckoned, was their giant-killer, the place where Dukakis would bring down Gary Hart. He would contest what the pros were calling the Lesser Antilles, the five neglected states scheduled for primaries or caucuses between New Hampshire in February and Super Tuesday in March; they would give Dukakis credibility as a viable national candidate.

Sasso and his Thursday nighters even saw rich possibilities in what might have seemed, at first glance, the forbidding terrain of Super Tuesday. Its sprawl alone was daunting, a twenty-state archipelago stretching from Florida to Hawaii, and so was its strong Dixie accent. The party centrists who designed it had dense-packed the schedule with Southern and border states, fourteen of them in a single day. Their conscious intent had been to rig the game against a Northern liberal like Dukakis and for a Southern moderate like, say, Sam Nunn—or, in his absence, Senator Gore.

But delegates were the chips in Sasso's game, and his single objective was to wind up Super Tuesday with more than anyone else at the table— enough to send Dukakis north and west wrapped in a cloak of inevitability. Massachusetts and Rhode Island had fortuitously scheduled their primaries for the same day. With a solid base thus assured, Dukakis's delegate hunter, Tad Devine, did a systematic analysis of all 167 congressional districts in play in the twenty states, isolating targets of opportunity where Dukakis might win outright or at least do well enough to pick off some delegates. The pieces came together in what his men called a four-corner strategy, with Texas, Florida, Maryland and Washington State as the corners. Solid showings there, coupled with his all but bankable victories in New England, would secure Dukakis's position at the head of the class.

The model thus was nearer Fritz Mondale's 1984 campaign than Gary Hart's: the strategy was victory by attrition, the means was organization over personality, and the *élan vital* was money, bushels of it, enough, if necessary, to buy the nomination. There was nothing very grand about Dukakis headquarters when it opened for business on three floors of a high-rise at 105 Chauncy Street; its tiers of cubicles and its constantly clanging elevators gave it the look of a law office of no great consequence. But its structure, its efficiency, even its language might have been copied whole out of a textbook on business administration. It was, its young volunteers liked to say, a goddam campaign *corporation,* with Dukakis as the product and Sasso as chairman of the board.

Its indispensable third man was Bob Farmer, a millionaire with a nearly unrivaled genius for talking people out of their own and their best friends' money. Farmer was himself an extravagant sort, with a permanent Florida tan, a wardrobe bordering on flashy and a Mercedes so pricey, he liked to complain, that it ought to give blow jobs. He was known on Chauncy Street for the size of his ego and the urgency of his appetites for food, drink and public attention. He had made his own fortune publishing workbooks, a business he had founded while still a student at Harvard Law and had sold at great profit when his interests led him deeper into politics. He had raised his first funds for the renegade Republican John Anderson's third-party presidential campaign in 1980. But he had drifted thereafter to Democratic clients, starting with Dukakis in 1982. He hungered, as he admitted, to be one of the movers and shakers, and, in the jaded view of some of his colleagues, the Democrats offered him more moving and shaking room.

His advertisements for himself, in print and on the political circuit, made him the object of some controversy at Dukakis headquarters and offended the governor himself. "I want this to be known as the *people* campaign, not the *money* campaign," Dukakis told Farmer one day in a wire-scorching call from the road. The blood drained briefly from Farmer's face; then he was back on the phone, calling all his friends to tell them the story.

Vanity ranks at least as high as conscience among political givers, and Farmer's basic recipe for raising money was accordingly heavy with butter. His own name for his technique, in fact, was "ego management." The day Dukakis announced his intent to run, Farmer had checked into the presidential suite at Le Meridien Hotel in Boston and had begun receiving donors, a dozen of them a day for a month. He didn't ask for money; he asked *them* to ask for money. Those who obliged were festooned with titles. A board of directors was created for the single purpose of luring a major Florida angel aboard. He was made chairman, and people who brought in $20,000 or more got to be board members—all 275 of them.

Farmer could be a formidable live presence; the contributors who trooped through headquarters took on a certain hunted look when he was around. But a telephone in Farmer's hands was what a Stradivarius had been in Jascha Heifetz's or a club in a caveman's—an instrument of art or punishment as the occasion demanded.

"You are the most important person I'll get to talk to all day," he would purr into the phone. He meant the most important at that moment; he would repeat the same line, one aide said, to as many as a hundred prospects a day.

"We need you to play a leadership role in this campaign and be part of our family," he would say. He meant, I want your money.

"You can be a major player," he would say. He meant there would be further flatteries if you ponied up enough—a personalized tour of the statehouse, maybe, or a chat on strategy with Sasso, or, for a really high roller, a private sitting with the governor himself.

"What can you do for me?" Farmer would ask. He meant, Don't just pledge the maximum $1,000 for an individual—go get more from your friends.

"You're a great American!" he would say, whereupon he would ring off, turn to his troops and do his own translation: "I just jerked him off for ten thousand."

No one was better at the game than Farmer, or more important to Dukakis's success; the governor's edge was not so much the brilliance of his strategy, Tubby Harrison would concede in hindsight, as the size of his bank balance. His fund-raising shop ran like a profit-minded multimillion-dollar corporation within the campaign. Farmer, as its star salesman, made the deals, and his partner, Kristin Demong, closed them, frequently offering donors a money-back guarantee if they changed their minds about Dukakis. There were no takers, and the money kept piling up, in large and reassuring heaps. A single fund-raising affair in Boston in mid-June harvested $2.1 million. Guests crabbed about the sparseness of the hors d'oeuvres; never, Demong admitted, had so many paid so much for so few shrimp. But the payoff came in the form of publicity at quarterly reporting time a month later. Dukakis's war chest had swollen to $4.2 million by June 30. No one else was close; if money was the first primary, Farmer bragged, Dukakis had won.

His apparatus was thus in place, monied, organized and strategically sound; the problem with his candidacy, as his own men recognized, was the faintness of its heartbeat. Sasso's quarterly memos to Dukakis continued to worry the subject of his soul quotient. It would not be enough to impress people with his record and his book-learned command of detail. He had to *inspire* them, Sasso warned. He had to work harder at it, spend more time with his speech coach; he was coming across as good, solid and gubernatorial when he needed to be forceful, compelling and presidential. He hadn't yet hit that high note, that thematic plane at which issues and positions transmute themselves into something called vision.

The strategic fallback of the campaign was that Dukakis could somehow get by without one. If charisma were the test, his handlers knew, he would have a problem. Their objective accordingly was, as Ira Jackson put it, to rewrite the rules of the game—to define, on their own terms, when you landed on Community Chest and when you went to jail. They would make character and competence the criteria; they would promote the myth of Mike Dukakis, a man of plain tastes, old values and proven talent for governing. His position at the back of the pack would shelter him from closer scrutiny until his message had had time to ripen; then, Jackson said, he would put on the afterburners and blow by everyone else in the race.

The first and most imposing figure in Dukakis's path was Hart, and there was a personal edge to their matchup. Hart, among friends, was contemptuous of Dukakis, regarding him as a man without ideas of his own; the governor, he would say, had no sense at all of what was going on. His feelings were known to Dukakis—there are few secrets in politics—and were reciprocated by him. He didn't like Hart. He didn't like the tales he had heard about the senator's unruly private life; his wife had brought some of them home from a woman-to-woman talk with Mrs. Hart during the 1984 campaign, and Dukakis had been scandalized. He didn't like Hart's pretensions to superior knowledge of world affairs, either. Dukakis didn't like conceding anything to anybody intellectually, least of all to a man he considered his moral inferior.

His air of grievance with Hart was monitored and subtly encouraged by John Sasso. Indignation was at least an emotion in an otherwise atonal public man; from his earliest days as a young reformer through his comeback race against Ed King, he had always been at his best fighting mad. Hart had never greatly troubled Sasso's sleep, in any case. Joe Biden worried him at times; Biden might get hot. Hart would not. Hart, in Sasso's view, wouldn't even last to the finish line. His candidacy was hollow, and somehow, somewhere, it would collapse.

What Sasso couldn't have reckoned on was the speed or the manner of the senator's undoing. He thought it would happen in New Hampshire, by popular vote. It came instead by Hart's own hand; Gary, in the words of one of Sasso's pals on Chauncy Street, shot himself in the testicles and folded his candidacy before it was one month old.

Fatal Attraction

THE FRONT-RUNNER had slipped his leash. Surging out of Turnberry Isle Marina aboard the pleasure boat *Monkey Business* one day late in March 1987, he set course from North Miami Beach to Bimini. The sun beamed, the sea sparkled, the campaign dropped far astern. The company aboard was congenial—William Broadhurst, forty-eight years old, a master of rest and recreation; Lynn Armandt, twenty-nine, proprietor of the Too Hot Bikini Shop; and Donna Rice, twenty-nine, an actress, model, sales rep and Phi Beta Kappa exercising her inalienable right to party. The Front-Runner wore scarlet trunks, and, as the day wore on, the sun turned his nose and cheeks a nearly matching red. When they docked their richly appointed yacht, he sat on a piling, and Rice, honey-blond and nubile, slipped into his lap.

Click: someone took a picture.

Later, the four shipmates ambled over to The Compleat Angler, one of Ernest Hemingway's old hangouts. The Front-Runner shook a pair of maracas, Broadhurst played the drums, and the young women sang "Twist and Shout."

Click: someone took another picture. Hey, why not? They were just party snaps for somebody's photo album; the Front-Runner had no way of knowing he would see them next in practically every newspaper and on every television newscast in America.

"I Never Wanted to Be President"

What had possessed Gary Hart? Pat Caddell, the cranky numbers genius who knew him well, called it a kind of suicide. Until that reckless day in the sun, Hart had had it all. No Democrat had started the campaign earlier, worked harder at it or put so much distance between himself and the rest of the pack. On the night of the 1984 election, even before the final count was in, he had picked up the phone and started recruiting. He had written a book about military reform and milled out a line of new ideas about arms control, industrial revitalization and competing with Japan; no one would be asking him where the beef was *this* time around. He had raised $2.1 million in campaign funds. He had worked on endorsements, a task he had considered beneath him in 1984. He had begun redoing his image as a distant and intellectually arrogant sort, a Kierkegaard in cowboy boots; he found it at once amusing and perverse when the media promoted him from "cold and aloof" to merely "enigmatic."

His strategy had been to control the campaign's forward ground before Mario Cuomo could come butterflying to life, and the plan seemed to be working brilliantly. By the spring of 1987, with Cuomo snuggled safely in his cocoon, one poll gave Hart a thirty-one-point lead over Jesse Jackson, his nearest rival for the nomination; another showed him beating either George Bush or Bob Dole for the presidency. The other Democrats were still mired hopelessly in single digits if they registered on the screen at all. Hart took a cocky swing through the South early on, talking to farmers, sitting among schoolchildren, paying court to Jimmy Carter. "Man of action!" he exclaimed during one hop, full of himself. "Get me in a stock-car race! These people are going to love me! I'm going to drive in a stock-car race—I'd like to see any of these other candidates do that!"

None of them got the chance; Hart's taste for action had turned him into his own worst enemy. Rumors that he had cheated on his marriage vows had tailed him from his earliest days in presidential politics, as George McGovern's campaign manager in 1972. They had done him no great damage; the old rules shielding politicians from stories about their pursuit of sex, drink and other fleshly pleasures had protected him. But something called character was becoming the new hunting ground of political journalism, and in the issue-free environment of 1987–88 nothing else seemed to count. The rules were changing, and Hart's people assumed he would conform to them. They figured he *wanted* to be president and would discipline himself.

What they hadn't reckoned on was the degree to which Hart placed himself above the rules. He had played by his own set in 1984 and had almost stolen the nomination; his problem, as his Hollywood chum Warren Beatty put it to him at the time, was that he had got famous too fast. He looked on his defeat then as a learning experience, not a rebuke; you *had* to run for the office twice, he told friends, just to make yourself known and to master the game. All the thread-pulling about his "character"—the trivia tease about how he had changed his name, fudged his age and borrowed freely from the John Kennedy book of mannerisms—was behind him. It had run its course in '84 without intruding seriously on his private life, and he seemed, three years later, to feel immune from further harm.

He was in some measure the Jay Gatsby of our politics, a man who had cast off his small-town, Bible-college past and re-created himself according to his own flashier design. He was fifty years old at the eve of battle, his shirt buttons strained across his middle, and his complexion was blotchy from too much time indoors, but Hart clung to his persona as the champion of a new generation with fresh political ideas and tolerant personal values; it was his mask, and what lay behind it was his business. There was a cavalier quality about him, an air bordering on contempt for the conventions of politics and political reporting. It was as if a campaign should be judged solely on its white papers, not on the strengths and weaknesses of the men who had written or commissioned them.

It didn't work that way anymore, as Bill Dixon, his campaign manager, tried to warn him. It was a given among Hart's people that there had been, as one put it, these *romances*. They joked about it sometimes, having no other recourse; Dixon, thin and tense as wire, worried that Hart's candidacy might, in fact, be scuttled by the loose lips of his own crew.

What they didn't need was Hart fueling the fire. You can't afford even the *appearance* of impropriety, Dixon told him.

"That is not going to be a problem," Hart said.

There were rumors that his name might surface as the Other Man in a notorious Washington divorce case, and that was only the beginning. The media, Dixon warned, might actually place him under surveillance.

"That's fine, that's fine," Hart said, whereupon, on all the evidence, he forgot it.

Other advisers were picking up similar danger signals. Hal Haddon, a

Denver lawyer and an old friend of Hart's, passed along a tip that one of the big newspapers was in fact thinking about staking him out.

"Figures," Hart said with a shrug.

He had told no one about his overnight holiday in Bimini, but those rumors washed in, too, on the rising tide. There had been talk in Florida, a friend at one of the networks told Hart's deputy political director, Joe Trippi, a bright young convert from Mondale '84. Hart had done a series of law lectures at the University of Florida, then dropped off the scope for a day. The gossip factory was humming. The network was considering tailing him the next time he showed up in the state.

The alert was brought to Hart's attention. There's no story there, he said, and nothing happened.

Not long after the Bimini run, Trippi and Haddon found themselves in Puerto Rico on an organizing trip. They wedged in some down time together to walk and talk on the beach. The amble stretched out for an hour, then two. Trippi was the new kid at Camp Gary, Haddon the old hand; Haddon had known Hart for more than twenty years, and Trippi found himself pouring out his worries to the older man.

"I can't go to Hart," he said. "I don't have a relationship with him. You're the only one who can."

The two paused for a moment, Trippi large and curly, Haddon square and compact.

"Well," Haddon said glumly, "I've done this before. The last time I went and talked to him was about three years ago, and he didn't speak to me for three months because of what I accused him of. I'm not pure on the subject. He's going to turn . . ."

His voice trailed off; he was picturing Hart's anger in his mind.

Still, he did try again, confronting Hart as soon as he got back to Denver. The senator, he felt, was like a bridegroom treating himself to a last, extended bachelor party before surrendering his freedom. It has to end, he told Hart. We've got to move up the wedding date.

In the past, when his people had given him similar advice, Hart had told them angrily to back off. He wasn't president yet, and he wasn't a machine they could run every minute; he needed space, he said, that *he* controlled. But this time Haddon's warning appeared to take. Hart's schedule showed a Saturday-Sunday trip to Puerto Rico in mid-May. Saturday was for politics. The Sunday entry said, "Day off with Broadhurst," and, Trippi guessed, Broadhurst's boating party.

Broadhurst—Billy B, to his friends—was a lawyer, lobbyist and fund-raiser well known for the quality and generosity of his entertainments; his seeming hold on Hart made some of the senator's people nervous, and so did their yacht trips together in the southern sun. Trippi had seen other, similar dates on the campaign calendar; it was, he thought, that blatant. But with Haddon's visit, they suddenly vanished. Playtime was over.

"You got Sunday back for politics in Puerto Rico," Hart's scheduler, Sue Casey, told Trippi at their next meeting. "He's not going on the boat with Billy."

Hallelujah, Hal, Trippi thought. You did it.

What Haddon had achieved turned out to be little more than a pause. Hart stayed in touch with Rice, phoning her several times, telling her how the media were roughing him up. A profile in *Newsweek* alluded to his rakish reputation, quoting a sometime adviser, John McEvoy, to the effect that Gary would be all right so long as he kept his pants on. McEvoy was speaking hypothetically, not from knowledge, but the story seemed to legitimate the subject, and others soon followed.

The floodgates of speculation opened while Hart was holed up writing his announcement speech, sometimes working at his high-rise law office in downtown Denver, sometimes in a small study at his log-and-stone house twenty-five miles from town. He had never liked being profiled in print, and the poking around in his bed linens only intensified his displeasure. The real problems facing the country wouldn't get discussed in the media, he complained to Billy Shore, his closest and most fiercely loyal aide. They were going to make *him* the issue; they were just going to pick him apart. He was a week out of Bimini and a week away from declaring his candidacy, and he was having real second thoughts. He began to wonder aloud whether he ought to be running at all.

In the end, he pushed aside his doubts. Reporters in tow, he went out to Red Rocks Park near Denver and, with his wife, Lee, and their daughter, Andrea, standing beside him, committed himself to the race. "Ideas have power," Hart said, looking oddly grim. "Ideas are what governing is all about."

The Friends of Billy B

For a short time thereafter, the senator's libido took second place to his unpaid 1984 campaign debts as an object of public inquiry, and his new candidacy seemed to find its land legs after a wobbly start. At the end of his first Southern tour, in April, his staff flew back to Denver feeling high. No one had seemed greatly interested in his sex life, and if anyone was, Hart had served up a preemptive answer—the *perfect* answer, his people thought—in a forthcoming story in *The New York Times Magazine*. "Follow me around," he had told a writer profiling him. "I don't care. I'm serious. If anybody wants to put a tail on me, go ahead. They'd be very bored."

On the weekend that story was due to appear, Hart left his wife at home and headed for Washington to work on an economics speech. What he didn't tell anyone was that Donna Rice was also winging into town. What he didn't *know* was that someone had leaked his secret to *The Miami Herald* and that his dare would be taken up even before it had been published to the world.

The tip came from a young woman in a call to Tom Fiedler, the paper's political editor. Fiedler had just published a piece attacking the rumor-mongering in the media about Hart's supposed adulteries, and it had caught her eye.

"You know that article you wrote about Gary Hart," she said, giggling nervously, "and the rumors about womanizing? Those aren't rumors."

"What do you mean?" Fiedler said.

She hesitated. "How much do you guys pay for pictures?" she asked.

Fiedler put her off, but she was back on the line next morning, elaborating her story. One of her best friends was involved with Hart. They had encountered each other at a big party on a yacht, she said; a day or two later, he had invited her out for a cruise; she was flying to Washington that very evening for a weekend with him.

This time, she offered supporting detail, and when Rice flew up late Friday afternoon, a reporter from the *Herald* was on the plane. Billy B and Linda Armandt met her at the airport. They picked up Hart at his place, dined at Broadhurst's on steak, corn and artichokes, then went back to Hart's town house. A *Herald* crew was tracking their comings and goings, though only imperfectly. No one kept a constant watch on Hart's back door, through which Broadhurst and the young women periodically issued; only the principals really knew who had stayed where with whom that night.

On Saturday, the foursome drove out to Mount Vernon and had a picnic on the Potomac; that night, Broadhurst and the two young women barbecued a chicken and took it to Hart's house for dinner. During the evening, Hart and Rice decided to take a stroll. As they stepped outside, the candidate saw someone in a dark parka walking their way, then abruptly doubling back. It was warm out, too warm for a heavy coat, and what had been a rather dim bulb blazed into light over Hart's head.

"My God," he said, "they're staking me out."

He grabbed Rice's arm and hustled her back inside.

"I don't know what they have, just that they're assuming I've been with Donna," he told the others. "I think it's best that until we find out more, you guys just leave."

They went out the back way, got into Broadhurst's car and slipped away unnoticed. Rice never heard from Hart again.

After a time, the senator came out the front door alone. He played tag with the reporters briefly, in his car and on foot, confirming his suspicions that they were following him; then he bearded them face to face. He looked nervous.

They asked about the woman.

He wouldn't give her name.

Had he spent the night with her?

"No."

Had he met her on the yacht?

"I won't deny anything."

You've been making all these calls to her—what were they about?

"Nothing."

Let us talk to the girl.

"No," Hart said, turning on his heel. "That's enough. I don't have to talk to you anymore."

The newsmen retired to their hotel to file what they had. Hart made for his telephone and started placing calls. Lee was first. He told her what had happened—by his account, nothing. There was no ducking and dodging, she told friends later, no I'm-sorry-but-we've-got-to-get-by-this-somehow-babe. Their marriage might have been bumpy, but, she said, Gary didn't lie to her; if he said nothing happened, nothing happened.

"I'm with you," she said. "We can keep going. I think it's important you become president."

"But, babe," he said, "you know I never wanted to be president."

Billy Shore was next, at his rented ranch house in the Denver suburbs. Shore, at thirty-two, was Hart's special assistant by title, his body man by occupation; a weekend off with his wife and his eighteen-month-old son happened no more than once every eight or nine weeks and was a rare treat for him. It was ten-thirty or eleven o'clock when the phone rang, disturbing his peace.

"My house has been staked out by some reporters," Hart told him.

Shore spread the word, and the senior staff gathered at Bill Dixon's apartment for an all-night crisis meeting. They popped beers and soft drinks. Music played low in the background, a counterpoint to their mood.

All they had then was Hart's sketchy version of the events. Some believed him, some didn't. All of them knew they had to find out what really had happened; if there was more to the story than Hart was telling, and the press beat them to it, they were cooked.

Dixon called Donna Rice, with his deputy, John Emerson, on an extension. Both men were lawyers, and the conversation had the edge of a cross-examination. Rice was exhausted, hysterical, sobbing, but Hart's people wanted to believe her, and her protestations of innocence sounded real to them. The problem was that they were dealing with appearances, and they needed to know *everything*. From her days as a model and a starlet in soap operas and commercials, had there been any—uh—photos? First she said no; then—well, there *was* that time she had posed for a saloon poster naked from the waist up, wrapped in a Confederate flag.

"Our Southern brochure," someone groaned.

They were starting a step behind the news, scrambling just to catch up. The *Herald* rushed into print on Sunday morning, without waiting to interview the two women—Broadhurst had offered them up on condition that the paper agree to delay the story—or evaluating its own surveillance procedures. It simply reported that Rice had spent Friday night and much of Saturday at Hart's place. What had or hadn't happened between them didn't really matter. The look of the thing did; it made an open issue of Hart's judgment, his credibility and his apparently slack view of marriage, and his people found themselves struggling to contain the damage.

Their preliminary strategy was to turn the tables on the paper by attacking its stakeout as sloppy and its ethics as gutter-low. But that would buy them no more than a day or two; the larger media herd would soon be thundering after the story of what really had happened that weekend, and Dixon flew out to Washington on the red-eye, determined to get the answers first. "If I find out he lied to me," he told a colleague, setting out, "I'll quit."

He made his way straight from the airport to Broadhurst's home, two small town houses merged into one. The place was a sumptuary's dream, with a patio bar, a hot tub and thirty places at table for dinner. There were five in help bustling among the antiques and the Oriental *objets d'art;* Lynn Armandt, in the official version, had come to Washington to interview for one of the jobs, as Billy B's social coordinator, and had brought Rice along for company.

Dixon got quickly down to cases. He had worked his way through law school as a licensed private detective, and he gave Broadhurst and Rice the third degree.

"What happened the last two nights?" he demanded. "Who slept with whom?"

Both of them swore that no one had been in the wrong bed. So did Hart when Dixon questioned him. Dixon believed them at first; he didn't know about Bimini until Monday, when Broadhurst told him the story. At Dixon's suggestion, Rice disclosed it to the world at a press conference in Miami. It would be his last service to Hart's candidacy; he felt he no longer knew *what* the truth was.

That night, Dixon called Hart from Broadhurst's house, where he was bunking. David Letterman was cracking late-night jokes about Gary campaigning his brains out. The papers had pictures of Rice modeling a bathing suit; judgment, as campaign press secretary Kevin Sweeney would say later, doesn't look that good in a bikini. The story was getting out of hand.

"I can no longer be of value as campaign manager," Dixon told Hart.

"We're all under a lot of pressure," Hart said. "Go take some time off and see if this is going to be a permanent decision."

It was. Dixon had just informed Denver of his resignation when Broadhurst found him in an upstairs sitting room.

"They don't know it yet," Dixon said, "but it's over."

The Siege at Troublesome Gulch

The scandal was slipping out of control by then, and reporters were beginning to ask where Lee was. The answer was that she had come down with a sinus infection and was holed up at the Harts' five-room cabin in Troublesome Gulch, a forty-five-minute drive from town; an address chosen in part for its catchiness had become only too appropriate. It hurt her to be pictured as a victim, too frail to cope and too wounded to be at her husband's side. Her illness was real and painful; her face was badly swollen, and if she went out looking like that, she told a visitor, people would say, Look—Gary *beats* her, too.

So she sat home with Andrea for three days, under siege by a media mob outside. Andrea, taking it hard, sat glued to the TV looking for news; occasionally, she would fling a shoe at the screen in anger. Lee couldn't bear to listen. Hart phoned her often. Her replies, according to a friend keeping her company, were quick and supportive: I love you. We're going to beat this thing. Let's go. Don't worry about me.

Not all of her crowd shared her forbearance. A troubleshooter from Hart headquarters arrived at the cabin one evening and peeked in through the screen door. A tall, stylish woman with a mass of dark hair was pacing up and down the living room, waving a butcher knife.

"Lee," she was shouting, "you've just got to cut his thing off!" The knife sliced downward through the air. "When you see him, just *bam!*—cut it off!"

"Now, you're being way too hard on him," Lee said between gusts of laughter. "I know Gary. He's naive about how things look, but he didn't do this."

"I don't care what you say," her friend repeated, "you've just got to *cut it off!*"

On the third day of the siege, she organized a picnic for a couple of chums in a meadow out back of the cabin. A clump of trees hid them from the press. They ate and threw a football around, and Lee talked openly about the conflict Gary had felt about running. He was running because he thought he could be a good president, she said, not because he wanted the job. He felt it was his *obligation* to serve—why couldn't people understand that?

Under the circumstances, it was difficult to tell just what Hart did want. Some theories were ribald, others serious. Some fastened on the senator's mother, a religious fundamentalist, who had wanted him to be a minister and had raised him to believe that he had a mission in life. That sense of mission had survived his passage from religion to politics: he had been given special gifts and was obliged to put them to the service of the nation. But the duty was not always a welcome one, measured against all he would have to give up. He seemed to his people to be pursuing the presidency with his mind, not his heart. It was as if a piece of him *wanted* to get caught, one of them said; if running was indeed his duty and it were taken away from him, it wouldn't be his duty anymore.

If so, his means of escape undid him; it was his wife who became the object of public sympathy, and she tried, with only modest success, to transfer some of it to him. As soon as she felt up to it, she slipped past the siege line in Troublesome Gulch on the floor of Trippi's Plymouth Voyager and flew out to New Hampshire to join her husband.

Hart by then had done a general defense before a meeting of newspaper publishers in New York, but he was about to face the working press for the first time since the story broke. The media were in full cry; his news conference was memorable mainly for its ferocity. The room was small, stuffy and overcrowded, the questioning smoky with indignation. Reporters could be least attractive when they were most sanctimonious, playing moral grand jury.

Did Hart expect his account of the weekend to be believed?

"I've written a spy novel," he said. "I'm not stupid. If I had wanted to meet with a woman in secret, I wouldn't have done it this way."

Would he take a lie-detector test on it?

"Give me a break," he muttered.

Did he think adultery was immoral?

"Yes," Hart said.

Had he ever committed adultery?

"I don't have to answer that," Hart snapped. He looked sweaty and taut, but under control.

That night at a small hotel in St. Johnsbury, Vermont, just over the New Hampshire line, the senator talked tactics over dinner with his senior staff and his local supporters. He had tried one more event that day, a town meeting in Littleton, New Hampshire, and had had to fight his way through the pack to get to his car, with Lee in his arms.

"They'll never stop asking me these questions," he said. "I'll never get by this. Anybody got any ideas?"

Trippi proposed buying a half hour of national television time. The story was bigger than *Dynasty;* everybody in America would tune in, Trippi told Hart, and it would be his show.

Hart's eyes lit up.

"The minute you do that," someone else said, "Dan Rather, Tom Brokaw and Peter Jennings will go on the air for the next thirty minutes and tear you apart."

"Yeah, yeah, you're right," Hart said.

There were other ideas; with each, Hart would brighten, then slump as someone poked holes in it. The campaign was going sour. Money was drying up. The party establishment was turning on Hart. His key supporters were mute.

"Maybe we should all go home," he said.

Oooh, this guy's out, Trippi thought. He sounds like E.T. He's not saying maybe anymore. It's the switch. *Pfft!*—it's done.

No final decision was made; the traveling staff and the Denver head-quarters team spent the waning evening wrangling by phone over whether to bring Hart home for repairs or keep him on the road. They were still talking when Paul Taylor of *The Washington Post* found Kevin Sweeney in a hotel bar on the New Hampshire side of the line and tugged him out into the lobby. Taylor seemed embarrassed, almost apologetic.

I don't know how to broach this, he began.

Uh-oh, Sweeney was thinking. It's the big, big one.

We have allegations of another woman, Taylor said, and we have substantial corroboration. We want to talk to Gary about it.

It was late, going on eleven o'clock. Sweeney said he didn't want to bother Hart without more to go on than that.

Taylor flicked on his laptop computer and started reading. We have her name, he said.

Sweeney struggled to keep a poker face in place. I've heard those allegations before, he said. Go ahead.

It's a detective's report, Taylor said. There was a name, a date in late 1986 and a lot of specific detail. The *Post* had confronted the woman with it. She had broken down, Taylor said, and admitted having had an affair with Hart. We have two-thirds of the story, he went on, and now we need the other third.

Sweeney scrambled for a phone to tell the others, knowing it was the last straw; the campaign was over. While Haddon called the *Post* to beg a day's time, Shore woke Hart with the news.

"This is really getting ridiculous," Hart mumbled, half digesting the latest allegation.

Later, he called Sweeney.

"It's never going to stop, is it," he said.

"No," Sweeney told him.

Hart hung up and turned to Shore.

"Let's think about going back early tomorrow," he said.

The road team laid down a line of retreat for him. The charter Learjet that had delivered Lee was still there. They tracked down the pilot, notified the airports at both ends of the journey, and scheduled an early escape; the press was left believing Hart would be touring a factory on schedule in New Hampshire. In the morning, the Harts, along with four close staffers, crowded aboard the six-seater and headed west. Hart stared out the window, a copy of Tolstoy's *Resurrection* in his lap. Shore wore a pair of sunglasses he had bought at the airport, figuring he might mist up. Sue Casey sat in the back. Tears were trickling down her cheeks.

At home, Hart took a two-hour walk in the woods to ponder his options. There weren't many, as his senior staff concluded in a day of meetings downtown. Maybe, someone said, he could go on national television, confess all and pray for forgiveness; maybe he could suspend the campaign until after Labor Day, hoping the flap would blow over. Some quickie phone-bank polling improvised by Paul Tully, the campaign's political director, splashed cold water on both ideas. Men found Hart's conduct merely stupid; women called it unacceptable, intolerable, unforgivable. Stupid they could survive, Tully figured. Unforgivable was fatal.

As the talk went wistfully on, Hart called in.

"I've got to make a decision," he told Dixon, who had come back to preside at the last rites. "I can't go on, with what's happening to my wife and children. What should I do?"

A dozen people crowded Dixon's office. "Anybody who thinks Gary should stay in this race," he told them, while Hart waited on the line, "give me your best reasons. Now is the time. Speak up."

There was total silence.

That evening, Hart went to work on his withdrawal speech. The more he thought about it, the angrier he got, and for a time he wavered. If I stay in, he told his people, I can lick it.

In the middle of the night, Warren Beatty called him and tossed another log on the fire.

"You're crazy," Beatty said. "Don't get out. There are a lot of people who think you have been wronged. Don't do it! You should tell them, 'Hell, no!' "

"Thanks, Warren," Hart replied. The staff-written text he had been working on was discarded, and he began to draft a hell-no speech instead.

Its bottom line was that he was quitting, but with a bang, not a whimper; his words were so defiant that staffers had to scramble to convince the press that he really did mean to drop out. He had gone to bed, he said, prepared to do a conventional withdrawal statement, "and then quietly disappear from the stage. And then . . . I woke up about four or five this morning with a start. And I said to myself, 'Hell, no!' "

There were whoops from campaign workers in the audience; they thought he meant to keep going. Hart looked startled. "No," he said, shaking his head. "No, no, no." The enterprise was over; he was an angry and defiant man, he said, who had refused to play the game, and he was being punished for it. The nearest thing he came to an apology was the glancing concession that he had made mistakes—"maybe big mistakes," he said, "but not *bad* mistakes." He was, in his recounting, more sinned against than sinning, the casualty of a process "that reduces the press of this nation to hunters and presidential candidates to being hunted. . . . If it continues to destroy people's integrity and honor," he went on, "then that system will eventually destroy itself."

His critique of the process and the press was not without merit; presidential politics had, as he said, become a kind of grand national sporting event, and the players in it, handlers and reporters alike, commonly agreed that it was crazy. But he was not a wholly innocent party. There was a piece missing from his speech, Sweeney thought: Hart never acknowledged that, with his recklessness, he had brought his problems on himself.

The Day of the Tortoise

Hart would attempt a comeback in December, going nowhere. If, as Pat Schroeder said, his fall had been almost like a Greek tragedy, his try at resurrection was merely pathetic. His candidacy had no real bottom in the electorate, no mass of voters who loved him, right or wrong. The media, having borne him aloft three years before, had dropped him without a parachute; his reentry lasted less than three months, whereupon he became the only presidential candidate in memory to drop out of the same race twice.

His passage from the stage in May had left the campaign in tumult. Jesse Jackson became the nominal front-runner, though with an invisible asterisk after his name; it stood for the white consensus judgment that he could not win. Dick Gephardt's standing in a *Des Moines Register* Iowa Poll shot up to 24 percent; he became the man to beat in the Iowa caucuses, well before he was ready. Joe Biden's pursuit of the Big Chill generation took on a new degree of plausibility. Bruce Babbitt tried on the mantle of New Ideas. Paul Simon's old ones suddenly sounded better; there was something comfortingly stable in his fusty speech and his homely ways.

Dukakis's stock ticked upward, too. He gained ground in Iowa and security in New Hampshire; people were saying for the first time that he was the *real* front-runner, no matter what numbers Jackson was putting up in the polls. Dukakis took a certain unconcealed pleasure in Hart's demise. "You must be shittin' me," he said, smiling, when one of his people brought him the news. But it meant he would have to get moving sooner and faster than anything envisioned in his strategy books. The hare had dropped out before the race had fairly begun, and the tortoise found himself ahead of the field too soon, exposed and alone.

Little Big Men

Running for president is like running for your life: almost any help is welcome. Before Congressman Richard Gephardt got under way, he went down to Plains, Georgia, to talk to Jimmy Carter. The trip was mostly a ritual, but the Carters sent no one home empty-handed. While Gephardt talked should-I-or-shouldn't-I with Jimmy, his wife, Jane, talked how-do-you-do-it with Rosalynn. "Go into the small towns in Iowa, just drive in," the former First Lady advised the newcomer. "Go to the local newspaper and introduce yourself, and be sure you take a bumper sticker. If they want to take your picture, you stand out in front and hold that sticker up. Then go down and introduce yourself to the people on Main Street."

Few politicians treated Jimmy Carter as a role model seven years after his ignominious fall, but the formula he had used in 1976 for moving from Main Street to Pennsylvania Avenue had, for many of them, become an obsession. For the candidate unknown beyond his home base, the dreamer long on ideas but short of money, the main attraction of the Carter method was its simplicity. From out of nowhere, you score on the night of the Iowa caucuses. In the media frenzy that ensues, you body-surf through New Hampshire. Then, as cash and workers come flooding in, a rising swell of momentum propels you the rest of the way to the nomination.

The scenario tantalized Gephardt, a strawberry-blond six-footer who arrived in Iowa with the grin of Tom Sawyer and the confidence of Norman Vincent Peale. It seduced Bruce Babbitt, a lanky Arizonan who pedaled across the entire state on a bicycle, hoping that Iowans would notice and think, Wow! Politics at its best! It lured Paul Simon, the junior senator from Illinois, a nice old guy who looked more like Pee-wee Herman than like John F. Kennedy and seemed to one of his own men to be running for president of the United Way. Of all the Democrats, only Michael Dukakis and Jesse Jackson had the resources—the power of money for the governor of Massachusetts, the power of soul for the preacher from Chicago—to work from a broader design. But when the tug came, they got out there, too, Dukakis in pinstripes, starched shirt and knotted tie talking up the virtues of Belgian endive; the ineffably urbane Jackson milking a cow.

If the caution in Mario Cuomo, Sam Nunn and Bill Bradley had kept them home, it sometimes seemed that the Walter Mitty in the others led them to Iowa. The impression was unfair. Each of them was experienced in his own way; each had a legitimate claim to the attention of their party. But the scuffling among them and their managers disclosed their common vulnerability. Each had started the 1988 campaign with a stature problem. The scramble to become known, to reach the top, would drive some of them to strike outlandish poses and others to hit below the belt. Each seemed to achieve his hour in the sun, then wilt under closer scrutiny. Round One of the contest would turn on a rather bleak question: Would anyone grow, in the public eye, to presidential size? Or would the winner win by default, simply for having survived?

The Power of Positive Thinking

On summer evenings in St. Louis when Dick Gephardt was still a freckled kid in a Cardinals baseball cap, he used to sit out on the front stoop watching the fireflies and talking first principles with his dad. Mr. Gephardt drove a milk truck. Get a good education, he told his son; make more of your life than your dad has. Mrs. Gephardt gave him a copy of *The Power of Positive Thinking*, Peale's famous primer on optimism. It captivated him. In an autobiography composed when he was fifteen, Gephardt wrote that he wanted to be a credit to his family, his country and his God. One day, an old friend took his mother aside and actually uttered the words graven into so many campaign biographies. ''Loreen,'' he said, ''you mark my words. That boy of yours is going to be president someday.''

And yet, in his forty-sixth year, Gephardt had still escaped the notice of most of his fellow countrymen outside Missouri, which he represented, and

Washington, where he served. He was not an obvious contender for the presidency when he started thinking hard about it in 1984; he had to get used to the idea first and then sell it to his wife and their three reluctant children before he could broach it seriously to anyone else. His ruminations and his travels stretched out for more than two years, a process he likened to getting into a swimming pool at the shallow end and walking toward the deep water. The first returns from his scouts on their prowls in search of campaign staffers were not at all promising. Mention his name, they reported, and people said, "Dick *Gephardt*? You gotta be kidding!"

They were dismayed. Gephardt was not. Sometimes, the thirty-second person you asked to take a particular job would be the first to say yes; still, he persisted, and his tenacity paid off. His first major catch was Dick Moe, a Washington lawyer who had been chief of Fritz Mondale's vice-presidential staff. Moe had been in five presidential campaigns, and his reading of Gephardt was positive. Sure, he could put an audience to sleep with his earnestness, but, Moe thought, he was a good listener, an unusual thing in a trade where most people preferred to talk. He was comfortable with himself. There had been presidents who fairly reeked of insecurity. Gephardt wouldn't be one of them, Moe guessed. Gephardt knew who he was.

Moe agreed to serve as an informal adviser, a lookout. He warned Gephardt that presidential campaigns bring out the worst in people: "Events are in the saddle, nobody is in control, the media are off in a frenzy—you've got to be ready for that." Moe could think of two people who would have had the gifts to tame the chaos for Gephardt. One was John Sasso, who was otherwise engaged. The other was Bill Carrick, then thirty-five, a South Carolinian of droll wit and shrewd political intelligence. Carrick had worked in Ted Kennedy's 1980 campaign and had joined his political apparatus two years later, waiting for him to run again. Kennedy didn't, and Carrick, hungry for action, was shopping for a candidate when Gephardt sought him out.

He liked Gephardt, once they had spent some time together; the congressman was smart, clean and disciplined, his ego was of a manageable size, and he seemed to have some feeling for what a campaign was about. His private life was an empty dossier; the pols back in St. Louis had dubbed him Little Dickie Do-Right for his good manners and his straight-arrow ways. But Carrick was blunt with him about his prospects, warning that he was a hell of a long shot. Gephardt might be a big deal on Capitol Hill, a six-term member of the House and chairman of its Democratic Caucus, but voters, journalists and party activists all had a mind-set that governors and senators were important people; congressmen were not.

Still, Carrick liked his looks and signed on. So did Terry McAuliffe, a lawyer, banker, broker and fund-raiser who had started in the trade shaking trees for Jimmy Carter as a law student of twenty-three. So did other prime draft choices: David Doak and Bob Shrum, two first-rate media-movers; Ed Reilly, one of the best of the younger polltakers; and Donna Brazile, a brilliant black field organizer who had worked for Reverend Jackson in 1984 and wanted to widen her experience.

Gephardt was the first of the Democratic candidates to reach Iowa; he spent more than two years working the entire circuit of the state's ninety-nine counties, promising to change the Me Generation to the Us Generation. The most famous thing about him then was the paleness of his eyebrows, which tended to disappear on TV; his own mother thought he ought to dye them. But he kept coming back with his outstretched hand, his Penrod smile and his apparently indefatigable faith in himself.

His crowds were small and, at first, mainly curious, but he drove himself through the routine—the short hops in small planes, the dusty sprints from farm to farm, the nights in anonymous motels. You had to do it, if you were Dick Who? and serious about winning. When you start, he said one day, riding down yet another back-country road to yet another barn rally, nobody believes you. You had to convince first yourself and then other people that you had a chance. If you didn't go everywhere, you might as well not go at all.

He sat rigid in the backseat of a borrowed sedan. Gravel spat up under the tires. The engine hummed drowsily. Long afternoon rays of sunlight exposed the red rims around his pale-blue eyes. He was fighting sleep, one more small act of will in an endless chain leading toward the presidency. Willpower was the most important thing in life, he said. Desire. Attitude. If you decided you were going to be something, you probably would be. You just had to lock on and say, This is what I'm going to be.

The drudgery bore dividends; in May 1987, when Hart fell by the wayside, Gephardt raced ahead of everyone in Iowa. It was too much prosperity too soon. His campaign had an unfinished look, and his support was dangerously soft, based more on familiarity than on love. People in Iowa thought he was a safe choice; they *liked* him all right, but once Hart was gone, they started shopping.

The Unimportance of Being Earnest

The shopping season was punctuated and occasionally enlivened by a series of candidate debates; they were the only way for a campaign to put points on the scoreboard before the primary season started. The candidates became a kind of traveling repertory company, available to any strategically situated newspaper, interest group or Democratic committee that invited them to come. There would be more than thirty debates before time ran out, and most of the candidates quickly wearied of them. It was hard to pick the winners, since Jackson typically dominated them with his rhetorical flair and was seldom rigorously challenged. The matchups instead had the aspect of gentlemanly boxing, the contenders feinting and jabbing for points with pillow-soft gloves; the objective at times seemed less to win than to keep from losing.

Not everyone succeeded. The road show made it onto network television out of Houston in July 1987, a full year before the convention, and it was the beginning of the end of Bruce Babbitt. He had his charms, chief among them a serious and curious mind, a respect for the difficulty of the real issues and a cheerful openness in addressing them. But the Houston debate revealed him to be, in the words of his press secretary, Mike McCurry, the Spuds MacKenzie of the campaign—the life of the party but a dog on TV. His head waggled. His eyes bulged. His gestures were awkward. His voice was an echo of Richard Nixon's. His Adam's apple bobbed like a yo-yo. Sometimes, wriggling and writhing in his seat, he slid entirely—some thought mercifully—off the screen.

His unease with the medium smothered his message and, very nearly, his candidacy. The only sign of approval in the hall audible to one of Babbitt's men was the sound of four hands clapping, his wife's and his campaign manager's. A group of voters registering their reactions on electronic people meters rated him at rock bottom; so did Sergio Bendixen, a senior adviser to Babbitt's own campaign.

Afterward, his manager, Fred DuVal, called his national chairman, Duane Garrett, for a review.

"I didn't know they had icebergs in Houston," Garrett said. "It was like the *Titanic*."

No flaw was quite so fatal to a modern presidential campaign. A sizable share of the growing population of handlers concerned themselves directly or indirectly with telemarketing, but some cases were harder than others, and Babbitt's bordered on terminal. Oh, shit, why am I in this anyway? he had asked himself, walking glumly back to his hotel room after the debacle in Houston. It was a fair question, given the degree to which politics had *become* television. The ridicule was harsh and universal. The campaign slid into a tailspin; the only thing America seemed to know about Babbitt was that he was that guy who flopped in Houston. People were saying, Bury him—he knew that. Read the obituaries. He's dead.

At low tide in his gloom, he retreated to his cabin in Sedona in the

Arizona mountains and, over a weekend, considered dropping out of the race.

"You don't quit when you're down," his wife, Hattie, told him. She had encouraged his candidacy from the beginning and had put her own successful career as a trial lawyer on hold to campaign for him. "Just do it," she told him. "Plow through it. It'll get behind you."

The next day, he called DuVal and asked to see the debate on tape. A showing was arranged at headquarters in Phoenix. Babbitt stared silently at the monitor; it was, DuVal imagined, like being slapped in the face.

"Well," the candidate said finally, "we got work to do."

DuVal, young and adoring, was near tears.

"If they can teach Mr. Ed to talk," Babbitt said, "they can teach me."

He had never really tried to learn before, or felt he had to. He had been elected governor twice with no flair for the medium and was unprepared for the new presidential politics; he had imagined it almost as a grand seminar, a battle of ideas at the level of the Lincoln–Douglas debates, and had found himself in a beauty pageant instead. Bendixen had badgered him in memos to do practice tapes for at least a half hour a day on the road, and his prep team in Houston had tried to get him to save some of his rehearsal time for style. "We'll move on to that tomorrow," he had told them. He didn't need coaching. His ideas were what mattered. The fuss over appearances was silly. It was part of what he was running against.

After Houston, his handlers rushed him to a video doctor, Michael Sheehan, an elfin Irishman who had begun as an actor and become a successful media coach. Sheehan liked Babbitt immediately for his mind and his honesty. But stylistically the governor was a mess, a judgment made plain to him in the weeks that followed in sharp and sometimes punishing terms. He moved *everything* too much; if you so much as raised an eyebrow on TV, Sheehan told him, you might as well dub in the sound of a thunderclap—the medium had that much power of magnification. In fact, as examination revealed, Babbitt had no voluntary control over his eyebrows at all. When directed to raise them, all he could do was bug out his eyes. Sheehan prescribed a regimen of eyebrow pushups, and Babbitt, chastened, did as he was told.

"Is this all style over substance?" Babbitt asked Sheehan. "Because if that's true, I'm going to be running with a handicap."

Sheehan did his best to help him overcome it. They worked on his smile, his frown, his vagrant waves of the hand—this little flipper, Sheehan called it, his manner as stinging as a ruler across the knuckles. "You're violating the frame again, Bruce!" he would screech at some mysterious twist or turn of the candidate's person. "I know, I know," Babbitt would say, where-upon he would try again.

The further question was what precisely it was he wanted to say once he had learned how to say it. He had been advertised from the start as something new in politics: an honest man who actually said what he thought regardless of the consequences. Babbitt had in fact staked out some controversial positions, arguing, for one example, for a means test for eligibility for government assistance. But he had fudged the touchiest question of all, the likelihood that some kind of new tax revenue would be needed to narrow the budget deficit and insure the economy against ruin. It was suicidal to talk taxes in a campaign, his people kept telling him, and Babbitt had come to believe them.

After Houston, necessity mothered invention. Babbitt met with his strategists one sticky day in July at the penthouse office of one of his Washington consultants, Greg Schneiders. The summer heat shimmered outside the windows. The power and the possibilities of the city below had never seemed quite so far out of reach. He had to do something bold, something unorthodox, or it would be lost to him, possibly forever.

The voices for daring came, ironically, from the Beltway professionals in the room, Bendixen and Schneiders, rather than from the young idealists serving Babbitt out of love. Houston, in Schneiders's view, had been liberating for Babbitt in the way Waterloo had been for Napoleon: he had nothing left to lose by taking chances. A major economic speech was coming up. It was an opportunity, almost an invitation.

"Don't tell me what you've been saying in the campaign," Schneiders told Babbitt. Schneiders was a smooth, handsome man with longish gray hair and a low-key bedside manner with a client; he had worked for Jimmy Carter in 1976 and was thus practically the only person in the room with experience in a winning presidential campaign. "In your heart of hearts," he asked Babbitt, "what do you *really* think ought to be done about the economy?"

Babbitt's eyes warmed. The next administration would have to lay on some kind of tax, probably on consumer purchases. "But I've danced around that," he admitted. "It's the kiss of death."

"Well, why not say it?" Schneiders asked.

"Really?" Babbitt said. "Everybody tells me not to." He looked stunned, like a freed prisoner blinking in fear at his first sight of the sun.

"I'm serious," Schneiders told him. "This is the image you have—that you take unpopular stands for what you believe. Why not carry it to its logical conclusion?"

Still, Babbitt hesitated; the idea was too new at first, and too controversial within his own campaign. The Arizona kids didn't like it. Neither did Bendixen's own partner, John Law. "This is hara-kiri!" he exploded when he heard about the scheme. "It's fucking *crazy!*"

The meeting ended without a decision. But Schneiders kept pressing the handler for a change, telling the candidate to forget the polls and the rules and speak his mind. There was no magic locket out there, he wrote in a memo to Babbitt, no single issue or idea that would carry the race. What people wanted was a leader, the kind of man willing to fight for what he thought right. It was the quality they found in the disparate figures of Ronald Reagan, Lee Iacocca and Oliver North; it was not their beliefs that had made them folk heroes so much as the ferocity with which they held them.

Babbitt's profile in courage, when he finally put it on, was thus in some measure machine-made—one more article of costuming in the masque we have made of our politics. He was not really enthusiastic about levying a tax on consumption; he had picked it from a list of options in part because reporters and intellectuals seemed to like it. But he got glowing notices for his bravery, and his handlers scrambled for more bold postures for him to strike, a *drumbeat* of them, Schneiders suggested, to go on for the rest of the year. The test was not so much that Babbitt believe deeply in them as that he feel "comfortable" with them. He couldn't outsmooth the other candidates, Schneiders told him. He had to own the franchise on strong character and straight talk if he was to win, or even lose well.

The search for drumbeats was entrusted to Babbitt's young issues director, Bart Gellman, with what he took to be a license to be outrageous. He retired to his apartment and started calling friends, academics, congressional staffers—anyone with an idea that no one else in politics dared speak. By late September, he was trying out twenty-three of them on his colleagues in a conference call. Not everyone was pleased. "Let's give five to each of our opponents and hope they use 'em," Garrett, the campaign chairman, said, and Babbitt himself shied away from some of them on frankly political grounds. But others found their way into his platform, with flattering effect. For a season, Babbitt became the darling of the academy and the press. Only the voters seemed not to notice.

He made a last, game effort to get their attention in the very forum that had been his undoing, a debate, in December, on network TV. After two years in the field, he was mired at one or two percent in the national polls. He needed a way, he told his people, to put the other candidates on the spot—to *force* them to take sides on his issues. Michael Sheehan, after some discussion, suggested calling on them to stand up for tax increases, and Babbitt, after some resistance, agreed. His seduction by the process was by then complete. He was willing to rest his declaration of independence on a bit of stage business provided him by his media coach; his final question to his people was not whether it was real but whether it would work.

It did, at least as theater, perking up what had otherwise become a tedious TV maxi-series. The debate, on NBC-TV, was well along by the time Babbitt found the moment and the resolve to go through with the stunt; his man Sheehan had dropped to his knees on the holding-room floor, praying, "Please, please, do it now!" He finally did, challenging the others to stand up with him and acknowledge that taxes would have to be raised. He clambered to his feet. Gephardt got halfway up, then plunked back down, blushing. The others sat frozen in their chairs; they looked, Babbitt thought, as if he had just invited them to face a firing squad.

"He did it, he did it!" his people cheered offstage; they screamed, hugged and slapped high-fives as if it were the nomination Babbitt had won, not just a debating point on a slow night.

"You fuckhead," Mike McCurry said as Babbitt left the stage. "We thought you weren't going to do it!"

Babbitt stared at his press secretary for a moment, shook his head and walked away.

His people would refer to his bit of stage business thereafter as "the moment," a victory to be savored and remembered. There would not be many more. Babbitt had decided, out of desperation, to play the game as it was—a game of appearances in which candor was one more tactic and authenticity one more disguise. His surrender was too late and his talent for performance too limited. The awkwardness that made him the most endearingly human candidate in the field was his ruin in the politics of 1988. Babbitt's candidacy had died in Houston at age one and a half, the victim of his infirmities on TV.

Instant Replay

By summer, Hart was gone, Babbitt going, and Paul Simon gasping for air. But professionals at politics are paid to worry, and the dog days of August 1987 brought new fevers of speculation among the front-runners, new phantom shapes in the night. It was Joe Biden's turn to step downstage for his brief moment in the spotlight—and, with a little help from his nervous rivals, to auto-destruct.

It had been easy to underrate Biden at first, to write him off as a superannuated boy orator of forty-four with a silver tongue and an under-worked mind. He was the best and most impassioned speaker in the field, save only Jesse Jackson, but his depth had long been suspect. His patter seemed too glib, his smile too flashy for seriousness; where Hart had had to promise people that he was really not a policy wonk, Biden had to persuade them that he was—or that at least he was smart enough to listen. He had, moreover, assembled an all-star team of paid consultants to help shape and run his race, among them the famously prickly Pat Caddell. Viewed from the inside, his command group at times was a demolition derby of colliding egos and crashing friendships. Outwardly, it looked rather *too* professional, too slick, too much a chapter of the Jockey Club; it became irresistibly tempting for the media to write Biden off as the creation of his handlers, an empty vessel for their ideas.

What he could do was fire a crowd with his appeal to the sleeping social conscience of his generation; he was beginning to move voters in Iowa, and his rivals began to sense it in the field well before it showed in the published polls. "Forget about Dukakis," Dick Gephardt told his people one day. "The challenge for me in this race is Joe Biden." He had seen it out there, felt it in his fingertips, and some private soundings by his polltaker, Ed Reilly, suggested he was right. Biden was taking hold, and his gains were coming straight out of Gephardt's hide.

The Dukakis camp was picking up the same signals at the same time. Biden had worried John Sasso all along, more than Hart ever had. Biden could get hot; the campaign Sasso had designed for Dukakis was like a mainframe computer in a climate-controlled room, smart, cool and efficient but vulnerable to a sudden rise in temperature. His anxieties were confirmed when Tubby Harrison brought in some fresh polling from Iowa and showed it to Sasso and his new national political director, Paul Tully, retrieved from the ruins of the Hart campaign. "Biden's not dead," Harrison said. He had youth, money, organization and a powerful generational message, and now fortune had further strengthened his hand. He was about to preside over the televised Senate hearings on the nomination of the conservative jurist Robert Bork to the Supreme Court, with the whole nation tuned in. There was nothing manufactured, nothing posed, about that, Tully said. That was history, right in your face.

The question was how to neutralize the threat. The answer, in the event, would be delivered up by Biden himself. The senator was an impulsive crowd-pleaser, a man for whom words were life and hyperbole was a permissible indulgence. His conversation was an undammed stream of consciousness; his approach to a more formal speech was chaotic, a round-the-clock seminar conducted, one adviser said affectionately, by a madman. The messiness of the process invited carelessness. There was, for example, the time Caddell and Mark Gitenstein, a longtime Biden staffer, brought him a draft of an important address in California. He was due to leave that day, but the speech was too long, and he started editing it, Biden style; he sat down on the floor of his study, furiously ripping pages apart and rearranging them into a circle of little stacks around him.

"Pages ten through eighteen under Roman numeral one," he mumbled. "Take out page five—I don't want to use that at all. One through seven, but without five, put that in two."

He looked up at the authors. They stared back at him.

"We're going to reorganize the whole thing," he said. "We'll do it on the plane."

The finished speech was a powerful one, a vow that the ideals and the convictions of the Big Chill generation would be renewed in 1988. But in the paper-shuffling, a quote from Biden's hero Robert F. Kennedy had crept into the final edition without attribution to its source; it was as if the senator were claiming the words as his own.

No one noticed then, or when, on another occasion, he cribbed from Hubert Humphrey as well. They didn't even catch him when he closed out a debate at the Iowa State Fair with a bit of moving if somewhat purplish prose from Neil Kinnock, the leader of the British Labour Party, on his struggle upward from the working class. The material had been a gift from William Schneider, a political analyst with the American Enterprise Institute, who had seen it in a Kinnock commercial in England and had brought home a videotape.

"You've got to see this," he told Biden's senior adviser Tom Donilon. "It's an amazing piece of political advertising."

Donilon agreed, and so did Biden when he saw it; he began using it regularly in speeches, always citing Kinnock as the source. It had become a regular part of his repertoire by the time he played the Iowa fair. But when he used it in his closing statement there, he forgot to mention its real author.

"Jesus, Joe," Donilon said, a pained look creasing his round boy's face. "You didn't attribute the Kinnock thing. We may get rapped."

Two weeks went by without anybody complaining. Biden was moving up fast in Iowa—his polls showed him up from one point in May to a virtual dead heat for first in mid-August—and the Bork hearings were about to begin. Donilon relaxed; the biggest thing left for him to worry about was whether Biden might be peaking too soon.

The problem was that Donilon's source, Schneider, had given another copy of the Kinnock tape to the Dukakis campaign. In late summer, Sasso called Dukakis's issues director, Chris Edley, into his office for a private showing—one of a series for senior members of the staff. Kinnock came on-screen, waxing lyrical about the pinched lives and the stubborn dreams of his forebears in Wales.

Edley felt himself shiver—the tape was that strong.

"Kinnock went up nineteen points in the polls after this," Sasso said. "Now let me show you something else."

He slipped another cassette into his office VCR. The video captured Biden in the act of snitching Kinnock's prose—even appropriating his ancestors.

Edley's jaw dropped. "Unbelievable," he said.

"Don't tell anybody else about this," Sasso cautioned.

Telling somebody was Sasso's job, or so he believed; some things had to be done in a campaign, he told a colleague, and he was the one who had to do them. The tale of the tapes had been buzzing on the gossip circuit for days; there were even copies of the Kinnock ad floating around. Sasso waited impatiently for the media to pick up the story. They didn't, to his great annoyance, and he decided to help.

At his direction, the two tapes were combined into one. He spoon-fed one copy to *The New York Times*. Jack Corrigan got a second to NBC through a middleman. Paul Tully flew out to Iowa and gave a third to the *Register*. All three came out with stories on the case of the purloined peroration. Only the *Register* acknowledged having been fed the tip and the tape by one of Biden's opponents; NBC and the *Times* made it sound as if they had come upon the story on their own.

Afterward, Sasso would insist gamely to friends that he had meant the tape only as a tickle—the political equivalent of a practical joke. If so, he miscalculated, and his crowd looked for reasons why. John was tired, they said. The race, with Hart's withdrawal, had sped up too much too soon; there were thousands of pieces demanding his attention, and his normal workday stretched out from twelve hours at the statehouse to eighteen on Chauncy Street. John, people said, was running faster and faster just to keep up. He was ripe for a mistake.

But his concern about Biden was well known on Chauncy Street, and his secretiveness once the story was out made it look as if he had something to hide. Patricia O'Brien, the campaign press secretary, was on the road with Dukakis and caught up with the story only when it broke. She showed it to the governor first, in a van crossing Iowa in a pelting rain.

"Governor, have you seen this?" she said. "This is going to be very important."

"Why?" he asked.

She tried to explain: the *Times* had put it on page one, which *made* it important. Dukakis seemed not to understand, but the story kept gnawing at O'Brien, and she phoned Sasso about it.

"What do you think?" she asked him. "This sounds ominous."

Sasso sounded oddly unsurprised.

Later that day, she checked in with her own office. There had been inquiries, her people told her. Tully had instructed them to plead ignorance—to say they knew only what they read in the newspapers.

The whole business began to sound fishy to O'Brien. Furious, she headed for Chauncy Street when she got home and confronted first Sasso, then Corrigan, then the two men together. They told her not to worry, they had made the tapes for themselves and for limited private circulation—to colleagues, Sasso said; to a friend, Corrigan swore.

"Look, guys," she told them, "I'm not going to be part of any lies. You're dancing on the head of a very crowded pin."

Sasso's "tickle," in the event, hit Biden with the force and the subtlety of a tactical nuclear weapon. The first story set off a kinetic run of follow-up reports, a kind of Chinese water torture transacted in the daily and weekly press. The day the Bork hearings opened, Biden's pilferings from Kennedy and Humphrey came to light. Then it turned out that he had inflated his college and law-school records; among other things, he had left out the F he had got for dolloping five pages out of a law-review article into one of his briefs without adequate credit.

Waist deep in the Shallow Muddy, Biden called a news conference, conceding that he had made mistakes and dismissing them—in, appropriately, a borrowed phrase—as much ado about nothing. But the mortifications kept spilling out everywhere, and the pressures were mounting inexorably for him to get out of the race with what was left of his reputation. He was sitting in a small antechamber during a break in the seventh day of the hearings, trying to vet a draft statement answering the latest charges about his academic record. Across the table, his Republican colleague Strom Thurmond was waiting to negotiate the order of witnesses for and against Judge Bork. At his elbow, Tom Donilon was holding a phone call for him; his New Hampshire coordinator was on the line, needing answers on how to steer through the storm.

"How's it going?" Biden asked Donilon. His eyes were pouchy and hollowed by fatigue.

"It's a real zoo," Donilon said.

Biden looked at him wearily. "Draft a statement," he said.

He agonized past midnight that night, his fight and flight reflexes at war with one another. Caddell, his friend of more than a dozen years, urged him to hang in; so did Governor Dukakis, unaware, so far as anyone knew, that his own men were part of the problem. Not many others encouraged him, and Biden, in the end, called his last press conference as a candidate. It was, he said, more important for him to stop Bork than to be president; the race, for him, was over, and he followed Hart from the field, the copycat joining the tomcat on the sidelines.

For days thereafter, the press tantalized itself with the further mystery of who had circulated the telltale video. Suspicion fell first on Gephardt's men, a line of inquiry encouraged by Dukakis's. In fact Gephardt's people hadn't even seen the tape until it played the network newscasts, but the rumors surfaced, and the damage to Gephardt's campaign was instant and long-lasting. His contributions tailed off. His momentum in Iowa stopped dead. His crowds turned growly, and it didn't seem to help him to deny all; when you did that, he thought, you sounded guilty, kind of like Nixon saying, "I am not a crook."

The silence at Dukakis headquarters on Chauncy Street was deafening; Gephardt was out there twisting slowly, slowly in the wind, and it did not serve the ends of the campaign to cut him down. But reporters were still nosing around the story, and as summer ebbed into autumn they were getting warmer.

Tully and Harrison left headquarters one late-September evening, heading home for the night.

"If you knew John Sasso had done the tapes but there was no smoking gun," Tully asked suddenly, "would you lie?"

"Shit, yes," Harrison answered, sensing exactly what the question meant; if the campaign had an indispensable man, it was John.

The next day, the truth finally hit the headlines: the tapes had issued from 105 Chauncy Street, and Sasso was behind it. Dukakis refused to believe the accusations at first. The campaign had been on a sustained high since Hart's withdrawal; the most visible danger to his success, as Eric Elbot had warned him only a day or so before in a van trip across Iowa, was his own air of cockiness. The governor was second only to Jesse Jackson in the national polls. Bob Farmer was raking in money, $8 million by early autumn. The unhappy business of Kitty's dependence on drugs had been put behind them; she had done a preemptive public confessional, following the new forms of politics, and had attracted vastly more sympathy than rebuke. John couldn't have done so foolish a deed, not when everything was going so well. Dukakis, on faith, denied it; so did Paul Tully, who knew better, at a luncheon with campaign contributors and in an interview with *Time*.

But the forty-eight hours that followed the first disclosure ravaged the campaign. Sasso, rumpled and exhausted, presented himself at Dukakis's office.

"Governor," he said, "the news is bad." The stories were true: he had given out the tapes.

Dukakis sat behind his desk in the wan afternoon light, lost in a stunned silence. Sasso had got involved in a similar mess once before, regaling some of his statehouse reporter pals with a crude audiotape making sport of the sex life of Dukakis's nemesis Ed King and his polio-stricken wife. Dukakis had been furious and had stripped Sasso of some of his authority. He assumed Sasso had learned his lesson.

"Why did you do it?" he asked, his voice edged with anger.

Sasso had no satisfactory answer, only his remorse. They would have to go public, Dukakis said, make a clean breast of it. But when Sasso offered to resign, the governor said no—he should take a two-week leave of absence instead.

Sasso went home thinking he would be allowed to stay on. Dukakis dragged himself to a million-dollar fund-raising party at Boston's World Trade Center, moving among the streamers and the straw hats with a thin and mirthless smile. He told no one what had happened except his lawyer friend Paul Brountas. Not even Kitty knew, though she suspected that something was wrong when they danced; he had no zest, no heart for it.

"Michael, what's wrong?" she asked him.

"I'm tired," he said.

It wasn't till they were home in Brookline that night that he told her what Sasso had done. They sat up late in the kitchen, nearly all night, talking about it. Dukakis spoke with Sasso by phone a couple of times, Sasso again offering his resignation. Dukakis again refused it, but his anguish was plain in his eyes and his cracking voice. He had by then painted himself, and Sasso, into a corner. His denial that anyone on Chauncy Street was involved had been accompanied by his implicit threat that he would fire anyone who was. John, by the governor's own decree, would have to go.

Sasso arrived for a senior staff meeting the next morning knowing the game was over. He found Francis O'Brien, a film producer and a comrade in the Ferraro campaign, one in a thicket of old friends who rallied around him. "We can do whatever you want," O'Brien said. He was pacing back and forth, a tiny leprechaun in furious motion. "If you want to stay, we'll arrange that. Or you can go. But either way, you're fucked. You're totally fucked."

Sasso moved on to the meeting. His colleagues were waiting for him, gathered around a conference table drinking foul coffee out of Styrofoam cups; the fund-raising party had gone well, and their mood was high. But it changed when they saw Sasso standing at the head of the table, his hands gripping the top of his chair as if for support. He looked like hell, his face drawn and tight.

"The governor will have a press conference at eleven," he said. "He's going to announce that I was the source of the Biden tape."

The room was still.

"I'm sorry I've let him down and you down," Sasso said. Then he turned and walked out. Tears shone in his eyes.

A feeling near panic coursed through the room. Edley stared into his cup; it felt to him as if a family patriarch had died.

"Is John going to be fired?" someone asked.

"He offered his resignation," Tully said. "The governor refused it, and he'll take a temporary leave." His eyes swept the room. The faces looking back at him mirrored their concern; they were mostly Sasso's people, not Dukakis's, and they felt a collective vertigo, as if the ground had opened under their feet. "Now, don't blow this out of proportion," Tully told them. "What Sasso did has nothing to do with the candidate and his voters."

While they dispersed, Dukakis sat ashen among his press people, preparing for his news conference.

"You're going to get whacked," one of them, Jim Dorsey, said. "It's going to be brutal. You're going to get hit hard on the integrity issue. Do you have the steel in your gut to get through this thing?"

Dukakis nodded glumly and went out to meet the press. His performance, in the view of Sasso's friends, was an exercise in moral overkill. Sasso's sin had been a mild one as dirty tricks go; Biden could fairly be said to have destroyed himself, on C-Span, where anyone with two eyes and one VCR could have caught him. But Dukakis himself had elevated a misdemeanor into a high crime. He accepted blame for the attack tape and offered Biden his apologies. Would Sasso stay on? Dukakis's words said yes. The reproof in his tone said no.

It was left to Sasso, in the end, to draw up the orders for his own execution. He phoned the governor that day. He'd *have* to resign, he said. So would Paul Tully; he had been caught lying.

Sasso, one friend said, had expected an argument, if only for old time's sake. To his shock, there was none. An aide walked in just after Dukakis had hung up. Kitty was with him, her chair pulled up to his desk. She had been furious at Sasso's miscreancy, insisting, by inside account, that he be fired. But she shared her husband's pain, now that it was upon them. Both were teary-eyed.

"John's gotta go," the governor said.

Sasso's curtain scene at a hotel across the street from headquarters was one last humiliation, a barbecuing by reporters who had been his friends and had fed on scraps of information at his table. Toward the end, one of them asked him why, having got into one jam involving a tape, he had done it again. Sasso took a half-step back and flinched, as if he had been slapped. Tears flooded his eyes. He turned and left.

His people had been watching on a TV monitor offstage. He asked them what they thought. You did fine, they told him. They took a back way out to shake the press, walking single file through the hotel kitchen, out into the street and back to headquarters. Sasso led them one last time, hunched into a steady drizzle. He sat in his office that afternoon, packing a few things and staring out the window. Friends lingered with him. No one said much; there wasn't much to say. "I can't believe this is happening," Sasso told them. By dark, he was gone.

His boys called during that night and in the days that followed, trying to cheer him. His hurt was plain. Sometimes he felt betrayed by a man he had considered his friend; sometimes he blamed himself.

"I let the governor down," he told John DeVillars.

You didn't do anything that other managers didn't do, DeVillars protested. It was no worse than going through *Congressional Quarterly* for evidence that Gephardt had flip-flopped on the issues.

"No, no, no," Sasso blurted, "I knew it was wrong the minute I did it."

Dukakis, bereft, managed to keep moving. Kitty was out that night; he cooked up a TV dinner for himself in the microwave, ate it in stony silence and afterward forced himself through a long-scheduled TV interview with David Frost. He looked and sounded awful. The next morning, he was on the road again, his cockiness fallen away and, with it, his pleasure; it just wasn't fun anymore, he told a traveling companion. A tour of Biden's strongholds in Iowa became a serial act of contrition, with apologies at every stop for what his best friend had done in his name. "Why did he do it?" he kept asking aloud on the long rides between tiny towns. "Things were going so well. We raised all that money. We had that great party." He looked out unseeing at the farm fields drifting by the windows of his van, the ranks of cornstalks dried a rusty autumn brown. "Why did he do it?" he asked again.

The Loneliness of the Long-Distance Runner

For weeks thereafter, Dukakis slid into a recession of the spirit, his thoughts turned inward on his pain. He stayed in motion, planting one foot ahead of the other according to the last memos Sasso had left him. But behind his stoic resolve his people could see he was, as one of them put it, walking wounded. He seemed to them to feel betrayed by Sasso; still, it was plain that he was grieving. His speeches wandered. His conversations with staffers on the plane would break off in midthought; he would turn away and stare silently out the window, tears in his eyes.

"You know, people say I lost a friend," he told one of them. "It's much worse than that. I lost a brother."

He had lost his support system as well; his trust in Sasso, and his dependence on him, had been the bedrock of his candidacy, and without him Dukakis felt lost. Susan Estrich, a straw-blond Harvard lawyer and law professor, had moved up from the issues department to occupy Sasso's corner office. It took some selling by her advocates to get Dukakis to accept her. Some people were telling him to go outside and get someone with more big-league experience. Estrich's résumé was mostly in policy, those unworldly back corners of presidential campaigns where people do white papers and worry about ideas. She was a talented inside operative with a tough, quick political mind. But she had never managed a campaign before and had never been especially close to the governor—not close enough, in any case, to have won his confidence or overcome his unease at having a woman in so critical a job.

The case *for* her was closed with the argument that Susan was family. She knew everybody on Chauncy Street. She understood the strategy. A newcomer would need time getting started; Dukakis was notoriously resistant to strangers, preferring the company of people he knew and the ring of ideas he had heard before. Estrich, if not a personal favorite, was at least familiar. She could keep things humming—so the argument ran—without losing a beat.

The subtext in the nominating speeches was the expectation among Sasso's crowd that Estrich would be head of a shadow government, someone to keep the chair warm until John came back and to keep an open line to him in the meantime. That he *would* be back was accepted as a given among his loyalists. They understood, as he did, that his banishment was necessary till they had got past Iowa and New Hampshire, both nice-people states, as Tully put it, with strong feelings about political trickery. But their common assumption was that he would return, perhaps by Super Tuesday, certainly by convention time.

The problem was that Estrich declined to play by their rules; she liked the word "manager" next to her name on the table of organization and refused to be a surrogate for Sasso, or Tully, or anyone else. She had never been one of Sasso's boys, who were, almost without exception, boys. Their bond had been formed at his poker table, their late-night games a rite of initiation into the brotherhood of statehouse politics. Sasso liked his politics the old-fashioned way, tough, ethnic and earthy. The games became a kind of testing ground, an audition for the big show; the *Wunderkinder* from the Kennedy School had to prove their manhood in combat with the street-smart pros. The play was serious, the talk macho, the betting heavy, the laughter raucous, the liquor free-flowing. Wimps were not asked back. Women were not invited at all.

Estrich, shut out, built on her own circle of connections. There was, as it turned out, more than one family on Chauncy Street, each clannish, jealous of its own position and chary of outsiders, and their frictions would become a debilitating chronic condition of the campaign. Estrich's circle was more Harvard than Sasso's, and less streety. There were women drawn to her by sisterly feelings; men who had not made it at John's card table and had found advantage in attaching themselves to Susan instead; new hires who owed her their jobs and their allegiance; older hands, like Corrigan, who seemed to feel they could run her. Her bunch circled the wagons when she took over, and Sasso's poker partners found themselves drifting out of the loop.

Sasso completed his own isolation, holing up at home with his battered feelings. He felt forsaken by Dukakis, cast into exile for the political equivalent of double-parking. There were days early on when old friends came around to buck him up and he sometimes refused to come to the door; it would be weeks before old Sass seemed to them to be himself again. Like the others, he expected Estrich to seek his advice or at least ask for his memos—the Bibles, his people called them, blocking out a detailed strategy for the campaign. His phone line to her was silent; others in the campaign stayed in touch, but in the eleven months of his exile Estrich called precisely twice. A time or two in the early going, Dukakis would ask her at a meeting what John thought about this or that problem. He seemed surprised that she didn't know.

What she could not do was replace Sasso in Dukakis's narrow firmament. His discomfort with her was painfully obvious. He needed his to-do memos; John had provided them, Susan didn't. He liked the sense, or at least the illusion, that he was making up his own mind in his own time; John gave him data, Susan gave him arguments. He wanted the feeling that he was in charge, not just, as he sometimes complained, a goddam figurehead;

John was deferential, Susan was domineering. She wore her rank on her sleeve along with her IQ, suffering even bright people badly; her impatience with them seemed magnified by her sensitivity to anything that looked like a challenge to her standing. Her manner grated on Dukakis, and his discouraged her. As fall faded into winter, he quit listening to her. By the spring of his nomination, they would barely be speaking.

Dukakis, in his loneliness, was committing a cardinal offense for a candidate: becoming his own campaign manager. He came to believe he had trusted Sasso too much, given him too much leeway. He didn't mean to make that mistake twice; instead, he reverted to the status quo ante Sasso, Dukakis as Duke I, poking into petty detail, turning aside advice and following his own cautious instincts. He was trying to be candidate, manager and governor all at once, and all three roles suffered. Riding back from a campaign event one day, Eric Elbot warned him against the folly of doing too much. Dukakis looked silently back at him. His answer was in his eyes: there was a weariness in them, a sadness, Elbot thought, bordering on despair.

His down mood showed in his performance. He was dragging himself through the campaign one day at a time, a visibly unhappy warrior who sounded more like a candidate for governor of Iowa than for president of the United States. "How are you feeling?" Marco Turbovich, a former state official who had joined the campaign, asked him one day. "I'm sad," Dukakis replied. He had limped through a debate in Miami in October, his eyes shadowed, his body slumped, his offering a wilted salad of old slogans. Afterward, Stanley Greenberg, an independent pollster monitoring public reaction, had bumped into Dukakis's communications director, Leslie Dach.

"Terrible," Greenberg said.

Dach mumbled something about the governor's exhaustion and fled.

Dukakis's gloom weighed down his candidacy through the deepening autumn. His public demeanor turned dour, his private humors petulant; he asked Nick Mitropoulos with almost childish impatience whether they couldn't fit in some time off for him to plant his cucumbers. His people eased up a bit on his schedule, giving him every other Sunday off, and saw that Kitty was with him more on the road. But his bleak look was at war with his optimistic speeches. His confidence had gone the way of Sasso's memos; he sounded less like the architect of an economic miracle than like its statistician.

The nuts and bolts of the campaign—fund-raising, field organizing, scheduling and logistics—remained sound. Bob Farmer was still raking in money, a million dollars in October alone; Jack Corrigan, as director of operations, kept the trains running on time. The damage instead was to its heart and its soul.

In their last memo to the candidate, Sasso and his kitchen cabinet had warned that the Massachusetts Miracle was going stale as a message. But with Sasso gone, there was no one who could persuade Dukakis that he needed to freshen up his presentation, and Paul Tully's exile robbed Chauncy Street of the man who might actually have provided the words and music; he and Tubby Harrison, working in tandem, had brought the campaign what little poetry it had. The new crowd had trouble just getting Dukakis's attention. The Miracle was working fine with the voters, he told them; only the press was bored. When they asked him what more he had to offer, what new language and themes, he kept demanding that they tell him. They tried, without success. Dukakis, in his gloom, wasn't listening to anyone except himself.

The Soul of a New Machine

One midnight in late autumn, a media consultant named Ken Swope sat in the dark in his office, staring at Dukakis's image on a television screen. Swope was an intense man with the wired-up synapses of a commercial-ad-maker and the hirsute look of a hippie, both of which he had been. His eyes were bloodshot and narrowed in concentration. He smoked, steadily and nervously. He had run through boxes of videotaped clips, playing them again and again, watching for some sign—any sign—of life, of heart, of passion. He was searching for the soul of Michael Dukakis.

Swope had never seen much evidence that the governor had one, and his first meeting with Estrich and her team a couple of days before had not been encouraging. Estrich had been trying for weeks to get Dukakis's speeches to a more inspiring plane. Her unhappiness was visible. She had tried lobbying the candidate herself, to no avail. She had brought in a Boston consultant, Tom Kiley, a rare visionary among the lawyers and process liberals on Chauncy Street; Dukakis liked him, but did not seem to act on his advice. She had commissioned a draft speech from her husband, Marty Kaplan, a Disney executive who had been Mondale's chief ghost; Dukakis had ripped out some of its strongest passages and still had not given it.

Seeking out Swope had been a kind of desperation move, a reach outside the insular Dukakis circle and, indeed, the standard political stylebook for something nearer Madison Avenue. There were risks attached, Swope having published a nasty magazine commentary on Dukakis's media campaign; the governor's chill first reaction, on meeting him, was, "How'd you get so hairy?" But he seemed to Estrich a chance worth taking, a way to fortify her own position on Chauncy Street and to kick-start Dukakis's idling candidacy at the same time. The ads then in hand were considered a disaster, so bad that their mutinous Iowa staff was pulling them off the air.

Swope thought there was still some mileage in the Miracle. The problem, he argued at his first meeting on Chauncy Street, was making the story bigger—moving it from past to future and from a state to a national stage. They needed, moreover, to show that Dukakis was more than its manager, more than a dull technocrat; they had to reveal in him the passion, the moral outrage, that it would take to lead a nation.

"Give me a chance to make more of an emotional connection," he said. "I want to show the passion in Michael Dukakis."

"Yes, yes!" Estrich exclaimed. "Move me! Move me!"

Swope retired to his office afterward with twenty hours of tape and a commission to deliver on his own promise. He saw in the first hour that it wouldn't be easy. Dukakis was stiff and preachy; he wasn't a bad speaker, Swope thought, but he had an unpleasant tendency to lecture. He was at his worst on his weakest subjects, foreign affairs and nuclear-weapons policy; his insecurity showed in his cockiness, the James Cagney posturing of a little guy trying too hard to assert himself. Swope was feeling nostalgic for his earlier ventures in politics, with George McGovern and Joe Biden, when something in a tape from Iowa caught his attention—a change in Dukakis's tone, a different look in his eye. The subject was oppression in Central America, and Dukakis was saying it was time to end the fiasco—time to stop the killing and start the war against poverty and injustice at home and throughout the region.

Swope rewound the tape and ran it again. *Let's end this fiasco . . . stop the killing . . . start the war against poverty and injustice . . .*

"Fuckin' A," Swope said softly, thwacking his knee.

He replayed the tape again and then again, seeing the anger in Dukakis's face, hearing it in his words. Later, he fished out another reel, the governor talking with equal feeling about the problems of the homeless. Swope felt a tingle of excitement, the onset of what his producer liked to call Ken's genius frenzy. He sat up all that night making notes, splicing tape and doing voice-overs, and for a week thereafter he rarely emerged from his office, even to sleep. His wife, who managed his shop, would leave him there nights with a plate of food on his desk and hope he would notice it.

Two spots emerged from his labors, one on Central America, one on the homeless, each relying on strong images of human suffering; the edge of indignation in Dukakis's voice-over was reinforced by the background music, selected for what Swope called its tension tone. The campaign liked them. So did Dukakis, when Swope screened them at the statehouse. The governor sat watching himself in silence, as if, Swope thought, he couldn't believe how good the ads made him sound; he *could* get emotional about issues without sounding silly. He asked for a second showing, then smiled broadly and said, "Wow!"

The ads played Iowa to positive effect, and Dukakis began using the material regularly in his speeches; even candidates can be moved by their better commercials and often try to reenact them in person, life imitating art. But their focus and their run was limited. The theory on Chauncy Street had been that if they could find the soul of that new machine called Michael Dukakis, a message surely would follow. It didn't, not for nearly a year, and by then it would be too late. John Sasso had been the one running for president all along, his friends would muse when the race was over. When he left the campaign, Dukakis found himself playing a role he had never really wanted in a script he had never mastered. Under the circumstances, there was not much for him to say.

Back to the Future

As the tale of the Biden tape sent Dukakis and Gephardt into their simultaneous swoons, Paul Simon had begun to climb. Till then, Dukakis's man Jack Corrigan, young and cocky, had derided the senator as the featured local attraction at county fairs. But with the first primaries drawing near, no one on Chauncy Street was laughing anymore; in their worst-case scenarios, Simon could win Iowa, ride east on the media tide and upset Dukakis in New Hampshire. The signs of their discomfort were received with glee at Simon headquarters. The tortoise has grown long, furry ears, the senator's media man, David Axelrod, said happily; the senator was metamorphosing into a hare.

If the metaphor was a bit mixed, so was the candidate. His rise mystified his own people; they asked themselves only half in fun whether it wasn't simply the Graceland Factor at work—people confusing *their* Paul Simon with the singer-songwriter whose album "Graceland" was riding high on the charts. Then fifty-eight, the senator was the oldest of the Democratic contenders and, in his ordinariness, the most comfortable. He wore antique bow ties and rumpled suits finely dusted with cookie crumbs. He spoke in a round, plummy bass more natural to funeral parlors than to modern politics, and as he made the rounds in Iowa he trailed a pleasant scent of licorice drops and shaving cream. On-camera, he looked like a waxwork of, say, Willy Loman. His earlobes were marvels of size and cantilever construction; his hair was slicked back in what his own children called the vampire look. Simon had, as one staffer put it, a great face for radio.

He was, or seemed, utterly uncalculating about what he said or did; some even thought him naive. He wasn't; even his decision to wear bow ties had been a calculation, one piece in the Our Town persona he had, by conscious design, created for himself. But the voters back home appeared to find his artful guilelessness a refreshing change in a politician. The year the Chicago Bears went to the Super Bowl, Simon announced at a press conference that, being from downstate, he was really a St. Louis Cardinals fan. Spontaneity in a candidate is not always valued by handlers, and one of Simon's demanded to know why he had said that.

They asked me, Simon replied.

In the event, no harm came of it; even heretical views are sometimes forgiven in politics if they seem honestly held.

The senator was a traditional heartland Democrat down to his home address—Rural Route 1, Makanda, Illinois—and his enduring faith in government as an instrument for righting social wrongs. He was as conspicuous among his postliberal rivals as a Victorian settee in a roomful of Bauhaus furniture. He advertised himself unabashedly as a real Democrat, "the Roosevelt, Truman, Kennedy kind," his earliest brochures said; Simon wasn't neo anything.

At first glance, nothing about him compelled serious consideration—not his musty look, or his meandering, homemade speeches, or his position in the back benches of the Senate. His advisers had told him he would be foolish to run, and so did some of the outsiders whose help he sought. Paul Maslin, who ultimately became his polltaker, said no when the senator first approached him; he figured Simon couldn't win and might, in fact, place his Senate seat in jeopardy if he did badly. Simon himself was talking up Senator Dale Bumpers, a fluent and well-regarded liberal from Arkansas. Even when Bumpers stood down, Simon dithered.

"I think we should have a meeting," he told his senior aide, Floyd Fithian, at two o'clock one morning.

"I think you ought to meet with *you*," Fithian replied.

Simon would encourage the view that he had been moved to run by a sense of mission, an obligation to the Democratic past. In fact, he had first talked to his brother, Arthur, about the idea in his days as a newspaper publisher in Troy, Illinois, years earlier, and when his wife, Jeanne, finally told him, "Go for it," he was more than ready. His campaign, initially, was staffed to fit his back-to-the-future design. He started with an older management group, people who, like Fithian, were roughly his contemporaries. It was they who cast him as the rightful heir to the party's lost heroes, not just another knock-off Republican like his rivals.

But a newer, younger crowd moved in during the summer and fall of 1987, bumping their elders into the background. They had got into the consulting business in the party's lean years, and they were, as Paul Maslin put it, tired of hearing about Democratic ghosts; it was time to give up the search for the next John Kennedy and nominate somebody reliable, somebody trustworthy, somebody real.

The ghost-busters could not and did not try dislodging Simon from his core belief in a government of good works. His ideas still came out of the old Democratic larder in old Democratic language, the insistent refrain "We can do better." What did change was his packaging. He was disconnected from the company of dead presidents and presented, with only minimal retouching, as himself—a crusading small-town newspaper publisher who had got into politics thirty years before out of conviction, not ego or appetite. He became, in his advertising, "Paul Simon, One of Us," the candidate as Everyman's Uncle standing against the tides of cynicism, greed and despair. His new slogan had an almost messianic ring: "Isn't it time to believe again?"

In a season that favored pliant candidates, Simon resisted being managed by anyone else; he had created himself as a public figure, and he remained, so he believed, his own best handler. His top hands were nearer his son's age than his own, a bunch of young squirts, one of them said, telling an old fart what to do. The senator graciously received their advice, then ignored it. He was especially naughty about preparing for debates; he was a street-corner politician, at his best talking to people singly or in small groups, not doing one-liners on TV. His inattention showed in his performances. He couldn't go on sleepwalking, Maslin told the others in despair, but Simon was lost in new-age politics, with its stress on polished surfaces and shallow prose. "You cannot convince me that how I look is more important than what I say," he complained.

He and his entourage went south to New Orleans in November for yet another in the interminable series of debates. His staffers left him in his hotel room with a huge briefing book, but he got restless as usual and went out into the streets in search of hands to shake.

"Whose idea was that?" Maslin asked Terry Michael, the campaign press secretary.

"His," Michael said.

The two men sighed. The time oozed away. There were two hours left.

"Jesus," Maslin said. Michael scooped up four aspirins from a room-service tray and gulped them down all at once.

They finally treed Simon in his room with an hour left and started throwing lines at him, a sharp question here, a shot at Gephardt there. The senator sat listening in a wingback chair, pen in hand, papers in his lap, his shined-up loafers splayed wide in front of him.

They concentrated what time was left on Simon's closing statement. David Axelrod, his media man, had done a draft, strong and gutsy, but Simon as usual had rejected it and written his own; all they could do was offer amendments.

" 'As I travel from the South to the Midwest to the North—' " Maslin began.

"Yeah, I like that," Simon said, picking up the thread. " '—I realize what we need is national leadership, basic leadership. That's what our party has always stood for. That's what counts.' "

"What's your punch line, Paul?" Maslin asked.

Simon read his statement.

Maslin shook his head. "You didn't use that you're proud to be a Democrat," he said.

Simon stared, immobile as a boulder. "I really felt uncomfortable doing that," he said. "My instincts are it's the party hack thing."

"You're really talking to reporters," Michael said. "The message you have to give them is, 'I'm a guy standing up for principles,' and in this context that line sounds like you're standing up for principles, not like you're partisan."

The statement, in any case, was forty seconds short, and Simon tried again.

"You didn't get in that black-and-white, North-and-South stuff," Maslin said. "That's very important."

Simon did his recitation a third time, getting in the black-and-white, North-and-South stuff this time, and his travels around the country as well. The words edged close to platitude, a hymn to children and the American dream, but as he read them in the fading daylight, he seemed caught up in their cadence. He nodded his head and tapped his feet in time; his fists clenched, and his deep voice trembled with feeling.

His performance that night would be listless, all feathers, Maslin complained, and no blood. It didn't seem to matter. He offered old simplicities, and his own obvious belief in them. Some people found the pitch sappy, but after Hart's misadventures with women, Biden's with shoplifted prose and Sasso's with covert operations, that didn't seem to matter, either. When Simon spoke, a lot of people were beginning to listen.

The Making of a Populist, 1987

Gephardt's people picked up the stirrings, and Bill Carrick flew out to Iowa to shake up the staff. His choice for state director was Steve Murphy, a gangly, spiky veteran of thirty-six who had worked the state for Ted Kennedy in 1980; he in turn was soon joined by Joe Trippi, who had put it together for Mondale in 1984. There wasn't anything wrong, Murphy thought, moving in, except the two things that really mattered. The first was the candidate's message; there wasn't one, not one that the voters could hear. The second was his ground organization, supposedly a showcase, actually a mess. His message, or, as Murphy called it, his nonmessage, was the harder to fix. He was treating Iowa as if it were his congressional district, trying to win it by knocking on more doors than anyone else; what he was saying seemed to concern him less than how many coffees he attended and how many hands he shook. His speeches plodded through his credentials, his travels and his views on the deficit and the balance of trade with the earnestness of an overprepared middle manager bucking for a promotion. Trippi listened to some of them on tape and found himself fighting off a mix of drowsiness and dismay. He shipped transcripts to the media men, Doak and Shrum, with a tart covering note. "Do you want to know why we are not moving in Iowa?" Trippi wrote. "Listen to the first four minutes of this speech and tell me what the message is. The best I can tell, the message is, 'I've been to a lot of places many times.' "

The problem was not easily tractable. Gephardt hadn't really had to run hard for more than a decade, not since his first run for Congress in 1976, and that had been largely a front-parlor campaign; he had never learned to move large numbers of people with his voice or his vision. His years on the Hill had fostered a certain stylelessness in him, a habit of thinking and speaking the language of a legislator. Dick Moe had warned him at the outset that he would have to "disenthrall" himself from Congress.

"Do you mean I have to resign?" Gephardt had asked.

"No," Moe had said, "but mentally you have to get out of this place."

In Washington, Gephardt's handlers caucused on how he could do better. Like Gephardt himself, they came from no-frills, working-class backgrounds; they sensed a well of frustration among voters of modest means after seven years of Reaganism. The particulars of the Gephardt record—trade legislation, farm legislation, tax-reform legislation—addressed their concerns without quite tapping their feelings. The dots needed to be connected into a single thematic whole, and Doak offered one in four words: "It's your fight, too." It would make Gephardt the people's candidate—and, with luck, the people's choice.

The persona was not a perfect fit. Gephardt was a quintessential Washington insider, blue-blazered and regimentally tied; his overnight rebirth as a populist hell-raiser amused some people who knew him and irritated others. It did not help that he sounded less like the man from Main Street than like the lawyer-legislator he had become, fluent only in the gluey language of Capitol Hill. A political scientist, Ethel Klein, was brought in from Columbia University to help guide his passage from what she called policy-speak through people-speak to passion-speak—from cold blood, that is, to hot.

Klein was a bright, taut, confident woman, the kind, she liked to say, who knew she was bright and worried that she wasn't a genius, and she wasn't afraid to treat Gephardt like an underachieving schoolboy. He was too macroeconomic, too used to talking to experts in a common tongue. "I don't understand trade," she would say. "Tell me about it." He tried, first with her, then with live audiences. The exercise helped break him of his dependence on abstractions and encouraged his search for exemplary stories, the metaphor that made abstraction real. The dislocations in agriculture were revealed in the tears of a family farmer who had lost his land and, by suicide, his son; the folly of the Pentagon's $2 trillion buying binge under Reagan came down to the tale of the GIs who, having landed on Grenada, had to buy a road map at a Mobil station so they could save the island from the Red menace.

With further prompting, Gephardt learned to put some feeling into his speeches, some righteous indignation at the government and the interests. Skeptics remained doubtful of his assault on the establishment, given that he had only lately been a proud member of it. Admirers likened the shift to Bobby Kennedy's from tough guy to tribune of the poor in the 1968 campaign. The man in the blue suit was still a milkman's son. He had his beginnings in common with ordinary voters, and he had begun talking to them in their own tongue.

Fifteen Minutes Apiece

THE REWARDS WERE SLOW COMING; in mid-November, Gephardt slipped back to third place in the *Register*'s Iowa Poll, trailing Simon by ten points and Dukakis by four. He managed to look brave about it, reminding himself that there was an ebb and flow in any campaign; his chances, after all, had improved from one in a million when he started to one in three that autumn. But the simple fact remained that Simon was going up while he was going down, and when his handlers urged tougher tactics on him, Gephardt was ready. At an NBC debate in Washington early in December, he turned on the senator, smiled his least pleasant smile and said, "Paul, you're not a pay-as-you-go Democrat. You're a promise-as-you-go Democrat. Simonomics is Reaganomics in a bow tie."

Gephardt was on vulnerable ground, having himself voted for the original Reagan tax cuts, and Simon's coaches had provided him with a counterpunch. "Dick," he was to say, "nobody knows voodoo like you do." The senator had mastered the line in rehearsal, but when the show went live he froze; the basic charge that he was promising more than the available money would buy was allowed to stand.

It mattered only fleetingly in the postmortems that Gephardt's attack had been as packaged as Wonder Bread and as subtle as a mugging. What counted was that Simon had come ill-prepared to defend himself, as he instantly realized; he left a postdebate reception early, trudged through a light drizzle to his office on the Hill, and sat up late over his work papers, thinking of things he should have said. The next morning, visibly angry, he called his young manager, Brian Lunde, and said they had to overhaul the prepping process. The campaign called in expert economic and political advice on how to square Simon's promises with the realities of the Federal budget. It was wasted motion. The senator's surge had crested; the Democratic race was playing out under Andy Warhol rules, fifteen minutes of fame for everybody, and while his fifteen were improbably hot as long as they lasted, they were running out.

The Six Percent Solution

Gephardt's were about to begin. His handlers gathered one night in November at Bob Shrum's house in Washington to talk about a new series of television spots, aimed yet again at defining who Gephardt was.

"We've got a candidate who's like a doughnut," someone lamented, "with a big hole in the middle."

"Let's throw a wrench in it!" Joe Trippi exclaimed, the light of inspiration flashing in his dark eyes. Gephardt had been trying on his own to make trade into a question of simple justice, not just numbers, and had called up research on what it would cost to buy various American products abroad. The list ranged from pens to personal computers, but the entry that had jumped out at Trippi was Chrysler's K-car; it was built to sell for $10,000 at home, but it would run $48,000 in South Korea, by the campaign's arithmetic, once Seoul had piled on nine separate taxes and tariffs.

They had their metaphor and, in a matter of days, their spot. The markup wasn't fair to American workers, and if Gephardt couldn't bargain the barriers down, he said in the finished ad, the Koreans would be left asking themselves how many Americans were going to pay $48,000 for one of their Hyundais.

The ad came just in time. The shoot was barely finished when Gary Hart jumped back into the race. Gephardt had always felt a measure of contempt for Hart, a man who seemed to him moved more by a hunger for celebrity than by a calling to public service. He had assumed that Hart would be back and was sure he would get nowhere. But in the first flutter of excitement, Hart rocketed to the top of the *Register*'s Iowa Poll with 29 percent, while

Gephardt's soufflé fell to 6. NBC stopped covering him entirely, and so, for a time, did practically everyone else; scenting death, the boys and girls on the bus had bailed out. "What's happening?" his own children asked their mother. "Is Dad going to lose?"

For a time known in the campaign as the Six Percent Days, Gephardt's normal optimism deserted him. His exhaustion showed. His edge was gone; his speeches relapsed into policy-speak. He didn't believe the numbers he was reading; the voters at that early stage were like leaves in a road, he thought, just blowing around. But polling affected people's perceptions of how you were doing. There were far too many polls, one every seven or ten minutes, it sometimes seemed to him, and they fed on one another; if one said you were doing badly, it would influence the next and the next and the next, until it became a self-fulfilling prophecy.

"Losing" was not one of Gephardt's favorite words; he got himself together over a holiday ski week with his family and worked out a final, all-or-nothing comeback. He pulled much of his field staff out of the South, emptied his Washington headquarters, and flung everybody into Iowa. Starting the day after Christmas, he blitzed the state with his ads, a powerful bio spot first, then "Hyundai" with the turn of the year.

The Six Percent Solution seemed to work. Slowly at first, then with a surge, Gephardt rose in the polls; by late January, he was back at the top and acting for the first time in weeks as if he really expected to win. You could see that transformation in a candidate, Trippi thought. The guy walks into a room and he's president of the United States, confident and in command; it was as if he had put on a suit of armor—you could hit him with a bazooka at point-blank range, and he'd think it just went *pong!* It happened to Gephardt the day the Secret Service arrived to cover him. Trippi, pleased, called Carrick.

"Bill, the switch," he said. "It just happened in front of my eyes."

"Joe," Carrick answered dryly, "it sounds like you might be getting emotionally involved with the candidate."

A Journey's End

If Trippi wasn't, Iowa was. A light snow fell on the morning of the caucuses; pale clouds floated past the sun the rest of the day. The turnout was heavy. That night, in the ballroom of the old Hotel Fort Des Moines, Paul Simon stood offstage, waiting to do a live-feed interview with NBC. The crowd out front was screaming. He seemed not to hear them. His shoulders slumped. His face was creased with fatigue lines. He was immobile, almost catatonic. Iowa was gone. His campaign was going down the tubes.

"Do you want a drink or something, Paul?" an advance man, Steve Rabinowitz, asked him.

Simon didn't move—didn't even blink.

Rabinowitz, alarmed, found his way to the senator's son Martin. "Your father needs some help," he said.

"He's got a lot to think about," Martin replied.

But Rabinowitz persisted, and after a minute or two Martin followed him back to where the senator was standing. He looked terrible. Martin hugged him, faked a wide grin and said, "Hey, Dad." The two embraced for a long, silent moment, and the trance was over.

So, in effect if not in fact, was Simon's campaign. He had wound up his run in Iowa expecting to win it; he could just sense it out there, he told his traveling staff, puddle-jumping across the state one last time. They had shared his optimism. He had had a bad patch during the winter, his spirits fading with his polls; his staff had enlisted his family and friends to pump him up enough to keep going. Then, as suddenly as they had soured, his prospects had sweetened again. The *Register* had endorsed him, his poll ratings had bounced back, and an upset had seemed within his grasp. The day of the caucuses, his brain trusters disappeared to compose a victory speech for him.

But their mood turned tense as they piled into a rusty Mustang for the ride across town to the Hotel Fort Des Moines. Daylight was going when they pulled up out front. The setting sun glinted on the State Capitol dome. "I just can't believe after all this, after coming so close, that we won't win," Maslin said. It sounded less like prophecy than prayer.

They gathered in a ninth-floor suite to watch the returns on two big television sets. Extra phone lines had been installed, and a walkie-talkie connected them with Simon. Sandwiches had been set out, and bottles of champagne nestled among the beers and Cokes in the sink, ready for a victory party.

It never came. At 7:45, CBS interrupted its programming with word that Gephardt was leading.

"Fuck," Maslin said.

A few minutes later, the first numbers went up; Gephardt had 33 percent, putting him ahead of Simon and Dukakis. In short order, ABC and NBC posted similar estimates. By 8:20, CBS would be back on the air, declaring Gephardt the winner.

Maslin was shaking his head.

"If these numbers hold up," Axelrod joked, "I think we should rework the speech."

Nobody laughed. The champagne stayed corked. In a suite up the hall, Simon told his family, "We're not going to get it." They tried to buck him up, but he seemed spent and beaten. He retired to his room. They could hear the clatter of keys from his battered Royal portable. As he did all his speeches, he was writing his own concession.

He had lost Iowa to Gephardt by a hairbreadth margin, but close, as one of the bromides of politics had it, counts only in horseshoes. Simon would linger in the field for two months thereafter, a ghostly presence going nowhere. Iowa had been the cornerstone of his strategy, and he had lost it. His secret hope, staying in play, was that a deadlocked party would turn to Mario Cuomo. His own fifteen minutes were over.

The Case of the Missing Cravat

Across town at the Starlite Village hotel, Gephardt's senior staff kept their own vigil in a third-floor suite overlooking the capitol. Three TV sets were going. Mountains of turkey sandwiches waited to be noticed. A bar was stocked with soft drinks, but the tension was thick, and some of his men slipped out to refill their glasses with something stronger. Not even Dan Rather's early bulletin awarding the state to Gephardt was enough to lighten the atmosphere.

"I wonder why the other networks haven't called it," Joe Trippi worried aloud. He had been in and out of headquarters all day muttering, "We're gonna win, we're gonna win," as if saying it would make it so, but now that it was happening he couldn't quite believe it. He held a victory cigar, unlit.

"I'm not smoking this," he announced, "till another one of them says we won."

"I hate this," Shrum said. "This is the real vote."

"You press people have to get ready," Ed Reilly said. His voice was taut. "Go live at eleven back East. Declare victory. Try to drive it."

A half hour later, ABC made its call for Gephardt.

"Ding dong, the Duke is dead, the Duke is dead," Trippi's wife, Katie, started singing beside him on the couch. She had worked on the Dukakis staff before they married.

Gephardt's family trooped in—his wife, his kids, his mother, his uncle

Bob Cassell. Cassell was an illustrator and had brought along a painting of the congressman in front of the Capitol. He wanted to present it at the victory party. Jane Gephardt inspected it approvingly.

"That's great!" she exclaimed. "I can't wait to find a place to hang it in the White House."

The high would not last out the week. Gephardt had bet his future on winning Iowa and had got no lift out of it at all, no surge of momentum to ride into the New Hampshire primary eight days later. The wayward press had run off chasing other hares: George Bush, who looked as though he might be finished, and Pat Robertson, who appeared to be taking off. There were no puff pieces on Gephardt in the papers, no cover portraits on *Newsweek* or *Time*—none of the traditional rewards of success in the caucuses. What press he did get was mainly hostile, picking up on the opposition charges that he was (a) a protectionist, (b) a fake populist and (c) a chameleon on the issues. They had expected two things out of Iowa, Bob Shrum said, a bounce and a fist. All they got was the fist, smack in the candidate's face.

Gephardt's "victory" thus bordered on pyrrhic; it had drained his treasury, denuded his field operations in the South, and sent him on to New Hampshire practically empty-handed. People were calling him a created candidate, a piece of merchandise manufactured by his handlers. Whatever could go wrong seemed to, and when the Simon campaign put up a new TV spot attacking him for having flip-flopped in his public positions, he blew up.

The spot that so provoked him was not an especially mean one, not, at least, by the back-alley standards that would govern the fall campaign. But the struggle for second place in New Hampshire, behind Governor Dukakis, was do-or-die time for both campaigns, and even a slap, under the circumstances, hurt like a haymaker. The candidates had converged at the Highway Hotel in Concord for a party affair. Word of the ad had caught up with Gephardt, and he stood scarlet with anger on a stairway, surrounded by baffled reporters, railing at a man he had only just left for dead on the prairie. "Paul Simon can take off his bow tie," he said, his face a frozen mask, "because he's just another politician."

Goddam—Dick Gephardt is losing it, Paul Maslin said, watching the spectacle unfold. He stole a glance at Mike Marshall, the Simon campaign's young field director in the state. They had a little secret, a plan for Gephardt's undoing, and he had just contributed to its success.

"Perfect," Maslin said. "He's totally set up."

Marshall shook his head, grinning. He smelled victory in the air.

Their scheme, in retrospect, would seem kiddish, a product of the hubris that seizes political handlers in hotel bars and restaurants late at night; in the beery air and the dim light, all things seem imaginable, even a client who does silly candidate tricks on command. Maslin and Marshall had been dining in a dark corner at the Backroom in Manchester only the night before Gephardt's outburst, conjuring ways to resuscitate their fading client. Yet another television debate was coming up that weekend at St. Anselm College. Simon's performances in these encounters had lately got so drab that his people prayed he wouldn't be mentioned in the morning papers. He had to do something showy to break through the numbing high-mindedness, his own and everyone else's.

"We cannot accept saying after the debate that he did OK," Marshall said. "We gotta do something that will kill Gephardt. *Keeel* him. Paul's gotta put on a long tie."

Maslin stared at him.

"Don't you see?" Marshall said. "This is what Coca-Cola pays these geniuses about—these gimmicks. But this is more than a gimmick. Let's use the long tie as a symbol of how quickly you can change your appearance."

Maslin leaned back. He was a veteran at thirty-two, an intense young man with combat ribbons from the Carter and Hart campaigns and a partnership in a new polling firm in Washington, but the stunt tickled the boy in him. "I'm just awed by it," he said.

Getting Simon to go along was quite another question; he was a bit of a troglodyte in contemporary politics, a stubborn unbeliever in the games handlers play. Maslin knew it would be a hard sell; still, he was excited enough to give it a try.

As it happened, an in-state adviser, Bob Shaine, had had the same brainstorm at the same time and had come to a prep session the day of the debate with a four-in-hand in his pocket. He showed it to Simon. The senator looked confused at first, but Maslin and Marshall jumped in, spinning out their stratagem. At the first opportunity, Simon was to undo his bow tie, clip on a full-length model and say, "Dick, I'm changing my image in seconds just by clipping this tie on. This tie represents how quickly you change your positions." The trick would steal the show. It would knock Gephardt out of second place; it might even win Simon the nomination.

Simon began to chuckle.

The rules of play for the debate forbade props, but Simon showed up that evening with the tie balled up in his pocket, and his people gathered around a TV monitor offstage to watch him administer the first recorded death by cravat in American political history.

He didn't. Slowball after slowball wafted by. The tie stayed buried in Simon's pocket. He was sleepwalking again, letting Gephardt dominate him.

"Goddammit!" Marshall exploded. "Goddammit!"

The show wound down. Simon did a reprise of his standard closing piece, an appeal for a government that cares. Then he walked off and rejoined his troops.

"I just gotta be myself," he said.

It might have been the epitaph for his campaign; to be oneself on television, in the politics of 1988, was always risky and often fatal. At the close, the tide turned back to Gephardt: he won the silver in New Hampshire by three points and, with it, a ticket to the next stop. Simon ran third and was mortally wounded. Babbitt finished sixth and went home.

Up the Down Escalator

Evening had fallen over Minneapolis. After a day of campaigning, Susan Estrich and Nick Mitropoulos of the Dukakis inner sanctum awarded themselves a drink with the campaign press secretary, Mark Gearan, at a hotel bar. The governor had done well enough in Iowa—the media, incredibly, seemed to be buying his feigned pleasure at having won the bronze there—and had watched with satisfaction in New Hampshire while his principal white rivals hacked each other to pieces. Now it looked as if he would finish off Simon in Minnesota and cripple Gephardt in South Dakota. The ice cubes clinked pleasantly, the smiles radiated self-congratulation. They were still savoring their good fortune when a young aide came rushing up.

"Gephardt has this incredible ad on television," he said breathlessly. "It's about Belgian endive."

Gephardt had struck on the Friday before the South Dakota primary, a stroke of timing much favored by political ad men for attack commercials: you caught your opponent going into the weekend, when the traffic departments at local TV stations shut down, and didn't give him the time or opportunity to respond. The spot needled Dukakis as a city boy who had once advised the hard-up family farmers of Iowa to solve their problems by growing Belgian endive. *"Belgian endive?"* a voice said at the end, dripping disbelief.

The ad was true, if trivial; the governor, on an early trip into the state in 1986, had indeed recommended that farmers diversify into flowers, blueberries and, yes, Belgian endive. But a certain tone was being set for the politics of 1988, a reliance on negative advertising by men who seemed unconfident that they had anything positive to sell.

The technique of bashing one's opponent was almost as old as the Republic—George Washington drew a bye—but new technologies had greatly expanded its reach and its destructive force. Television particularly, in the hands of the new managers, was the equivalent of what napalm might have been in General Sherman's: you could scorch a lot more earth with a lot less wasted time and motion. For people who made their livings winning elections, the weight and the literal accuracy of the charges involved were of secondary importance. A well-made negative ad attacked one's adversary like a stubborn virus, breeding doubts that lingered long after the particulars were forgotten. The issue was not whether it was fair or germane but whether it worked.

The endive spot did, and thus justified itself. It hit Dukakis in his most vulnerable spot, his self-esteem: the governor dreaded ridicule and reacted badly to it. When the ad first went up, Kip Scott, the state party chairman, called Will Robinson, Dukakis's deputy political director.

"You see it?" Scott asked.

"Yep," Robinson said. "We got trouble."

They did, with the voters and with their own candidate. "I never said that," Dukakis exploded when Estrich told him about the ad. In fact he had. Estrich urged him to fight back. Dukakis refused. He had rejected the temptation to go negative up to then; it ran against his prim reformist impulses, and the Biden affair put cleanliness even nearer to godliness in his eyes. On Saturday morning, his brain trust pushed him to run a commercial attacking Gephardt. He still refused. We're having this nice little conventional war in South Dakota, Robinson thought; the other guys are going nuclear, and our missiles are stuck in their silos.

Before the endive ad, soft voters had been breaking 65 percent Dukakis's way. The next day, the figure fell to 23 percent. On primary day, Joe Trippi phoned a chum at CBS News from Gephardt's charter Learjet, en route to Waco, Texas.

"Can you tell me anything?" Trippi asked.

"You're blowing him away."

He was; the final returns would give Gephardt 44 percent of the vote to Dukakis's 31.

There had been bad blood between the two campaigns from the beginning, intensified by the swivet over who had done Biden in, and the men on the Gephardt plane burst into whoops of pleasure. Their first poll in Texas showed Gephardt winning. Another in Florida placed him only four or five points behind. They were leading by a point in Georgia. Victory was, or seemed to be, in reach.

But hostilities in campaigns, as in war, have a way of escalating. Gephardt's little TV spot had bought him short-term advantage in South Dakota, but at dangerous cost; he had, as Ethel Klein put it, picked a fight with a *real* army and invited retaliation in kind against his own outmatched campaign. The day after the South Dakota primary, the brooding Dukakis snapped to attention, called a top hand and apologized for not having counterattacked.

"I learned my lesson," he said. "I won't let it happen again, anywhere in the country."

It was a lesson his people had been trying for weeks to drive home. Their smiles at finishing third in Iowa had masked what had in fact been a bitter disappointment. Some of them had expected to win, and when they had met with the Dukakises late that night at the Savery Hotel in Des Moines, they had scolded him heatedly for not having put more juice into his presentation.

You never adequately defined yourself, Estrich had told him. You never went negative.

I've been in this business twenty-five years, Dukakis had answered finally, his voice a hoarse shout. I know what to do.

His people were accordingly pleased by his anger at the endive ad. They figured South Dakota might have been a lost cause anyway, with or without Gephardt's spot. But blaming his advertising gave them the argument they needed to get Dukakis fighting mad. With Super Tuesday two weeks away, he told his people to go nuclear.

"It's not going to be pretty," he said, almost sadly, and it wasn't.

The Song of the South

For MONTHS, THE MONEY BOYS had been looking for a centrist in shining armor—no moonbeam merchant, no liberal, no wimp; just a kindred Democratic spirit they could go out and buy the nomination for. The hunt had been going badly, and the members of Impac '88, a high-rollers' combine pulled together by a Maryland developer named Nathan Landow, were beginning to lose heart. They gathered in thinning numbers one spring evening in 1987 in a beige-on-beige hospitality suite at the Grand Hotel in Washington, pouring themselves generous drinks and chattering in the discouraged tones of thoroughbred racers inspecting a paddock full of plugs.

Dukakis? Another Northeastern liberal. Babbitt? A space cadet. Gephardt? No presence. A nonstarter. Hart? People *still* didn't know who he was—it made you nervous. Biden? He's so hot on TV, you had to turn the set off two minutes after he came on. Simon? Simon *who*? Cuomo? Bumpers? Chuck Robb? Where were they now that their party needed them?

They descended eight floors to receive the latest supplicant for their favor, expecting yet another in a gallery of losers; some were still reading their press packets in the elevator to find out who he was. And then, into their dining room walked the junior senator from Tennessee. The guy had presence written all over him: he looked like a quarterback, thought like a Southerner and talked like a corporate CEO. He shook every hand in the room; he told a divinity-school joke about unscrewing the inscrutable; he discussed Central America and arms control, knowledgeably; he flashed his acquaintance with the new technologies; he ticked through all the buzzwords—competitiveness, communications, the service economy. But he didn't talk down to them. You could *understand* him.

"Great!" said Buddy Temple, a Texas businessman, wagging a finger in Senator Al Gore's direction. "Just what we've been looking for. He's it—he's the one!"

In a week, Gore was back for a second sitting, this time with checkbooks in evidence around the table. In less than a month, he would be off and running for a prize he had coveted all his public life.

The White Knight

From the time he first ran for Congress at twenty-eight, everyone around Albert Gore Jr. knew he had his eye on the big white mansion down the hill. He was ambitious, smart, serious, confident and pedigreed. His father had preceded him to the Senate and had served there with distinction for eighteen years. He was thus a child of the Washington aristocracy, though he had not traded on the name since his first run for Congress as a twenty-eight-year-old in 1976; he had been just plain Al, not Albert Jr., ever since.

He was also the youngest man in the field; he turned thirty-nine during the two weeks he allowed himself to meditate on declaring for president in the early spring of 1987, and even then he was three years younger than Jack Kennedy had been when he first announced in 1960. He was late coming to the table; he didn't seriously consider running until Senator Bumpers, his fellow Southerner, had made up his mind not to. Even then, Gore worried whether his youth would be a handicap in purely political terms; he guessed that people might think him previous in his ambition. When his father had first told him he would be in good field position for 1988, he had replied, "Dad! What do you mean? That's frightening. Absolutely not."

But his hesitance had more to do with timing than with modesty, and the harder he thought about the idea, the better it began to sound. He had never been overwhelmed by the field taking form, certainly not after Bumpers stood down from consideration; it struck him that Thomas Jefferson was not in the race, only a job lot of mortal and, in his view, limited men. He felt he had something to offer that they did not, a deep understanding of arms control and of the opportunities it presented for working profound changes in United States–Soviet relations. He was growing that sense of destiny required of men offering themselves seriously for president; he was, a friend said, moving toward the conviction that he couldn't wait because America couldn't wait for him.

There was, moreover, an empty spot for him in the group portrait of candidates assembling for 1988—an opening for a white, male and preferably Southern centrist who could call a generation of disaffected Democrats home. The party had won a majority of the white vote in a presidential election only once since the death of Franklin Roosevelt, in the aberrant Lyndon Johnson landslide of 1964. George Wallace's third-force candidacy had split away sizable numbers of whites four years later, with social values as his issue and race as his subtext, and Nixon and Reagan in their turn had diverted the stream to the Grand Old Party; by 1984, two white Americans in three voted Republican. The Democrats had become, in one widely held view, the party of the blacks, the unions, the liberals, the social engineers and the loosened behavioral codes of the 1960s. They were, or were seen to be, losing their last purchase on the white middle class, and a wing of the party was in search of the hero who could win back the strays.

The part had not been written for Gore. The men more commonly mentioned were Sam Nunn, Dale Bumpers and Charles S. Robb, the promising ex-governor of Virginia; Gore had to assure his own manager, Fred Martin, that he wasn't really running for vice president. But the strategists and bankrollers bent on moving the party rightward found him a more than acceptable substitute white knight. Gore was attractive, well-spoken, tough-minded and yet not *so* conservative as to split the party mainstream from its left or its past. He wasn't really very conservative at all, though his angels and his packagers preferred not to notice; except in matters of military preparedness and fiscal prudence, his voting record had a distinctly liberal cast.

The issue in his own mind was never whether he could handle the presidency. His parents, having themselves made their way up in the world from threadbare beginnings, had bred confidence into him. What concerned him was whether he could get the job, and at what human cost. He canvassed more than two hundred people in his budgeted two weeks of meditation, among them Fritz Mondale, who knew just how bad it could get. The picture they drew of the process was mostly a grim one, a prospect of a year or more torn loose from his life and his family. But Gore was ambitious, even driven, and he seemed to friends to rationalize away the negatives. Deciding to run for president was sort of like buying a warm puppy, Roy Neel, his administrative assistant, guessed. You take it home, you try it out, and you can't live without it; you forget that the puppy is going to pee on the rug.

Gore's wife, Tipper, the crusader for cleanliness in rock lyrics, was all for the idea. Their four children were less sure, and the family met around the coffee table in their peach-tinted living room in Arlington, Virginia, to talk through their worries.

Karenna, the oldest at thirteen, seemed the most concerned. Her first questions, as the child of a political household, were pragmatic. "Dad," she asked, "how do you think you can get any more publicity than Gary Hart when no one knows you?"

But there were personal matters too, the anxiety of children at a change in the settled order of their lives. Kristin, nine years old, got out a yellow legal pad and wrote "Dad's Decision" at the top. Then she drew two columns, headed "For" and "Against."

Under "For," she wrote: "He wants to. Help the country."

Under "Against," the downside: "Some people may think he's too young."

"We don't want our friends to look at us different from now," Karenna said.

Kristin wrote that down, too.

There was, moreover, the matter of their privacy. "When is Social Security going to start following us around?" eight-year-old Sarah wanted to know. She meant the Secret Service, but she had the idea.

Albert III, the baby of the family, allowed that it was all too much for him. "Can't you wait till I'm five, Dad?" he asked. He was then four.

Gore decided finally to jump in. But the realities of running proved tougher than he had imagined. He was himself a novice in national politics, with a novice manager in Martin, a slight, owlish Ph.D. in American history whose main prior experience had been as a staff man to Mario Cuomo and Walter Mondale and a speechwriter for Geraldine Ferraro. Their first miscalculation was that the debates would be the perfect launching platform for him, a show window for his size, his self-assurance and his command of geopolitics. What they didn't anticipate was that, in the high-pressure world of presidential politics, the sight of a dais or a television camera would turn him into solid teak.

The problem mystified his handlers. On duty, in Tennessee, Gore had been known as a poised, loose and likable campaigner; off duty, he enjoyed a joke, a dance, a long evening of conversation and Calvados among friends. But with his graduation to the big time, he looked as stiff as a mannequin and sounded as stuffy as a pedant. It was a measure of his rigor mortis that when he confessed having tried marijuana as a much younger man, it seemed less scandalous than humanizing; he wasn't just a walking GI Joe doll who had to tell people he had soul. The guy just tightened up, one of his strategists said, mystified. He promised to work at it, but a man who has to practice looking comfortable rarely does; it was as if he were trying to offset being so young by trying to act middle-aged.

Gore's further gamble was that he could ignore the strategy books that had lately governed Democratic primary politics. Ordinarily, someone who had been lost among the "others" at the back of the pack in Iowa and had placed fifth in New Hampshire wouldn't present much of a threat to anyone; the book said you had to do well in the table-setting early rounds to get anywhere at all. But Gore bailed out of Iowa, announcing at a party dinner there that its caucuses were a playpen for special-interest groups, and maintained no more than a low-budget presence in New Hampshire. His game plan turned instead on dominating Super Tuesday—the Big Bank, as he called it—by presenting himself as the regional favorite son of the South.

His course required that he swing right as well, muffling what was liberal in his record and talking up what was not. As Senator Gore, he had put forward an imaginative arms-control proposal to shift from multiple- to single-warhead missiles, giving each side a terrifying deterrent but neither the means for a first strike; the idea had been well received by liberals and conservatives alike. But as candidate Gore, playing to the conservative white South, he repositioned himself as a lonesome hawk in a dovecote— an advocate of a muscular defense, a champion of America's military adventuring in Grenada and Libya, a convert to nonmilitary aid to the Contra insurgency in Nicaragua.

To make sure he carried the point, he began turning the debates into target shoots, accusing his rivals of being soft on defense. He and his people insisted that his stance was both principled and wholly consistent with his record. But he had in fact begun his campaign in more moderate terms; his subsequent hard-lining was seen even among his own men as a political ploy, an attempt to please his angels in Impac and his target voters in the South. His competitors were not pleased by his sudden tougher-than-thou positioning. In one of the debates, when Simon scolded him for knifing his brother Democrats, Dukakis leaned over and told the senator, "Good job."

There was a hollow core to Gore's Southern strategy, a missed connection with the voters. As late as January, two-thirds of the Southern electorate didn't even know he *was* a Southerner; he was just another guy in a blue suit running around doing dozy lectures about treaty terms and weapons systems. With the turn of the year, Jack Quinn, a refugee from Hart's campaign, and Bruce Reed, a speechwriter, sent him a memo urging him to broaden his offering—to stir in "a dose of responsible indignation" in support of working Americans. Nothing happened; economic policy was Gore's short suit, and in the heat of the campaign he relied mostly on what he knew best.

"Al, that puts people to *sleep,*" one consultant warned him; there was no payoff in the new politics for knowing your stuff.

"Well, they don't want Pablum," Gore replied sniffishly.

He could be that way, difficult for his managers to manage. He relied instead on his own instincts and on the advice of his wife and his parents, known among the hired help as Senator Sir and Senator Ma'am; he would carry a new idea back to them, and it would disappear, as if, an aide thought, into a black hole. The pros, as one of them confessed, wanted style and glitz. The Gores preferred substance, and the senator continued to deliver it, with all the fire and dash of a class valedictorian.

With his back-of-the-pack finishes in Iowa and New Hampshire, his campaign had a themeless, rudderless look. People were saying, and writing, that he had made a big mistake by passing on the prelims, that his Super Tuesday strategy had blown up in his face. He had to do something; his moderate-turned-conservative look wasn't selling, and a *new* new Gore soon emerged from its chrysalis in a conference room at his Arlington headquarters, a people's politician who sounded as if he were reading Dick Gephardt's lines. The campaign borrowed a million dollars for a brilliantly timed and targeted television buy and brought in Ray Strother, a high-powered media man with Southern roots, to shoot some new spots.

Strother thought Gore was, or ought to have been, a storybook candidate—a guy with the looks, the mind, the education, the family, everything an adman normally hopes for in a client. But one key element seemed wanting in him. Great politicians, like great generals, had a boldness about them, Strother thought, a stroke of daring. Gore did not.

His new ads tried to inject some. His positive ads reintroduced him as a neopopulist who would fight for working people and make corporations face up to responsibilities beyond earning profits. His negative spots were aimed at Gephardt. The campaign's calculation was that only three men were going to emerge on the other side of Super Tuesday. Dukakis was sure to be one of them. Jesse Jackson would be the second. Either Gore or Gephardt would be the third, and Gore accordingly went after Gephardt with that extra ferocity born of desperation. By the last four or five days, while everyone else except Dukakis was scratching for money, Gore's spots were running at saturation levels across the South.

The game was a suspenseful one to the end; he won his first victory in Wyoming three days before the big event, but it was not until the last weekend of the campaign that his phone banks in the South began to pick up positive signals.

On primary night, Gore sat up with his family and his backers in a suite at the Opryland Hotel in Nashville. We've pulled off the impossible, he told himself, watching the returns; he had won five Southern and border states, plus Nevada for good measure. At midnight, he tuned in a special edition of Ted Koppel's *Nightline* on ABC-TV, expecting to bask in the electronic glow of triumph. But George Bush's demolition of Bob Dole was the top news story that night. No one had even mentioned Gore's name until, a few minutes before the end of the show, Koppel asked his guests whether there was anything they had missed.

Well, Peter Jennings said, I suppose Al Gore's finish constitutes a minor surprise.

With that, Koppel signed off.

Victory Through Air Power

At an elegant little restaurant in Boston called St. Cloud's, Tubby Harrison, ordinarily a nice man, squeezed his glass of vodka so hard his knuckles turned white. A month before Super Tuesday, his thinking was running to the medieval. "We'll cut the balls off him," he said. "We'll hang him over the fire so his toes will be singed. We'll never let him forget it. If he comes on negative, he'll *die*."

The object of the polltaker's disaffection was Richard Gephardt, and the instrument of torture would be television advertising. The congressman had brought it on himself. The Dukakis campaign had picked up reports that tapes labeled "Endive" were waiting in television stations all over the South, a bit of intelligence that was duly reported to the governor; his people wanted to keep him pumped up for a fight.

It helped their cause that Dukakis had long since come to dislike Gephardt for having said mean things about him; the congressman, he told one adviser, was just not a nice man. The two had met in a face-to-face debate in August, an event so charged with loathing that even the arrangements had bordered on war; aides drifting past Sasso's office had heard him on the phone to Gephardt's people, screaming, "Fuck you! . . . Fuck you! . . . Well, fuck *you!*" In the main event, Dukakis had won on points, his seconds thought, but lost on manners. He had, in the prophetic words of a memo "to MSD" from his staff, "come very close to snideness. . . . Winning the debate doesn't pay off if you come across as unlikable in the process."

By Super Tuesday, his people led him up the escalator to open war. One obvious line of attack was Gephardt's history of changing positions on a wide range of economic and military questions, the stations on a learning curve if you liked him, a profile in opportunism if you did not. But how did you put the evidence into a commercial and get anyone to watch it? The day after South Dakota, two of Dukakis's media men, Dan Payne and Mike Shea, arrived for a meeting in Estrich's office on Chauncy Street with a brainstorm: use an acrobat to do *real* flip-flops, and leave the details to the voice-over.

The idea was unconventional, and Dukakis's people had to persuade themselves that it would work. Should the acrobat jump over a sawhorse, maybe? Or bounce on a trampoline? Would the acrobat *look* like Gephardt? Would he have red hair? Wouldn't the old weathervane trick be a safer, clearer way to make the point—the politician shifting positions with every change in the wind? Strategy meetings in the Dukakis campaign had developed an abnormally high yammer level in Sasso's absence, and a want of daring as well, but you *had* to ask questions like that; in the new presidential politics, the styling of a television ad was vastly more likely than the content of an issues speech to separate the winners from the losers.

With some hesitation, Estrich finally signed off on the idea. But Tubby Harrison worried that it wouldn't work alone. He had done some interesting polling in Arkansas and found what he thought was a way to turn Gephardt's populism against him. The survey showed that support for an unnamed Candidate X, a close match for Gephardt, dropped from 19 to 4 percent when voters were told that he took money from organized interest groups. Harrison saw the outlines of an ad in the numbers. The acrobat spot was great, he told the others—"but first we gotta prove he's a whore."

Till then, Dukakis himself had resisted going after Gephardt for accepting contributions from corporate and other political-action committees; his people in Iowa had had to plant questions at his meetings to get him to say anything at all on the subject. But Estrich had quietly delivered a list of Gephardt's PACs to Ken Swope, the media man, and when Harrison proposed doing a whore spot, Swope was armed and ready.

For a time, he sat silent at Estrich's round table, a blank legal pad staring up at him. "It's your fight, too," he wrote at the top; that was Gephardt's slogan, and Swope was about to destroy it. People were talking back and forth, but their voices were hollow echoes. Swope was in a trance, his ballpoint pen flying over the empty page.

Estrich asked what he was writing.

"Don't bother me," he told her.

"What have you *got,* Swope?" Tom Kiley demanded.

Swope ignored him.

Leslie Dach tried to snatch his pad away. Dach was, in the words of a colleague, an unedited man; he was known backstairs on Chauncy Street as Baby Dach for his peremptory ways. But Swope brushed him off and kept scribbling. He was already screening the commercial in his mind, the visual a list of Gephardt's corporate contributors, the voice-over saying, "Kinda makes you wonder—is Dick Gephardt really fighting your fight? Or theirs?"

His script was approved on the spot, and, at Estrich's direction, a memo from Harrison outlining it was hand-delivered to Dukakis on the road. The cover was marked CONFIDENTIAL to give it an important look, and the Arkansas poll data was double-underlined. Dukakis read it on his campaign plane, and finally said yes.

Both spots went quickly into production. Payne's producer held auditions and chose a high-school gymnastics coach for the lead part in the flip-flop ad; they sprayed red paint onto his hair, dressed him in a suit and taped him doing forward and backward flips. "Hmmm," Dukakis said when the media people showed him the finished ad. He seemed not to get it, but everyone else liked it, and he said yes again; the high-school gym teacher with the painted red hair was to become one of the key players in the destruction of Dick Gephardt.

Ad schedules are an open secret in high-stakes politics; they are easily available to anyone with a friend at a TV station or a minimal level of skill at deception. Dukakis's two spots were accordingly packaged with innocuous names—the PAC ad was called "List," the acrobat "Record Hop"—and sent around to the targeted media markets. The PAC spot went up first, a week before Super Tuesday; the flip-flop ad was booked to go on a few days later, a surprise second punch.

"We'll hit him so hard he won't be able to get up again," Estrich told the others.

Events would prove her right. The campaign's strategy from the beginning had been to hoard money in the early primaries; by October 1987, Sasso had banked $3 million in a certificate of deposit for Super Tuesday alone, declaring it untouchable. In the event, Estrich spent only $2 million of it, resisting pressures to go for broke.

"You want a million?" Bob Farmer asked her nervously over dinner one night. "I can give you another million."

Estrich shook her head. "We can win without it," she said.

Their one-two attack on TV was in fact quite enough to undo Gephardt; it puts him on the defensive, the worst of all postures in politics. The campaign's own intelligence sources were sending daily reports to Chauncy Street on where Gore and Gephardt were placing ads. Gore was of secondary interest, although, on hearing that he was planning to run some anti-Dukakis spots, Estrich called Gore's man Martin to warn him away.

"Fred," she said, her voice raspy, "we hear you're airing negatives in the South. If that's true, we're gonna beat the shit out of you."

"Are you threatening me?" Martin asked.

"No," Estrich said. "I'm *telling* you: if you air, we'll beat the shit out of you."

The ads ran anyway, but the Chauncy Street regulars shrugged them off; their main concern, for tactical and personal reasons, was to run Gephardt out of the race. With Florida and Texas looking solid for Dukakis, the campaign started matching Gephardt's media buys even in states they had no real hope of winning. If that meant more states for Gore, so be it; they could dispose of him later, in the North. Gephardt would be forced to bleed his treasury just to stay competitive in his *best* Super Tuesday states. There would be nothing left for him to spend in Dukakis country.

Slo Mo

The attack caught Gephardt unprepared, strategically and financially. If Gore had gambled everything on the South, Gephardt had banked too heavily on Iowa and New Hampshire; the pursuit of what George Bush once unluckily called Big Mo got nowhere. No one had been scared out of the race except Bruce Babbitt, who had never really been in it. Gephardt was nearly tapped out; he had spent himself broke for next to nothing.

Not all his people had read the handwriting on the wall, or, more accurately, on the spreadsheets. Carrick was a South Carolinian, a home-boy on the Super Tuesday terrain. If you get through Iowa, he had assured Gephardt, I'll get you through the South. At their headiest, in the wake of their stolen victory in South Dakota, they thought they might actually sweep the region, or at least enough of it to break Dukakis's back; they went into the governor's prime target states, Texas and Florida, playing to win.

They underrated the PAC ad at first, figuring that no one would really care. But the two spots taken together had a slower, more corrosive effect, which was precisely the intent of negative advertising; the specifics mattered less than the toxic aftereffect, the vague memory among voters that they had heard something bad about the guy in the crosshairs. The spots, moreover, were running across the region, not just in Dukakis's target states. It was scorched-earth politics, an assault on Gephardt's character in states Dukakis had no chance of winning; the governor was going for the kill.

Finding a way to respond was harder than divining Dukakis's intent. Dukakis and Gore were outspending Gephardt by a factor of two or three dollars to one; he no longer had the money to defend himself, let alone get out his own hey-look-me-over bio ad or his populist economic message. His media people scraped up enough money for a desperate counterstrike, a ten-second mini-spot charging that Dukakis, in smearing an opponent, was once again up to his dirty tricks. Before it aired, Ed Reilly, the polltaker, called Joe Trippi on the road and told him to be sure to clear it with Gephardt first.

"If we put it on," Reilly said, "it just severs any chance of Mike Dukakis ever selecting Dick as VP. He'll hate him the rest of his life—that's the kind of guy he is."

The message made Trippi uncomfortable, but he passed it along.

"Well," Gephardt said, "he's not going to be *my* vice president, either."

The chance that he would be choosing a vice president was by then slip-sliding away. While he defended one flank against Dukakis, Gore hit him from the other. The crossfire was murderous. Gephardt was a blank slate out there, Reilly thought, and the other guys were writing bad things on it; they were going into every market where Gephardt had any strength at all and just blasting the shit out of him.

Gephardt's men were like generals in a bunker in a losing war, watching their lines collapse and their holdings fall away. His poll rating in Florida dropped twenty-one points in less than two weeks. Oklahoma seemed promising one day; the next, it fell to Gore. On the Sunday afternoon before Super Tuesday, Gephardt sat with Bob Shrum in a hotel room in Dallas, watching television for an hour and a half. They saw three of Dukakis's spots and three of Gore's, but none of their own. That night, Reilly called from New York. The bottom had fallen out in Texas. It was gone, too.

On primary day, Reilly took a last look at his numbers, then did a conference call with the headquarters cadre in Washington and the traveling party at a Howard Johnson's in Miami to broach the scale of the catastrophe. It was all caving in on them. They were going to get their tail whipped, and they didn't have the money to survive it.

Afterward, Bob Shrum and Dick Moe went to Gephardt's room. They knew Gephardt felt down, but they had to begin thinking about what he could say that night, how he could handle the scale of his defeat. Shrum was near tears.

"It'll be OK, Bob," Gephardt said, the loser comforting his second. "It'll be all right."

That night, he flew home to await the bad news. It was, in the end, worse than they had imagined. Of the day's twenty-one contests, he won only in Missouri and ran second in Oklahoma and American Samoa; everywhere else, he was lost in the dust, nineteen to seventy points behind the leaders. He vowed the morning after that he would keep the campaign alive, "until," he told his people, "they cut my head off." In practical fact, they already had; before the month was out, Gephardt would be back in St. Louis, filing for a seventh term in Congress.

He was, as he came to believe in hindsight, one more casualty of the game as it was played in the 1980s: a contest in which the qualities of a man's mind and record counted for little as against the frequency and the cleverness of his ads. He had managed to get his positives out in retail states like Iowa and New Hampshire, he mused one gray spring day after his withdrawal; people had liked what they saw of him, and he had done well. He had added a biting attack ad to his repertoire in South Dakota and had done well there too.

But Super Tuesday, with its vast sprawl, had been practically all air wars, a duel of videos in which the candidates were the bit players and their packagers the stars. Gephardt had been outspent and outslickered in the one game that counted. Nothing else seemed to him to have moved the numbers—nothing he or his rivals said in their speeches, nothing the media said about them. It was all paid TV, he said, his tone more clinical than sad. If you had the dough to do it right and get it out, you won. If you didn't, you went home.

"We Really Kicked Ass"

In Boston, where the Dukakis people threw their victory party, Susan Estrich was laughing, swearing, gesturing, dominating the room. There was a lot to toast and a lot to drink. "We really kicked ass," Estrich exulted. "We really kicked ass."

Younger aides who thought of her as a forbidding figure watched with open wonderment, but Estrich had earned her celebration. She and her team had executed the four-corner strategy set in place by Sasso and the old crowd, toughing it out with *sangfroid* and discipline, and it had paid off handsomely.

North Carolina was a disappointment; Chauncy Street had hoped nearly to the end to win, but Gore's ads had hurt there, and Dukakis slipped back to third. But Sasso had identified the two biggest Southern states, Texas and Florida, as the prime targets, and Jack Corrigan's field operatives had organized them brilliantly. One small measure of their nothing-to-chance intensity was the courtship of Annie Ackerman, the septuagenarian political boss of one of the condo clusters in North Miami Beach. At its peak, Ackerman wrote her granddaughter's phone number on a scrap of paper and gave it to Greg Rothschild, the young Dukakis worker assigned to cosset her. Greg was a cute boy. He phoned almost every day. He could give a nice girl a call, maybe take her to dinner.

But I already have a girlfriend, Rothschild protested when he got back to headquarters.

You take her out anyway! his superior, Steve Rosenfeld, roared.

On Super Tuesday, Ackerman's condo went for Dukakis. So did all of Florida, plus Texas, plus six other states and American Samoa. Dukakis's day was made. Gephardt had been annihilated, his reward for having offended the governor's pride; the only state he got was his own.

It would be a considerable while before the consensus judgment of politics caught up with the real meaning of the returns. Al Gore's six states were widely posted on the scoreboard as a great victory, when in fact his people had privately hoped for eight or nine to send them north with something like momentum. Fortune had not smiled on their plan. They had presented Gore as the champion of the New South, but there were in fact two New Souths on Super Tuesday, one his, the other Jesse Jackson's. The senator, like the rest of the white candidates, had conceded the black vote to Jackson and had discovered too late that there weren't enough white votes to go around. The reverend carried five Southern states, one more than Gore, and so effectively knocked the props out from under the senator's candidacy.

Gore would campaign quixotically on for six more weeks on begged and borrowed money, only once finishing higher than third. His "victory" on Super Tuesday had been an illusion to which he and his family council were prey. So, for a time, were the media. Gore's performance, and Jackson's, obscured Dukakis's in the early commentaries on Super Tuesday. The oracles of television did not declare the governor the big winner that night. Anchormen talked instead about a brokered convention.

Running Long,
Running Strong

HE STOOD UP FRONT WORKING THE CROWD, a tall black preacher turned to politics, ministering to the left—and the left-out—of his wounded party. "Why am I so close to workers?" he wondered aloud. "Because I *am* a worker. I *understand* cooking on a hotplate, no health insurance, bathroom in the backyard, slop jar by the bed. I *do* understand. Born to a teenage mother, looked down on and disrespected. I *do* understand." Heads nodded, eyes grew bright with tears. No other Democrat talked the way he did; none of them could. "I wasn't born in the big white house, I was way over down in the slums. But the slum wasn't born in me and it was not born in *you*." His long fingers drummed the side of the podium as he felt the connection click. "I'm running long, I'm running strong. Got my second wind. I've just begun to fight." And now they were on their feet, feeling the words, moving toward him, calling him in a swelling roar—"Jesse! Jesse! Jesse!"

See Jesse Run

The new Jesse Jackson sounded better and looked stronger than the unsure novice of 1984. His two decades as a black leader and his astonishing maiden run for president had, he liked to say, put him alongside Ronald Reagan as the best-known people in the world; you turn either one of them loose anywhere on the planet with only a dime in his pocket, and he'd be home free. No other Democrat except Hart had Jackson's name recognition, and, as a new campaign approached, the arbiters of the conventional wisdom simply assumed that he would run again. He had, in the common view, never really stopped.

But Jackson didn't mean to go it alone. For big decisions, he liked war councils, serial gatherings of preachers and politicians, old friends from the movement days, Young Turks from the cities where black political power had taken hold. His canvasses stretched out from the summer of 1986 well into the early months of 1987. " 'See Jesse run?' " he asked them, a rhetorical question posed, like everything he said, with rhetorical flair. "No, we're going to run together or we're not going to run at all." For those whose faces said, Oh, no, not again, he had a reply: there were six million unregistered black voters out there, more than enough to tip the balance. That base was just waiting for a "progressive" candidate. "We can win," he said. "This ain't protest. It's not symbolic. It's not pride. This is *real.*"

Could he really win? Electability, in the Jackson campaign, became a loaded word that meant different things to whites and to blacks. For many whites, it was a comfortable euphemism that cloaked the race issue: the reality that the white majority was not yet prepared to vote a black man into the White House, not Jackson or anyone else. For black leaders, the issue was more subtle. To some, Jackson looked like a problem in the guise of an opportunity. On the one hand, he had brought a stirring and powerful voice for their common concerns to the national dialogue at its highest level. On the other, he was not merely black but hot, a bull in the china shop of multiracial coalition politics. It had become axiomatic among many white and some black leaders that his candidacy was at cross-purposes with the effort to win back those stray white voters called Reagan Democrats; it was said that the party might not win without Jackson but that it surely would not win with him.

Jackson had grown since 1984, both as a man and as a political force. His first candidacy had been a predominantly black enterprise, the civil-rights movement raised to the plane of presidential politics; it had sometimes been said that he was running for president of *black* America. Not everyone in the Family, as a loose national network of black leaders called themselves, had liked that idea. His moral and political impulses had never been more than a synapse apart. His admirers chose to believe that he was moved first by what was right and only then by what was advantageous.

His detractors, the first time, had figured it was the other way around. Some of his old movement allies had thought Jackson an ego-tripper, seeking attention and glory for himself; some black politicians regarded him, not without envy, as a show-timer trying to crash their game at the top.

But the 1984 campaign had established him against all odds as the first serious black candidate for president, and there was every reason to believe he would do better in 1988. His candidacy and his postprimary crusading had helped register two million new voters, mostly black and Democratic, and they in turn had helped return the Senate to Democratic hands in 1986; his base in black America was larger and more fiercely loyal than ever.

He had, moreover, worked hard to reach beyond it, crisscrossing America to witness with striking workers, dispossessed farmers, peace marchers, people with AIDS; usually, he was the only presidential aspirant in sight. His ecumenism won him growing respect among liberal whites. The battered left wing of his party had grown tired of the bloodless rhetoric of a technocratic age, tired of Democrats pretending to be Republicans; some came to see Jackson as the last resonant voice of traditional Democratic issues and values.

His way with the Family was accordingly easier. Some of his brothers and sisters in politics still resented his claim to preeminence but saw the folly in denying him; they knew they could expect trouble in their own election campaigns if they did. Mostly, the opposition he had encountered in 1984 melted away. As he made the rounds of black political caucuses in state after state, demanding solidarity as his asking price for carrying on, he found it. Jackson had, as one old hand at Democratic national headquarters put it, become the movement; the common objective was to leverage what power blacks had in the party, and the reverend was running the only game in town.

One last, elusive figure was Andrew Young, Jackson's comrade in denims from the old days soldiering with Martin Luther King Jr. He had been a skeptic in 1984, and, as 1988 approached, Jackson courted him actively, as if Young's approval were a kind of validation for his candidacy, a posthumous blessing from Dr. King. Young remained hard to get. He had chosen his own more orthodox road in politics and had become mayor of Atlanta, and he told Jackson in an early phone call not to waste time trying to convert him.

"I'm with you as much as I can be," he said. "I think we have different roles."

Jackson kept trying. The two men talked again, before the primaries began, when the reverend was in Atlanta for a meeting; their conversation took on the tonality of a negotiation, an effort, Young thought, not at alliance but at détente. Young had long been an advocate of what he called the Jewish strategy in politics; it was, he believed, in the interests of any minority to have friends at court, as the Jews seemed to, no matter who got elected. Blacks needed to be positioned in every camp, not just in Jesse's; it was important, he said, that Jackson not be the only Democrat talking about the things they cared about, issues like hunger, apartheid, women's rights, child care.

"Oh," Jackson said, "so you see yourself as kind of a roving linebacker, plugging all the holes on defense?"

Young grinned. "I hadn't thought of it that way," he said, "but I like that. And I don't have any problem with you being the quarterback. In fact, I support you and encourage you in that role."

Jackson said that was fine with him. But Young was never quite sure with the reverend. He was always so restless, always acting like a guy with an agenda. Young liked him personally, but Jesse was . . . The thought trailed off. Jesse, finally, was Jesse.

He was, first, a lavishly gifted man, bright, handsome, eloquent, difficult and driven. He lived in constant furious motion toward the goal he had set for himself, which was to be taken seriously as a leader among leaders. He was Ralph Ellison's Invisible Man demanding to be seen and heard; where other candidates longed for the power and majesty of the presidency, Jackson appeared at times to be running for respect, for black Americans and himself.

He could be single-minded to the point of wintriness in its pursuit. Some associates thought that two personalities were struggling within him. One was the Jackson everyone loved, the quick, laughing, self-deprecating man, Jesse as the brother on the block; he seemed in those moments to slip out of his public persona, to unburden himself of the size and weight he had achieved in the world by his own wit and daring. But if you crowded him, tried to get too close, he could switch in the blink of an eye to *Reverend* Jackson, formal, aloof, almost priestly, standing on his dignity. He could be so affirming, one old friend mused as the campaign got started, so big-brotherly when he let himself be, but sometimes he could just look at you, and you wanted to go crawl up *under* the airplane.

His candidacy was not the foregone conclusion everyone thought it would be; when he finally did declare his candidacy, in October 1987, he was the last man onto the field. He had had moments of doubt—moments when it seemed too risky; moments when he worried about all the media attention to what used to be considered private lives; moments when he thought it might put too much stress on his wife, Jackie, and the kids. He had been dogged for most of his public life by rumors of extramarital adventuring, and the fall of Gary Hart made it plain that no corner of a man's "character" was off limits. As late as the day before he announced, Rex Harris, director of Jackson's Rainbow Coalition, warned supporters that a major newspaper was about to print some allegations—a lot of garbage, Harris called it—about Jackson's supposed infidelities. It came to nothing, and Jackson joined the race.

There would be days down the road when his campaign seemed improvisational, governed by the instincts of the candidate. But there was an underlying design to the enterprise; its metaphor was a marathon run, not a quadrennial series of fits and starts, and its unlikely model was the rise of American conservatism. Its theoretician, Frank Watkins, a longtime Jackson adviser, saw parallels between the reverend's campaign in 1984 and Barry Goldwater's in 1964: each had shown that a base of ideologically committed voters, properly energized, could have an impact on a national election. But, Watkins felt, you needed more than just principles and programs; you needed a candidate, a *vehicle,* to make something of them. The conservatives had found theirs in Ronald Reagan. The progressives were discovering Jesse Jackson. He had been their Goldwater in 1984. In 1988, he could be their Reagan.

Almost from day one, his second candidacy had a more professional look than his first. It had a whiter hue as well, since blacks had been largely shut out of the business of running presidential campaigns; Jackson soon found himself in the curious position of having to deny that he was discriminating against them. The leading black figure in his campaign was its chairman, Willie Brown Jr., the powerful speaker of the California State Assembly. Its manager, Gerald Austin, a consultant who had helped Richard F. Celeste to the governorship of Ohio, was white. So was its foreign-policy adviser, Robert Borosage, a recruit from a Washington think tank, and its domestic-issues man, Mark Steitz, a congressional budget expert who had worked for Gary Hart. And so was Jackson's unofficial guru, Bert Lance, the wily Georgia banker-politician; the reverend called him day and night for strategic direction and horse sense at points of crisis.

Jackson's own performance had improved with practice, to a point where, at any assembly of the candidates, he was the dominant presence. The amateur of 1984 had compromised himself with a single careless remark to a reporter, a reference to Jews as "Hymies" and New York as "Hymietown"; his apologies had been late and sounded grudging, and his campaign had been knocked off balance. The professional of 1988 had installed a Jew as his manager and made the search for "common ground" among *all* the party's constituent groups the leitmotif of his campaign.

In debates, his gift of gab put his rivals in the shade; the form was made for his skills at the theater of politics, and so was the gray backdrop provided him by the opposition. When he found a powerful emotional issue in the spread of drugs, the others followed along in his train. When they fell to bickering among themselves, he was the statesman, chiding them for degrading the process with their rat-a-tat. When, as only occasionally happened, they challenged him on his ideas or his inexperience, he came as well prepared as they with smart answers. He had, he said at one debate, dealt with more world leaders than anyone running—and, unlike George Bush, *he* had met them when they were still alive.

With a swell of optimism, the campaign's master plan called for raising $10 million and earmarking $2 million for media on Super Tuesday. The money did not materialize quickly or easily. On a wing, a prayer and a pittance, Jackson flew into the primaries. He started stronger than in 1984, winning friends among beleaguered white family farmers in Iowa. He ran fourth there and in New Hampshire and second in Minnesota, Maine and Vermont, all, in practical terms, white states.

Then he exploded onto the friendlier soil of Super Tuesday, the homeboy come back to his native South. His $2 million fantasy budget for media had melted away to $100,000, a hairline fraction of what he had hoped for and what the others were spending. He made poverty a virtue; his was, he said, a poor campaign with a rich message, and its payday was richer still. He ran first or second in sixteen of the day's twenty-one primaries and caucuses, and his 27 percent market share of the aggregate popular vote was bigger than Dukakis's or Gore's.

He felt, with some justice, that he was being put through a series of proofs that no one else had to answer. There was some tactical advantage to being the one black candidate in the race, a grant of immunity to frontal assault; the others dealt with him gingerly or not at all. But as a black man, he felt himself carrying the weight of sociology as well as politics. He had had to pass the race test, the electability test, the seriousness test, all with the mass media keeping score, he thought, and when he had finally started winning, he found himself confronted with the same frustrating question that had bedeviled him four years earlier: What does Jesse *want*? That he might actually want what the white candidates wanted, to be elected president, seemed too outlandish for the press to take seriously.

Then came the Michigan caucuses.

"It's Real Bad"

"Jesus," Dan Payne wondered, "where are all these black people coming from?"

Payne, Dukakis's amiable media man, and his senior colleagues had gathered around Susan Estrich's conference table to celebrate what they all presumed would be their victory in Michigan. Outside, a hard March rain splattered Chauncy Street. Inside, there was only numb silence. No one tried to answer Payne's question. No one knew.

They needed a big win in the industrial North; they had failed in their first try, in Illinois eleven days earlier, and had redoubled their efforts in Michigan, mounting the nearest they could manage to a zero-defect campaign. Their field operatives had made a quarter of a million phone calls, sent 500,000 pieces of mail, diligently worked union members and power brokers in Detroit and Lansing. Coleman Young, Detroit's black mayor, was notoriously unfond of Jackson and was helping them behind the scenes. Their polls were looking good. They had arrived at 105 Chauncy expecting victory, banking it in advance. Tubby Harrison had brought a bottle of Polish vodka; Estrich had set out a bowl of candy, sweets for the sweet. How could they possibly lose?

But they *were* losing. Their polls and their hubris had betrayed them, and so had their messageless campaign; it was money power against soul power, and soul was winning. Ken Swope, the adman, was frantically switching channels searching for news. What there was kept getting worse. Jesse Jackson, Payne thought, is kicking the crap out of us; they had got whammed by a goddam locomotive when they weren't looking.

They had at least known there would be problems in Illinois. They had, to be sure, underestimated the degree of difficulty there too. In the cocky aftermath of Super Tuesday, the Chauncy Street crowd started referring to the race as the Land of the Living Dead; they imagined, for a time, that they might even beat Paul Simon there and all but wrap up the nomination. But Illinois was Simon's home, and Jesse Jackson's, and Dukakis had rarely seemed quite so much an Alien Life Force as he did in their earthy territory. John DeVillars, who had scouted the state, warned the governor in a memo that he needed to put more meat into his message and more heart into his performances—some show of empathy for people suffering through hard economic times. The advice was largely ignored. No moaning and groaning, Dukakis regularly instructed his speechwriters; he was running a nice, optimistic campaign.

He had never been much good at feelings, anyway. The morning after Super Tuesday, his people had booked him and Kitty for breakfast with a group of unemployed steelworkers at a café called the Lion's Den, set in a wasteland of gutted factories and rusting cars on Chicago's South Side. The intent was to show on camera that he cared, but he looked as much at home in his dowdy suit and wingtips as a teetotaler in a saloon. He talked at the workers, not with them. His words flowed in a fast stream, all commas and no periods. Occasionally, he remembered to ask the workers a question, then forgot to listen to their answers.

The gap was never bridged, not, anyway, in Illinois; his best TV spot featured a large bricklayers'-union leader conceding up front that Dukakis was "not your shot-and-beer kinda guy" and only then proceeding to the sell. The governor believed nearly to the end that he was connecting. He was not, and on primary day he straggled in third, behind Simon and Jackson.

His campaigning had gone no better in Michigan. His command group had begun coming unglued after Illinois, the family feuding over who was to blame for his defeat there, and Dukakis's faith in them, already strained, was near its end. He responded by freezing them out and retiring to the statehouse in one of his pettish moods. It was hard to get him to campaign in Michigan, and when he did, his message and his manner were flat; to his impatient young speechwriter Bill Woodward he sounded less like a political leader charting a vision than like a lawyer laying out a case. He did a rally late in the week in Hamtramck, a largely Polish-American enclave within Detroit. There was a big welcome sign, his name spelled out in kielbasa sausages, but the crowd was small and apathetic, and he came away discouraged. I don't feel good about Michigan, he told Estrich when he got home.

His instincts proved right. The first sign of trouble had come in at ten that morning, when Will Robinson, the deputy political director, called from Detroit. A few days earlier, nursing a beer at the Hotel Pontchartrain, Robinson had predicted expansively that Dukakis would obliterate Gephardt; it was the congressman's last stand, and it would end about as happily as Custer's. No one had been sweating the Jackson problem at that point, but on caucus day there was panic in Robinson's voice.

"There are hundreds of black people turning out," he told Jack Corrigan. "We're gonna get killed."

"Talk to me," Corrigan said, trying to slow Robinson down. At thirty-one, Corrigan was a cool, practiced operative, a Sasso holdover who had attached himself to Estrich; some people on Chauncy Street thought he, not she, was really running things. Robinson was his opposite, a tightly wired man, addicted to chocolates to pacify his nerves.

Corrigan couldn't calm him. Their polls had shown them going into the caucuses with a lead of from ten to fifteen points over Jackson, but there had been some warning signals; their phone banks were running into more refusals to talk, and their tally of "number twos," voters leaning to Dukakis, had dropped sharply over the past several days. By caucus day, it was plain that Jackson was mustering a silent electorate, people the polls hadn't reached. They were turning out in huge numbers on a blustery day, Robinson said. It was fucking incredible.

"You're panicking," Corrigan said, dismissing him.

Robinson hung up feeling sick. He and Coleman Young had been to a Greek-American fund-raiser the night before, fifteen hundred people cheering wildly for Dukakis. "See how excited these people are about Michael?" Young had remarked, watching them. "I got a whole city like that for Jesse." Then Jackson had flown in from Wisconsin to work the black churches and the housing projects, the rock-solid citadels of his campaign.

Robinson closed himself in his cubicle for ten minutes, getting his head together; then he began rechecking his phone banks, taking calls from frantic aides at caucus sites, funneling reports to Boston. Their tone was increasingly pessimistic. No one wanted to believe them. "Sure, if you're sitting in downtown Detroit, you're gonna see mostly black people," Payne said, mostly reassuring himself. "Detroit is a black place. It ain't like Boston—they actually *run* things there."

Estrich, always anxious on election days, had been queasy all week about this one. Kitty Dukakis wasn't helping her nerves, phoning in for reports and reassurance. Estrich had no ready answers. She looked ashy.

"Relax," Tom Kiley told her. "We'll be OK."

Someone took a poll of the room: Who thought they were going to win? Kiley's hand shot up. So did Payne's and Tubby Harrison's. Estrich and Leslie Dach sat still.

The lingering doubts eased a bit when the first returns gave Dukakis 45 percent of the vote, Jackson 35. The numbers were safely inside their own projections. There, goddammit, Kiley thought; why are these people driving me crazy?

But new numbers were coming in every ten minutes, and Dukakis's were going straight south; all their calculations were coming unglued. The phone rang with reports of stunning turnouts for Jackson in outstate congressional districts, not just Detroit. Payne and Kiley flipped through *The Almanac of American Politics,* trying to match districts to cities whose names they knew.

"Where are these places?" Payne muttered. The answers were surprising: some were industrial cities like Flint, some college towns like Ann Arbor.

A vista of defeat was taking form before their eyes, like a slide coming into focus on a screen; the lead Dukakis had counted on in the suburbs and the countryside would not be big enough to offset Jackson's big-city vote. The networks, slow to pick up on the arithmetic, were projecting Dukakis as the winner. At eight, Robinson phoned in the results from Detroit's two biggest congressional districts: nearly 50,000 people had voted, more than 90 percent of them for Jackson. In 1984, only 22,000 voters had turned out in the entire city.

Harrison's vodka had turned into an anodyne; people were getting slowly and quietly drunk. When the final tally was in, Jackson had 54 percent, Dukakis 29.

"Shit," Estrich said.

She busied herself for a time moving bodies—putting her issues chief, Chris Edley, on the plane with Dukakis to juice up his message; moving field staffers to the next battleground states. Her demeanor was brisk and businesslike; she juggled visitors and phone calls, carrying on three or four conversations at once. But as she was leaving headquarters she let down her tough facade for just a moment.

"It's real bad," she told Corrigan.

Then she headed out into the rain with Kiley and Harrison, for drinks and dinner at St. Cloud's. The table talk carefully avoided politics. It was too painful to state the obvious: that their insurance policy on Dukakis's nomination was the fact that his last substantial opponent was black.

The End Game

THE SENIOR HANDS on Chauncy Street gathered nightly before a television set at evening-news time in the aftermath of Michigan, looking for meaning in the dance of images and numbers before them. It was, one of them thought, as if a tidal wave had hit them—as if they were in the hold of a ship watching the water flood in through the portholes. One night, Jackson's face appeared, dark, sweaty and handsome, filling the screen with his passion. He was exhorting yet another big, multiracial crowd to quit the battleground of race and follow him onto the common ground of mutual interest. At the close, he shouted hoarsely, "I love you!"

"I *love* you?" Dukakis's people echoed, a chorus of unbelief.

"Fuck," someone said. They had just spent four heated hours back at square one, group-groping inconclusively, as usual, for the why of the Dukakis candidacy; they had been chewing the subject for more than a year, and Jesse had just delivered his message in three words.

"We might as well give up," someone else said.

There was an edge of panic in the room, a sense that not only the vocabulary but the known ground of politics was changing before their eyes. The press, with its fondness for comeuppances, was feasting on the governor's; the message coming out of Michigan was that, with all his money and all his organization, he couldn't buy inspiration, affection or, perhaps, the nomination. "I'm not going to try to outscream Jesse," the governor had told them, as if he could; it was quite beyond his inner resources to fight fire with fire. They were up against an American original, Ira Jackson was thinking, a man unlike any in presidential politics since William Jennings Bryan, and Michael Dukakis, of all people, was the vessel history had chosen to face him. History appeared to have a sense of humor. *Now,* Jackson was wondering, what the fuck do we do?

Happy Days Are Here Again

Finding answers was made psychically more complicated by the fact that the last remaining man in their path happened to be black. Since Super Tuesday, Dan Payne had been thinking over the irony of going one on one against Jackson. Dukakis's people traced their liberal roots back through Mondale, Kennedy and McGovern to the great romantic flowering of the civil-rights movement in the 1960s. Did they want to spend three months trying to beat a black man for the presidency? The thought made Payne and some of his colleagues uncomfortable, but it was what they had to do. It was, Payne thought, sort of sad.

It was lucky for them as well, in the cold reality of American life and politics. Jackson was a member of not one but two dispossessed minorities, as a black man and a spokesman for the Democratic left. His ideology allowed Dukakis plenty of room to position himself to the center; the governor had studiedly muted his own book-learned liberalism from the beginning, and Jackson's history of excesses of word and deed in behalf of his causes made him the perfect foil. A vote for Jackson was no longer just a protest vote for a movement preacher after Michigan; in one stroke, his victory certified him as a serious candidate for President and made it all but impossible for him to win.

Dukakis had counted on Michigan for the momentum that would, finally, make him unbeatable. It hadn't happened, and winning another backyard victory in Connecticut three days later hadn't helped. The campaign seemed stalled. A number of key endorsements dematerialized, among them Mario Cuomo's. A planned push for superdelegates—party leaders with free passes to Atlanta—had to be postponed. The media were predicting a brokered convention again, with Jackson prominent among the brokers. After Illinois and Michigan, Dukakis couldn't afford to lose another big state; the veneer of inevitability had been a powerful inducement for otherwise unenthusiastic Democrats to vote for him, and it was beginning to flake away.

It's end game, Tubby Harrison thought, reviewing his numbers. He called Jack Corrigan to talk about the next important round, in Wisconsin.

"We've got to win this," he said.

"You didn't tell anybody that, did you?" Corrigan asked coldly. The iron rule in politics was to raise the stakes for the other guy, never for yourself.

Shortly after Michigan, Estrich finished a tightly reasoned, two-page strategic memo on how to win Wisconsin and walked it to Dukakis at the statehouse.

"Well," he said, needling her about their misreading of the Michigan polls, "we were really geniuses until five o'clock, weren't we."

Estrich was not amused; her own interests, as well as Dukakis's, would be on the line in Wisconsin. Some Democratic heavyweights were beginning to ask if and when the governor might bring Sasso back; Dukakis had chosen to carry on as is, but both he and Estrich needed a win to change their luck. Her memo recommended that he spend an entire week in the state, concentrating on blue-collar towns and talking about what four more years of Republican rule would mean to working people. He should avoid attacking Jackson, she said, and he should put a push for endorsements on hold; his bandwagon would be considerably more appealing once he started winning again.

His chances in Wisconsin looked better in her memo than on the ground. Three weeks before the primary, Corrigan had tried telephoning state headquarters in a dusty old warehouse in Milwaukee. No one had answered. Furious, he flew out to see what was going on. It turned out that there was only one phone, and its wall jack was broken; incoming calls were not getting through. Corrigan scrambled to plug in help, but things had improved only marginally when, toward the end, Will Robinson was called back from vacation to help out. There were no phone banks, no mailing lists—only a few green kids to work what had become the battleground state.

Shit, Robinson thought, looking around.

"Where are you coming from?" a young intern inquired.

"Michigan," Robinson said.

"Oh," the intern said, looking sorry he had asked.

Reinforcements poured in from Chauncy Street, and Dukakis campaigned as if his candidacy hung on the outcome. Even his habit of refusing advice and his rule that he spend half of every week at his desk in Boston were suspended; he worked the state for six days, so hard that by the end he was sagging against podiums to hold himself upright. He seemed to his people to borrow energy from the fight; if his own persona was indistinct, Jackson gave him someone to define himself against, someone *not* to be. Gradually, his labor began to pay off. Dukakis's late polling showed him far ahead, but the spin doctors on Chauncy Street kept the numbers to themselves. The official line was that the race was tight, and when Dukakis wound up winning by nineteen points, the disinformation added luster to the victory.

New York was harder, a journey into a Byzantium of warring egos and court intrigues; the key to winning or even surviving there lay, as Dukakis's streetwise field director Paul Bograd put it, in finding ways to step around the bullshit. It wasn't easy. It required, for example, that Dukakis pay court to Mayor Edward I. Koch, calling on him at his official residence, Gracie Mansion, and pretending to enjoy a plate of chocolate-chip cookies the mayor had baked for the occasion. Dukakis left imagining that he had pleased Koch, more, certainly, than Koch or his cookies had pleased him. He hadn't; the next day, Koch endorsed Al Gore.

Dukakis made a similar pilgrimage to Albany five days before the primary to see Mario Cuomo. Their relationship had been a scratchy one almost from the beginning; Cuomo seemed to hold both Dukakis and his Miracle in light regard, and the Dukakis team in turn was offended by Cuomo's relentless cuteness—his refusal to choose sides, his acts of aid and comfort to various enemies, his public flirtations with the possibility of a draft at the convention. It was plain, in any case, that he wasn't going to endorse anybody before the primary. Dukakis's visit was accordingly a *pro forma* one, which didn't improve his spirits; neither did the fact that Cuomo kept him and his party waiting for ten minutes past the appointed time for their audience.

They had been led through a labyrinth of marble halls to a vast reception room for the meeting. The building dwarfed their red-brick statehouse in Boston; its sheer scale and ostentation were intimidating, and so was Cuomo when he finally burst big and smiling into the room, striding across the thirty-foot expanse of floor to greet them. He towered over Dukakis, his hand engulfing the candidate's. Dukakis puffed out his chest and put his hands on his hips, the banty-rooster pose he struck when he felt intimidated or self-conscious about his size. Cuomo seemed to sense his discomfort. He led the party on a guided tour of the art and artifacts, Dukakis strutting along behind him.

Their way led to a huge ceremonial desk at one end of the room. Cuomo, smiling broadly, pushed a button. A little platform popped up behind the desk.

The platform had been built for the late Governor Thomas E. Dewey, Cuomo explained. Dewey had needed to stand on it when he talked to reporters, because he was so short.

Dukakis was silent as stone. Some of his people thought the slight was innocent, some thought it intended, but they could feel his pain.

In the end, Cuomo's abstention didn't matter, and Koch's endorsement of Gore turned out to be a blessing in disguise. Gore's campaign had, in one Dukakis staffer's phrase, become a rolling Alamo by then, and it finally died in the mayor's smothering embrace. With the senator in tow, looking uncomfortable, Koch raked up memories of Hymietown and of Jackson's embrace of Yasir Arafat of the Palestine Liberation Organization when they met in 1979; Jews, His Honor said, would be *crazy* to vote for Jackson. His remarks inflamed the city's already polarized race relations, at greater cost to Gore and to himself than to Jackson. The senator's polls ticked upward briefly in the first flush of the endorsement; then, with a little prompting, his white followers began figuring out that a vote for Al amounted to a vote for Jesse and switched their custom to Dukakis instead.

If stepping around the bull droppings was indeed the key to success in New York, only Dukakis wholly succeeded. He conceded the black vote without a fight, visiting Harlem only once, and resisted pressure from his Jewish supporters to get tougher on Jackson; he limited himself to some oblique remarks to the effect that competence was more important than charisma. His posture made him the healer in the field, and Gore, by association, the divisive figure. On primary day, Dukakis beat Jackson by fourteen points. Gore limped in third with just 10 percent of the vote, the preeminent victim of the poisonous campaign waged in his behalf. Two days later, he dropped out of the race.

Estrich as usual had spent a nervous week worrying about the outcome. She had persuaded Tubby Harrison to fly down with her on primary day, tempting him with the prospect of a well-stocked bar, but they had sat silent during the flight. Tubby, in the window seat, had watched the great sprawl of the city rise beneath them, wondering silently how they could win the fucking thing—it was so goddam *big*. Only when the exit polls had confirmed their victory had they finally loosened up. Estrich, vindicated by the numbers, poured herself a drink, then another.

"Hey, you guys," she said, looking around the room. "It's good to be with you guys. Just us. All alone."

Their triumph was complete: New York, in effect, delivered Dukakis the nomination. But the governor, cautious to a fault, would trudge on through the remaining primaries at a time when he might have redirected his campaign against George Bush. The day after the New York primary, he took the Green Line to work as usual. Everyone else was medicating hangovers with heavy doses of aspirin and euphoria. Dukakis was all business.

Chris Edley, the issues man, phoned to congratulate him. "Governor," he said, "we're walking around with our feet six inches above the ground."

"Well," Dukakis replied, his tone short, "get back to work."

The governor, in fact, didn't allow himself to believe in his victory until well along in the primary campaign in Pennsylvania in April. One day in Pittsburgh, before his first one-on-one debate with Jackson, he found himself in a college music room, being prepped by his deputy issues director, Tom Herman, on the essentials of electric furnaces and continuous slab casting. Eyes glazed, he got up and walked out.

"I think you should consider extending the voluntary restraining agreements, Governor," Herman shouted after him.

There was no answer, only the sound of Dukakis poking around the music locker next door. In a few minutes, he returned with a sousaphone around his neck and shoulder and a trumpet in his hand. He tossed Paul Brountas a pair of drumsticks; then, drawing on dim memories of his days in the Brookline High School band, he raised the trumpet to his lips and belted out "Happy Days Are Here Again."

The Tough Side of the Mountain

The field house in Steubenville, Ohio, was still ringing with Jesse Jackson's fiery cadences. "You know who he is?" shouted Jim Bailey, a white workingman festooned with Jesse buttons. "He's Harry Truman, that's who he is. He don't take crap off of *any*body."

That spring, whites of similar mind turned up in Montana, Oregon and California, sunburned men in baseball caps balancing their kids on their shoulders and roaring, "Ac-tion Jackson! Ac-tion Jackson!" As the campaign neared its finish, Jackson surveyed their opaque white faces through the windows of his motorcades. He had seen people like them before. Sometimes they voted for him; sometimes they disappeared.

"There are those schizophrenic white folks again," he said one day in Oregon. "I wonder what they're gonna do *this* time."

Jackson divided the white electorate into two categories: the top drawer and the bottom of the heap. The first included white liberals, the Boston-Washington crowd, the sort who had gone to Simon and Dukakis. They couldn't make the break, he mused; they said all the right things, wore all the right clothes, went to all the right concerts, said all the nice things about Dr. King, quoted all the right philosophers, and then, in the end, they had told him, "Hope you win, but I know you can't." And then there were the working-class whites, hard cases hurt by Reaganomics: landless farmers in Iowa, laid-off auto workers in Kenosha, Wisconsin. Jackson had spoken up for them and marched with them, and they seemed to respond with genuine affection.

The problem was that their friendship didn't dependably translate into votes. For an intoxicating time after Michigan, Jackson thought he was the front-runner. His picture made the covers of *Newsweek* and *Time,* a standard index of who's hot and who's not in politics; he came to believe that he could actually win the nomination in a three-way race with Dukakis and Gore. He called Bert Lance from Kenosha. "Something is happening," he said; the state was only 3 or 4 percent black, and he was turning out big crowds everywhere.

But the workers there soon started deserting him, moving to Dukakis. On primary day, a fourth of the whites stood with him, impressive but not nearly enough to keep him close or even competitive; he lost to Dukakis by nineteen points. It particularly pained him when Kenosha fell. He had walked picket lines with the jobless workers there, and they had still voted their color. They were going through turmoil, Jackson thought sadly. They looked at him and *cried* because they couldn't vote for him. They feel locked, he thought, culturally locked. They're voting for him and pulling for me.

By the time he reached New York, fatigue was creeping up on him, and so was bitterness. He had registered all those voters in 1984 and since, contributing greatly to the party's resurgence in 1986, and no one reciprocated; not a single governor or state chairman had endorsed him. When Koch sloshed mud at him, no one came to his defense, not the major media or the party leadership; in Jackson's view, they just gave the mayor free rein to be destructive, without so much as a word of rebuke.

In the silence, the temptation to hit back had been enormous, and had been heightened by the frustrations of the campaign. He had got bad advice to stick to the city, close to his natural base, and had largely cut himself off from the white vote upstate; Dukakis carried it without a serious contest from Jackson *or* Gore.

The night of the primary, with the numbers charting Jackson's rout still coming in, the hotheads in his entourage urged him to cut loose. So did the celebrants at his primary-night party at the Sheraton Centre; waiting for him, they chanted, "Down with Koch! Down with Koch!"

In Jackson's suite, a worried aide slipped into a bedroom and put in a call to Bert Lance at home in Georgia. People were really pushing Jesse, he said. They wanted him to lash out at the mayor.

"I don't think it's a good idea," Lance said.

"You'd better talk to him, then," the aide said.

He made his way to Jackson and put him on the line.

"Nobody's spoken out on this, Bert," Jackson said. "People really think I ought to go after Koch."

"Whatever you do, just don't do that," Lance told him. "You need to be mature. You need to be positive. Bigger than the folks who tried to tear you down."

Jackson took the advice. His speech that night was at once passionate and forgiving, a plea against cynicism, anger and despair. "We've come too far now," he cried hoarsely again and again; too far to retreat from the high ground they had seized. The crowd was exploding with every line. Aides were flashing grins across the room at one another, jabbing the air with their fists. "Dr. Martin Luther King's heart is rejoicing tonight," Jackson was saying. "We're winning. We've climbed the tough side of the mountain, and we can keep on climbing, step by step by step." The room was ablaze with his fire. Only his people understood that it was his valedictory as a serious candidate; black against white was the race he could not win.

That night Jackson set the tone for the rest of his campaign. At times, he seemed drained; friends worried for him and begged him to slow down. He didn't. In one lyrical speech after another, he tried to set a populist agenda for the Democrats, attacking the nation's weakness for drugs, its profligate defense spending, its creaking health-care system. His objective, in his *mano a mano* with Dukakis, was to draw distinctions without creating division; he could not afford to be seen as a spoiler, so he aimed much of his fire at the Republican opposition instead. His people hoped the voters would get the message—that the courage to change priorities was what leadership was about.

He had moved from electoral to prophetic politics, and as he did, the threats on his life proliferated; some days, members of his Secret Service detail had to nag him to wear his bulletproof vest, explaining only that they wouldn't ask if they didn't think it was important. Jackson seemed at once haunted by and impervious to the danger. He visited with some Los Angeles gang members late in the campaign, and one of them put the matter to him bluntly: "Look, man, we really appreciate your coming here and talking with us, but if you keep this up, they're gonna *kill* you—do you understand that?"

The room was silent for a moment. Two of Jackson's sons, Jesse Jr. and Jonathan, sat in the back, impassively watching.

"They can kill me," Jackson said, "but don't you think I know that? I've already outlived all of my contemporaries from the sixties."

Neither would he countenance talk of losing; he was, he said, in the business of removing the ceilings on dreams, of keeping hope alive. But he could count, and he understood that the race had ended the day the field had narrowed to two. The contest wasn't Jackson versus Dukakis, in his view, or Jackson's ideas versus Dukakis's. It was Jesse versus Stop Jesse, the massed opposition of party, press and money, he believed, and after New York they didn't need the bad words anymore; they could use all the right words about the good of the party and the prospects for fall and still convey the message. He had outlasted all the others, Simon and Gephardt and Gore, only to find himself in a rigged two-handed game.

His consolation was his feeling that his message was winning even as the messenger was going down to defeat. In the view from Chauncy Street, Jackson had become a sparring partner, someone to beat up on every week; you could predict the outcome of any given primary, a Dukakis operative said, by checking the number of black voters in the state. For Jackson, the campaign was the thing, not the weekly box scores. His candidacy, Bert Lance reflected late in the game, wasn't the kind that began with a ribbon-cutting and ended on the short end of some primary somewhere. Its existence alone was a victory, and, Lance mused with some wonderment, it ain't stopped yet.

Stirring the Pot

In the last legs of the journey, Jackson gained a standing in white and black America that had largely eluded him in the past. On a dais in San Francisco that spring, Andy Young, the old doubter, found himself moved to tears by one of Jackson's speeches. He spoke of having gone to an AIDS march in Washington, standing with the dying against the plague; none of the other candidates had been there. His words had almost a religious quality, Young thought, a brave and dangerous clarity that reminded him of Dr. King. The two men embraced afterward, and later that night, at their hotel, Young had an aide hand-carry a private letter to Jackson's suite. "You make me feel proud and humble when I hear you speak," he wrote. "Martin would be proud, too. You have my full endorsement as the moral voice of our time."

For Jackson's more ardent followers, recognition was no longer enough. He was putting breathtaking numbers on the scoreboard for a black preacher with no experience in public office; by the season's end in June, he would have amassed seven million votes, nearly a third of them from whites, and eleven hundred convention delegates. His advocates felt that his just reward would be the vice-presidential nomination; there was no *rule* guaranteeing favorable consideration for the runner-up, but there were precedents, Lyndon Johnson and George Bush among them, and Jackson's legions felt that his time had come.

Their demands boiled up before he was himself ready to address the question. His defeat in New York had knocked his command team off stride; people had got rattled, one aide conceded, and mistakes started happening, failures of strategy, slips of the tongue. In an off-guard moment, Willie Brown told *The Wall Street Journal* that Jackson's showing entitled him to be considered as a running mate for Dukakis. Gerry Austin had said the same thing to the traveling press. Neither aide had checked with Jackson first, and he was furious. At a heated staff meeting, he directed Austin curtly to knock it off; to start talking him up for vice president with the primaries still on was to concede the game to Dukakis before it was over.

Jackson was in fact tantalized by the idea, though even among his senior staff he hid his feelings behind his impenetrable Reverend Jackson mask. It piqued his sense of irony when old-guard Democrats starting saying, wishfully, that Jesse wouldn't really *want* the vice-presidency—it wasn't good enough for him. He chuckled at the notion. Merely being mentioned for the job was a kind of recognition, he said one day late in May, crossing the tarmac at the Albuquerque airport; it was a measure of how far mama's boy had come. He used to caddy, thirty-six holes, not eighteen, carrying those big, heavy bags; used to be a waiter when he was growing up. Now they were saying the vice-presidency of the United States wasn't big enough to suit him. They must have thought he was crazy.

The morning after the last big-state primary, in California, he declared the season of the convention open and promised to play a leading role, bringing pressure to bear on the leadership, the platform, the rules, the very direction of the party. The game was a delicate one, a tightrope walk between imperatives. His core group, on one hand, was pushing him to demand the vice-presidency as his due; his political instincts, on the other, told him to be the statesman, not the spoiler, and consolidate the ground he had won. Timing was everything, as Bert Lance kept warning him in their three-a-day phone conversations. His position, as Lance told him, was like Michael Jordan's in a basketball game. As wonderful as his moves are, Lance said, ol' Michael don't have but twenty-four seconds to shoot. He can't hold the ball—the rules won't let him. The clock is ticking. The longer you hold that ball, the more people will be around you trying to take it away from you.

The last hurdle placed in Jackson's path was the presumption in the party establishment that, being Jesse, he would do something disruptive. His mood worried Bob Beckel, who, as Walter Mondale's trail boss, had handled negotiations with Jackson in 1984. Beckel respected Jackson, but he had known for a long time that the reverend had it within his power to pull the convention and the party apart if he chose to. That spring, he had phoned Sasso, an old comrade, hoping to back-channel some advice to Dukakis. Personal relationships were important to Jesse, he said. Dukakis should spend plenty of time with him. If he wasn't a serious contender for the number-two spot, they should level with him and say so.

By mid-June, Beckel's fears had grown worse; Jackson by then had asserted his right to be considered for the ticket, and Beckel invited him to dinner at Petitto's restaurant in Washington to talk about it. Jackson showed up, as often happened, with a couple of friends. Beckel asked whether they could speak alone.

"Let's take a walk," Jackson said. They stepped out into a vestibule on the second floor. Jackson asked Beckel what he thought.

Once Senator Simon had dropped out of contention, Beckel said, Jackson wasn't just representing black America anymore; he had become the leader of the progressive wing of the party. It was a big responsibility, and he had to take it into account as he considered the vice-presidency.

Jackson listed carefully. He seemed flattered.

"Look," Beckel said, "there are a lot of people who want you on the ticket. I'm worried that your people feel so strongly about it that even if you *try* to turn them off, they're not going to listen."

"We'll have to wait and see," Jackson said. He wanted to be considered seriously; it wasn't time to be doing any turning off, not yet. "Sometimes," he said, "you have to stir up the pot."

He's ready to cooperate with Dukakis, Beckel thought as they parted. The ball was in the governor's court; the outcome would turn on his finesse in handling Jesse.

The Veep Perplex

The Dukakis campaign, as it happened, wasn't ready for diplomacy yet; they had grown too used to thinking of Jackson as the last opponent in a long, debilitating war. The primary season had finally ended in California in June, the governor emerging from it in an oddly flat mood; his nomination by then had been long since sealed, and George Bush was already rehearsing attack lines for what would be a memorably negative campaign. There was no champagne in Dukakis's rooms at the Century Plaza in Los Angeles, no victory feast—only a soup-and-salad dinner for himself and his children. A bouquet of flowers lay on the table, the card unopened. A bottle of aspirin was attached to the stems.

Downtown, at the Biltmore, his senior operatives in the state sat staring red-eyed and dozy at a television set, watching a pro basketball playoff game and waiting for returns. Their party fare was Diet Cokes and room-service sandwiches. A staffer was logging in results from the field, one fat number after another for Dukakis. A voice on the TV said New Jersey had gone big for the governor, delivering nearly enough delegates to put him over the top. Then Bush came on, delivering *his* victory speech. One of Dukakis's men, Paul Pezzella, walked over from the couch to watch.

"You next, buddy," he told the face on the screen. He turned back toward the others. "I can't wait to get this guy," he said.

In the days thereafter, Dukakis's relations with Jackson seemed to get worse, not better. They were, as Jackson would complain, two ships passing in the night. Where the other candidates had made a point of chatting him up during the long march through the primaries, Dukakis had been distant, treating Jackson as just another opponent; the word from his management on Chauncy Street was not to cave in to the reverend's demands. Success only hardened their disinclination to cater to him, and so did Jackson's continued campaigning after the primaries were over; soul politics was not well understood on Chauncy Street. They didn't *need* to deal with Jesse, Tad Devine, the delegate-chaser, said with a shrug. If Dukakis won enough delegates, he wouldn't need Jackson at all.

The chill was part political, part personal. Their uninterest in Jackson's feelings began with their view of how the party could best get back in play for the presidency, a view at war with his. They were mesmerized by the battle for the hearts and minds of the Reagan Democrats, those Southern whites and urban blue-collar workers who had bolted the party in 1980 and 1984; if their return to the fold was the solution to what ailed the Democracy, as the Dukakis command believed on faith, then Jackson was part of the problem. But there was the further fact that "The Reverend," as Estrich icily called him, could be exasperating to deal with. You could never satisfy him, she said. Grant him a concession, and he'll be back for more; give him a minute, and he'll take up your whole day.

There were those who thought a day of her time or the governor's well worth the investment, but the peace process, when it finally happened, got off to a sputtery start. The first attempt to get Dukakis and Jackson together socially, for a family Fourth of July dinner in Brookline and an evening at the Boston Pops, was a fiasco. The Dukakis people forgot to send someone to meet the Jacksons at the airport. No one had mentioned the appropriate clothes; the Jacksons came dressed up and found their host and hostess in casual gear. No one had consulted them on the menu; the Dukakises served a milk-based chowder, to which Jackson was allergic, and poached salmon, which he didn't like.

The talk, to his further annoyance, was determinedly small. He wanted to open conversations about the vice-presidency, but when he finally got Dukakis alone in the living room, one of the governor's daughters walked in. "Dessert?" she asked sweetly, and the moment was lost.

In fact, while Dukakis was careful to maintain appearances, he had no intention of putting Jackson on the ticket; the received wisdom of politics was that doing so would be tantamount to driving over a cliff. Finding the *right* running mate was a problem that had preoccupied the governor's advisers for more than a year. Sasso had charted a course in an early strategy memo, and the new management on Chauncy Street had elevated it to dogma. As a Northeasterner and a stranger to Washington, the line went, Dukakis would do well to pick a Southern senator, someone who could help win back part of the South and then open doors for him on the Hill once they were elected. Sam Nunn of Georgia and Lloyd Bentsen of Texas were obvious possibilities. Jesse Jackson, given the rules of the hunt, was not.

Dukakis had turned the talent search over to Paul Brountas, his friend and senior adviser. Brountas brought substantial strengths to the job. He was a corporate lawyer, respected in Boston for driving hard bargains. His owlish eyes peered out through grandfatherly spectacles, seeming to miss nothing; he spoke in a soft voice, and he knew how to keep a secret. He in turn assembled a squad of accountants, lawyers, even private eyes. A background-research staff on Chauncy Street worked under security rules so tight that the others called them the Manhattan Project; even the governor's daughter Andrea was shown the door when she strayed onto their floor.

Brountas's own inclinations followed Chauncy Street's; he too heard the siren call of the South. Over breakfast in Los Angeles the day after the California primary, he gave Dukakis a long memo on forming a ticket. Among other things, he mentioned Jack Kennedy's choice of Lyndon Johnson. The whiff of history appealed to Dukakis, who was fond of comparing himself to JFK. The memo itself was neutral. The underlying directional signal pointed south.

But Dukakis wasn't ready to be steered. In the first euphoria of victory, he came to believe that he had considerable leeway in filling the ticket, that he didn't *have* to make a purely political choice. His first favorite was Senator Bill Bradley, the Rhodes-scholarly ex-jock from New Jersey, who wasn't interested. His second was Lee Hamilton, an Indiana congressman of intelligence and promise, who lacked a tradable name. With his lead over Bush beginning to soften, Dukakis agreed to a number of joint appearances with contenders of more visible heft: Al Gore, Dick Gephardt, Lloyd Bentsen and John Glenn. At one point, his staff floated a trial balloon suggesting that Glenn was the one; it soared so high so fast that they had to loft another, this time for Gore, just to pop the Glenn bubble.

The show played badly. Reporters began remarking in print that the Dukakis gavotte was starting to look as stagy and as clumsy as the Mondale minuet of 1984, the series of driveway photo ops that had led to Geraldine Ferraro; it was a comparison Dukakis had consciously set out to avoid. A bare week before the convention, he called a last caucus at his place in Brookline with Brountas, Estrich and Corrigan to settle the matter. Kitty had set out coffee, iced tea and a bowl of candy on the kitchen table. The governor came in from mowing the lawn, still in his Bermuda shorts. Brountas was just back from Washington, where he had met with Jackson. He had deliberately put the reverend last on his interview list, to minimize the time available to him for mischief-making. Still, Brountas had maintained the forms, assuring Jackson that he was being taken seriously as a prospect and that he would be told the answer before he read it in the papers.

In fact the answer had always been no; of the seven nominal finalists, only Bentsen and Glenn were then seriously in play. The kitchen council went through their list one last time, reviewing strengths and weaknesses. The tick marks fell into place for Bentsen. He had figurehood in Washington. He gave them a shot, so they persuaded themselves, at the South. He had already beaten Bush once, in 1970, for an open Senate seat in their home state. He had impressed Dukakis and Brountas with his dignity, his maturity, his confidence. Bentsen was the goods.

It was nearly midnight when Dukakis went around the table, pointing to each of the others by turn.

Brountas was first. He liked Bentsen. So did Kitty, and Estrich, and Corrigan.

"That's my choice," Dukakis said. The deal was done; at six-thirty the next morning, he reached the senator, who was home shaving, and offered him the job.

Missed Connections

The phone that never rang was Jesse Jackson's. Two days before the choice was settled, Donna Brazile, who had migrated from Jackson to Gephardt to Dukakis, had gone to the governor's top people and begged them to level with Jackson right away. Don't start no race riot, she said; tell him the choice is X, if that's the way it's going to be, and ask him for his support. No one did, and no one bothered inviting Brazile to a staff meeting the day the decision was announced. The networks were already on the air with the Bentsen story when she phoned a friend from Operation PUSH, Jackson's home organization in Chicago.

"Oh, my God," her friend said. "Jesse doesn't know. He's on the way to the airport."

"He knows," Brazile said; the others had assured her of that.

"No, he doesn't," her friend said.

Brazile was, as she would say later, one mad bitch, but she contained her anger and ran downstairs. "Jesse doesn't know," she told a staffer. "Find him. Reach him."

They both worked the phones, too late. Jackson was in Cincinnati, bound for Washington; the first he heard the news was when reporters waiting at National Airport told him it was Bentsen. At a press conference later, his response was frosted with irony. He was too controlled, too mature, he said, to be angry at the slight.

His supporters were not; their reaction was quick and heated, and Dukakis found himself in the bull's-eye. He was unfortuitously booked to address a convention of the National Association for the Advancement of Colored People (NAACP) in Washington. Some red-hots at the convention were painting up picket signs calling him a racist and a member of the Ku Klux Klan.

"Should I apologize?" he asked his staff at an emergency meeting in his hotel suite just before he was to go on.

Brazile waded in, demanding to know how they had gone wrong. Brountas said he had given Jackson's phone number and his departure time to Estrich, and she in turn was to have given it to Dukakis. Estrich said she had got only the number, not the time. The fabled Dukakis machine had slipped a cog, and Dukakis had begun making his courtesy calls fifteen minutes after Jackson had left for Washington.

"Why didn't you tell me he was leaving before?" Dukakis exploded.

Brazile studied the players one by one. It wasn't deliberate, she thought; it was insensitive. These people were from *Boston*. They don't think about black people. Race was an afterthought for them. They thought of Jesse just like they thought of Gephardt or Gore.

The damage potential was scary; Jackson was seething, and the party leadership began worrying that he would take his revenge at the convention in Atlanta, raising a ruckus about the platform and the rules. The unity of the party and perhaps the outcome of the election were, or seemed to be, at stake, and a gallery of Democratic eminences from Jimmy Carter to Mario Cuomo to Tip O'Neill pressed Dukakis to meet the reverend and try to pacify him.

The two men, in fact, had a mutual interest in accommodation, but by the time a meeting was finally arranged for Dukakis's convention suite in Atlanta, their relationship was badly bruised. It took more than an hour to ventilate their differences with each other. Toward the close, Jackson said that what he wanted was a "partnership" with Dukakis. Dukakis refused. He was thinking law and Jackson was thinking soul; they didn't even have the meaning of the word "partner" in common.

Jackson tried to translate it into everyday usage. " 'Hey, partner! How ya doin', partner?' It's like your friend, your buddy," he said. "Somebody you trust, not some legal relationship."

Dukakis sat stiff and uncomfortable through the linguistics lesson. The word plainly made him nervous; he had been told too often that anything resembling a partnership with Jackson would amount to kissing the Reagan Democrats goodbye. It was only when the clock was running out on their meeting that he asked Jackson straight out for his support. I want you, he said. I need you. I need your millions of supporters. I can't win within you.

They cobbled together an understanding that some of Jackson's people would be integrated into the governor's general-election command. Jackson himself would get a plane for his campaigning in the fall. The agreement was only cosmetic, and the word "partnership" was never mentioned at a press conference afterward; most of the treaty terms would sooner or later break down.

But each man had what he wanted: Jackson a position of respect in his party, Dukakis the peace and good order of the convention. Jackson took the stage on his night surrounded by his children; seeing them together,

Dukakis felt something in common with him for the first time. Jackson's speech, far from an incitement, was an eloquent summing-up of his campaign—a call to the party to remember the poor and the disfranchised, a summons to his own followers to keep hope alive. His mood would be spoiled later by the governor's carelessness of his feelings, but his week at the convention was a sustained high. He ran into Jack Corrigan one day and grasped his hand. Corrigan had been running things for Dukakis in Atlanta, directing the rules and platform negotiations with Jackson's people. He was tough and intense, obsessed with numbers, uncomfortable with passions that could not be quantified; when a colleague had fretted shortly before the convention about Jackson's hell-raising potential, Corrigan had answered, "Fuck him."

When they finally met, the two men stood for a long moment, eyes locked, each trying to stare the other down.

"I'd like to take you out to the back alley," Jackson said.

He paused. Corrigan stood his ground.

"To pray," Jackson said, grinning broadly.

Corrigan, who rarely smiled on duty, grinned back.

A Place in the Sun

The apotheosis of Michael Dukakis at the Omni Coliseum in Atlanta was a masterpiece of stagecraft, the last, best work of the marketers who had created his candidacy around him. It was widely assumed, like everything else in his long march to the nomination, to have been a triumph of management. It was in fact a triumph *over* management. Behind its smooth corporate facade, the Dukakis campaign was perilously close to falling apart.

By the end of the primaries, Dukakis had lost faith in Susan Estrich and the new crowd on Chauncy Street. Corrigan had all but taken possession of the campaign and, to the extent anyone had it, access to the candidate's ear. Dukakis was treating Susan like a blithering idiot, Tom Kiley thought sadly, cutting off her monologues and ignoring her advice; when he wanted to feel assured that the convention was in capable hands, he brushed her aside entirely and reached out to the old crowd she had shut out of the loop. Even Sasso was invited to Atlanta, though never into the governor's presence. Just having him in town was to the campaign what a security blanket is to a child, a source of comfort against the ghosts of the night.

But Dukakis could not bring himself to reinstate Sasso; Estrich and

Brountas fought the idea hard; Estrich was said on Chauncy Street to have burst into tears at the mere suggestion that it might happen. Sasso's friends had mounted a first push for his return shortly after Super Tuesday; some, in fact, assumed he would be back any day. Sasso had asked Dukakis about it at the time.

"I don't know, I don't know," the governor had replied. "It'll be a big story in the press."

So Sasso had returned to exile, waiting for Dukakis to call. He didn't. What advice Sasso had was back-doored into the campaign through old poker partners who had survived the putsch, men like Corrigan and Mitropoulos. To be openly associated with him on Estrich's scorecard was to risk being cut out of the action; to advocate bringing him back was a capital crime.

Sasso and his allies tried again to effect his return at the close of the primary season, and were rebuffed again.

"The Republicans will kill me," Dukakis told Sasso this time.

You're right, Sasso thought. But they won't kill you about *me*.

The freeze-out would continue even in Atlanta. Sasso thought he had finally engineered his return, and had even begged a leave from his boss at Hill, Holliday to rejoin the campaign. He wasn't asked. The person most responsible for getting Dukakis nominated would spend most of his time at the convention holed up in his room playing poker with his boys and staying out of sight. The governor would ask him afterward to work up a plan for the first hundred days of a Dukakis presidency. Sasso was insulted. He suggested to his wife that they take a summer place they had been talking about on Martha's Vineyard; he was no longer interested in doing anything for Dukakis at all.

But if he was unwanted, the members of his pokerklatsch found themselves suddenly back in demand. A month before the delegates started gathering, Dukakis invited Ira Jackson over to Brookline and asked him to work up an acceptance speech. Jackson was one of the orphans of the Estrich regime, stamped with an S for Sasso and shut out of her decision-making circle. He felt flattered at being asked back, and was only slightly daunted at the task that had defeated the campaign from its beginnings: finding the poetry in Dukakis's pedestrian prose.

The themes they discussed were largely the same old hodgepodge Dukakis had used all along—jobs-and-opportunity, the Massachusetts Miracle, the Best America that was yet to come. I don't want to reinvent the wheel, the governor cautioned Jackson; he was plainly bent on holding the party together by being as unprovocative as possible. Jackson met with his fellow outcasts from Sasso's old kitchen cabinet and immersed himself in the Greatest Hits of the Democratic past. Each of the best had a powerful idea at its core: the New Deal, the New Frontier, the Great Society. Jackson pondered their formulations and came up with a couple of his own: the New Citizenship, and an Era of Greatness.

With the muse of ghostwriters upon him, he dispatched his wife and children to a Holiday Inn downtown and sat up alone at home all one Thursday night working on a draft. On Friday, he presented it to the old-boy network, then worked all night again incorporating their changes. On Saturday, he delivered the text to Estrich.

"It could use some help," she said, scanning it; she remanded it to *her* network for surgery.

Jackson went away mad, swearing he would never work another minute for the campaign. But the day before Dukakis was to deliver the speech, Nick Mitropoulos called him from Atlanta.

"Get your ass down here," Mitropoulos said. The speech was a mess. Dukakis needed him.

Jackson threw some things in a bag, caught the next plane south and walked into the middle of an impasse. Four different people had tried their hand at redoing the speech, and Dukakis in turn had picked and hacked at their work. The product was a tattered crazy quilt of thought and style. Dukakis wouldn't deliver it.

Jackson and Bill Woodward, officially the chief speechwriter, worked frantically on a rewrite, with help after midnight from Jack Kennedy's rhetor-in-chief, Ted Sorensen. The next day, Dukakis spent two and a half hours rehearsing it to a small group of aides and advisers; it did not escape their notice that Estrich was nowhere in sight.

Dukakis seemed on edge, flaring at distractions, his tunnel vision fixed on the speech. The team in the holding room was startled by his rudeness, his brusque "I know" whenever an aide tried to introduce him to something or someone new; behind his back, members of the stage crew mocked him, snapping, "I know, I know" at one another. At one point, he spent five minutes debating with himself whether to call the idea of trading arms for hostages "crazy," as his text proposed.

"Crazy?" he muttered. "No, that's not it."

A pause, more muttering.

"Yes," he said finally, "it *is* crazy."

He read on. Ira Jackson was yelling at him from the sidelines, "We need something more personal here. . . . We need something community here. . . . We need something family here." Aides methodically tried to fill in emotions and dab in some soul. Dukakis wasn't much help. He would joke publicly later that Kitty had fallen asleep while he practiced a final draft, an attempt to keep expectations low. In fact, it didn't seem to matter how eloquent the words were; in his monotonic delivery in rehearsal, they dropped thuddingly to the floor.

The hardest problem of all was to get him to register emotion. His people solved it the only way they knew how, by programming feeling into him. At dinner before he delivered the speech, his family and a few close aides tried gently to prime him.

"Think of your dad, how proud he would be on this night," one of them said, grasping for inspiration. "He's the only person who's missing."

Then, holding their breath, they sent him to the hall. Behind the Omni, Tad Devine was holed up in a campaign trailer. He had fifteen operatives on phones, wired to whips on the floor; they in turn would coordinate chanting and applause. On stage, Dukakis's cousin Olympia, the actress, warmed up the crowd. Then a video biography went on, making much of the governor's immigrant roots and his plain lifestyle; his period snow-blower, in a cameo appearance, became a national symbol overnight.

Dukakis finally entered, to Neil Diamond's "Coming to America"; technicians cranked the bass high enough to shake the auditorium floor. His route, by prearrangement, led him through the dense-packed rows of delegates on the floor; he seemed to draw emotion from them. He scaled the podium and stood there for a long time, as his handlers had cued him to do, saying nothing. His eyes shone in the floodlights. He waited until the crowd quieted. Then he got out his ragged collage of lines and turned them into the best speech of his life.

It was not an enduring work of political literature; Tubby Harrison had read the text in his box seat at the Omni, waiting for Dukakis to go on, and had told the others, "This sucks." Neither was his pitch perfect, tactically speaking. His most memorable line was also his most dangerous, a dec-laration that the election was not about ideology, it was about competence. His strategy books had been saying the same thing from the earliest days of his candidacy, but it wasn't something you told the world; it was like inviting the other side to say yes, it is, too, about ideology, and to hit you with their whole arsenal of hot-button "values" issues. Sasso, in exile, hadn't known of the line until he heard Dukakis deliver it.

"How the hell did that get in there?" he asked Tom Kiley afterward. "Those Republicans are gonna shove that line right up our ass."

But only inside players seemed to notice the defects. The night belonged to Dukakis; the speech was the culmination of years of careful marketing, and the reviews next morning were nearly unanimous raves. For one memorable time in his long campaign, he appeared to have feelings, and let them show. His voice cracked when he mentioned his father; his prompters had hoped for precisely that. When he finished, Kitty and the kids rushed up to him; the Bentsens came in; then Jesse Jackson, his wife and their children were there standing by him, and Gore, and Gephardt, and Babbitt, and Simon. The balloons came tumbling down. It was like getting a dozen curtain calls on opening night at the Met, Ira Jackson was thinking offstage, and the first wave of polls would reflect it: Dukakis came bursting out of Atlanta with a seventeen-point lead over George Bush.

The governor himself, in his moment of triumph, hadn't needed to wait for the survey results. "It doesn't get any better than this," he said, stepping down from the podium to rejoin his entourage. It would *have* to get better, one aide told him at the time.

It didn't; his triumph of theater at the Omni sent him forth expecting victory and unprepared for war.

PART THREE

THE REMAKING OF GEORGE BUSH

◻━━━━━◻

Miles:	*Who is he?*
Jack:	*I have no idea.*
Becky:	*His face, Miles. It's vague.*
Jack:	*It's like the first impression that's stamped on a coin. It isn't finished.*
Miles:	*You're right. It has all the features, but no detail, no character, no lines . . .*
Jack:	*He's a blank. Waiting for the final, finished face to be stamped on him.*
Theodora:	*But whose face? Tell me that.*
Miles:	*I think we could all use a drink.*

—INVASION OF THE BODY SNATCHERS, 1956

Don't Worry, Be Happy

THERE HAD BEEN A TIME, at the very beginning, when George Bush had doubted himself—when he thought he had been undone by this thankless supporting role in the 1984 campaign. The election had been an occasion for joy for his party; the president had vaporized Walter Mondale and had made it possible for dreamers to dream of a permanent Republican majority. But the victory had been Reagan's, not Bush's, and it left the taste of ashes in the vice president's mouth. He had been pushed nearly off the screen by the first woman ever to make a major-party ticket, and when he did get noticed he often wished he hadn't been; he came across in the press as a terminal second banana, a spear-carrier with no real gift for politics and no principles or passions of his own. The autumn of Reagan's glory had been a trying one for Bush. To one associate he seemed, in his gloom, to feel fatally damaged by it.

The resuscitation of his hope began with a visit by his old friend Nicholas F. Brady to the Bush family compound in Kennebunkport in the weeks after the voting. The family house on a rocky spit of land called Walker's Point on the Maine coast had been special to Bush since the summers of his boyhood; it was a place of peace and continuity, and he had retreated there in the waning autumn to rest and brood. He was still low in spirit when

Brady, a former senator and a prominent Wall Street investment banker, found him there. The job Bush had sought through two years of running and four more of waiting seemed to him more distant than ever from his grasp. There were days when he talked about giving up the quest—just stepping aside to make way for somebody younger.

"Let's see what we can put together," Brady said, trying to lift him from his gloom. *He* would start assembling the machinery to put Bush back on track toward the nomination. The job was doable, he thought, and Bush found himself drawn along in his friend's optimistic train; all he had needed was for someone he trusted to tell him he really could be president.

Rudy Vallee Meets Willie Nelson

The vice president had never been a particularly happy warrior; campaigning, for him, was a sweaty necessity you had to go through to get to the seemlier business of governing. He attacked politics like a plate of spinach or a chapter in Hegel, because, if you meant to get ahead, it was good for you. What was wanting in him was any visible show of pleasure in the game or its players. He hired professional handlers, one thought, as he might engage a gardener or a garage mechanic, to do a specific task and leave; he was generous, even friendly, to them and submissive to their advice, but they were not expected to stay to dinner. Their usefulness ended, with their wages, on Election Day.

He knew, nevertheless, that you had to have them, and with the revival of his spirits he beat his rivals to some of the best in the business. His first choice to oversee the campaign would have been James A. Baker III, an old and dear friend who had managed Ford in 1976, Bush in 1980 and Reagan in 1984; if the first two had been losers, the last, if Baker did say so himself, had been a flawless campaign. But he was happily employed as secretary of the Treasury, a lofty distance above politics, and he was reluctant to get back down into the trenches unless he had to. So it was Lee Atwater who was summoned instead to Bush's office that Christmas season and asked, barely six weeks after the windup of the last campaign, to manage the next one. The leap from number three on Reagan's table of organization to number one on Bush's was irresistible for a hungry young man of thirty-three, and Atwater said yes.

On the face of it, he and Bush made a dissonant pair, a Willie Nelson duet with Rudy Vallee. Atwater was a Johnny Reb among Yankees, an alley fighter in a Marquess of Queensberry campaign. He came with a reputation as, charitably put, the Peck's Bad Boy of American politics; his hero was Richard Nixon, and his specialty in his intermittent graduate studies was the theory and practice of negative campaigning. Tales of dirty trickery followed him from campaign to campaign, and while he regularly denied them, he was not above cultivating his legend as a predator or trading on it. It was, for example, a well-advertised fact that he reread Machiavelli twice a year; it was as useful to him as to a spitball pitcher to be thought to be up to something shady. But there was no question at all about his will to win. If you knocked him down once, an old Carolina pal said, you'd better be prepared to keep his ass pinned to the canvas, or he'd come up gut-punching and hurt you.

Not everyone in Bush's circle felt comfortable with the choice, and Atwater's stop-at-nothing aura was only one of their concerns. There was the further awkward fact that two of his partners in the consulting business, Charlie Black and Roger Stone, were working for Jack Kemp; the connection did not trouble Bush, but it bothered his son George Jr., and he said so at a weekend planning retreat for the family and staff at Camp David early in 1986.

"How can we *trust* you?" George Jr. demanded point-blank.

Atwater pacified him by making room for him at headquarters, as an ambassador to the red-meat right; it was better, he figured, to have the boss's son inside the tent pissing out than outside pissing in. But the day George Jr. reported for work, he found himself jaw-to-jaw with Atwater again. *Esquire* had just done a long piece profiling Atwater as a self-seeker untroubled by conscience or scruples—"all grit," the story said, "all blood on the floor and don't look back," George Jr. had discussed the story with his mother, and they had agreed that, to phrase it gently, Lee came off as something less than a mature political organizer. The story had, in their judgment, reflected badly on Atwater, the campaign and, by extension, the vice president, and there were to be no more like it.

"You need to earn your spurs through performance, not interviews," George Jr. scolded.

The stories stopped, and peace was restored.

Atwater, as it turned out, was not really in full charge, or even first among equals; he was instead one of a half-dozen men who would govern the campaign and would each have direct access to the candidate. They called themselves the G-6, a play on the Group of Seven leading industrial democracies, and they ruled by consensus rather than fiat, each respecting the others' territories. Atwater's was tactics. Bob Teeter's was polling. Craig Fuller, recruited from the president's staff, took charge of the

OVP—the Office of the Vice President. Robert Mosbacher Sr., a Houston oilman, ran fund-raising. Roger Ailes, a Manhattan media consultant, had custody of the candidate's image. Nick Brady played Best Friend, the peer who had no identifiable interest to serve except Bush's and so could speak to him plainly, man to man.

They were plagued from the beginning by the buzz in politics that Bush couldn't get elected anything on his own, a suspicion to which some of them fell prey at least some of the time. He was a *terrible* campaigner, a close associate said, a case study in hyperkinesia run amok. His public service had been practically all by appointment, not popular demand, and was further compromised by an odd absence of footprints in his path from office to office. He appeared to be asking people to vote for him because he was the front-runner, having waited so loyally for so long. The claim that it was his turn had some weight, given the royalist tradition in Republican politics. But in a new age, pretenders to the presidency were supposed to come equipped with something called "vision," not just the low number in the Takachek line.

Bush's weaknesses as a candidate were accepted as a given by his campaign command, and they compensated by designing an elaborate corporate structure around him. The atmosphere at its headquarters on Fifteenth Street in Washington was all thick carpets and quiet phones, a member of Bush's family complained, preferring something a little less investment-bankerly. Its own apparatchiks called it Bush Inc., and it was, like the Mondale campaign of 1984, a temple of organization raised by managers and marketers unconfident that the merchandise would sell itself. In their plan, Bush would win his party's nomination as Mondale had won his, by the sheer overwhelming force of management, money, connections and vice-presidential prerogative.

The Connecticut Pinstripe-Suit Thing

The first labor before them was the remaking of George Herbert Walker Bush. There were those who thought, as one member of the campaign command suggested only half facetiously, that they might start by losing his two middle names; they were the token of his privilege, his silver-spoon beginnings as the child of old family and old money. No matter that he had served his country bravely at war, or that he had parlayed a grubstake from his family connections into his own fortune in oil, or that he had been at least nominally a Texan for forty years; he was still burdened by what

Atwater, in frustration, called the Connecticut Pinstripe-Suit Thing, the look of the wellborn gentleman down from the manor to mingle with the common people. His blue bloodline and his gilded references clashed with a strain of populist chic in our politics; we have lately favored citizen candidates who, like Jimmy Carter in 1976 and Ronald Reagan in 1980, ran against Washington as if it were an enemy capital, and Bush was all wrong for the part.

None of his rivals was a true populist, either. But Bush's establishment aura clung to him as stubbornly as if it had been sewn into his tennis whites and Topsiders. He was a WASP's WASP, a senior adviser said; he was chauffeured cars to grammar school and boating summers in Maine; he was baseball at Andover and Skull and Bones at Yale; he was the Petroleum Club in Houston and the old-boy network in Washington; and all of it showed, in his bearing, his manners, his eagerness never to give offense. The clubhouse chatter of politics, even with women newly around, still used the language of a boys' locker room, and the words that stuck most cruelly to the vice president were "preppie," "weenie" and "wimp." It was once said of him, by a famously earthy Republican governor, that he was the kind of guy who would get out of the shower to take a leak.

His very calling to politics had about it the strong odor of *noblesse oblige* as against commitment to an idea or a cause. He got into it initially as a matter of civic concern, like raising money for the local Y, his wife said, and he had kept scaling rungs thereafter, more, apparently, in quest of affirmation than of state power. It struck David Keene, a senior official in his 1980 campaign, that Bush was a man without an agenda—that he was more interested in the processes of decision-making than in the results. In this, Keene believed, he belonged to the tradition of good-government Republicanism that flowered in the Northeast with the turn of the century. It was a WASP tradition, born in civic anger at the abuses of the big-city Democratic machines. It placed its faith in rule by wise men, men of substance and judgment. If you sought them out and sheltered them from pressure by the bosses and the interests, they would, in their wisdom, do what was right for the Republic.

"If I were elected," Bush would tell Keene in their days together, "I'd bring in the best people—"

"Fine, George," Keene would respond, "but what are you going to tell them to *do*?"

The question never got answered, not to Keene's satisfaction—he defected to Dole for 1988—or, apparently, to voting America's. Bush's only memorable words in his first run for the White House had been his allusions to Reagan's "voodoo economics" and to his own fleeting "Big Mo" in the early going. The Mo had soon run out, Reaganomics had become the law of the land, and Bush had disappeared into the trackless waste called the vice-presidency. It was said of him, heartlessly, that he and the office were made for each other—that his passage through *all* his government jobs had been trackless beyond his indisputable gifts at making friends for himself and overseeing bureaucracies for his patrons. He had never been out to bend history; he spoke of politics instead as a system of challenges and rewards leading ever upward toward the White House, and the vice-presidency was one more station on the journey, a place where you served your time and waited your turn.

The result, when he announced for president, was a widespread puzzlement as to why. He did have his reasons, a senior campaign strategist said, real and heartfelt reasons; the problem was that they were satisfactory only to him. He wanted to be president, this counselor supposed, because he was a decent man with relevant experience, sound values, concern for his country, and a sense, inculcated by his father, that he had an *obligation* to serve. Men had run for president on far less worthy grounds, but Bush's motives did not translate well out in the marketplace, where the voters were. It sounded elitist and even arrogant, in this view, to *present* oneself for president as a matter of duty and to expect the thanks of a grateful nation in return.

Bush hated it when people nagged him about what he called the Vision Thing, his apparent incapacity for saying where he meant to lead the nation in what remained of the twentieth century. His difficulty flowed in part from a deep reticence about self-promotion. It was thought unseemly in his tribe to brag or be a know-it-all, and when he felt himself venturing near the line, talking about his achievements or his feelings, it was as if he could still hear his mother's admonitions against presenting oneself as "the Great I-Am." His modesty was becoming in personal encounters, but it was a disability in politics, and so was his accompanying eagerness to please. In a public setting, one adviser thought, Bush worried too much about that one person out there who might dislike him; in consequence, he softened everything, so as not to make anyone mad.

What vision he did offer was largely borrowed from his patron, the president. Bush had led his whole public life that way, shuttling regularly between right and center in campaign years as fashion required, but he was not truly an ideological sort; once situated in a job, he would go about trying to solve problems as practically as he could without breaking faith, philosophically, with his employer. He said in the earliest days of his campaign that the country didn't *need* a new direction—it already had one, thanks to Ronald Reagan, and Bush would stay on the master's course. The theme song his people ultimately would choose for his fall campaign was the Bobby McFerrin ballad "Don't Worry, Be Happy"; if its lyrics were sardonic on close listening, its title summed up Bush's message.

He thus entered the field, against the settled conventions of politics, as the candidate of the status quo. His me-too posture was well suited to the primaries, given the party's nearly reverential feeling for the president, but Bush's handlers tried regularly to persuade him that he would have to paint on a bigger canvas in brighter colors for the general election. The results were not encouraging. When Atwater brought in some megatrendy thinkers and writers to talk to Bush about the future, he emerged saying, "I guess the bottom line is that it's exciting."

Bush, to be sure, had *values,* as inbred as if they were part of his genetic code. He could fairly claim, in his early sixties, to have lived an exemplary life of service to God, country and family and to the gentlemanly ideals of honor, achievement and common decency. He and his four-generation clan lived the sort of picture-book home life Reagan only talked about; his proudest achievement, he liked to say, was that *his* children still came home. His thoughtfulness was legend among people who knew him; a whole network of Republicans felt bonded to him less by his policies and positions than by his small kindnesses—the handwritten notes of condolence or congratulations, the spontaneous phone calls just to say hello.

But friends and colleagues searched in vain for a body of political beliefs all his own, or even a simple grocery list of problems and solutions that excited him. Reagan handed him one almost as a gift in their earliest days in office, assigning him to chair a task force on regulatory reform. It was a tremendous opportunity, Keene told him at the time, a chance to open his own front in Reagan's popular war against big government.

"I don't see it that way at all," Bush complained. "It's all paperwork—dull, dreary stuff."

Other assignments followed, on drugs, terrorism and crisis management, each with its own ripe possibilities for keeping Bush's name in the papers. He attacked each of them dutifully, and left his mark on none. He had *never* played to the crowd, he once protested, not at the United Nations or the CIA or anywhere else, and he wasn't about to start in the vice-presidency. He was there to serve Ronald Reagan, period, he said, and when the two of them were not alone in the room he chose to recede into the shadows. Even in the sanctuary of the Cabinet, a friend at the table said, George never seized an issue or argued a position at all.

The result of his low-profiling was the perception, in Washington and beyond, that he had no profile at all. His man Fuller mourned aloud at the eve of the campaign that Bush had been emasculated by his office; the closer he stood to Reagan, the less he seemed to have an identity of his own.

It did not help much when, in 1985 and 1986, he went off courting the leaders of the far secular and religious right, trying rather too ardently to persuade them that he was not really a sheep in wolf's clothing. The vice president's admirers, including, it was said, his wife, were unhappy with his show of Heepishness, and Bush himself canceled one booking, telling his handlers, "Fuck 'em. I ain't going. You can't satisfy those people." Still, he kept trying to, at debilitating length. His rewards were courteous applause from the red-meat conservatives he played to and sour notices practically everywhere else; even Atwater, who had planned the tour, came to regret it. Bush was lampooned in the comic strip "Doonesbury" for having put his manhood in blind trust, and the conservative columnist George Will likened him to a lapdog—a slight Bush never forgave and was not allowed to forget.

His quest for identity was made more difficult by his pallor as a performing artist, a visible unease whenever he got in front of an audience or a camera. The case that a pretty face and a pleasing style have become decisive in modern media politics has been overdrawn; among the major-party nominees in the video age, only John Kennedy and Ronald Reagan can be said to have been truly telegenic. But Bush was a particularly hard case—a man who, as his friend and former media adviser Robert Goodman put it, was without public style.

He had, in fact, been trying for ten years to master the medium, almost from the day he first set his sights on the presidency. The struggle had been a discouraging one. He could be magnetic in small rooms, which were his natural element; there he had something like charm as the novelist Albert Camus once defined it—a way of getting the answer yes without having asked any clear question. But in larger settings he regularly fell victim to what his occasional speechwriter Peggy Noonan thought of worriedly as the Chucklehead Factor—a proneness to accident that diverted attention unfairly from his years of achievement to his moments of silliness.

His gestures turned awkward on public view, his voice sounded strained and high, and his hold on words and syntax went slippery. He had a positive gift for stumbling from first-form preppisms like "deep doo-doo" to postgraduate howlers, as when he set out to say that he and Reagan had had some setbacks; it came out, "We've had sex." Even his efforts to slip out of the Pinstripe-Suit Thing and be one of the guys were undermined by his ineloquence and his breeding. He professed concern to a staffer, for example, that Gary Hart might—*wink! nudge!*—"waken the sleeping pussy factor" with his sex appeal and run everybody else out of the race. For Bush, the R-rated argot of politics was only too plainly a second language.

The net impression he left, too often, was one of weakness, and the effect was heightened by the rice-pudding texture of his politics. Bush was heir to Reagan's legacy but not to his size or his passion. His own people warned him bluntly that he came across as bland and—ah—wimpish. It was, in his eyes and theirs, a bum rap; he had proven his manliness as a bemedaled warrior and a nearly self-made oil millionaire. But his steel did not show on TV; he seemed literally to shrink under the eye of the camera and the glare of the kliegs. In real life, he stood a slim-lined six feet two, an inch taller than the president. On television, Reagan diminished him by his sheer commanding presence; people meeting Bush for the first time kept telling him, "Hey, you're *tall*—I thought you were a little short guy."

The image question was not lost on Bush, and the business about his looking small was, for him, its metaphor. Gotta do better, he told himself, as if it were a problem in technique rather than soul. You had to work on the mechanics of it, he told a visitor to his retreat in Kennebunkport. You had to figure out how to come across as what you *are*, and not what somebody else *thinks* you are.

But he refused to accept that television was all there was to politics. He felt good about himself and his prospects as he prepared for battle. He had already been through a lot, the Iran-Contra thing and all that; he had been hammered on in print and on the air by people who didn't even know who he was. If things were as bad as people said they were, he thought, he would have been starting out third or fourth in the polls. But in spite of everything, he was still number one, still the front-runner, so, he imagined, *something* was going right.

There were those who questioned whether he had the skills or the strength for the long march ahead—he knew that. But on his own checklist, he had never felt more determination, more *drive,* in his life. That fire in the belly, I've got it, he thought; nobody's going to outhustle me; those guys who were down there where I was eight years ago, with asterisks next to their names in the polls, they're not going to work any harder than I do. You just had to keep moving forward, he told himself. Tell the truth. Don't get discouraged. Do your best. Be what you are. Resist gimmicky advice. Just have faith, have confidence, he told himself, and he did.

He knew, for openers, that he would be a good president—better than *any* of the rest of them, he said, 'cause I can listen and then I can make up my mind and I can stay with it. He was well thought of where it counted most, among his peers. Sure, he thought, it might get a little—well, *grubby* out there on the trail, but he had the respect of the leading men of the nation and the world, and next to that all the superficial business about his image didn't matter very much.

If I don't measure up, he thought, if I'm not quite as charismatic as the media people think I should be, I've done my best. He had worried himself into an ulcer once in his life, as a young businessman in Texas, and he wasn't about to do it again; you'd spend your whole time churning if you brooded and quaked about the possibility that you might lose. Maybe some people in the country didn't understand him yet; maybe, as the preseason polls suggested, they even found him boring. If so, he mused, gazing eastward from his patio in Kennebunkport into the hard northern sunlight glinting off the sea, it was just a challenge. It was one more challenge between him and that horizon out there, he thought, and with a little help from his friends he would make it.

Dink Stover's Schooldays

Help had arrived that summer in the brassy, billowy person of Roger Ailes of Ailes Communications Inc., a mid-Manhattan image factory with a strong subspeciality in teaching even the most refractory politicians and businessmen to sell themselves in speeches and on TV. Ailes had a reputation as the Rodin of the small screen, a sculptor who could turn the plainest clay into figures of size and raw power; he was the magician who had made even Nixon look good on television back in 1968 and had nursed Reagan through a case of the shakes after his discombobulated first debate with Mondale in 1984. With the approach of a new campaign, he ranked with the masters of his craft, both as a maker of ads and as a remodeler of men. Everyone wanted Ailes, and he found himself in the comfortable position of having the candidates—all but Pat Robertson—audition for *him*.

He found it painful choosing among Bush, Dole and Kemp—so painful that, for a time, he considered sitting out the race entirely. When he finally did settle on the vice president after two sittings, ideology had little to do with it; Ailes had none during business hours. Neither was it decisive that Bush Inc., of all the campaigns, seemed likeliest to stay the course and keep writing the checks for Ailes's pricey services. He picked Bush instead because he *liked* him, man to man.

He knew Bush would be a challenge; at the time he signed on, everyone was telling him that the guy couldn't win, that Bob Dole would wipe him out. But Ailes figured that *all* the contenders would be challenges, and the vice president had strengths he felt he could work with. For one thing, Ailes thought, he wasn't nuts the way some candidates are; he wasn't running to exorcise some demon inside himself. He was a real person, the kind of guy you could call at three in the morning if you were in trouble and he'd be there inside a half hour. He was a winning product, Ailes thought. He had substance—he just didn't know how to get it out. If everyone in America could just sit down with the guy in his living room for two minutes, there would be no contest: he would win by a landslide.

The problem, as he knew, was that national campaigns don't happen in living rooms, unless they got there on TV. You had to sell a candidacy to a mass audience, and Ailes didn't need a highlight film of Bush's past miseries on stage and screen to know what he was getting himself into. He knew you couldn't invent a personality for a client, and he made it his rule, only slightly elastic, not to try. Bush was no John Wayne, but, Ailes believed, he might play as Gary Cooper—strong, silent, slow to anger, tough in a fight.

Ailes's commitment, once he came aboard, was total; in a trade plied mainly by mercenaries, he thought of himself as a freedom fighter, willing, he liked to say, to give his life for his clients. He was an affable sort off duty, a man of serene ego and lusty appetite for the foodstuffs of that innocent past before cholesterol counted. Häagen-Dazs ice cream was a particular weakness, freely and guiltlessly indulged. If there was none around, anything caloric would do; once, when Lee Atwater was calling room service on the road, Ailes told him, ''Just tell them to send up page one of the menu.''

But the mountain of flesh he inhabited turned volcanic in battle. ''Roger, you just love combat,'' his wife, Norma, told him. It was true; for him, politics was war, which was the secret of his success.

He was closest to Atwater in warrior spirit among the men who made up Bush's G-6; Atwater was the kind of guy who drowned everything he ate in Tabasco sauce, as if he liked even his food to fight back. In the beginning, at least, the two of them made a natural pair, a couple of *arrivistes* with land-grant educations and bruised knuckles in the manicured society of Bush Inc. Ailes had ambitions in the theater—he had produced the award-winning play *The Hot l Baltimore* off-Broadway—and Atwater was only an unfinished dissertation away from a Ph.D. in political science. But put them in a campaign, Ailes's friendly competitor Robert Goodman thought, and they became tank commanders—two tough boys you wouldn't want to meet in an alley after dark.

Ailes had a particular genius for television, having been in it all his adult life. He had scrambled from prop boy to producer of the old Mike Douglas talk show and from there, at the age of twenty-eight, into the council of Madison Avenue soapflakes salesmen charged, in 1968, with the creation of a New Richard Nixon. He had never actually run media in a presidential campaign, but his legend had grown, along with his girth, a pewter-gray goatee and a long winning record. Businessmen happily paid him $6,500 for twelve-hour courses in public speaking. Politicians signed far larger checks for his time, which routinely came to a hundred hours a week. His price for the Bush primary campaign was a below-market $25,000 a month. The sweeteners included $2.5 million in commissions on advertising placed through a separate media-buying firm he had founded, plus the prospect of *serious* money if Bush made it to the finals in the fall.

What Ailes offered in return was his mastery of his basic medium. He had understood in his first campaign, for Nixon, that politics had *become* television, a performing art in which only the gifted or the well-coached would survive, and his apprenticeship in daytime talk TV had refined his sharp, blue-collar instincts for what—and who—would play in Peoria on a twenty-six-inch screen.

The Case of the Vanishing Vice President taxed even his gifts at transmogrification, but with patient nurturing a New George Bush did begin taking form. If no one was likely to mistake him for Superman, he did make a fair approximation of Clark Kent, a straight and solid man with a hint of unsuspected strength hiding behind the rimmed glasses and the square gray suits. Most politicians came to Ailes with formed habits of speech and stagecraft, and he could be brutal with them. "That looks stupid, but go ahead if you want to," he would say, and with particularly recalcitrant students he would wave toward an open window and ask, "Can you fly?" Bush was different, a man who needed to be jollied, not bullied, into shape. Bush *knew* he had a problem, and he made an unusually disciplined patient, willing to take his medicine obediently and on time.

He hadn't always been so pliant; relays of coaches had tried over the years to refashion him without success, and he had come to be known in the industry as, stylistically speaking, a lost cause. Ailes began by instructing Bush to forget everything he had been told. He all but abandoned his New York offices for Washington and saw the vice president between twice and ten times a week, a course of doctoring tantamount to intensive care. The vice president talked too fast when he got excited, his words rising in pitch and tempo like an audiotape on fast forward. Ailes slowed him down, which deepened his voice to something nearer presidential timbre. His body language was as out of sync with his words as Richard Nixon's gestures or Jimmy Carter's smile. Ailes trained him in the tricks of nonverbal communication—how to show calm with a smile, and strength with a stab of the hand; how to convey an air of command simply by sitting straight up on the forward edge of his chair; how to steady his darting gaze and lean into the camera in a debate or an interview, as if invading the enemy's space; how to size up an adversarial situation in seven seconds and then take charge of it.

In prepping for debates, Ailes worried little about the usual practice of burying a candidate in briefing books; they were mostly makework for the issues staff, an unacknowledged ghetto for grinds in most campaigns in the age of the sound bite and the bumper strip. Any career public servant as seasoned as Bush, in Ailes's experience, knew the basics cold. He did believe in heavy rehearsal, but mostly to shorten and sharpen answers and to embed them in memory. You didn't want to load a guy up with substance; the issues people could always come in behind with their white papers and fill in the blanks.

Ailes preferred putting Bush through what he called pepper drills, rapid-fire Q&A exchanges that quickened reflexes, pruned out verbiage and got the adrenaline pumping. It was a truism in politics that only masochists and C-Span junkies would watch the early debates end to end; what most of America saw was the snippet of highlight tape on the evening news. Ailes accordingly cared less about the sixty or ninety minutes of cross-chat than about creating the single memorable moment—the bold line or the bravura gesture that would get you those thirty seconds of free airtime and bump everybody else off the screen.

No one could stage-manage Bush in unstructured settings, not Ailes or anyone else; the Dink Stover in him would keep popping out, the boola-boola style and speech of the old-boy Yalie forty years on. He would always be that way, one of his strategists worried; there would always be these little *splashes,* the off-pitch remarks that reinforced all the stereotypes of him as a rich, pampered and not very deep patrician adrift in a non-U world. His gaffes were innocent enough singly, but their danger grew in direct proportion to their number and to the larger uncertainty as to what it was he stood for. For long intervals, the dominant impression of the vice president was the sum of his mistakes; the ambush parties of reporters out on the trail watched as avidly for him to say something silly as they did for Kemp to be boring or Dole to be mean.

Bush did not disappoint them. Even his attempts to joke away the problem or to fix it by mastering the language of workaday America kept getting him into what he might have called deeper doo-doo. At the eve of his announcement, he traveled through Europe, a perfect showcase for Bush as statesman, and blew it with a single careless remark—a wisecrack suggesting that Moscow's auto mechanics were better than Detroit's. The response was a new Motown Sound: a low growl to the beat of no hands clapping.

It did not help that Bush had long had sticky relations with the trend-makers and soul-searchers of the national press. He had never borne criticism well; he was afflicted, a senior adviser said, with rabbit ears, a term of art in baseball for a player who lets booing or bench-jockeying get to him. Another man who had known him for years in politics and government guessed that the vice president was indeed still Pres Bush's little boy, still the Connecticut schoolchild trying hard to please an exacting and forbidding father. It was important to him, in this view, that there be nothing negative in his report cards for his dad to fasten on, not so much as a question about his penmanship or his spelling. They had to say George is good, George is decent, George is trying hard, George's manners are fine, George has a great future, George has earned straight A's, George is an all-round wonderful boy; if there was a single note of doubt or criticism, his father would be displeased.

Bush's fuzzy identity was one consequence, this colleague supposed. He wasn't really a fuzzy *person*, but if you were trying to make everybody like you, you came out sounding that way. The further and more troublesome cost was a widening divide between him and the media. Their *job* was to criticize, his colleague went on, and if your notices came out sixty–forty favorable, you were ahead of the game. Most politicians understood that. Bush did not. For him, reporters were the teachers writing bad reports home; every one of them was thus a threat to him, his friend said, and his anxiety, turned outward, became anger—sometimes vengeful and often profane.

He had the further misfortune to be running in a season when the question of "character," roomily defined, had become a preoccupation of the press. The public rationale for the rise of psychojournalism was the belief, supported in some measure by polling, that character is what elections are fundamentally about; the private considerations included the staleness of the post-Reagan political dialogue, the boredom of the media with the issues and personalities, and the libido of Gary Hart. No corner of a man's life or psyche was private anymore; the people, or their servants in the press, had a right to rummage through everything from tax returns to bed linens for evidence that this candidate was a secret swinger or that one a closet millionaire. The full Freudian field check had, by 1988, become a part of the electoral process, and no one was immune. But where most of the others found it an irritant, Bush saw it as an act of war. The questions that most absorbed the character inspectors on *his* trail had to do with his strength, and when *Newsweek* raised them on its cover the very day he announced for president, he exploded.

The headline read, FIGHTING THE "WIMP FACTOR," and the accompanying profile of the vice president went straight to the core question about his candidacy: whether he was man enough for the job. That the question existed was not news; Bush's own managers had worried it, sometimes with him in the room, and it was familiar to anyone who had read "Doonesbury" or watched a Johnny Carson monologue over the past eight years.

But the term "wimp" in headline type was a fighting word to Bush—a kick in the gut, Ailes thought—and the timing of the story redoubled his fury. Like most candidates, he had expected a free ride from the media on his declaration day, a chance to frame his own state portrait in the most flattering way; it was as if a holiday from hard scrutiny had become an entitlement, not just a convention of political reporting. You don't call a man a wimp on the day he announces, the vice president grumbled months later. No, *Newsweek* and that evil cast of characters who ran it up in New York had strayed way over the line, and he would punish them for it; he would, he said at the time, think of it every day of his presidency if he won.

The W word blackened his mood on the flight down to Houston for his kickoff ceremony and dogged him from stop to stop thereafter. The ceremonial itself, in a third-floor Hyatt ballroom, was an oddly flat affair, and, while his words were eloquent on paper, Bush smothered them in his prosy delivery. His message was that Ronald Reagan had led America out of the high winds and heavy seas of the Carter years, and that he was the man to hold the ship on course. "I'm not much for the airy and abstract," he said, as if to apologize for his plainness of speech and imagination. He was instead a practical man, he said, promising "strong, steady, experienced leadership" in the same general direction. America, in Reagan's sentimental vision, had been a shining city on a hill. Bush appeared to be offering himself as its city manager.

His launch played to polite, tennis-tournament applause, and the balloon drop afterward in the atrium was hardly more inspiriting; a third of the balloons had deflated by the time they touched the lobby floor. It seemed a harbinger of the glitch-ridden week that followed. It was a measure of Bush's luck that, on the seventh day of his candidacy, the stock market crashed around his and his patron's ears.

Bush's message, to the extent he had one, was drowned out by the background noise; the tour played to cool reviews in the press and to delighted smiles among his rivals. Richard Wirthlin, for one, couldn't believe his eyes or his man Dole's good fortune. Those golden days, those free chances to control the political environment, don't come again, he thought, not from the day you announce until the night you accept the nomination. Bush had squandered his moment, Wirthlin though. He had no touch, no feel, no instinct for politics; the Man Who Would Be President—quite possibly, Wirthlin granted, a *good* president—was making the kinds of mistakes you expect from a first-term congressional candidate.

The Karate Kid

The diagnosis, as it developed, was prematurely terminal. The new George Bush, redone under Ailes's direction, was waiting in the wings, and only the face was familiar; the aura of mastery was not. He made his entrance late in October in the season-opening debate in Houston, a made-for-TV production on William F. Buckley Jr.'s *Firing Line*. He did everything Ailes had taught him, sitting forward, squaring up, lowering his pitch, looking into the camera, getting out his rehearsed button lines no matter what he was asked. He dominated the stage from a first exchange on why he clung so tightly to Reagan—"In our family," he said, "loyalty is a strength, not a character flaw"—to his closing appeal for support as the seasoned co-pilot who knew how to land a plane in a storm.

Not even the New Bush could win them all. In the blood sport we have made of political debate, everyone stalks the front-runner, and no one brought more zest to the chase than the man bringing up the rear, Alexander Haig. The general, being a realist, knew it would take a miracle for him to win. But he had his reasons for slogging on from Rotary lunches to retirement communities to beg votes, and George Bush was one of them; he saw it as his patriotic duty to keep Bush out of the White House. Bush struck him as a man who had gone from job to job getting his ticket punched, nothing more, and now he was swaddling himself in Reagan's skirts. He had never made a difference, Haig thought, never stood up on his own. By Haig's measure of the man and the times, Bush wasn't strong enough to be president.

So the general lay in wait, and in a debate on NBC-TV in December, a mass assembly of all the candidates of both parties, Bush walked into his sights. The subject was the vice president's role in the sale of arms to Iran; his case for himself rested importantly on the claim that he was usually somewhere else when the important decisions were made, and Haig went at him like a district attorney attacking an alibi.

"George," he teased, "you've claimed to be the co-pilot of this administration. . . . Were you in the cockpit [in the Iran-Contra affair], or were you on an economy ride in the back of the plane?"

Bush was caught off balance. The audience was laughing at him. He wobbled through a response, a scrambled replay of his mistakes-were-made-but-not-by-me defense, with puzzling asides on the rising quality of American intelligence-gathering and on the praiseworthiness of Reagan's air strike against Muammar al-Qaddafi.

"George, you haven't answered my question," Haig needled.

A chime sounded.

"Time's up," Bush said, palpably grateful; he had had to be saved by the bell.

It was plain who had won *that* night's battle of the highlight tapes, and, more important, who had lost. Afterward, Haig bumped into Dole's campaign chairman, Bill Brock, looking as happy as a kid at Christmas.

"Al," Brock told him, "I'm going to get Bob a little statue of you and put it on his bureau so he can kneel down and say his prayers of thanksgiving every night."

Mostly, Bush did better. He came off in his clippings as a kind of golden-years Karate Kid, a late-blooming prodigy at the martial art of debate. It helped that Bush was the most underestimated man in our politics since Ronald Reagan before 1980; he had only to survive a debate unmarked to be counted a winner, since no one thought he had it in him to do more. A great deal of the credit was accordingly heaped on Ailes for feeding him lines, shaping his posture and scouting his sets in finicky detail; it mattered, for example, that the water be unsullied by ice cubes, since ice constricted the vocal cords and sent Bush's voice back up to his squeaky old heights. But the *sensei* could not accompany his pupil onto the mat. When the lights came on, Bush was alone in their glare, and he did well simply by doing better than expected.

He fought by Ailes's rules of war, the first of which was to seize and hold control of the ground. Ailes thought of himself as the brawler among the coat-and-tie boys on Fifteenth Street, a guerrilla fighter in the war room plotting the Normandy invasion. In his rules of engagement, you got into the trees and kept firing, even when you were out of ammunition. When there was no one else to shoot at and nothing left to shoot with, you could always take aim at the media; they were as easy and as friendless a target as a tin can on a fence rail.

Their target, as luck would have it, was Dan Rather of *CBS News;* he was the living symbol, in conservative circles, of the power and presumption of the media, and, to their delight, he presented himself for the kill. Rather had been working on an inquiry into the story of the veep, the Ayatollah and the Contra *comandantes,* and in January CBS put in for an interview with Bush—an extended sitting, the network said, to be edited down to five minutes or so of tape for a "profile" of the vice president.

"Ab-so-lute-ly *no!*" Ailes exploded at a staff meeting. You could never trust TV guys in a tape situation. They weren't on your side; they could edit your guy into oblivion. *"Jesus,"* Ailes said. "No, no, no!"

The request was rejected, and after fitful negotiations Bush's men followed up with a counteroffer: Rather could have his interview, but it would be live or nothing.

Not all of them celebrated when the network said yes. Lee Atwater, for one, didn't like the smell of it. He was a medley of tics and twitches even in repose, all flittering fingers and jouncing knees, and the Rather interview looked to him like a setup.

"I'd really watch that guy," he said when Bush phoned in from New Hampshire the day of the telecast.

Bush laughed. You're wrong, he said; he had known Rather since Texas, twenty-five years before, when Bush was in oil and Rather in local news.

"He's a fair man," the vice president said.

"All right," Atwater answered. He was still nervous.

Ailes wasn't. Teeter had alerted him the night before that they were caught in a classic bait-and-switch; the word was around that the subject would be Iran-Contra and that CBS was going to open up half the show for it, Rather's piece first, then the interview. Ailes made some calls, confirming the rumors; one mole told him that people were running around the network boasting that they would take Bush out of the race. The warrior in Ailes wakened, and when Air Force Two landed in a snowstorm at Andrews Air Force Base that Monday evening, he and Fuller were waiting. The limousine ride to town was the only chance they would have to prepare Bush for the likelihood that, as Ailes predicted, Rather would be coming at him like a mad dog.

Bush seemed insufficiently worried. "I've answered the question five hundred times," he said. "I don't see any big deal."

"This *is* a big deal," Ailes said. "All they have to do is press you on dates and bullshit that you haven't had time to review, and you're gonna look like you don't know what you're talking about. If somebody asked me what I had for lunch last Thursday, I wouldn't know, but I'd look guilty trying to think about it."

"No, no," Bush said. "Dan Rather is a good newsman. He won't do that."

"Hey," Ailes said, "his job tonight is ratings. His ass is on the line. He doesn't care about you. If he thought he could get away with it, he'd *shoot* you."

The message registered, and Ailes used their time in the car to get Bush ready for combat. "Don't accept *anything* Rather says to you," he said. "Don't accept the premise of any question—I don't even care if it's *right*. Stay on the offense the whole time and wear him out." He studied Bush. The guy wouldn't fight unless he got mad, and what dependably would get him mad was the feeling that he was being treated unfairly.

"Watch the opening piece," Ailes told him. "That'll get you up."

As it happened, Ailes had thought about what to fight *with:* a notorious incident several months earlier when Rather, on location in Miami, had got sore at having his newscast held up by a tennis match and had walked off his set to call New York to bitch about it. The tennis match had ended in his absence, and CBS, with nothing else to put on the air, had gone to black—an empty screen—for six minutes. It was the ultimate embarrassment for a network, as Ailes reminded Bush; Rather would deny afterward that that had been his intent, but he caught the heat for it.

"Look," Ailes said, "he's trying to judge your whole vice-presidency by this stuff. That's like judging *his* whole career in broadcasting by six minutes when he acted like an asshole."

A sixth sense had told Rather that Bush might use the story. He expected the vice president to come at him a hundred miles an hour, he said during his own weekend warm-ups for the interview, and when someone asked what about, he answered simply, "Miami." The prospect did not deter him. The Iran-Contra story went on first and was as tough as its advance billing. Watching at Bush headquarters, Pete Teeley, then the campaign press secretary, called it a five-minute attack commercial.

The interview that followed more nearly resembled a prizefight, the anchorman hammering away like Mike Tyson, the vice president dancing, dodging and rope-a-doping like Muhammad Ali. Rather jabbed. Bush filibustered. "Let's talk about the record," Rather demanded. "Let's talk about the *full* record,'' Bush demanded back, meaning those parts of the record tending to exonerate him.

"I don't want to be argumentative, Mr. Vice President,'' Rather said deep in the proceedings.

"You do, Dan,'' Bush replied.

"No. No, sir, I don't.''

"This is not a great night,'' Bush said, '' 'cause I want to talk about why I want to be president . . . and I don't think it's fair—''

"And, Mr. Vice President,'' Rather broke in, "these questions are designed—''

"—to judge a whole career,'' Bush said, "it's not fair to judge my whole career by a rehash on Iran. How would you like it if I judged your career by those seven minutes when you walked off the set in New York?''

He had got the time and place wrong, but his aim was true. Rather looked stricken.

It's over, Teeley thought, watching at Bush Inc. The interview kept going, but Bush had the initiative, and it was Rather instead who lost hold of his emotions. "You made us hypocrites in the face of the world,'' he scolded near the end, his voice strained and rising. He had become, in that moment, a straight man in an Ailes scenario; he had allowed himself to be baited over the line from reporter to bully, picking on Mr. Nice Guy. When time ran out and he cut Bush off in midsentence, it sounded rude and sealed Bush's victory; only the opposition and the op-ed commentators noticed that Bush still hadn't answered the questions.

The Old George Bush made a brief appearance in the aftermath, overwound and overstated. It had been Tension City out there, he would say later, just like combat, and he didn't mind letting the world know how he had felt behind his forced on-camera smile. "Well, I had my say, *Dan*,'' he said, yanking out his earpiece and flinging it over his shoulder.

A CBS sound man rushed over to tell him the mike was still live. Bush seemed not to hear or care.

"He makes Lesley Stahl look like a pussy,'' he said.

"I wish you'd wait to say that until we're off mike,'' Ailes said with a nervous approximation of a laugh.

"The worst time I've had in twenty years of public life,'' Bush said. "But it's going to help me, because that bastard did not lay a glove on me.''

The tape wound on, catching every word.

"I'm really upset,'' Bush said, plowing ahead. "You can tell your goddam network that if they want to talk to me, they can raise their hands at a press conference. No more 'Mr. Insider' stuff.''

The brief glimpse into his innards nearly spoiled the show; it became fair game to ask, as Bob Dole did, how Bush would handle Gorbachev if he got so agitated by Dan Rather. The vice president ultimately apologized for his language, and, months later, he would put in a quiet call to Rather; the message was, No hard feelings.

But nothing could spoil the flush of victory that night at Bush Inc. The phone lines at Black Rock, CBS's corporate tower in mid-Manhattan, were abuzz with calls supporting Bush and denouncing Rather; the vice president's poll ratings in Iowa and New Hampshire bumped visibly upward; even Atwater's kinfolk in South Carolina were on the line, reporting, scientifically enough to suit him, that no one was talking about anything else. It was a defining moment, Atwater thought, a show of sinew and spine just two weeks before the Iowa caucuses. That night, he and his comrades congratulated themselves on the death of the Wimp Factor and the baptism by fire of the New George Bush.

The Last Angry Man

□══════════════□

ON A CRISP FALL MORNING in New Hampshire, in the third year of his still unannounced quest for the presidency, it came to Robert Joseph Dole that he might actually wake up one day in the White House. In time, his glimpse into the future would be seen less as revelation than as mirage; Dole had the ill fortune to be running against Ronald Reagan's vice president, and his campaign from the beginning had been a mirror of his own gnawing insecurities about himself, his support troops and his chances. But as he settled into a seat in a roped-off section of the dining room at the Sheraton Tara Wayfarer Inn in Bedford, he permitted himself the fleeting fancy that it could happen after all. Iowa was looking good, the polls were narrowing in New Hampshire, and a new top-management team was moving into Dole headquarters in Washington—the third and, the senator dared hope, the strongest.

The air outside sparkled like crystal in sunlight. Ducks glided by on the stream just beyond the windows. The trees were afire with autumn reds and oranges. The day was mellow, and Dole's mood, for once, seemed to match it.

''I think things are happening,'' he told his breakfast companions, the core group of his New Hampshire operation.

Glances flickered around the table; people who knew Bob Dole were not accustomed to hearing optimism from him, not, anyway, about himself or his prospects. Dole, at sixty-four, was a man of the last generation in our politics, not the next, and he carried more than his share of its history and its scar tissue. His life had been formed in the want of the Dust Bowl and had nearly ended on a battlefield in Italy in World War II, when his arm, his shoulder and his dreams were shredded by enemy fire. The fact that he was alive at all was a triumph of his will and his furies over the ruin of his body, and his rise to the Republican leadership in the United States Senate had been the product of forty years of unremitting struggle.

His success had not altered his contingent view of the world, or of how much he had to lose in the caste-conscious life of Washington if his run for White House failed. "I don't want to be a eunuch in this town," he had told friends, starting out. His people had come to doubt that he would *ever* really gamble what he had to get where he wanted to go. His first try, in 1980, had been a dismal failure, and he still felt burned. Inside his Washington figurehood dwelled the small-town Kansas lawyer with a crippled arm and stunted expectations, and the faintest gleam of belief in his eye was more welcome to his handlers than a bump in the polls or a bite on TV.

The gleam had been lit that October morning by his sense that things were beginning to move for him in New Hampshire. It was supposed to be Bush country, but Bush, to Dole's undisguised delight, was stumbling through his first week as a declared candidate, and a new state poll for the senator's campaign showed him only eleven points behind.

He canvassed the table to see whether the others shared his up feeling.

"Bob, we're not up here to finish second in New Hampshire," Tom Rath, a former state attorney general and a senior adviser to the campaign, told him.

Dole turned to Warren D. Rudman, a Senate colleague who was about to endorse him and bring along his own state organization.

"I think Tom's right," Rudman said. "If you come out even close, you've won—and that means you've got a fifty-fifty chance to be the next president of the United States."

Dole ducked his head and rolled his eyes, then came up smiling. "I think maybe you have something there," he said.

It was, his people thought afterward, the moment the quest became real to him at last. "I've got to begin thinking about what I do if I get this," he told an acquaintance in the days that followed. He had begun, for the first time, to look into the mirror in the morning and see President Dole smiling back.

The All-American

In a season of false hope, one source of Dole's optimism was the failure of Jack French Kemp to emerge as the rightful heir of Ronald Reagan. George Bush, who felt *he* answered that description, dismissed Kemp privately as a lightweight, and Dole had in the past considered him a mere irritant on the Hill, a smarter-than-thou complainer who had sat around picking nits while the *real* leadership wrote the president's program into law. But in the early betting on 1988, a fair-sized stack of smart money had said that Kemp would give Bush a serious fight for rights to the Reagan estate. Kemp, it was said, was suited from his coif to his monogram for the role of JFK in a remake of the Nixon–Kennedy campaign of 1960; *he* would be the man of vigor, optimism and young ideas—Republican ideas, this time—vying with an incumbent vice president to succeed a revered but spent old man.

The wish scenarios written around him had reckoned everything except the odds; everything had to go right for Jack, his campaign chairman, Ed Rollins, mused early on, at a point when everything was already going wrong. Kemp's candidacy had been born with a stature gap between him and his two main rivals, one the vice president, the other a pillar of the Senate; he was running from the House, which hadn't sent a member directly to the presidency since Garfield, and a major fraction of the electorate knew him best, if at all, as some guy with blow-dried hair who used to play pro football. His organization had more stress fractures than an orthopedic ward. His money managers were spending him into debt, profitlessly. His speeches, on bad days, were as long as Hubert Humphrey's and as hard for laymen to comprehend as quantum physics. His handlers, long before the end, had given up on him. The election was still a year and a month away when Rollins looked around, shook his head and told himself, It's *over*.

Rollins at forty-four was a ringwise veteran, chunky, bearded, balding and tough; he had been political director in the Reagan White House and had managed the president's reelection landslide, and he knew winners from losers when he saw them. The Kemp campaign, in his regretful view, was a loser. He had known from the first that Kemp was a long shot, but he had signed on anyway, partly because Bush hadn't called, partly because he liked both Kemp and the challenge. The misgivings came later. He felt at times like a hood ornament with a fancy title and no real power; what authority there was reposed with his friend Charlie Black, the campaign manager, and even that was compromised by Kemp's preference for the company and often the advice of his movement conservative friends. "Jack, you're like Luke Skywalker," a favorite, Jude Wanniski, the supply-side theoretician, assured him. "Throw away all the programming and all the polling and let yourself go." Too often, he did.

He was, moreover, addicted to good news, which was what he preached out on the circuit and what he liked hearing back from his advisers. Rollins's view was more somber, and in the summer of 1987 he set down his doubts in an eyes-only memo to Kemp on what was wrong with the campaign. The answer, simply put, was everything, from grand strategy— there was none—to the nuts-and-bolts mechanics of politics. The organization, in Rollins's appraisal, was totally flat; headquarters had "no real direction," spending was under "no real control," fund-raising was "far from ready," the home-office payroll was too big, the field staff was too small, and scheduling was a "political disaster" waiting to happen to Kemp the day it finally wore him out.

Worst of all, Rollins wrote, the whole edifice was built on a series of false premises, the first and most dangerous of which was that Bush would be knocked out early. "George Bush is in the race to the end," the memo said. "He will not quit; Jim Baker and others who have a vested interest in a 'Bush presidency' won't let him." False premise number two, in Rollins's view, was that Kemp could win as Gary Hart nearly had done in 1984, doing well in Iowa and New Hampshire and riding the resulting media wave to victory. "The odds are very high that we'll end up like Gary Hart," Rollins wrote dryly, "in debt and not nominated." They were running an incumbent-style campaign, expensive and presumptuous, when a long-march strategy was called for; they would come out of New Hampshire with no plan, no money and no field organization to bring in the 1,139 delegates they needed to win.

A further problem, less easily repaired, was the candidate himself. Kemp *had* a vision, unlike most of his earthbound rivals, but its form kept getting lost in the Babel of his thoughts on the merits of, say, a basket of commodity prices. "We still don't have a clearly defined message," Rollins wrote. "You've got to sit down and write out: Why should you be president? What is it that you want to run on? What [do] you think a Kemp presidency will try to accomplish? Why should voters trust you with the country's most important office? What is your vision of America in the future? After you've answered these questions, we have to narrow your stump speech down to six or seven topics and repeat them over and over again.''

Rollins's timing was unfortunate: he hoped to discuss the memo with Kemp one Friday afternoon early in September, just before the candidate was due to go watch one of his sons quarterbacking a high-school football game.

"Boy, I'm stunned by this," Kemp said, scanning the white paper. "I guess I need to do something, huh? Why don't we talk about this next week?''

They never did. Someone hands you a grenade like that, Rollins thought, you at least got to ask some questions, but that wasn't Jack's way; he was out there on the road, mistaking applause for votes, and he didn't want to deal with the core problems of his candidacy.

"Ed, you and Charlie get together," he said. "You got to work this out. Make it happen.''

Without his intervention, nothing changed. Black's in box was a black hole, the result of his trying to do everything himself. The ideologues were at war with the professionals, the pros at odds with each other. The money people were reduced to shaking out today's envelopes to keep Kemp afloat through tomorrow. Everyone found someone to blame, most often the candidate, for his sins and their own; in the age of the hired operative, their implicit message to him was, Leave us alone and we'll get you elected.

Kemp kept his oblivious distance from the brewing troubles until, at a senior staff meeting that September, they blew up in his face. The trigger issues, in retrospect, would seem trivial as against the real problems dragging down his candidacy: the ideologues were unhappy with a proposed ad campaign, in the saccharine mode of Reagan's "Morning in America" spots of 1984, and some of the pros were upset at Kemp's having chosen a finance director without Black's OK. But both sides landed on Kemp—just beat the living shit out of him for two solid hours, Rollins thought, watching at ringside—and the worst of it was that Jack just sat there and took it.

No other candidate Rollins knew would have tolerated the scene; Bob Dole would have put a bullet between the eyes of the first guy who got out of line, he guessed, and George Bush, wimpy as he was, would have whistled a halt to the uprising. Jack didn't. His style was consensus rather than command, which, Rollins thought, was why career legislators make lousy candidates and probably lousy presidents. The closest Kemp came to putting up a fight was when he suggested that Wanniski go find some other candidate to sell his horseshit ideas. Otherwise, he listened, reasoned, cajoled, whined and grumbled; it was Rollins instead who finally called time.

"I realize every candidate needs to be critiqued," he said angrily, "but this is just horseshit. If you're not here for Jack Kemp, get the fuck out."

The meeting sputtered to an end. Kemp looked stricken. Rollins felt numb.

"Jack," he said, "I've been in this business for twenty-five years and I've never seen a mutiny. You've just had a mutiny. I got to tell you, I lost a little respect for you."

Rollins retreated to France for a week's R&R. Kemp went back to the road for repairs to his bruised ego. He really believed that he could sail home on the irresistible tide of his ideas about low taxes, a good-as-gold dollar and unfettered free enterprise, and when his audiences clapped or cheered he thought he was winning; he didn't understand that in politics, unlike football, *everybody* gets applause. He had caught the bug, and it had inflamed all his worst traits as a candidate—his all-pro ego, his slack self-discipline and his logorrheic way with words.

He could still act like the pampered college jock, which was bad enough. He insisted, for example, on his $100,000-a-month chartered jet when the campaign was sliding into hock, and he seemed more concerned that it be stocked with the right sandwiches than that there be a big crowd waiting when he got where he was going; Jack, Rollins thought, could be a real pain in the ass. But his star temperament concerned his handlers less than his evangelical style. When the supply-side spirit was upon him, he seemed unable to begin or end a speech or to translate what came between into workaday English.

Breaking him of his habits became a preoccupation of the campaign; they called it behavior modification, only half in fun, and nagged Kemp about it relentlessly with only minimal reward. Even a conversation with Kemp could be like listening to a tape recorder, his congressional soulmate Newt Gingrich of Georgia thought. A podium went to his head like a double Dewar's to an alcoholic's; his blue-sky, growth-and-opportunity conservatism would come spilling forth whole, at a thick-throated tenor pitch, as if there might never be another chance to tell the good news.

"If I could remove two-thirds of your knowledge and three-fourths of your vocabulary, I can make you into a decent candidate," Rollins told him.

Kemp would listen, nod, do one or two dynamite speeches, and then the spigot would go on again; he would be out there filibustering crowds to sleep, dropping non-negotiable names from Maimonides to Hannah

Arendt and scrambled jockonomic metaphors about how, in the 1970s, Malthus had been on offense in the world.

Kemp's defense was that it wasn't a matter of talking too much—it was having so much to say. He was out there offering something new, even *radical,* and he felt in consequence that he had to explain himself from A to Z every time he got out there. He came belatedly to understand that a campaign was thirty-second sound bites or five minutes with the guy from *The Des Moines Register;* you couldn't pour everything into every speech or every answer.

His addiction to overstatement was, in his own view, a mistake of the heart. He wasn't just another politician wrapped up in his survey research and his organization charts; he wasn't a coattail conservative like Bush, or a bitter-medicine conservative like Dole either. He was a man of ideas, a motivator, he mused one autumn day, crossing central Iowa in the backseat of a rental car. He was the guy out there with the message, the one who could light that fire, and if he sometimes ran on too long, well, that was his idealism talking—*youthful* idealism even if he was fifty-two years old and going gray. The real battle hadn't been joined yet. When it was, when the polls and the jockeying had been forgotten, he believed, the guy with a vision was going to win.

But his fading youth came off more nearly as boyishness, in his handlers' eyes, and his vision grayed out in speeches that made twenty-two points badly instead of three points memorably and well. If you didn't look and sound presidential, Rollins thought, it didn't matter if you had all the answers; politics was about appearances, 80 percent imagery and 20 percent issues, and Jack kept wanting to turn it the other way around. His tutors put him on what they called the Word Diet, enforced by a digital stopwatch they gave him to carry. He kept leaving it on lecterns, a signal of his unhappiness; still, under its unforgiving liquid-crystal gaze, he slimmed his road speech down from thirty-four minutes, on the average, to twenty-two.

But Kemp was not always so apt a pupil. He was still the quarterback at heart, accustomed to having the last word in a huddle, and his campaign was run according to his headstrong ways. A Kemp strategy session reminded his friend Newt Gingrich of a faculty senate meeting, a windy colloquy on interesting ideas in the Western world when there was still an election to be won. When his managers did corner him for a discussion of how he might actually win it, they found themselves in a constant and usually losing war for his attention; he would sit there taking calls, ordering Cokes, spinning off ideas and only occasionally listening to what he was being told.

His campaign scraped bottom, psychically, in December. His numbers were stagnant, his survival was mortgaged to banks, and his underattention to his handlers was showing in debates. His usually irrepressible spirit began to droop; he started to talk nostalgically about how much fun it had been running for Congress back home in Buffalo, focusing on issues instead of all this tiresome, tedious, somewhat boring business of where you ranked in the polls. The news from headquarters was unrelievedly bleak, and Rollins didn't have the heart to tell Kemp what he *really* believed—that the time had come to pack in his candidacy, come out for Bush and try to preserve a future for himself. If he quit early, he could be viable for vice president, or a Cabinet job, or maybe senator from New York, and live to run for president another day. If he stayed in and took his lumps, it could be all over for him for good. Jack could be history by spring, Rollins thought; he might never be heard from in national politics again.

But you didn't tell your candidate that, not before he had even climbed into the ring; Jack had too much of his life and his pride invested in the campaign, and, Rollins guessed, he wouldn't have listened anyway. So the enterprise slogged on, and for a time at the turn of the year fortune seemed to be smiling on it. Kemp's speeches sharpened, and when he backslid, his press secretary, John Buckley Jr. said, it wasn't a battle anymore; his people simply teased him out of it. "Thirty-year T-bills are at 9.6 percent," he told a group of senior citizens, who visibly wondered what he was talking about. His traveling party ragged him afterward—"T-bills? *T-bills?*"—and he took their meaning; at the next stop, he found it sufficient to say that interest rates were too high.

He showed flashes of fighting spirit as well, though he had to be persuaded to go on the offensive. His offering was Reaganism sunny side up, drained of the grievance at its core, and getting personal ran crossgrain with his sense of who he was and how a campaign ought to be. Everyone, even his wife, Joanne, was after him to speak up more on what made him different from Bush or Dole, but he resisted. When his media people brought in some tough TV spots attacking the two front-runners, he said no; if he couldn't win on the force of his ideas, he didn't deserve to win at all.

"You've been running the ball off tackle," Newt Gingrich told him at one of an interminable series of meetings on the subject. "You have to start throwing it down the field."

"We're doing better than everybody thinks we are," Kemp protested. "Let's not start getting negative."

Jude Wanniski backed him up; what Jack had to sell, he said, was a vision of opportunity and growth spreading out from America around the world.

"Jude, it's all over," Gingrich said. "We can have all the worldview in the world, but if nobody hears it, it's not going to get us anywhere."

"The day after we win the New Hampshire primary is the day the spotlight comes on Jack Kemp," one of the pros, Roger Stone, agreed. *"That's* when Jack Kemp comes out with all the positive stuff."

Kemp was skeptical, until the day in January when he tasted combat himself and discovered that he liked it. The arena was a debate at Dartmouth College; Bush and Dole had both come after him hard, and he had countered well, drawing a line in the dust between their dour, line-item conservatism and his own expansive new model.

"You were great," Dole told him afterward.

Kemp beamed. He had drawn the big boys' fire; he was in the race at last. That night, on the plane back to Washington, he reached forward to the seat ahead of his and tapped Rollins on the knee.

"Get the ads on," he said. "Get the ads on."

The ads went on, and Kemp began climbing in the polls; by mid-January he had broken into double digits in New Hampshire, close behind Dole in the scramble for position as the leading alternative to Bush. But Kemp's season in the sun, like Dole's, was illusory. He was challenging Bush for rights to the Reagan coalition, and in a party as sensitive as theirs to the rightness of things, he reflected afterward, that simply wasn't done. It was as if there were a rule somewhere that if you hadn't lost once, you hadn't earned your stripes. You're a good candidate, people kept telling him, and you're a nice guy, and you'll have another chance, but this is George's turn. Kemp was left standing in line; he had invited the Reagan majority to a party, a Grand New Party, and nobody came.

Faith, Hope and Uncharity

Bob Dole sat snowbound in the VIP lounge at Andrews Air Force Base one day in 1987, killing time with a copy of the day's *Washington Post* until the roads to town could be cleared. Dole had announced his candidacy a couple of days before, pointedly offering America "a record, not a résumé," and the story that caught his eye had to do with Bush's response—a plaint that he had a record, too, going all the way back to his days as a combat flier in the war. Dole smiled. It always pleased him to get under George's skin, and the *Post* had just made his day.

"Looks like we're drawing him out a little," he called across the room to his spokesperson, Mari Maseng. "He's getting a little testy." He rolled his eyes playfully. "We have a few more goodies for him," he said.

But his pleasure faded as he reread the part about Bush's tour as a Navy pilot. Dole's war had been a disfiguring experience, a wound to his soul no less than to his body. He had learned to talk about it only lately and with great pain, and here was George sounding off again about how he had got shot down at sea on a bombing run against the Japanese. A lot of guys did that, Dole thought, and a lot didn't come home. His face darkened. *He* wasn't running around with a big sign on his back saying, "I got shot, feel sorry for me," but George seemed to think that he had to; every time he opened his mouth, so it seemed to Dole, he talked about climbing out on that burning wing and parachuting into the Pacific.

"Sickening," Dole said. "He wasn't even hurt, was he?"

If Pat Robertson's campaign ran on faith and Jack Kemp's on hope, Dole's was marked from the first by its uncharity—a vein of resentment whose prime target was the vice president. It was too much to say that Dole *hated* Bush, his people gamely insisted. But "disdain" was not too strong a word for his feelings; he considered his rival a soft, untested man who had coasted through life on his family's wealth, his Ivied pedigree and his establishment connections. There had been nothing privileged about Dole's mean beginnings in the little prairie town of Russell, Kansas. His father, he liked to say, went to work in overalls every day of his life, and nothing since had come easily for him, not money, not position, not life itself. His way up had been steep and, in part by his own choice, lonely, and his campaign became the lengthened shadow of a haunted and driven public man.

His packagers presented him as a retrofitted if not quite a new Bob Dole, a far cry from the hit man blamed by some for having blown the 1976 election with one bitter aside about the dead in "Democrat wars" from Verdun to Vietnam. It was said that time, success and a good second marriage had mellowed him, and his quest for the presidency, his friend and adviser Tom Rath thought, was one more rung on the ladder, a kind of final validation of who he was and what he had made of himself. But the rigors of his passage had left their mark on the man, and it showed in his candidacy—in his fear of losing all he had won at such great cost, in his brooding reluctance to trust anyone else with anything affecting his life and fortunes, and most of all in the dark undercurrent of anger playing just under the surface of his campaign.

His chances were diminished from the start by his inability to let go of his position as leader of the Republican minority in the Senate. The job was more than power and perks to him; it had become his card of identity in Washington, his claim to size and somebodyness. Some of his handlers saw its usefulness as a showcase for Dole as leader, engaging with the great issues of the day while Bush hung back in the shadows of the vice-presidency. But running for president had become a full-time, four-year occupation in modern politics. You had to bet your life on it, and Dole's fear of falling held him back from scaling the heights.

His ambivalence had shown from the first seedling days of his candidacy in 1985, when he sat down with the chairman of his political-action front, Don Devine, to address the threshold questions about running. Devine had brought along a list of talking points, ticking through them one by one till they got to the last note on the page. "Choice—legislator or president?" it said, and Dole had to make it.

He balked. He was majority leader then, arguably the king of the Hill, and he wasn't giving it up.

You *have* to choose, Devine told him. He could keep the title, but not the day-to-day detail work, not if he wanted to be president.

Dole wouldn't budge.

Devine gnawed at his cigar. He was talking to a guy who carried a hundred-dollar bill around in his shirt pocket, a psychic hedge against the day they came and took it all away. The Senate was something he had. The presidency was something he wanted, but it was a long-odds gamble.

"What are you going to do?" Devine asked finally.

"Both," Dole said, and the case was closed.

The tug of war between his dreams and his doubts would never be fully resolved. For a time in 1986, he seemed to his people to be making the psychic leap; but with the return of the Democrats to power in the Senate that November and his own step down to minority leader, he relapsed. "The one thing that counts is that Bob Dole is going to be a player in this town," he told Devine, and being a player meant hedging his bets. It meant tending to his business, or what was left of it, on Capitol Hill.

Devine sensed then that it was over, and nothing in the months that followed changed his view. "Bob Dole has decided that he will accept the Republican nomination and the presidency if it does not interfere with his Senate leadership role," he wrote in a despairing memo to himself in December 1987, with the Iowa caucuses less than two months away. "This means he will not win the nomination, although it could fall in his lap by the mistakes or inadequacies of other candidates."

Dole's legislative mind-set not only fractured his time and attention but colored his candidacy as well. He was at least as tongue-tied as Bush trying to frame a word picture of the American future under his stewardship, though he was rather better-humored about his prosiness; once, passing a Pearle Vision Center in an Iowa shopping mall, he joked aloud about going in and buying one. He thought it quite enough to offer himself as he was, the consummate Washington insider, absorbed less with the poetry of politics—the Vision Game, he called it—than with the art of getting things done. People didn't ask him about vision in Iowa, he grumbled one day aboard his campaign jet. They asked him what he was going to do about the farm program.

On the record, his outriders defended his want of any message more inspiring than his knowledge of the folkways of the cloakroom. But the poesy gap was a matter of intense private concern to his command. Devine and David Keene, both passionate movement conservatives and both senior advisers to the campaign, pushed earliest and hardest for a rationale for a Dole candidacy, a set of identifiable goals and—yes—the V word. "We are not saying anything very important," Devine warned the senator in a memo in August 1987, and the campaign was stagnating as a result.

What Dole *had* been offering was the next best thing, a moving evocation of his pinched boyhood in Kansas and his thirty-nine-month passage through the shadow of death during and after the war. If it was not quite a vision, it was a statement of the values that had formed him, values of archetypal force in the American imagination. It was easy to forget, hearing him, that he had last lived in Russell twenty-seven years before and that he had become a man of wealth and high station in Washington, with a flat at the Watergate and a condo in Florida. He stood, in his speeches, for two of the great mythic strains of our national past: for the indomitability of the individual spirit and the good-neighborliness of the small midland town.

He had been reluctant at first to talk openly about the rough places in his biography—to see, as he ultimately conceded, that you couldn't just fly into town, pass out your brochures and expect people to know who you were. His wounds were a particularly tender topic for him, as raw in memory as they had been in war. It smacked of weakness, in his mind, to go out hustling votes with a sling on your arm, a cane in your hand and a flag wrapped around your shoulders. He wouldn't even accept help buttoning his shirts or tying his ties, let alone beg strangers for their sympathy, and he didn't want to start now. His people had to trick him into discussing the subject at all, planting questions at his town meetings in Iowa. His replies were spare at first, but his comfort level rose as he felt himself connecting with his audiences. There are more people out there like me, he thought, than like any of the other candidates—people who can relate to someone who's known some bad times along with the good.

He seemed to his managers to have hit his stride beginning with a speech in Grafton County, New Hampshire, in the spring of 1987; it was as if he had opened a shuttered window onto the wintry landscape of his past. It became easier for him thereafter to speak of what it had been like growing up in the Great Depression, the family scraping by on his father's modest earnings from a butter-and-egg store and his mother's from giving sewing lessons. He talked about the scars of war, physical and psychic, and about how the people of Russell had collected money in cigar boxes to pay for his recuperation. He remembered his earliest days in politics, when, as county attorney, he had reviewed the welfare roll every month and seen the names of his grandparents on it; they weren't lazy, he said—they were just tenant farmers who got old and couldn't make it anymore.

So he knew something about people with problems, he went on, and it had softened the edges of his conservatism with compassion. "Remember as you're climbing the ladder to look back at the people who aren't even on it yet," he said. The response surprised even him; the normal course of prudence in Republican politics was to sound hard-nosed in the primaries and save the compassion for the general election, but Dole's show of feeling for the afflicted seemed to him, beginning in Grafton County, to be working for him.

Something had changed for Dole, or so Rath sensed; the warm response to his new tack seemed to certify to him that his candidacy stood for something larger than his own ambition—that it embodied the longings of plain, decent, workaday Americans everywhere. His offering till then had been the promise of something vague called leadership. His confessional in Grafton County added a measure of that third dimension called soul. His people encouraged him, and by the time he formally announced for president in November, his humble roots and his homely values had become the conceptual framework for his campaign.

Russell High Versus Andover

Dole went home to Russell for the launch, speaking from a platform at the intersection of Eighth and Main; he was within eyeshot of the drugstore where he had been a soda jerk in his high-school years for two dollars a week and all the ice cream he could eat. The morning was cloudless and biting cold. A banner proclaiming that IT ALL BEGAN IN RUSSELL snapped in the autumn wind, and when Dole had finished his stock tour of the issues he came back to the sense of commonweal he had learned there as a child of hard times and world war; he would, he said, be "sensitive to the needs of the left-out and the down-and-out in our society as they try to fulfill their own dreams."

It was implicit that he was not, as he put it privately, the silver-spoon candidate in the field, his thinly coded term for George Bush. There was not much to distinguish them from each other as public men, given their close positioning in the Republican center right and their common membership in the Washington peerage, so Dole fastened on the differences in their bloodlines and their careers in government. He was the man of the people, elected to every office he ever held and accountable on the public record. Bush, in his typology, was the perpetual protégé; his success had been largely the grant of men of power, and his achievements had to be divined between the lines of his résumé.

But with the turn of the year, the Dole command began pushing for some point of contrast with Bush more vivid than their dueling pedigrees. His most conspicuous single attempt till then, on the Reagan-Gorbachev treaty to pull their theater nuclear missiles out of Europe, had been a flirtation with disaster. The treaty was enormously popular, but only Bush among the contenders embraced it outright. Dole, playing minority leader, refused to commit himself until he had first read the fine print, and the others said no; the vice president stood alone in the field as Reagan's ally in the quest for peace.

Dole's handlers knew he would have to edge back into the picture, and the White House opened a way: a carefully framed tableau in which Dole would meet privately with Reagan to talk about the treaty, then descend to the White House briefing room and endorse it with the president at his side. But Dole kept finding reasons of policy and pride for drawing back from the arrangement, and no one bothered to let Bush in on the plan—not until Reagan himself broke it to him over their regular Tuesday lunch at the White House. Bush was apoplectic. He left Reagan's table steaming and sent for Chief of Staff Howard Baker, who had been Dole's predecessor as Republican leader in the Senate.

"Was this an idea Bob Dole made?" Bush demanded. He was shouting.

No, Baker replied, it came from the White House.

"It's a dumb idea!" Bush shot back, proceeding, in unbuttoned language, to explain why.

He's out of control, Baker thought, retreating finally to shelter in his own office a few steps down the hall. He summoned his deputy in charge of communications, Tom Griscom, who had first proposed the rapprochement with Dole.

"Go make peace," Baker said. "He's beside himself."

Griscom tried. The deal, he told Bush, had been a matter of legislative necessity, not presidential politics. No one was taking sides with Dole.

"Well, I don't agree with it," Bush said. "It was a mistake."

As Griscom headed for the door, he reminded Bush that *he* had got to meet with Gorbachev during the chairman's visit to Washington. It was Dole who had complained then, bitterly, at being left out.

"Goddammit," Bush exploded, "I had every right to be there. If that sonofabitch Dole doesn't understand that, fuck him!"

The veep had always had a reputation among the president's men as a bit of a crybaby; one of them, a veteran of the Reagan campaigns of 1980 and 1984, refused an assignment to Bush's plane, considering him too petty and vindictive under pressure to be endured at such close quarters for so long. But Griscom was no less stunned by the violence of his response. He slipped out into the corridor, dazed, the air behind him still blue with obscenities. Bush had lost it, he thought. He was berserk. He was crawling the walls.

Bush's people tried furiously to put a stop to the Ron & Bob Show, floating the story, at one point, that Baker was angling for vice president or secretary of state in a Dole administration. Reagan stood fast, Dole was nursed through a last, nearly terminal attack of the dithers, and the pageant played out largely as written. The pictures on the evening news and in the morning papers caught the president and the senator together, allies in the cause of peace.

Baker's out to get me, Bush groused at his next lunch with the president.

Reagan tried to soothe him, but Bush wasn't having any. Baker and his crowd, he said, were secretly tilting toward Dole.

The news of his displeasure found its way back to Dole headquarters on L Street in Washington. For one rare moment in the campaign, everybody laughed.

The smiles were short-lived; all the senator had done was catch up with Bush on one issue when he needed most of all to show where they *differed*—why, that is, the voters should choose him over the man who was first in line for the job. He needed to get out front on something, an agenda identifiably his own. The problem was persuading him. Dole had never taken direction easily from his own people; he seemed, in his self-doubt, to wonder how smart they could be if they were working for him. So, as they sometimes did on sensitive questions, they found someone they *knew*

Dole would listen to. They took him to see the Zen master of negative politics, Richard Nixon.

Their pretext for luring Dole down from New Hampshire for the pilgrimage to Saddle River, New Jersey, in January 1988 was to let the former president vet a major foreign-policy speech he was to do the next day. Their hidden agenda was to let him hear from the Old Man himself that he needed to pick some fights with Bush on real questions of policy and state. Nixon liked Dole, a self-made man with a history and an outlook not unlike his own, and was quietly advising his campaign; his channeler was its sometime chairman, Robert Ellsworth, who had served him in happier times in high-level government and diplomatic jobs.

He received Dole and his party in the library at his home, a handsome room of bare brick walls and shelving heavy with works of history, biography and politics. His guests made themselves comfortable, Dole lounging in a patterned navy cardigan, Ellsworth and Bill Brock loosening their neckties and draping their suit coats over the backs of their chairs. Nixon, by contrast, wore his formality like armor; he kept his houndstooth-check jacket on and buttoned, and his dark tie stayed tightly knotted in his white shirt. He scanned Dole's speech text wordlessly while the others took coffee or tea and nibbled at cookies. He offered a couple of suggestions; then, for two hours, he talked attack politics, scribbling notes to himself on the remnants of a four-inch-thick legal pad as he spoke.

What Dole had done thus far had been good, he said. "You've established that you came from modest beginnings and achieved great heights. You've established that you're a strong, effective political leader. What you have to do now is draw some sharp distinctions on important issues between yourself and Bush." It would be risky, Nixon conceded, given Bush's affiliation with a popular president, but the larger danger was that the vice president would win by simple inertia. "You *have* to take risks," Nixon told Dole, "if you're going to get this nomination."

Dole agreed, or seemed to; he felt he had already begun the process. It could be done, he said. It had to be done.

Not much *was* done in the days thereafter. There *were* no large issues separating Bush and Dole, no great ideological or programmatic divide; the real differences between them had less to do with their politics than with their manifest dislike for each other. Dole, in Bush's eyes, was a creature of Congress, a trader, not a statesman, and a small-spirited man besides; the campaign was just going to be *mean,* he complained to a friend going in, and he hated the thought of it. Bush, in Dole's view, deserved whatever he got. Everything about him offended Dole, from his pampered boyhood to his royalist campaign for president. "Were *you* ever chauffeured to kindergarten?" he asked a young aide one day. Well, George was, and the attendant odor of privilege brought out the bruised underside of Dole's spirit, the strain of bitterness and self-pity embedded in him by hardship and war.

The great debate between them reduced itself accordingly to personalities, not issues, and Dole's heart was plainly in it. Everything in the vice president's life seemed to Dole to have been handed to him, all gain with no pain; even his storied résumé was a catalogue of fancy titles on an otherwise blank page. If someone asked Dole his proudest achievement, and he said being in the Senate, he thought, people would justifiably reply, "Big deal." But that, in his view, was what George was doing. Ask him what it was he had done at the CIA, say, or what were his five proudest achievements as vice president, and he'd be hard pressed to answer; he hadn't done or decided anything.

It was an ill-kept secret in the Dole campaign that his people considered him potentially his own worst enemy. They had warned him early on that he couldn't reprise his performances as Gerald Ford's designated hitter in 1976 or as the wisecracking also-ran of 1980; he was a real player this time, with vastly more to lose by spoiling the matured and mellowed new look they had spun around him. All campaigns are reductionist, one of his strategists said, and if Bush versus Dole came down to Wimp versus Whiner in the public mind, the Wimp would probably win, if only for having been at Reagan's side.

The senator listened and tried hard, in the early going, to behave himself, joking, sometimes, that he would one day publish a book of all the things he hadn't been allowed to say. There were days, indeed, when he overplayed the role of Mr. Manners. He went into the first major debate so overtrained at niceness as to seem, in his own morning-after review, "sedated." He wished aloud afterward that he could go one on one with the vice president alone. Just have a head-on for a couple of hours, he said, an edge rising in his voice. Nobody in the room but George and me.

The pain of containing his demons by then was beginning to show. If there were no differences worth talking about between him and the other candidates, he wondered one late autumn day, what was the use of voting? Why not vote for us all? His reserve started to chip, and with the onset of winter it broke. He tweaked Bush almost daily for everything from his head start at birth—"*I* didn't have rich and powerful parents"—to his sideline seat in the administration. Maybe Bush was vice president, but when Ronald Reagan wanted something *done,* Dole said, it was Bob he called, not George.

At times that winter, it became surprising when Dole *didn't* burn the vice president. "Your guy's boring today," a reporter told Tom Rath one day in New Hampshire; Bush had taken a shot at him, and Dole hadn't replied.

Rath repeated the remark to Dole a bit later, in a car speeding up Route 111 from one stop in Salem to the next in Hampstead.

Dole rolled his eyes. "I've been good, I've been good," he protested. "Don't you think I've been good?"

"I know," Rath said. "You've been very good."

But being good had its limits, and Dole crossed them practically the moment he climbed out of the car to visit a drug-rehabilitation center. A TV reporter quoted him the latest from the veep—that when Reagan had needed a running mate, it had been George he called, not Bob.

"Was it collect?" Dole asked.

The rat-a-tat continued and at moments took on the hard edge of class war—a conflict setting Main Street against Wall Street, Russell High against Andover, a life of struggle against a life of *noblesse oblige*. The skirmishing suited the purposes of Bush Inc., casting Bush as Han Solo against Dole's Darth Vader. The marketing division at Dole headquarters was a great deal less pleased; anything that wakened memories of the senator in his old chain-saw-massacre mode was as welcome there as a root-canal repair.

But Dole seemed unable to contain himself for very many days on end. When his advisers warned him that the constant chivying made him look small, he waved them off. He had discussed the subject with Bob Strauss, the Democratic power lawyer, he said; the two men were chums in Washington and poolside buddies in Florida, a friendship that transcended party in Dole's mind, and Strauss thought his daily Bushwhacking was just great. He ought to do more and more of it, Strauss had told him, and that was exactly what Dole intended to do.

He did do more, and the results showed in his numbers. His name recognition rose, but so, for the first time, did his negative ratings in the polls, from next to nothing to a worrisome level in the space of two or three months. Dole was becoming his stereotype, a composite of his barbed-wire jokes and his dead-serious flashes of anger. The senator was shooting at George Bush and wounding himself.

The Disorganization Man

They called it the Great Dole Bumper Sticker Commission, and for its short, unhappy life in 1987 it revealed the chaos in the house that Bob built—a disorder radiating outward from him to the farthest reaches of his campaign. Dole's managers of the moment had decided that what he really needed was bumper stickers, something in smarter hues than the clichéd red, white and blue. Two media consultants, Alex Castellanos and Mike Murphy, spent the next two months churning out mockups—enough, Castellanos guessed afterward, to plaster every Republican bumper in America with its own one-of-a-kind variation on the basic theme. Each new design and color scheme was handed up the line to the senator. Each came bouncing back down to its creators with vaguely framed directions to try again.

The reasons for Dole's unhappiness were never made plain, until Castellanos, hip deep in dummy stickers and rejection slips, began asking questions. Dole, he discovered, had received each new mockup with grunts, shrugs and noncommittal comments. His people simply assumed, from long and fearful exposure to his humors, that he was displeased and wanted something better. In fact he didn't much care then or later, when, after months of scholastic debate, his people finally settled on stickers in yellow and blue. The senator, had anyone had the nerve to ask, was partly color blind.

That the question reached his desk at all was a measure both of his own compulsion to meddle in the minutiae of his campaign and of the sometimes paralytic terror he inspired among his hired help. He had come a long way from his spiky early days in the Senate, when a colleague did cloakroom jokes about how Dole couldn't peddle ass on a troopship; in his late middle age, he was no longer famous solely or even mainly for his ungovernable angers or his acid tongue. But he was still known in his Capitol office as the Ayadolah, both for his intrusive involvement in detail and for his carelessness of the feelings of the men and women in his employ. He was, some of them thought, carrying the campaign with his personal appeal and destroying it with his private conduct. At least one of them, a senior hand at headquarters, concluded long before the issue was settled that Dole should never be president.

Dole conceded that he would have to watch himself once in office—that he would probably be tempted to get involved in more things than a president ought to. In the campaign, temptation usually won. He was bad at delegating, and though he regularly protested that he was getting better, he knew it was a problem. His success had always seemed perishable to him, as if Bob Dole of Russell were living in the middle of a mirage; he was afraid to entrust it to anyone's hands but his own.

The result was that, as Wirthlin put it, he was forever getting into the thick of thin things. There was, for one flagrant example, the time he discovered that a staff man had bought a $2,000 billboard in Houston, in hopes that Bush would see it on a visit home and get mad. The amount was petty cash in a badly overspent campaign, but the senator was angry, and the billboard became an issue at the highest levels of his management. He constantly second-guessed his handlers, sometimes brutally and in public, and when his disappointment in them became terminal he didn't fire them—he dealt directly with their subordinates or brought in new layers of management over their heads. Lines of authority blurred, since no one finally had any except Dole. Factions formed, each with access to the senator, none with his full confidence. Third-rank staffers did campaign business without notice to their bosses. "Senator Dole told me to go to South Dakota," they would explain when asked, or "Senator Dole told me to send those mailings to Kings County."

Dole's hand was heaviest on matters of scheduling, with chaotic results. The demands of the Senate made advance bookings difficult, and even when they were laid on, Dole kept vetoing them on short notice; he trusted the seat of his pants more than all the battle maps and computer models at his headquarters. On a successful three-day fly-around in Texas in the summer of 1987, he abruptly scrubbed a last stop in Austin for a news conference.

But it's the state capital, his people said. It's where the political reporters are.

Dole fetched up a Texas map. "We've done Houston, we've done Dallas," he said, "but we haven't done anything over here." He was pointing at Midland, Bush's old town, in the western reaches of the state. The date in Austin was canceled, the plane was diverted to Midland, and Dole played a lonely airport scene to three or four surprised local cameramen.

It was probably fated that so chronic a delinquent would come to grief in so complex an enterprise as running for president. His idea of an organization, David Keene guessed, was himself and then everyone else; the term "Dole organization" was, in fact, an oxymoron, and the cost to the enterprise was visible from its very earliest days. Bob Ellsworth, an old chum on the Hill in the 1950s, had been around at the beginning, and so had Devine and Keene, two Beltway pros with combat seasoning and inside moves. What was missing was a big-picture strategist. Dole's choice for the role, and Ellsworth's, was John Sears, a veteran of the Nixon and Reagan campaigns, but the match was never consummated; there were too many nay-sayers on L Street, and Dole, who loathed personnel squabbles, would not knock the necessary heads to make the appointment happen.

By then, most of the other name Washington professionals were committed elsewhere, and Ellsworth found himself in charge of the campaign. It could fairly be said that Dole had thus got the kind of management he had always wanted: the kind he could rule or overrule on his own unpredictable whim. Ellsworth had never coveted the job and brought no obvious credentials to it, beyond his intelligence and his thirty-year friendship with the senator. His deliberate working habits were formed in government, not politics; he was, and was seen on L Street as, an office temporary warming the chair until someone more clearly suitable could be found. He was a friend occupying a space where Dole needed a peer—someone who, when he shouted, had the standing, the experience and the nerve to shout back.

The net result was something like the ''Before'' chapter in a time-motion study; decisions that needed thought were made in seconds on Dole's fancy, while questions that required speedy attention moldered for months awaiting answers from Ellsworth and his overburdened deputy, Bill Lacy. By midautumn, when help finally came, the operation looked to one senior adviser like an overgrown Senate campaign, all busyness with no apparent purpose and no movement in the polls.

One of the newcomers, Wirthlin, was asked to take a quick look around and do a report on what needed to be done. His thirty-page appraisal concluded as diplomatically as possible that the campaign needed work in nearly every sector, from its lack of a theme to its faulty strategic assumptions to the simplest ABC's of scheduling the candidate and handling the national press. His private view was less guarded. The enterprise, he thought, was in as sorry a state as you could possibly imagine short of actually sinking; it was amazing that the senator was even in the race.

The Bickersons

The man recruited to keep him in it was William E. Brock, the sometime senator from Tennessee, and an implicit part of his brief was to save Dole from himself. Brock too was new to the business of running a presidential campaign, and he brought a Southern-gentlemanly gait to the job, a fondness for short Fridays and long weekends boating or tending his roses. But he was, or seemed to be, the missing peer in Dole's circle. He had come to town as a shy young congressman in 1963 and had enjoyed a long, honored run ever since in politics and government, most recently as Reagan's secretary of labor. A tour as Republican national chairman in the seventies had been a particular triumph of modernization; it was sometimes said that Brock had reinvented the political party as a high-tech fund-raising and people-moving machine.

His Washington résumé was thus nearly a match for George Bush's, and so were his ambitions: he sometimes fancied himself as secretary of state, friends said, or even president. He had the stature, or so Dole's people believed, to look the senator in the eye and tell him he was wrong. "Bill *Brock?*" Dole himself had exclaimed when his chief scheduler, Judy Harbaugh, first mentioned the name. He laughed, as if he found it hard believing that so grand a figure would want to work for him.

Brock's own circle was at least equally surprised. He and Dole had never been close and were not at all alike; his friends simply assumed that George Bush was more Bill's sort. But Bush had been a disappointment to Brock in their years in Reagan's service. George was easy enough to talk to, he told associates, but there was no substance in it; you couldn't interest him in serious issues like trade or competitiveness, questions Brock felt belonged on the national agenda. The last straw had been the Iran-Contra affair. Brock had watched the congressional hearings from a hospital bed, recuperating from repairs to two detached retinas, and was horrified at how so misbegotten a series of decisions had got made. When he was up and around, he asked Lee Atwater why Bush hadn't pounded the damn table in protest at the time. I don't think there's an answer, Atwater told him, and Brock went shopping for another candidate.

Friends worried for him when he signed on with Dole. Their common response was that the match was crazy; the hour was too late, Bush had it won, Dole was a people-eater, and Brock could only get hurt. But need drew the two men together. Brock was looking for an engine to hook his own ambitions to, and Dole wanted someone with size, skill and a full Rolodex to bring some plausibility to his raggedy campaign. Brock's marquee name and his Southern accent made him irresistible.

Dole accordingly was on his best behavior during their mating dance, a series of four meetings in late summer and early fall. His sales pitch, in fact, was more nearly a cry for help. He had a campaign full of dedicated people, he told Brock, but they were young and inexperienced, and everything was sputtering as a result. No one was making the judgment calls. They weren't getting it done in the South; the support was there, Dole felt, but it wasn't coming together. The scheduling was incomprehensible, at least to him.

"I don't know why they send me to one place as opposed to another," he said. "There doesn't seem to be any logic to it or any pattern. I have to make a lot of those decisions myself. I shouldn't. I don't want to, and," he told Brock, "that's what I need from you."

There were, Brock saw in hindsight, warning signals that Dole was not wholly reformed. "I'm not going to just say, 'OK, call me, wake me when it's over,' " he said; he liked to know what was going on in his business, and he wasn't about to delegate everything. But he seemed really to mean it when he said that he couldn't be candidate, speechmaker and minority leader all at once and still run the campaign.

It didn't take either man long to see that their partnership was built on illusion. Dole was not the penitent sinner Brock had seen in him, and Brock was not the hands-on, combat-ready player Dole thought he had hired; he saw himself floating above the fray instead, as a high-concept senior adviser. The tip-off came when, early in his tenure, Brock proposed convening a bipartisan forum of several hundred leading thinkers to blueprint the first 180 days of a Dole administration and to ponder the needs of the nation in the year 2000. A reminder from a colleague that there was still an election to be won seemed not to trouble him. If they lost, Brock replied, they could always give the study to George Bush.

The tonic effect of his arrival was short-lived, both for his client and for the organization he had inherited; he appeared to the holdovers to be breaking eggs without knowing how to make an omelet. His early hires came in well above market prices, at an average annualized rate of $60,000. They were known in Dole's Senate office as the High Rollers for the roundness of the numbers on their paychecks and the loftiness of the offices in which Brock installed them, two floors above the old campaign executive suite on L Street.

"We're spending too much money," Dole complained as the overhead mounted.

You *have* to, Brock replied; it was better to hire one person at $100,000 a year than ten at $10,000 each, because they already had the ten and the campaign was an unmitigated disaster.

But the ballooning payroll at headquarters ate up the campaign's cash reserves for mail and media, and the advent of the High Rollers made the old crowd feel unwanted. Their suspicions seemed to them confirmed with the arrival of Norman (Skip) Watts as political director at $10,500 a month plus a rent-free condo in the Virginia suburbs and air fare home to his family and his law practice in Woodstock, Vermont, every weekend. His qualifications for the job were not plain even to the candidate he was to serve: he had been out of big-time national politics since 1976, and some fieldwork he had undertaken for the Dole campaign in New England had not gone well. He fucked up Vermont and Maine, Dole said in his cutting way; we might as well put him in charge of the country. But Watts came aboard anyway, displaying his disdain for the old guard like a battle flag; it was his belief, thinly veiled, that Brock should have begun by firing them all.

When tales leaked that some of them *would* be fired, Keene, as one of the prime targets, marched on Dole's Senate office to protest. "For Christ's sake," he said, "can't you see what these guys are doing? They're coming on, and what they're telling you is that everything's fucked up. If you win, it's because they straightened it out, and if you lose, it's because the other guys fucked it up."

Dole heard out the harangue, but did nothing; there was, as Keene recognized, not much he *could* do. For one thing, the Brock-Watts-Wirthlin critique could not be lightly dismissed. The old leadership *had* been soft; nothing had been getting done. A third of the money allowed by law for the entire primary season was gone by the time Brock's team arrived, and it took a three-week review of the books to figure out what it had bought. The answer was not much—so little, indeed, that someone raised the possibility of embezzlement. Skip Watts laughed. The old guard, he said, wasn't smart enough to steal.

Brock's further life insurance was the lateness of the hour and the desperation of the cause. But he was too genteel and Dole too driven to make the match work very long; the Odd Couple metamorphosed into the Bickersons practically overnight. There was friction early on when Brock refused to mix it up with Lee Atwater on TV, viewing it as beneath his station; there was, he said huffily, no sense getting into a pissing contest with a skunk.

"If Brock won't do it, I will," Dole grumbled.

His image doctors winced. They had hoped that Brock would do the hatchet work for him, but Brock seemed not to want to get his hair mussed; his enemies on L Street guessed that he was trying to save a place at Bush's table with his mannerliness, just in case.

There were further sparks over Brock's attendance record. He was technically a volunteer, a two-day-a-week part-timer overseeing the paid professional staff. But a presidential campaign had become a total-immersion pursuit in the 1980s, and the senator was not amused by Brock's habit of disappearing from his desk, for a private business trip to Japan, say, or a Christmas holiday in the islands. Dole was a dawn-to-midnight workaholic; his idea of R&R, a colleague said, was an hour's sunning on a Capitol balcony. "I hope we don't hear any more about Caribbean vacations," he groused aloud. The message didn't get through, and Brock's truancies continued.

So did Dole's micromanaging, and Brock was forced to spend too much of his limited capital too soon trying to stop it. "If you want to win this thing," he scolded when Dole tried to cancel out of an appearance at the Republican Governors' Conference, "you're going to have to do it right." Brock won that one, at a price; you always paid for your victories, an older Dole hand said, and the cost was almost always the same—more second-guessing, more back-channeling, more countermanded orders, more random dialing from the candidate to subordinates two and three tiers down the line.

The senator finally crossed Brock's threshold of tolerance in January, during a bad patch in the campaign. Bush's lead was still where it had been two months earlier, a new strategy paper from Wirthlin reported, and Dole's mood was as bleak as his numbers. His wife, Elizabeth Hanford Dole, had quit her job as Reagan's secretary of transportation to campaign for him; they were coursing the landscape like two unguided missiles, a staffer said, running everyone ragged with their wearying pace, their sudden changes in scheduling and their stubborn resistance to advice. Brock had warned Dole once about the dangers of fatigue, to which the senator had dryly replied that there would be time enough for rest if they lost. The formula, he said, had always worked for him in the past.

The bill finally came due the day he arrived in Vermont, road-worn and sullen, for a breakfast with some key supporters and found himself addressing a half-empty room. He had been typically late agreeing to the date, leaving his people just two days to put it together, and an ice storm had depressed attendance still more. But Dole went on a radio show afterward and blamed his volunteer Vermont ground troops for having let him down.

Brock was furious. "You've got to think about what you say, think about the effect it has on people," he lectured Dole. "Understand that you're really tired. Understand that there are people who are breaking their hearts for you, doing everything they know how to do. They're going to make mistakes, I'm going to make mistakes, and the candidate is going to make mistakes, and we all have to live with that."

Dole seemed chastened by the dressing-down, enough, for a time, to modify his behavior. But the respite didn't last. Both Doles kept pushing themselves and their schedulers too hard, trying to crowd in more events than they could effectively do, and it no longer mattered what Brock said to dissuade them; it was tough, as Skip Watts had put it during an earlier siege, to tell which senator was running things.

So they lumbered on toward Iowa as they were, a top-heavy dinosaur of a campaign, with Dole's candidacy riding on the results of the caucuses there. They had to win New Hampshire too, Wirthlin argued in his strategy book, and ride the wave south on Super Tuesday; if they lost badly there, it would be over. It all sounded doable on paper, in Wirthlin's determinedly hopeful prose, but it wasn't. They didn't have the resources, on the ground or in the bank, and it was too late to put them in place.

Skip Watts knew it. From his office at headquarters, he had looked down the same road past Iowa through the prism of his estrangement and seen only impending doom. New Hampshire was impossible, the South was about as seaworthy a vessel for Dole's hopes as the *Titanic,* and what passed for morale was shot: it had gone the way of the misspent money and the phantom field staff.

The first votes had yet to be cast when, late in January, Watts chatted with his wife, Jill, in his office. "Easter in Vermont," he promised her. Bob Dole might think he was going to be president, but he was finished, and Watts was sorry he had ever left home.

Running for
President of Iowa

IT WAS ONLY A BEAUTY CONTEST in the provinces, five months before the first
real voter was to cast the first binding vote for the Republican nomination
for president. But foreplay can be, or seem, as important in modern media
politics as in love, and the suspense was getting to Lee Atwater, gnawing
at his innards and pebbling his palms with sweat. Atwater had spent three
years designing a strategy of inevitability around George Bush and had
come out to Ames, Iowa, to witness its launch in a straw poll at a party
fund-raiser. What he saw instead, gazing down from his perch just under
the rafters at the state university field house, was a Pat Robertson camp
meeting—a noisy assembly of Christian soldiers with Styrofoam hats and
stickers that read I WAS THERE WHEN ROBERTSON WON.

A brass band was playing the theme from *Rocky* when Atwater turned
to his deputy campaign manager, Rich Bond, sitting beside him. There was
murder in his eyes and a sharp edge to his Carolina drawl. Bond had made
his reputation in Iowa, micromanaging it for Bush in the 1980 party
caucuses and stealing away with a victory over Ronald Reagan. Iowa was
why Atwater had wanted Bond in the first place. Bond was supposed to *own*
the place, and now this—Pat Robertson starring in *Rocky V.*

"God, where are our people?" Atwater groaned.

Bond scanned the bleachers. There were pockets of Bush loyalists around, but they were like the last holdout garrisons in a conquered country, overrun and irrelevant.

"We're dead," Bond said. He thought Lee might strangle him.

Atwater's angst, as it happened, was turned inward. Bush's run for president was the first Atwater had managed himself, a token that, at thirty-six, he had arrived at the top of the political consulting business. He meant to stay there. He was a taut, wiry young man, an assemblage of exposed nerves and bony angles in constant jangly motion toward the next straw poll, the next primary, the next victory to add to his twenty-eight-and-four lifetime won-and-lost record. Atwater *liked* those numbers, quoting them frequently; he had made it in politics because he couldn't stand losing and so rarely did. Ideology meant little to him, beyond a filial respect for the conservatism of his Southern boyhood, and governing did not interest him at all. The game was everything to Atwater, and losing made him physically ill. There were only two places at the end of a campaign, he liked to say: first and other. It was accepted among his competitors and even his friends that Lee would do anything—*anything*—to be first.

His drive to win was reinforced among his comrades in the campaign by the suspicion that Bush could not afford to lose—that he might be, just as his rivals said, a hemophiliac who would bleed to death if you nicked him. Bush's claim to the presidency rested heavily on the principle of primogeniture, the right of the crown prince to succeed the king, and on his loyalty—*blind* loyalty, he once said—to Ronald Reagan. But Bush hadn't been elected anything on his own since winning a second term in Congress twenty years before, in a safe Republican enclave in Houston. He had tried twice for senator and once for president, failing each time, and his electability remained an open and nagging question.

He could prove it only by winning, as early and as often as possible; inexorability was central to the playbook Bush's men had written for him, and anything that detracted from the appearance of success, even a rinky-dink straw poll in Ames, was enough to tie a knot in Lee Atwater's gut. Atwater would insist long afterward that he had *never* liked the smell of Iowa; he had hung out there for four days in March 1987, talking to people, and had come home thinking it would be infertile ground for Bush. In fact he was putting heavy emphasis on winning the state—*unbelievably* heavy, he said that summer—and Ames in September had seemed a tempting setting for an ambush. A similar straw poll there had started Bush toward his upset victory in the caucuses in 1980. The remnants of the Bush

Brigade, the homegrown organization that had led the charge then, were sure that it could be done again, and Atwater had let himself be persuaded that they were right.

Down to the eve of the Presidential Cavalcade of Stars, as its sponsors grandly called it, the house seemed, in fact, to be well papered with Bush votes. Twenty-eight hundred tickets had been sold by then, at twenty-five dollars each, and the vice president's handlers were sure they could turn out nine hundred people—enough, they reckoned, to win. As it turned out, they had miscalculated. The day of the cavalcade, the Dole and Robertson campaigns loosed a last-minute rush on the ticket office, buying up nearly two thousand more seats between them. By starting time, the crowd had swelled to six thousand, four times the turnout in 1980. What had begun as a sideshow had taken on the scale, the decibel level and the rowdy unpredictability of a runaway party convention.

It was the first game of the 1987 pre-season, and the first time Bush had deigned to share a platform and a microphone with his rivals. All of them came except Al Haig, and from their perch beneath the rafters Atwater and Bond watched with rising anxiety as the candidates took their turns downstage. It wasn't Bush's own pale performance that disturbed his men. It was instead the sheer foot-stomping, hand-clapping, praise-the-Lordly intensity of the Robertson crowd rocking the field house with their fervor.

Bush's men had glimpsed them before, in the summer of 1986, when Robertson had ambushed *them* in a first round of precinct caucuses in Michigan. The campaign had had to go to court to win what they had lost in the field, and Atwater had resolved that it wouldn't happen again, certainly not in Iowa; his early guess was that at caucus time, Robertson would taken an eight- or ten-point bite out of everybody's ass *except* Bush's.

But Ames was a déjà vu for Atwater, a scary reaffirmation that the invisible army was real—real enough, anyway, to stack a meeting or swamp a precinct caucus. Robertson people wept if they had forgotten to bring IDs and fell to their knees in prayer for sinners who strayed to Bush. The vice president's passionless candidacy couldn't match that. More than two hundred of his people went home without troubling to vote; the hour was late, the lines were long, and Robertson by then looked unbeatable.

Their votes might at least have helped bring Bush in a merely embarrassing second instead of a humiliating third. The vice president and his party didn't stay to find out. They were on Air Force Two, headed home for Washington, when the count reached them: 1,293 for Robertson, 958 for Dole, and a dispiriting 846 for Bush.

Rich Bond sat brooding in the back of the plane for a time, wondering whether he had a future at Bush Inc. He had always preached that if you did the little things well—if you got out all the mailings, and wired up all the phone banks, and hung your literature on all the doorknobs—the big things would naturally follow. But the people on the ground in Iowa, under his mostly absentee landlordship, had lost their competitive edge since the brief glory days of 1980. The little things hadn't got done, the boss had been embarrassed, and Bond was in the bull's-eye, feeling very alone.

The Bush connection was vital to him, or so he had given his friends to understand; his livelihood as a political consultant depended on his surviving and making his mark. Rich, one intimate said, had fallen victim to a common occupational disease in the 1980 campaign: he thought he was a peer in his candidate's eyes instead of merely a tradesman selling his services. He had followed the vice president into the White House and, in this account, had wound up on his ass the first time a *real* peer forced Bush to choose sides; if his pals in the industry hadn't found a place for him at the Republican National Committee, he might have been back in New York doing state-assembly races. His personal goal in 1988, his friend said, was more realistic—to be *seen* as an insider, even if he wasn't one, and to trade thereafter on the perception.

He had first to make peace with Lee Atwater, his sometimes bitter competitor in the business of politics. They had made the alliance work mostly because they needed each other; it had evolved from an armed truce to a viable office relationship. But Ames could put them back at square one, Bond thought. The word in the industry was that Atwater accepted blame about as happily as he took defeat; there was always someone else between Lee and disaster. Lee was in the forward cabin with the Bushes on the flight home from Iowa. He could be saying *anything* to the old man.

After a time, Bond steeled himself and walked up front. Bush was there, with his wife, Barbara, and their son Marvin. Atwater was still with them. Their mood was subdued. Bush, gallant as usual, tried to be nice about the pratfall; it wasn't, after all, the end of the world.

"Mr. Vice President," Bond said, "I really feel I let you down, and I take full responsibility for what happened."

"I'm the campaign manager," Atwater interrupted. "*I'll* take full responsibility for it, and," he went on, glancing at the Bushes, "I've told them that already."

Bond's relief was short-lived; whoever took the blame, he was going to have to clean up the mess, and the prospect was not a welcome one. Iowa was history for him, his long-ago apprenticeship for the big show back

East. He had a wife and two kids, and a home going up on Shelter Island, and he had not reckoned on another winter at the Hotel Fort Des Moines.

But it was made luminously plain to him that that was where he was going to be. The word, as sometimes happened, came not from the vice president or his campaign manager but from Barbara Bush; she was her husband's partner in politics, tougher and less forgiving, some thought, than he was, and her wish was presumed by the hired help to be his command.

"So, Rich," she said, smiling sweetly, "when are you going back to Iowa to manage the vice president's campaign?"

"Immediately," he said, smiling manfully back.

"Good," Mrs. Bush told him. "That's what George and I want."

The Imperial Vice President

Three days later, Bond found himself back in Des Moines with his bag, his rental car and his thankless commission: saving the state for Barbara Bush's husband. It was going to be hard. The vice president tried clumsily to joke away his defeat in Ames, guessing, to the horror of his staff, that his supporters had been off playing golf or attending their daughters' debutante parties. Bond's private estimate was less cheerful. He was a political bricklayer, a meticulously detailed organization man, and a quick look around told him that the Iowa campaign needed reconstructing from the ground up.

He had spent his first forty-eight hours on the road, putting seven hundred miles on his odometer and several fresh worry lines on his still boyish brow. What he heard in his one-man canvass was mostly bad news. The state operation he had inherited was in disrepair, the result of slack supervision from headquarters and low morale on the ground; it struck him that half the people he talked to were discouraged and the other half merely mad. The campaign had counted on the survivors of the old Bush Brigade of 1980 as a dependable base, but they weren't insurgents anymore; they had become the establishment and had taken on the slightly flabby look of a fraternity reunion ten years on. It was like fighting a second guerrilla war, one of Bond's line officers said, or courting your wife a second time—the old fire just wasn't there.

Neither was the George Bush who lit it, the '80 model road-runner prepared to shake any hand, buss any cheek, dandle any baby and cosset any town councilman in his frenetic path. Time and incumbency had changed him; to Bond's dismay, he had become the imperial vice president, sealed inside his cocoon of staff men and bodyguards. In the process, he had let Bob Dole make off with his old playbook, right down to Bond's petitpoint management style. The buzz around the political community was that Dole's man in Iowa, some homegrown farmboy named Tom Synhorst, was the Rich Bond of 1988, and Bond didn't like it. He was polite enough when they met one evening on the skywalk in downtown Des Moines, but as he moved on he told a companion, loudly enough for Synhorst to overhear, "I'll take care of that little shithead."

He had first to deal with the vice president's own men, the praetorian guard separating him from the people. Iowans were spoiled by their prominence on the political calendar, and while Bush sailed by them in his motorcade, Dole was catering to them; some people were telling Sally Novetzke, a former state chairman and a prime Bush supporter, that they had met the senator four or five times. It was Dole who was getting out to the farm country, she had warned long before Bond's arrival; it was Dole who was making his calls to county chairmen, volunteering his box-office name and presence for ribbon-cuttings and bean feeds. But whenever she had raised the alarm, the old crowd had laughed her off. Dole, they assured her, wasn't going anywhere; he had tried in '80 and hadn't even registered in the polls.

Bond, knowing the territory, didn't need persuading. One of his first prescriptions was that Bush spend more time visiting the state and less in his limousine when he got there. He was a blunt and demanding man, and he found himself frequently at sword's point with the agents of the imperium—the Secret Service men who secured Bush's person and the vice-presidential staffers who looked after his dignity. They were too much into their travel manuals for Bond's down-to-earth taste, and too little concerned with the needs of the campaign. There were days, Bond thought, when their main worry appeared to be lining up enough yards of blue draping to assure the candidate a suitably vice-presidential setting.

The regal manner of the campaign served only to remind Iowa that Bush was the vice president, and Ronald Reagan's vice president at that. Reagan's popularity had been dragged down by the state's laggardly economy, and it was no longer thought wise by survivalist Republicans to advertise oneself as his obedient servant; the statewide winners in 1986 had in fact distanced themselves from him. The case for letting some daylight show was forcefully put to Bush in the early fall at a private meeting with forty-five key supporters at a Holiday Inn in West Des Moines. Their main advice to him was to get out of the president's shadow and carve out some space of his own.

Bush listened attentively. He promised the group that he would run an underdog campaign from that day forward, scrambling as if it were 1980 and he were an asterisk again. But he wasn't going to start criticizing the president, not now; no way.

He had thus made himself Reagan's hostage, for better or for worse, and his men knew that the process they called "separation" could not be rushed. So Bond settled for the next best thing: disengaging Bush from the vice-presidency. They were behind in Iowa, he thought, and they had to run that way; they had to put on a lean, mean, third-and-long campaign. Under his sandpapery nagging, the Secret Service finally lightened up a little, and Craig Fuller's vice-presidential staff made room in Bush's schedule for more Iowa time; by the end, he would have spent seven more days in-state than he had in 1980, when running for president had been the only job he had.

For a brief season, he even got out of his armored Lincoln and into the late-autumn sunshine, where he could at least fleetingly be seen, touched and videotaped. He chatted with truckers. He shot baskets. He did radio call-in shows. He jogged with the boys' and girls' track teams at a high school, announcing, with a grimace, that it was fun. He did a series of "Ask George Bush" forums in school gyms and church halls—"kind of a Phil Donahue kind of thing," he said at one stop. "Hopefully a little cleaner act." The questions were mainly slow-pitch softballs—what, for example, he thought were the most important parts of being president—and the answers as a result were whatever he felt like talking about. The clips played well on TV, and if they didn't precisely recall the touchy-feely campaign of 1980, they at least affirmed that Bush was alive and well inside the airless confines of his office.

The trouble was that none of it seemed to help, not the refurbished road show, nor the improved performances in debate, nor even the tableau of Saint George slaying Dan Rather on network TV. All they were doing, one of Bond's men reckoned, was firing up people who were already fired up; his poll charts looked mostly like the flat-line electrocardiogram of a failing heart patient. Morale ebbed with his ratings, and people in the campaign were beginning to say that maybe Bush was the problem—that he would never carry Iowa unless he let go of Reagan's coattails.

But Bush held stubbornly to his Ron-and-me line, and when it didn't click he seemed at a loss for anything else to do. The tour drifted on, one character in search of a script, and Rich Bond found himself forced back to basics. The way to do Iowa, in his formulation, was organize, organize, organize, and then get hot at the end. He couldn't guarantee the big finish, but he could keep laying his bricks, one by one, so that everything would be in place if it happened.

The lights burned late in his ground-floor office in Des Moines most nights, revealing Bond alone at his desk like a figure in a lonely Edward Hopper townscape. He kept the blinds open, his advertisement to passersby on Grand Avenue that the campaign was still in business. Some of the old Bush Brigadistas—the wine-and-cheese crowd, others in the party called them—were eased gently aside. New faces appeared, and the little things Bond wanted done got done. Doors were knocked. Phone calls were made, thousands of them, from a warren of cubicles partitioned with sheets of Styrofoam. Mailings went out, among them, at the end, a sophisticated "caucus kit" with a letter from Bush, a set of instructions on where and how to vote, and a computer list of neighbors who might be peer-pressured into going along.

It all had the look of 1980, but it wasn't working, and Bond knew it. The engine he had constructed wouldn't run without fuel: some reason for Iowans to choose Reagan's surrogate when they had fallen out of love with the real article. The rationale wasn't there, and what passed for a strategy in the waning days came down to needling Bob Dole, trying to bring out the Mr. Hyde who was said to be slumbering fitfully in his bosom. In this, the campaign was a great deal less squeamish than the vice president. They were going down the tubes, a headquarters operative in Washington conceded, and the whole gestalt of the campaign became Let's Get Dole to Blow Up.

The men from Bush Inc. tracked the senator through the final week, monitoring his moods and his fatigue level until, five days before the caucuses, they had reached what looked like critical mass. At that point, a broadside issued forth over the name of Bush's state chairman, George Wittgraf, with the plain purpose of driving Dole wild. It said, in a sledge-hammer language, that the senator was mean-minded, crony-ridden and rich—and added that, while nothing illegal had been found so far, his wife's finances were under Federal scrutiny.

The statement turned out to be a casebook example of the folly of spitting into the wind; it did stir up Dole's furies, but his anger looked righteous for a change, and it was the Bush campaign that came off as mean. Dole's man Kim Wells could barely believe his eyes or the senator's good fortune when the fax machine just beyond his door coughed up a copy of the statement. Wells, a lawyer of thirty-eight with a straight-ahead mind and a symbiotic kinship with Dole, was the resident agnostic among the wizards and alchemists who people a modern campaign; he believed that informal judgment and common sense are surer guides to politics than all their formulas, numbers and spells, and what his common sense told him was that the Bushies must be in trouble. We've got to be ten points up, or they wouldn't be doing this, he told the others. Atwater might be mean, but he wasn't dumb. They were behind, way behind, and they were trying as a desperate last resort to pull Bob Dole's trigger.

The scary second reaction, for Wells and everyone else in Dole's service, was that it might work. The statement caught up with the senator's entourage at a high school in Latimer, Iowa, where he was booked for a speech on education. A press conference followed, always a dangerous setting for Dole in one of his distempers, and his people crowded him into a broom closet—the only private space available—to try to moderate his response.

"You're sorrowful, not angry," his press secretary, Mari Maseng, told him, almost imploringly. It would play better if he just expressed his hurt at the insult to his wife and left it at that.

If her advice registered, it didn't show in Dole's performance. "Either George Bush is responsible for this kind of campaign," he told the press, waving a copy of the offending document, "or he is totally out of control. . . . I want George Bush to hold this in his little hand and say, 'I stand by every word.' "

Bush didn't bite, and the senator was still smoldering the next morning. He sat in the back of the Dolemobile, the campaign nickname for the camper he used on short hauls, plotting his revenge on the way up Route 9 from Osage to the airport at Mason City and the jet waiting to fly him home. His mood didn't require mind reading; his people could clock the rise in his bile level by the drumbeat of his fingers on the table. By the time he reached his office on the Hill, his plan was set, and he couldn't be talked out of it. He had always wanted a piece of Bush, one on one; if you flushed him out of the shelter of his office and his life of privilege, you could show him up for what he really was—weak, indecisive and uninformed.

Dole tested his theory that day in the most public arena available to him: the floor of the United States Senate. Bush was in his place as presiding officer when Dole came churning toward him, waving Wittgraf's statement under his nose.

"Did George Bush authorize this?" Dole demanded. "This is mean, mean stuff. We're running for president here."

"You were picking on me," Bush said. His face was pale as vellum, a mask of disbelief. His eyes flickered from Dole's to the middle benches and back.

"Did you authorize it?" Dole pressed.

Bush said he had done so, but without having read it first.

"Here, read it," Dole said, poking the release at him and walking away.

The vice president's handlers were no happier with the scene than the senator's. Their timing had been bad, a week too late to hurt, in the Dole camp's estimate, and their pitch was worse; the sheer stridency of their attack had succeeded mainly in making Dole the aggrieved party and Bush, through his Iowa proxies, the mudslinger. The campaign had fallen victim to an attack of collective stupidity, a senior hand at headquarters reflected after the fact, and this time nobody wanted to admit having been in the loop. The corridors at Bush Inc. echoed with the sound of footfalls scuttling backward. Suspicion attached to Lee Atwater as naturally as iron filings to a magnet; his vice in a campaign had always been a tendency to overkill. But the wagons circled around him and the vice president, and Wittgraf, a small-town lawyer of normally mild speech and manner, was put out on an ice floe to take the blame alone.

It wasn't quite the hot finish Rich Bond had had in mind. The lights still blazed late in his office on Grand Avenue, but he remained a bricklayer without an architect, someone with a vision of what the pieces, once in place, were supposed to convey. By the end, he seemed homesick for his family back East and perilously close to burnout in a lost cause. They were going down the tubes in Iowa, and Lee's people in Washington had to start planning against it, preparing a comeback in New Hampshire and the South.

Beginning three weeks before the caucuses, Bond had been on the phone regularly to the headquarters crowd, steeling them for the inevitable. They might still run Pat Robertson a good race for second, he believed nearly to the end, but they were going to lose Iowa, and it was going to be bad. Bush was going to have to win the nomination somewhere else.

Hunting George Bush

Tom Synhorst woke up at four o'clock the morning of February 8, too wired to go back to sleep and too early for racquetball and steam at the Y. So he started the biggest day of his young life in politics doing the only thing there was to do: he scrubbed the bathtub in his apartment in Des Moines. When he finally got to the morning *Register* over coffee, the page-one headline advised him IT'S CAUCUS DAY IN IOWA, but that was hardly news. He had come reluctantly back from Washington late in 1986, at the personal request of

Bob Dole and his own boss, Senator Charles E. Grassley, a farm-grown Iowan like himself. He was Dole's man in Iowa, and the caucuses had been the central fact of his life eighty hours a week for more than a year.

He had thus become a player in the midwinter madness that descended on his home state every four years—a plague of candidates in breathless pursuit of voters, visuals, bites on the news, bumps in the polls and something called momentum to wave at the unfortunates living in next states in their path. The actual results of the caucuses were much overrated, as Gary Hart, say, or George Bush could attest from recent experience. The prize for winning, or doing Better Than Expected, came to not much more than a few days' bragging rights in the media and enough chips to keep a candidate in play for another hand. Those candidates who *had* successfully made Iowa a springboard to nomination had been few in number, Democratic in persuasion and—except for Jimmy Carter, once—losers in November.

But candidates in both parties built whole strategies on pleasing the voters there and in New Hampshire, simply because they cast their ballots before anyone else. It was three-card-monte politics, a game of illusion played for high stakes on small tables. Two marginal states had set themselves up as the testing grounds for presidents and had made the players believe it; their joint 3 percent of the population, by Wirthlin's arithmetic, got 32 percent of the major-media coverage in the 1984 nominating season. Everyone in the political industry, candidates and correspondents, knew it was crazy, and yet practically everyone came. Attention was as aphrodisiac to office-seekers as green baize to a gambler, and not many were brave or foolish enough to say no to its allure.

For Bob Dole, more than most, Iowa was life or death, and Synhorst had as much volition in the matter as a soldier in the Light Brigade. His orders, simply put, were, Win or else, and as he started up Locust Street toward his office at seven o'clock, he brooded one last time on his checklist of worries. How good were his own troops—kids, for the most part, spirited but untested in battle? How big was Pat Robertson's invisible army? What was Rich Bond up to? Synhorst *was* the Rich Bond of 1988, a hungry and combative whiz kid looking to make a name for himself by putting on a picture-perfect campaign, and the rivalry between the two, challenger and champ, had got personal and bitter. It would be real sweet to win, Synhorst thought, and shove it down Bond's throat.

He was blessed with the better merchandise, at least for the Iowa market. Dole came from nearby Kansas, not Kennebunkport, and was unencumbered by Bush's air of majesty or his association with Ronald Reagan. The

Bush crowd seemed to Synhorst as out of place in rural Iowa as visitors from Mars; he himself had fled the farm for the city as soon as he got old enough, but when he slipped into a Bush rally unnoticed and heard an imported country singer warming up the crowd with a string of barnyard jokes, he felt patronized and angry. Dole, by contrast, belonged. When he told a crowd of farmers or factory workers that he was one of them, or spoke about his own beginnings in an outback farm town, he had a credibility for Iowans that all Bush's court magicians couldn't conjure or buy.

Dole was, moreover, a workhorse campaigner, on those days, at least, when you could pry him loose from the Senate and put him on the road. Synhorst had developed his own technique for dealing with Dole's hot-and-cold-running humors, which was to stand forcefully up to him; if you showed him a glimmer of doubt or weakness, he'd be on you like white on rice. But Dole, once in-state, didn't need much handling; he understood that, as he put it, you run for president in Iowa as if you were running for sheriff, and he did, materializing at every bean feed or pork roast he could find. When he did tamper with his schedule, canceling a fund-raiser in Hardin County, say, for a trip to Puerto Rico, Synhorst put him straight: "You just don't do that in Iowa." Most days were better. By caucus time, Bob or Liddy Dole had been to ninety-seven of the state's ninety-nine counties at least once, and had gone back to the most populous two-thirds for return engagements.

Dole was supported in Iowa by the elaborate infrastructure Synhorst had set in place under him. Caucus politics is a retail business, a specialty in which the priciest TV ads count for less than painstaking organization, and organizing was Synhorst's line; it was a matter of competitive pride with him that he and his kiddie corps would beat Rich Bond at his own game. They were green, yes, but willing, and Synhorst had run them long and hard; by the finish, they had the hollow-eyed look of volunteers in a sleep-deprivation experiment. It was a token of their seriousness that, when state campaign chairman Steve Roberts invited them to his house for a Christmas party, no one drank more than a couple of beers. There was work to be done, and they were back at their desks on Locust Street, clear-eyed and combat-ready, by eight that evening.

Synhorst oversaw them with a furious, elbows-out intensity, with eyes only for the bottom line. As a teenage boy, he had cried when Nixon resigned, and while he had since come to understand the reasons, he remained a sore loser. He was not, as he freely admitted, a people person. His passion instead was politics; in a choice between winning friends and winning votes, he would take the votes. His recruits on the ground were prepared to walk through walls for him, but he struck sparks in Washington with his blunt talk and his demanding ways. "That little bastard is a pain in the ass," Skip Watts told a field staffer who had chanced to ask what Synhorst would be doing after Iowa. "I'm getting rid of him."

Bill Brock, as it happened, had already tried, dispatching a series of consultants to the state in the fall of 1987 to peer over Synhorst's shoulder and prepare the case for his removal. But Dole's strong lead in the polls certified that his people on the ground were doing something right, and, besides, the senator liked Synhorst; he was a kindred spirit, a man as driven and as driving as Dole himself had been as a thirty-year-old starting up the ladder from the lower rungs. Leave Iowa alone, Dole signaled the new-broom bunch on L Street. They did, and Synhorst survived.

There were times in his fourteen-month run when even he seemed to wonder if it was worth the price. His innards tightened like piano strings in anticipation of each new Iowa Poll in the *Register*. He lost fifteen pounds, and his suits hung baggily on him, as if he had mistakenly wandered into a big-men's store. His chums from Senator Grassley's office were alarmed seeing him when he came home to Washington for Thanksgiving dinner; he sat at one end of the table, pallid and spent, staring absently into space.

"What are you doing?" his host asked him, trying to cheer him up. "Counting caucus attendees in Keosauqua?"

It had been a year since Synhorst had thought about anything else.

The last months of the campaign had been a ride on an emotional roller-coaster, his spirits rising and falling with the fluctuations in his own nightly tracking polls. Bush had actually crept ahead of Dole three times in the backstretch, once when Reagan and Gorbachev shook hands on their missile treaty, again when Rich Bond's shop got out a well-done statewide mailing, and finally after the vice president's tangle with Dan Rather on *CBS News*. Synhorst had watched the brawl on a set at headquarters and had been exultant at Rather's tough introductory piece on Iran-Contra; with each new jab at the weak spots in Bush's story, Synhorst had pantomimed a prizefighter throwing body blows at an imaginary opponent. But his mood had turned queasy at Bush's counterattack and Rather's overheated response to it.

"Oh, stop, stop," he begged Rather's image on the screen.

It didn't stop, not for nine minutes.

"Oh, shit," Synhorst had groaned.

The harm, by then, had been done; within forty-eight hours, Bush had popped eleven points ahead in Synhorst's tracking, and his man Wittgraf was on radio suggesting, in effect, that Dole and Rather were twins separated at birth. But the encounter had come at least a week too early to do the vice president any lasting good. His lead melted quickly, like an ice sculpture at a lawn party, and when his Iowa people put out their statement attacking the Doles with five days to go, Bush was undone by the backlash; he fell from seven to thirty-five points behind in two days.

Dole's man David Keene was accordingly in a buoyant mood when, on the Saturday before caucus Monday, he bumped into George Bush Jr. at the Des Moines Marriott.

"Nice coat," George Jr. taunted, inspecting Keene's winter-weight green camouflage jacket. "Is that bulletproof so you'll be able to get out of Iowa alive?"

"No, George," Keene needled back, "this is a hunting jacket, and that's why I'm here."

The sense that the hunt would end in success, by then, was palpable on Locust Street. That night's tracking showed Dole still twenty-one points up, at 43–22. Synhorst's stomach unknotted, almost; all that remained to be done was to pray for clear skies and activate the machinery he had so carefully set in place.

The weather was not cooperating when he arrived at his desk in an abandoned suite of law offices downtown at seven twenty-five on caucus day; the morning was sullen and snowy, and the forecast was for one to three inches. Bill Brock, nervously pacing the lobby of the Marriott nearby, felt daunted by the weather. Synhorst, as an Iowan, did not. Sitting in his bare-walled office, a quiet island in a sea of rumpled denim and empty fast-food cartons, he signed checks, shuffled papers, tidied up and waited for his fourteen months' handiwork to kick in. He had, by the end, organized 2,100 of the state's 2,586 precincts and had identified 62,000 possible Dole workers, each indexed on a three-by-five card and regularly recharged with phone calls and mailings. Synhorst's high-side estimate was that 50,000 would be enough. In the event, he would need only 40,000, and his troops were primed to get them out.

He spent the morning on the road with the Dole entourage, a farewell tour that began in a big, drafty outbuilding on the Synhorst farm forty miles from town. His mother had baked up cookies for everyone, and a wood stove struggled bravely to warm the crowd of seventy-five or so waiting for a glimpse of the man Abe and Sally Synhorst's boy had been working so hard for. "If I win tonight," Dole told them, standing before a mound of bagged soybean seeds, "the medal ought to go to Tom Synhorst." Dole was notoriously stingy with compliments, as tight as Mike Dukakis picking out a new suit in Filene's Basement. Synhorst's ears burned.

He followed on to a shopping mall and a Chamber of Commerce luncheon, but by two he was back on Locust Street, dropping his overcoat and jacket on the floor in one corner and slipping into a well-worn blue cardigan. The carpeting at headquarters was strewn with pennies left there for him to find—he considered them lucky—and a bouquet of flowers was waiting on his desk; their perfume mingled with the scent of victory gathering on the air. David Keene was drafting talking points for press consumption, one set headed WHY DOLE WON and another WHY BUSH LOST. Kim Wells was hunched over a word processor, polishing a foreign-policy speech for the next day. The word was out that Bush knew he was cooked, that he was fleeing the state for New Hampshire without waiting for the returns.

"I think we're going to beat his ass," Synhorst told a supporter who had called in for news. "I think Robertson may even beat Bush."

The suspense, indeed, was no longer whether Dole would win but how gracefully he would handle victory. His public rancor toward Bush had become the source of rising alarm among his people, and a couple of nights before the caucuses Keene had written him a memo on the importance of cutting it out. All that negative stuff had to be ended, done, gone by Monday night, Keene said, because when Dole woke up Tuesday morning the whole landscape was going to be different: people were going to be looking at him seriously for the first time, measuring him as a potential president rather than one more candidate rooting around for votes.

Dole had read the memo, then given it to Bill Brock to look at. Brock handed it back.

"Read it about six more times between now and New Hampshire," he said.

The concern was lost in the wash of the evening's good news. Only Dole seemed subdued in the face of his success; he was like a climber who, having made it halfway up a high mountain, looked down and saw only how far he had to fall. He was awaiting the returns with his family when Dick Wirthlin found him in the tenth-floor presidential suite at the Fort Des Moines. Wirthlin, a cautious soul, had been troubled for weeks by the softness of Dole's lead in the state. The numbers were written in sand on the seashore, he had been telling people; here they were, betting the farm on Iowa, and he wouldn't gamble a single penny on winning.

It had taken the early returns to make a believer of him. On caucus night, for the first time, he was smiling.

"Well, what do you think about this, Dick?" Dole asked.

"Senator," Wirthlin said, "I think we've got a good shot at it."

The mood in the presidential suite remained nonetheless measured as the numbers came in. Someone had taped a photo poster of Dole on the dining-room wall next to more formal portraits of Ford, Carter and Reagan, and Mari Maseng was calling him "Mr. President." But Liddy Dole was fighting a heavy cold, and Dole looked drawn and exhausted, longing for nothing quite so much as a day off somewhere in the sun. "Feels good," was the most he could manage when a reporter asked his reaction to the returns. In two past tries at national politics, he hadn't learned to say anything except "ouch."

Tom Synhorst was not nearly so restrained. He was at his desk in the late afternoon, worrying about the snow in north-central Iowa, when word came in that Dole had broken Bush's double-digit hold on New Hampshire and closed to within seven points. He and Floyd Brown, the campaign's Midwest regional director, traded wide smiles and high fives; if Iowa fell, and then New Hampshire, the senator was on his way.

At seven o'clock, Synhorst went to his own caucus site, at a retirement community near downtown, and saw the fruits of his labors: a pointillist sea of blue-and-gold DOLE FOR PRESIDENT lapel stickers stretching from wall to wall. He knew then that they had won, not just his caucus but the state. He waited for the count to make it official. Then he stepped outside into the snowy night and whooped, loudly, for joy.

Marching as to War

When the last caucus-goers in the nethermost hamlets in Iowa had stood up and been counted, the numbers indeed belonged to Bob Dole: a first-place finish, a 37 percent market share and a satisfying two-to-one rout of George Bush. But the louder hosannas rang at the International Trade Center downtown on Eighth Street, where the followers of Pat Robertson had gathered to cheer his arrival in presidential politics. The candidate's beaming face could be seen on a surreal square of television screens four sets high and four wide; in its pale light, three men embraced in a tight triangle, heads bowed together, each chanting his own prayer for God's blessings on the campaign. Their words, and Robertson's, were lost in the din of celebration. A man who had been widely discounted till that night as a stray from the electronic sawdust trail had finished a solid second to Dole, turned out more voters than any of the Democrats—and very nearly undone the vice president of the United States.

From the moment he announced his candidacy in the fall, with $10 million on hand or in play and 3.3 million names on his run-Pat-run petitions, Robertson had been like a new-money billionaire at a garden party in Newport: he was too brash to be welcome and too big to be invited to leave. The schizoid reaction he provoked among old-line Republicans was akin to what the white Democratic establishment felt toward his fellow divine Jesse Jackson. There was on the one hand their unease with Robertson's origins in the television ministry, as head of a cable network and host of a gently evangelical talk show called *The 700 Club*. Religion and politics had traditionally made a bad mix, and, at a time when televangelists seemed to be falling daily from grace, the downside looked steeper than ever. Yet there were, on the upside, those tantalizingly round numbers his people kept quoting: the 37 million households plugged in to Robertson's Christian Broadcasting Network; the 50 to 70 million Americans who called themselves evangelicals and whose language Robertson could plausibly claim to speak.

He spoke it, indeed, with a fluency polished over twenty-seven years on TV. His off-camera life more nearly resembled Bush's in its privilege than the lives of most of his followers; he too had been the son of a United States senator, had gone to the best schools and had made a handsome success in business. But as a public man, he was a latter-day populist, an heir to a two-century tradition of grievance against the ruling elites of New York, Washington and, more recently, the libertine sin towns of California. He offered himself as the voice of the flyover people between the oceans, the hard-working, flag-flying, God-fearing common men and women who felt their faith, their families and their values under siege in an immoral age. They were, as a campaign T-shirt proudly announced, a silent army, and when 27,000 of them materialized at the caucuses to vote for a nearly perfect stranger to worldly politics, they made believers of the skeptics overnight. "There's a lot of us," one of them, a Dubuque lawyer, said, "and we're real people."

For them, Robertson's amateur standing was not a negative but a prime virtue, his certification that he was real people, too. "I am not a politician," he would tell his audiences, to amens and loud huzzahs. He was instead a public moralist, a scold on the whole range of hot-button issues from abortion to anti-Communism, and, while he had secularized his speeches for a new and larger audience than he had played to on CBN, they still held some of the fever heat of sermons under a revival tent. He became, on these occasions, the preacher he said he had left behind in his studios in Virginia Beach.

His aim, he said, was to "restore the greatness of America through moral strength,'' and he proposed to start by driving the usurpers from the temples of power. The schools would be cleansed of the secular humanists and reopened to God; the Department of State would be purged of the one-world socialists; the Pentagon would be repopulated with leaders dedicated to fighting Communists, not accommodating them. The Federal government, in the world according to Pat, had few valid functions except rolling back the Red tide to the borders of the Soviet Union. He saw no reason why the budget couldn't be cut by $100 billion in his first year and balanced by 1991; the people could deal with the ills of American society, in their homes, schools, churches and communities, without Washington's meddlesome help.

His core supporters were commonly pentecostal and charismatic Christians, people for whom church was the center and religion the first fact of daily life. But his message was not limited to what his more secular campaign manager, Marc Nuttle, called ''that one little pinpoint'' on the map of American conservatism. It spoke to a far wider audience of the spiritually disfranchised—ordinary men and women whose children went to prayerless public schools, whose living rooms were invaded by sex and violence on TV, and whose eyes were assaulted by porn shops and abortion clinics anytime they drove downtown.

The strength in their numbers was less clear in the polls than in Robertson's vivid imagination. He had had nine years to think about it, since the days when he first fell prey to what an old CBN associate thought of as Pat's presidential fantasy, and he had persuaded himself of their rich potential. There were enough of them, he believed, to make the Republican Party something vastly larger than a country club for the elite, which was what he felt it had become, or a chapel for evangelical Christians, which was what he was often accused of wanting it to be. They were, he said, the makings of a new Republican majority—an ecumenical rainbow coalition of the right as big and durable as Franklin Roosevelt's governing majority had been in the 1930s and '40s.

Since his arithmetic could not be proved or disproved, he was received by the Republicans as gingerly as Jackson by the Democrats; their respective parties presumed that each man would lose, and hoped that his followers would hang around for the general election. Where Jackson's baggage was the color of his skin and his politics, Robertson's was the klieg-lit hue of his ministry. There had always been an implicit wink in Ronald Reagan's sermons, a note of tolerance for the weaknesses of the flesh. Robertson's sounded as if he meant every word; his life's work praising the Lord and rebuking the fallen on TV defined both the strengths and the limits of his appeal, and the duality colored his campaign from beginning to end.

He tried for the most part to make the best of his old vocation by making as little of it as possible, often disowning or denying his more florid utterances in the service of the Lord. He quit the ministry in preparation for the race and dropped the honorific "Reverend." In his new life, he preferred to be known as a "Christian businessman," a term his own polling showed to be more palatable to voters than "television evangelist"; the latter label carried negative ratings, in other surveys, of 70 to 85 percent. A passage relating how God had once told him to stay out of politics was excised from a new edition of his fifteen-year-old autobiography. His everyday speech was customized to reach two audiences simultaneously, one pious, the other temporal. It dwelled on "traditional values" and "basic moral principles," button words for the Christian right, while barely mentioning God at all.

It pained Robertson to be thought kooky or scary, or to be caricatured as, in his word, some bluenose trying to impose his own straitened moral code on America. It was chief executive he was running for, not chief pastor, he argued, and his beliefs, while proudly and deeply held, were a private matter between him and God. But he remained lashed to his past, those not-long-ago days when he had healed the sick, prayed away hurricanes and prophesied nuclear war as a prelude to the Second Coming, and in the age of audio- and video-tape he was not allowed to forget it. His negative ratings began as the highest in either party, and were driven higher still by the unhappily timed scandals in the electronic church. His opponents, welcoming him for the public record, spread the word privately that it was not a campaign Robertson was running—it was a *jihad*.

He found himself, in consequence, trying to run from his old calling even as he traded on it, but those Eastern media liberals kept dragging it out of the closet; even the night of his triumph in Iowa had nearly been spoiled by it. He had been eager to brag on his success and had beaten his rivals in the day's second most important race, to be first at live-feed interview time on the networks. Dan Rather had been respectful on CBS, though Robertson had baited him fearfully during the campaign, and Peter Jennings had been a great gentleman on ABC. But Tom Brokaw of NBC had raked up the old stereotypes again, referring to Robertson straightaway as a television evangelist and asking whether he was getting political advice from God.

Robertson had flared. The question was in poor taste, he thought, like walking in on a man having a party and dumping a load of garbage in his living room; Robertson considered himself a nice man, as pleasant as can be, but he wasn't taking any of that mess anymore. "If you don't mind, I think it's the last time I want to be called a television evangelist," he had told Brokaw, visibly agitated. He was a religious broadcaster and a candidate for president, and to use a label as belittling as the one Brokaw had hung on him was an act of "religious bigotry."

He had in fact proven himself to be a savvy secular politician, a state-of-the-art campaigner with a clear message, a devoted following and a mastery of both the techniques and the uses of modern telecommunications. His own manner on-screen was reassuring, talk-show cool as against hellfire hot; he made more intimate eye contact with a camera, after a quarter-century's practice, than with a live audience ten feet in front of him. Free audiotapes broadcast his words—300,000 copies of his set speech were distributed in Iowa and New Hampshire alone—and five-dollar home videos intercut scenes from his rallies with shots of the war in Nicaragua and the tenderloin district around Times Square. His fund-raising and voter-targeting apparatus was the envy of most of his rivals; he had begun with mailing lists bought from CBN and culled from the petitions begging him to run and had kept building outward from there.

But his real strength lay hidden at the grass roots, beyond measure by conventional polling or political analysis; he had been no more than a phantom presence in Iowa until the day in August 1987 when his state chairman, Drew Ivers, and his Midwest campaign director, Marlene Elwell, had decided it was time for him to go public. Elwell had come by Ivers's place in Webster City looking for what she called a key to the door in Iowa, a prelude to a full-scale assault on the caucuses. Ivers, a plant geneticist and a longtime party activist, had suggested the September straw poll in Ames. There were risks in moving the invisible army out of the front parlors and the church basements into the open: it would put Robertson's rivals on notice that he was for real. But Elwell had seized on the idea, the buses had rolled to Ames, and Robertson had been born yet again, as a serious contender for the nomination.

His standing had been reinforced by further strong showings in the prelims, in Michigan, Florida and Hawaii; if his followers were novices at politics, they had learned networking in their churches, and their skill at organization, coupled with their passion for their cause, made them a force anywhere people gathered within four walls to vote. Robertson was sometimes victim to dangerous flights of fancy about how powerful a force. He predicted early on that he would get seventy thousand votes at the caucuses in Iowa, more than twice Bush's winning total in 1980; he had raised the ante for himself in the Expectations Game, a beginner's mistake, and he soon had to back down to sounder ground—the vow that he would turn out "whatever it takes to win."

If his math was awry, his belief that there *was* a silent army remained unshaken; he was confident from the first that he would do better than the numbers he kept putting up in the *Register*'s Iowa Poll. He had only fourteen paid staffers in the state—Paul Simon, on the other side, had more than 150—and his own time there was closely rationed; sometimes, his campaign bus jounced through the back counties without him, a ghost ship showing the colors in place of the candidate. What Robertson had instead was his people, starting with 38,000 names culled from his petitions, and an organizational infrastructure of cell groups in the churches and subscribers to CBN. His man Ivers plotted their growth in numbers along a slowly accelerating curve, drawing in religious and secular conservatives alike. His canvassers were still identifying supporters the night before the caucuses, well after the other campaigns had quit the hunt.

More than most campaigns, they were dealing with people who had dropped out of worldly politics or had never voted at all, and their approach was carefully soft-sell. No one attending a Robertson meeting was asked what party he or she belonged to, or what church; the talk instead was of home and family, where, as Elwell put it, the pain was. Neither was Robertson's clerical past loudly advertised; it was well enough known to believers, and, at a time when TV preachers were widely suspected of harboring either too much or too little piousness in their bosoms, the image of Robertson in the pulpit was not thought to be his best recruiting poster. Robertson's early TV spots were, in fact, designed to get the "Reverend" out of people's minds, Ivers said, so that they would focus on just plain "Pat" and his message. His closing print ad in the Iowa papers juxtaposed his picture with John Kennedy's on facing pages, with captions reminding voters that JFK too had been called unfit for the presidency "because of his religion."

The campaign, like its advertising, was made to look, sound and feel inclusive. Its style was more familial than churchly; for one televised debate, Robertson's people laid on more than a thousand parties across the state so that his voters could be together and cheer him on. The mysteries of caucus politics were explained and explained again in ABC language accessible to the shyest first-time participant. "In every precinct, which is the voting area around where you live," Robertson would tell his audiences, "people are going to assemble in Iowa for what are called caucuses. . . ." The lecture series in Political Science 101 ran on almost to the hour of the voting; the first stop for Robertsonians that evening was typically a potluck-and-prayer dinner, with a program including a last refresher course on what to do at voting time.

Robertson himself had planned a big finale, a two-day helicopter tour of forty cities, towns and hamlets. Fortune did not cooperate; he was grounded by a balky chopper and a brewing snowstorm, so he switched to his bus for a grinding twenty-stop, dawn-to-midnight circuit ride. His spirits seemed undiminished. "If I win Iowa on Monday," he said, "I promise you I'll be the next president of the United States of America. . . . Just give me the pleasure of seeing Dan Rather's face when he has to announce it." The bus rolled on, to Fairfield and Ottumwa and Corydon, and finally, on Sunday morning, to a black Baptist church in Des Moines. The last, an aide said, was a calculated choice. The media would never make fun of a black congregation for being demonstrative in their faith; black people, the aide said, were *expected* to shout and wave their hands in church.

Robertson's second-place finish the next night, if not precisely a victory, was quite enough to impress Dan Rather, humble George Bush and bury Jack Kemp and Pete du Pont, his principal rivals on the right. More important, it had accredited the formerly reverend candidate for president as a serious player at the table. His mood was accordingly buoyant as he flew east aboard his leased BAC jet. Its interior had been handsomely appointed by the Robertsonian who owned it, with teak furnishings, French doors and a Tiffany-style lamp, a setting appropriate to Robertson's new station.

That station was in a large measure illusory. Iowa had proven only that Robertson could pack a caucus, not that he could win a primary; that test awaited him in New Hampshire, and its rocky soil was not his most promising ground. But he seemed untroubled, lounging in a swivel chair in jeans and a CBN warm-up jacket with his plain-English Bible at his side. Bush hadn't beaten him anywhere, and now, by all accounts, the vice president was badly, perhaps mortally, wounded. All Robertson could say, he told a reporter along for the ride, was, Follow along and watch the numbers as they went up on the scoreboard. He had the support of the basic people out there, mainstream people who worried about schools and drugs and teenage pregnancies and Communists kicking America around; everybody, that is, except the liberal media. Just keep looking at the tote board, he said. The Bible Belt South lay just over the next horizon. It was Robertson country, and he was going to win.

Poppy Redux

TWO NIGHTS OUT OF IOWA, Bob Dole sat up late with some of his traveling staff in his rooms at the Hilton in Merrimack, New Hampshire, nursing his road-weariness with a cup of hot coffee and a feast of good news. Its bearer, once again, was Dick Wirthlin, and its makings lay in the looseleaf binder spread across his knees, the returns from his latest scan of the state. Wirthlin had believed from the first, and had argued in his strategy memos, that Dole had to beat Bush significantly in both Iowa and New Hampshire—that he was a 90 percent sure bet to win the nomination if he did and a nearly certain loser if he did not. Iowa had, relatively speaking, been the easy part. New Hampshire was tougher, a state where, as a rival strategist put it, a Dole candidacy was like an organ transplant destined for rejection; only a month earlier, Wirthlin's polling there had shown him eighteen points behind. But the Iowa results had jarred the chessboard and rearranged the pieces in Dole's favor.

"Senator, you've known me now for close to eighteen years," Wirthlin said, looking up from his numbers. He was a smallish man with a wan, indoor look, and his voice was soft in the room. "You know I don't make predictions lightly. But," he went on, "we're going to win this thing." There was even a chance that Bush would once again limp in third.

Dole smiled. "Are you willing to bet your company on that?" he teased.

"Senator, that's pushing things too far," Wirthlin said. His high-tech, high-price polling and marketing firm was no joking matter to him; his billings to the Dole campaign alone, to the distress of some of the old guard there, would come to $500,000, and politics was no longer the major part of his business. But he was no less sure of his ground. Dole was on his way to the victory he had to have.

"Well, great," the senator said. "I'll go to sleep. Wake me up next Wednesday."

He meant when the primary was over; if Wirthlin was right, Dole would be the odds-on favorite for the nomination.

Through the Looking Glass

That he was even within dreaming distance of winning was a measure of the powers of magnification applied by the media to his victory and Bush's perceived collapse in Iowa. The caucuses there were no more than a test market, a kind of hyperinflated focus group attended by 110,000 people. But the mutual needs of the new consultant class on one hand and satellite-dish journalism on the other had turned modern politics into a hall of mirrors, in which reality on the ground counted for less than its image on television. On caucus night, the network anchors had used verbs like "humiliated" to describe what Dole had done to the vice president, and the drumbeat continued in the week thereafter, fed by tracking polls from New Hampshire. The effect, for the Dole campaign, was intoxicating. Not even witting wanderers among the mirrors were immune to their powers of illusion; for five disabling days, Dole's seconds gazed into the looking glass at their imminent ascent to glory and believed what they saw.

The realities of New Hampshire had been unfriendly from the beginning; Dole's original aim there had been merely to prevent a Bush blowout and survive to fight on more hospitable ground. For starters, New Hampshire was not Iowa. Its granite heart still belonged to Ronald Reagan—his eighty-plus approval ratings were near the canonization level—and Bush's strong bond to New England gave him the home-court advantage for round two. His steady twenty-point lead in his own pre-Iowa polling reflected the difference in terrain, and a rock-solid field organization provided a form of insurance against disaster. Where Dole had Senator Rudman in his corner, Bush had Governor John H. Sununu in his. Both were popular in the state, but it was one of Lee Atwater's rules that governors made better catches than senators; senators, once elected, disappeared to Washington for six years, where governors stayed home and kept their organizations constantly fine-tuned for the next campaign.

Bush's advantages were imposing, and as game time approached, a confidence bordering on cockiness infected his headquarters command. Some of his ground troops got nervous toward the end, as ground troops will, about the stately pace of his scheduling and came down to Washington to complain. Their first stop was the Office of the Vice President, where Craig Fuller and Bob Teeter gave them a civics lecture on the importance of Bush's time and the loftiness of his station. Lee Atwater, who had listened in, told them afterward to forget it, go home and keep doing what they had been doing.

"This meeting was a complete waste of time," he said. "All you guys got to worry about is: fuck Dole."

The Dole campaign, by sharp contrast, had started late and fared badly, a casualty of the chaos on L Street and inertia in the field. Paul Jacobson, one of several aides on loan from Rudman, reported for work as regional press secretary in May 1987 and knew from a first look around that it wouldn't be fun. What passed for Dole headquarters was a dingy, twenty-eight-step walkup with sagging floors, a balky computer system and no air conditioners or window screens. The full-time staff consisted of one paid organizer with sixty-two names in a box of index cards. Finding more required setting up phone banks, but they got mired in internal infighting. Too few calls were made early on, as a result, and too many at the end; a Washington staffer found one whole bank of volunteers working from identical lists, phoning the same irritated voters again and again and again.

Dole's paid-media campaign was similarly lost in the bureaucratic Byzantium on L Street. It took his adman, Don Ringe, three days of door-knocking at headquarters to get a simple radio spot approved, and TV ideas moved more slowly still; with little more than a month till primary time, a lone bio spot was the only ad in the can. Ringe, an abrasive sort who had worked in TV news, had wanted to do some talking-head pieces— eye-contact shots of Dole speaking directly into a camera. But he couldn't beg or bully his way into the candidate's presence for the necessary warm-ups. Dole instead had walked into a studio one day in January and taped the spots cold, with predictable results. They came out as bland as vanilla pudding; Rath and Rudman, Dole's two prize allies in New Hampshire, hated them, and both the spots and their *auteur,* Don Ringe, were soon cast over the side.

With just eighteen days left before the primary, two separate command groups, each unaware of the other, sat down four hundred miles apart to review what scripts were on the table. The more senior of the two, led by Dole and Brock, met in Manchester and agreed on a number of ads, among them one called "Little Old Lady"; its subtext was Bush's profane post-script to his set-to with Dan Rather, and its protagonist was an elderly woman on the phone to a neighbor, remarking how Bob Dole didn't take the Lord's name in vain or use crude words about women. Tom Rath had a couple of ideas about improving it, and when the session broke up he called the campaign's new communications director, Larry McCarthy, a former Ailes associate who had been brought in over Ringe's head.

"I want to work on the 'Little Old Lady' spot," Rath said.

"*What* 'Little Old Lady' spot?" McCarthy answered, mystified. He had met in Washington that very day with Wirthlin and Ringe, who was still around as a production subcontractor, and they had rejected the ad; none of them thought it would work.

Nothing else seemed to be working, either. The fleeting optimism Dole had felt in the fall gave way to the gloom of winter, and he worried his people constantly about the flatness of his campaign; you just knew, he said, that if one more poll came out, you'd still be stuck around twenty and Bush would be up around forty.

"Don't get discouraged," Rudman, a regular recipient of his phone calls, would tell him. "Go to bed."

Dole, unappeased, worried on.

He was, as ever, a part of the problem, making and breaking dates on short notice and imposing his own temperamental rules of the road; he would not travel by car, for example, if the drive time was more than a half hour. But his advancing was no more proficient than the rest of his campaign, and the days of two-car motorcades delivering him to small and listless crowds did little to improve his dark moods. He went out knocking on doors in Manchester one frosty Saturday morning. Not many opened. "They must have looked out the window," he said. After a half hour, he gave up trying and went to lunch.

There had been stirrings of life in the state before Iowa, and the rush of euphoria on caucus night had swept doubt and caution away. Tom Rath, a stubby man with a cherubic face and a cheerful manner, was waiting on the tarmac at Concord Municipal Airport the next morning as Dole's plane taxied in. However the race came out, Rath was thinking, every campaign deserved a day like this one, one day's pure pleasure to redeem the months of unrelieved stress. He watched Dole come down the ramp, tired but obviously pleased with himself.

"We got this won yet?" he asked Rath.

"We're gettin' there, coach," Rath said.

His confidence was less than complete. He and Senator Rudman had dined with some others in Manchester the night before, and while the news from Iowa had cheered the table, they felt a little stab of anxiety about the way just ahead. As trial lawyers by training, they planned campaigns the way you prepare a case: you start by putting yourself in the other guy's position and wondering what the hell he could do to you. What Bush could do to Dole, the two agreed, was paint him as a friend of the tax collector, a sin just short of child molestation or cannibalism in the canons of New Hampshire politics. The senator had supported the 1982 tax bill, the biggest increase in history. So, reluctantly, had Ronald Reagan, and, presumably, Bush, but a cleverly done ad campaign could make Dole look like a pickpocket stealing back the Reagan tax cuts of 1981.

The concern was not a new one in the campaign; Wirthlin in his strategy papers and others in endless meetings had identified taxes as a target of opportunity for Bush. But no one had pushed hard for ads or anything else inoculating Dole against attack on the tax issue. L Street was a great deal more concerned with the vice president's big edge in the polls on foreign-policy and defense questions. The strongest spot in production for New Hampshire was one called "Gorbachev," picturing Dole as tougher and steadier than Bush would be sitting across a table from the Soviet general secretary. There was nothing on taxes at all.

Rath was unhappy, and so was Rudman; the senator, in fact, didn't much like anything they were putting on the air, and he was less restrained than Rath had been about saying so.

"How are things going?" Dole had asked him on the ride in from the airport to the statehouse for a speech to a joint session of the legislature the morning after Iowa.

"Well," Rudman had answered, "I think things are going well, but I have to tell you right now, I'm unhappy with the media. My God, this is a presidential campaign, Bob, and I don't think our commercials are all that good."

Dole hadn't disagreed, but his text that day, in keeping with the higher strategy emanating from L Street, was a red-meat manifesto on foreign policy. A chance to confront the tax question head on, in the first-day flush of media attention, was lost; his rote promise not to raise income-tax rates amounted to little more than clearing his throat for the body of his speech, on the praiseworthiness of the Star Wars antimissile system.

The nagging continued, and by Wednesday morning Rath, haggard and

puffy-eyed, finally got Brock's attention. With Kim Wells, they drafted a
short, sharp insert on taxes for Dole's standard road speech, just enough
for a thirty-second spot, and Larry McCarthy was directed to scramble a
camera crew to Nashua to tape the senator doing it live at a candidates'
forum. McCarthy in turn called Don Ringe and dispatched him to Boston
to rent an editing room; the weekend advertising deadlines for New
England stations were closing in, and they were going to have to put
something together fast.

The problem with the production was its star. The language Wells
handed him was strong—"If you want to see toughness, let the Democrats
try to raise taxes"—and the punch line was a flat pledge to veto any increase
that reached his desk. But Dole arrived in Nashua heavy with fatigue, the
toll of too many long days on the road. His normally muscular presence
before a crowd deserted him; his face was ashy, his voice quavered, his bad
shoulder drooped, his speech was rambly, and when he got to the new
material he mangled it. "I would say if you want to see toughness," he
said, "just let the Democrats try—just let the Democrats try to lower—
uh—to scuttle the lower tax rates Republicans in Congress got passed for
President Reagan."

The take was a bad one. Ringe, in Boston, did what he could with it,
editing it into what he considered a serviceable ad; maybe it wouldn't win
any Oscars, he thought, but it would work in a crunch. No one else liked
it even that much, and while Dole did better at a new shoot at the University
of New Hampshire the next day, his camera crew did not. The videotape
was a technical mess, a surreal sequence of Dole seen at a great distance,
off to one side of the frame, talking into a cavernous echo chamber of a hall.
The remake never got made, and with one weak version in the can and
another on the editing-room floor, the campaign was left dangerously
exposed to attack on a sensitive issue.

Later, there would be finger-pointing, each of the principals finding
someone else to blame. In the flush of the moment, the question seemed
moot. A winter storm was brewing, and the stations were shutting down
their ad-traffic departments early, setting Thursday-evening and Friday-
morning deadlines for new spots. Dole's people did not press hard for more
time; they took no for an answer and were seduced past caring, in any case,
by the tidal flow of voters moving their way. Wirthlin was saying they
didn't even need a tax ad; the issue didn't seem to be cutting in his polls,
and the ad they had would have lost votes, not won them. The hard-edged
"Gorbachev" spot, by contrast, had tested well with Wirthlin's focus
groups, even among women, and it wound up dominating Dole's weekend

ad rotation. Wirthlin had the tax spot pulled from the one Boston station that had received it, and it died unseen.

It was easy, in the euphoria, not to worry. Dole had been five points behind Bush the night, at midweek, when Wirthlin told him he was likely to win. By Friday, he was five ahead, and all the straws in the wind appeared to be blowing his way. Al Haig came out for Dole that morning; he did not bring many votes with him, but his four-star blessing helped the senator with his national-security problem, and it played to a captive audience of snowbound correspondents and cameramen with nothing else to report.

That Friday was the zenith for Bob Dole—as good a day, Wirthlin reckoned the next morning, as any in the history of presidential campaigning. Wirthlin was waiting outside Conant High School in Jaffrey while Dole was speaking inside; snow was blowing on a stiff breeze, but the day was alight with sunshine, and its warmth matched his mood. Bush's people had been doing everything wrong, he mused. They had been trying to change his image overnight, transplant him from the backseat of a limo to the cab of an eighteen-wheeler, and the result was no image at all; it was mush, and the vice president was all but finished. It was, Wirthlin thought, like seeing the sun, the moon and the stars all perfectly aligned. There was one chance in a hundred that Dole would lose, and a fair possibility that he would blow Bush away.

The edifice, as it turned out, was as glittery and as perishable as an ice palace in spring, and by the time Wirthlin got airborne for a trip home to Washington it had begun melting. Everything in Bush's campaign was clicking, even the implausible photo ops of the vice president doing malls and driving semis. Rumors were flying that Roger Ailes had roadblocked thirty minutes on practically every station serving New Hampshire for a Saturday-evening special; Dole's media people, sometimes posing as Ailes employees, made some calls and confirmed that it was true.

But the worst news of all was waiting when Kim Wells came back from a two-day emergency trip home to Kansas. A crisis was brewing, and Brock, not for the first time, was somewhere else. Wells found Tom Rath in the lobby of the Merrimack Hilton, looking grim.

Bush had got on the air after the supposed deadlines with an ad attacking Dole on taxes, Rath said. Dole had nothing on to answer it with. They hadn't even tried.

Wells was furious, with himself for having been out of touch for two days and with the message people for not having banged heads at the stations to put something up. It was just an absolute crock, as Wells would put it to

Dole when they got together later. The deadlines could have been bent, and *any* ad would have been better than no ad; the quality didn't matter, as long as you could hear the words and see that it was Dole talking.

The postmortems made too much of the ad that didn't run as the *cause* of Dole's fadeout, when it was more accurately a symptom of all that ailed his campaign. Partly in self-defense, Wirthlin would do his own autopsy with his own money after the primary, going back to the soft and undecided voters who had flooded to Bush in the closing days. Taxes, according to his figures, had moved some votes but not many. The decisive issues instead were Bush's close identification with Reagan and Dole's vague resemblance to Nixon; the words people chose to describe the senator included, commonly, "arrogant," "vindictive," "smart-alecky" and "mean."

Dole thus had met the enemy and it was he; the problems of his candidacy traced finally to the candidate and to the campaign he has fashioned in his own image. He had come out of Iowa playing catch-the-wave politics, riding as precariously as an amateur surfer on the currents of fashion, and when the tide turned against him he had no resources left—no message, no strategy, no depth on the ground in New Hampshire or anywhere else. It was a high-risk game, and in his heart he knew it. He had, in fact, been first to sense the bad vibrations, wondering aloud to Rath at midweek, while the surge was still on, why he wasn't ahead yet. It was only Thursday, Rath had reminded him; Gary Hart, the model for all catch-the-wave campaigners, hadn't passed Fritz Mondale until the weekend before the primary in 1984.

Dole had remained unpersuaded, and the numbers proved him right. Wirthlin was the first to see them, at his home in McLean, Virginia, early Sunday morning. Things had gone sour. The bounce had died. Dole's line moving down the charts had met Bush's moving up. The race was a dead heat.

Wirthlin considered and quickly dismissed the possibility that there might have been some sampling error. The sample was fine. He had been wrong.

He called Dole. "We had a very bad Saturday," he said.

The glass was always half empty for Dole. He had felt it coming. He hadn't needed to be told.

He arrived in a sour mood for a last pre-primary debate at St. Anselm's College in Goffstown; his performance was Dole at his worst, as acid as lemon and as growly as a bear. His people had seen the forum as a last chance to answer Bush on the tax issue, but Bush was too well coached to raise it face to face; it was Pete du Pont who blindsided Dole with the question and dug the hole a little deeper.

Du Pont had brought along a copy of a no-tax pledge, a standard-issue oath as necessary to office-seekers in New Hampshire as a visa to travelers to Russia. Some of du Pont's staff had wanted him to force it on Bush, but by luck of the draw they were seated too far apart. So du Pont shoved it at Dole instead, and Dole broke one of the hornbook rules of political debate: he accepted it.

"Sign it," du Pont said.

Dole look flustered. He stared at the paper for a few seconds, then tried to make a joke of it, a play on his own hesitancy about supporting the INF Treaty. "Give it to George," he said. "I have to read it first."

The audience laughed, but Bill Brock, looking on, felt his stomach knot up in a ball. Dole should have wadded up the pledge, thrown it on the floor and responded that his own promise not to raise taxes was good enough. Instead, Brock thought, he had shown a dangerous, even fatal glimmer of ambivalence on the single question most dangerous to his candidacy. Brock was dying inside. The primary and the presidency were slipping away. He thought he was going to be ill.

The Empire Strikes Back

Lee Atwater sat dazed on the edge of a bed in a hotel suite in New Hampshire, oblivious, so it appeared, to the command-level crisis meeting going on around him. "I think we're going to be all right," he kept saying. "I think we're going to be all right." He had come out of Iowa looking shellshocked, not so much by the fact of Bush's defeat as by its devastating scale. The vice president's candidacy had tumbled into free fall, and the hunt for scapegoats had already begun. I can't believe they'd shit-can me before South Carolina, Atwater was thinking, but the word was about that Bob Teeter was trying to accomplish just that. Atwater's future was on the line with Bush's, and there he sat on the edge of the bed, saying, without visible conviction, that they would probably be OK. He had been chanting the same mantra all week, and some of his colleagues, having heard it before, were actually laughing at him. He seemed not to hear. Lee's out of it, one of them thought. He's in a trance. He's panicked.

The vice president himself had been gracious in defeat, and Atwater had appreciated it. A candidate could have come out the next morning and said, "Atwater, you're the campaign manager, you messed this thing up," whereupon Atwater would have had to find two or three underlings to blame; the dog would be kicking the dog all over the lot, he thought, and the campaign would really have been in shambles. But Bush, a notoriously sore loser, had arrived in New Hampshire on caucus day with upper lip stiffened. "I don't want to see any glum faces around here," he said, debarking from Air Force Two, and when the traveling members of the G-6 visited him a bit tremulously in his rooms at the Clarion Somerset in Nashua at seven the next morning, his mood was still forbearing.

"Look," he told them, "I don't want to point fingers at anyone. Let's stay upbeat. We've got eight days here. I want us to sit down and figure out everything we need to do to win, and then let's get out there and win."

As it happened, the pieces were in place to do just that. Atwater could have been in a coma all week instead of working through a four- or five-day downer; he had prepared the ground in New Hampshire so well that Bush could have prevailed, if necessary, without him. Atwater had understood from the first that the state was crucial to the vice president's hopes—that all his brave geopolitical talk about building a Southern fortress as a fall-back was meaningless if New Hampshire fell.

"If we win there, we're going to win the nomination," he told his state political director, Will Abbott, the day Abbott signed on early in 1986. "If we lose there, we're going to lose the nomination."

Abbott had moved in immediately and begun seeding the grass roots, a year and a half ahead of Dole's people. When Governor Sununu was recruited in 1987, by Atwater's design and Bush's five-year courtship, the game was all but over. The governor brought, along with a large ego and a lordly attitude, the strongest private political army in the state.

But in their first maundering days out of Iowa, it was easier to see New Hampshire as the burying ground than as the launching pad for Bush's ambitions. For a time, Sununu appeared to be the only man in the campaign, or, indeed, the state, who seemed really to believe that the vice president was going to win.

"We come out of Iowa with a twelve- to fifteen-point loss," Atwater had asked Sununu before the caucuses; "what can you do in New Hampshire?"

Win it, Sununu had replied.

Not even the eighteen-point final margin in the caucuses appeared to have dismayed him. He and his wife, Nancy, had caught up with the Bushes in the restaurant at the Clarion on caucus night, joining them for coffee after dinner. The Bushes had seen the drift in Iowa in the day's first exit polls, and their mood, unsurprisingly, was heavy.

Bush asked Sununu whether they could salvage New Hampshire.

"I'm confident that it's going to happen," Sununu said. "You can relax."

"You really believe that?" Mrs. Bush asked, her skepticism showing. "You're not just saying it?"

"Yes, I believe it," Sununu said. The organization he had been nurturing for a year would deliver. It was going to work out.

Confidence otherwise was not in abundant supply. Bush's steady 40 percent share of the polls, public and private, through much of 1987 had melted down to 22 percent by Friday, five behind Dole. Retrieving voters you had had for a year and a half and then lost was the easiest trick in politics, Atwater would say afterward. But you had to plug back into them with a good message, and for the first seventy-two hours, with Atwater fogbound and the others flying blind, Bush appeared to have no message at all.

His speeches wandered. His voice regressed to its old, reedy whine. He spent one day telling his audiences that, as a fellow New Englander, he was one of them, a line openly purloined from Dole's Iowa speeches. "It was supposed to be funny," he had to explain afterward. "Maybe nobody got it." He disappeared to Washington the next day, to change his laundry, he said. His mission in fact was to be seen and photographed keeping his weekly lunch date with Reagan; in the absence of any other clear strategy for his recovery, Bush's hold on the president's coattails grew tighter and more desperate than ever.

His revival, according to people who knew him, began with a hard look inward, at the regal manner he had encouraged in his campaign and at his own Poppy-knows-best conduct as a candidate. "I stared into the abyss and decided something had to change," he would confess afterward, and that something, he understood, was himself.

The Good George Bush, the man at the center of a loving family and an army of devoted friends, had a less appealing flip side well known to old-timers in his service. He took direction poorly and in ill humor; there was, he complained one day, a tendency among his aides to handle him, as if he were Ronald Reagan, and he didn't need it or like it. Older hands around him thought that a bit of handling was exactly what he did need. But there was a streak of insecurity in George, one Reagan-Bush veteran thought; he would get all bent out of shape with the hired hands if things went wrong and throw a tantrum if you told him he was the one who had screwed up. It took the trauma of his defeat in Iowa to humble him. He was scared enough to listen to people who knew better, a key campaign strategist said. For a change, George Bush did as he was told.

He was handed a moving new script, the work, principally, of the party's poet laureate, Peggy Noonan. But his strongest stage direction came from the unlikely person of John Sununu, a stout, plain and self-possessed mechanical engineer who had labored through his own eight-year losing streak in New Hampshire politics to get elected governor in 1982. Sununu was unloved in the statehouse for his domineering ways; legislators, privately, called him Havana Fats, for his birthplace and his build, and wore lapel pins with his likeness, captioned WILL ROGERS NEVER MET THIS MAN. It hardly mattered. The people liked him well enough to have reelected him, twice, and in the crisis of the Bush campaign his knowledge of their tastes and his own habit of command became precious assets. Everyone else was stumbling around wondering what the hell to do next, his friendly adversary Tom Rath reflected afterward, and there was Sununu, saying, "Follow me, boys." For two or three days post-Iowa, Sununu *was* the Bush campaign.

The down payment for his help was a real place at the table, not just on a Bush-for-president letterhead; the G-6 became, de facto, the G-7. The further price was Bush's agreement to forget about the perks of his office and hit the streets like a hungry Amway salesman. The governor was an advocate of the photo-on-the-mantel theory of politics: if someone had a picture of himself and the vice president over his fireplace, he was going to work awfully hard to make it a picture of himself and the president. But the pictures would never get taken if you weren't out among the people. Bush had to get out of the cotton batting—the limos, the ropes, the blue backdrops, the uptight bodyguards—and run what Sununu called a see-me, feel-me, touch-me campaign right down to the finish.

Sununu had been arguing just such a course for a year, with only intermittent success; like Rich Bond in Iowa, he kept bumping against Craig Fuller's concern for the proprieties of the office and the comfort of the candidate. The rules provided that there be no days longer than ten hours, including ninety minutes of down time, and no day trips hitting more than three cities; if winning meant Bush's having to work twelve hours a day, one in-state operative said in disgust, Fuller would choose losing.

After Iowa, resistance crumbled; Bush was on the ropes, and if he had to put on funny hats and shake ten thousand hands, as Sununu kept hectoring him to do every morning, he was prepared to do it. On one manic Thursday, he set out in a blue parka and a baseball cap, worked a forklift at a lumberyard, moved on to Cuzzin' Ritchie's Truck Stop for a cup of coffee and took his celebrated spin in an eighteen-wheeler, with two ulcerous-looking Secret Service men clinging to the sides. "Wait till you see the sky-diving," Sununu joked, looking satisfied. The attempt at soul-transplant surgery provoked smiles at Dole headquarters, but they soon evanesced; the visuals of Bush playing workman began a five-day run in which he dominated every broadcast medium from drive-time to radio to network TV.

His revival seemed complete when his new speech emerged from Peggy Noonan's word processor three days out of Iowa. Noonan had made a considerable reputation ghostwriting for Reagan, catching his voice with nearly perfect pitch in part because she believed in him. She had planned to sit out the primary season. She was a working mother in her midthirties, with a husband and a baby boy at home in the Virginia exurbs, and none of the pretenders had moved her at first glance the way the president had. She liked her politics passionate, a Manichaean struggle between darkness and light, and no one auditioning, not Bush or anyone else, seemed as ideally suited as Reagan had been for the part.

She hadn't even known Bush until she signed up for a road trip with him on Air Force Two in 1986, mostly out of curiosity. She did a speech for him, and was invited forward to his cabin with the other writers. She was struck instantly by the difference between the big, attractive man sitting across from her and the smaller, more pallid figure she had seen on TV; he was long, tall and *cute*. She still refused a full-time job in the campaign, but the writer in her was intrigued by the challenge of teasing the *real* him into open view. She helped with his announcement of his candidacy, and when she heard him on the radio from New Hampshire, floundering through his deadly I-am-one-of-you routine, she reached for the phone.

"Do you want me to join you?" she asked him.

The answer was yes, and when Bush returned from his day trip to Washington she was with him. What Bush needed to focus on, in Noonan's view, was his long executive experience and his differences with Dole on the issues; if he could not reawaken that old Reagan magic, he could at least convey that he was a good, solid and well-credentialed fellow with sensible political views. She sensed a latent affection for him in his audiences— *really* latent, she conceded, but there to be tapped. She could almost feel people thinking that this poor guy was in trouble and needed their help, and her rewrite of his staple speech sought unashamedly to beg it of them.

Her prose, and his delivery, were in fact most affecting in their humility, a trait not previously conspicuous in what had been a smug, we're-number-one campaign. His attack on Dole was sharp-edged, three jeers for the senator's claim to be a "leader" when the institution he purported to lead was out of control. But what was really new was Bush in an apologetic, even a confessional mode. He was offering himself warts and all, he said, quoting a phrase of Oliver Cromwell's, and he did not hesitate to display them. He had a tendency, he said, to be taciturn, "to avoid going on with great, eloquent statements of belief. . . . But let me tell you, don't take that private side of me for lack of passion, lack of conviction about the United States of America. There may be better orators out there, but nobody believes more strongly. I don't always articulate, but I always do feel."

He might, for the first day or two, have been talking to empty rooms, so far as the press, the polls and his own managers were concerned; only Sununu among Bush's men seemed to believe that the sky wasn't really falling. The governor's evidence was primitive as against the sophistication of the fancy network surveys tracking Bush's downhill slide; he placed his trust instead in the John Sununu Shopping Mall Poll. He had worked the crowds at some mall stops with the campaign, asking people whether they were going to vote for Bush. No one was telling him, "No way," which meant, ipso facto, that things couldn't possibly be as bad as the press seemed to think.

His voice was lonely at first, but as Bush recovered his own footing so did his men. Jim Baker, from the discreet distance of his office at Treasury, phoned Teeter and Teeley with an idea from his 1980 Bush-for-president playbook: a telecast of one of the "Ask George Bush" forums the campaign was conducting around the state. The device had been effective in Bush's first, failed run for president, Baker remembered, and Teeley, who had been there, agreed.

They had, moreover, the perfect producer in Roger Ailes. His first job in politics had been doing "man-in-the-arena" shows starring Richard Nixon in 1968, the candidate on his feet fielding questions from an audience of polite civilians instead of reporters in war paint, and the format was second nature to him. He was walking through a case of pneumonia with a 102-degree fever, but he directed the taping on Wednesday night and spent forty-eight sleepless hours thereafter editing it down to thirty usable minutes.

The further trick was getting people to tune in, and Ailes's device was known in the trade as a roadblock. He bought simultaneous half hours for Saturday night on all but one of the TV stations serving the state, leaving dial-switchers, Atwater gloated, with *Hee Haw!* as the main alternative to George Bush. Every soft voter on Will Abbott's lists got two calls urging him or her to watch, and four busloads of young volunteers papered the malls with fliers advertising the show. The audience was large and the effect electric. You couldn't get through to headquarters that night, Teeley remarked afterward; the lines were tied up with Bush voters wanting to come home.

The second, more devastating strike in the media war was the attack ad on Dole. It was called "Straddle" for its two-faced image of the senator and its audio message: the charge that he had waffled on defense, oil-import fees and, sin of sins, raising taxes. It was a curiously inartistic piece of work, thrown together in a single night. But its aesthetics meant less to Ailes than its punch, which was substantial, and its late-hit timing, which, according to plan, would leave Dole no time to get out an effective answer.

Getting the stations to accept it after their deadlines, the problem that so buffaloed Dole's people, proved a great deal easier than selling it to Bush. He had never liked negative campaigning, and, like the more genteel members of his command group, he was still raw from the backlash against the campaign's attack on the Doles in Iowa.

The arguments flew back and forth through the week, Atwater, Ailes and Sununu leading the charge, the others on the G-6 resisting. The tension between hawks and doves had always been there, and was particularly sharp between Atwater, the ultimate operative, and Fuller, the consummate staff man. With Lee, a colleague said, it was always let's do the interview, let's get those commercials on the air, let's do one more thing; but if there was even an element of rolling the dice in it, Bush would go cautious, and Craig would be right there reinforcing him. "You don't need to do this," he would say, and Bush would reply, "You're right. Tell Lee no way."

This time, however, the numbers argued powerfully for risk, and the doves started coming around, first Teeter, then the others; by the end, Bush was all but alone with his misgivings. The clock was running when, late Friday afternoon, the hawks made their last pitch to him in his suite at the Clarion; it was the day the campaign touched bottom, and, they argued, they had to do something. Dole was on the air with a spot called "Doonesbury," in homage to the comic strip that inspired it; it featured George Bush's image fading into invisibility, with a voice-over questioning what it was he had done in all those impressive jobs.

You *have* to answer negative ads, Atwater said. It's core, fundamental politics.

Bush remained hesitant. Could the "Straddle" ad be documented? Were all the facts correct?

Atwater said they were. His research director, Jim Pinkerton, had put together a ten-page concordance to the commercial. They had Dole's voting record nailed all the way back to his opposition to the Kennedy tax cuts of 1963.

Bush received the information unmoved. "I just think it's negative," he said. "I just don't know if it will work."

The meeting wound down, and Atwater, disheartened, went jogging in the Clarion's parking garage, the only area he could find sheltered from the blowing snow outside. In midrun, he saw his friend and partner Roger Stone, a Kemp man, smiling at him.

"You guys aren't going to make it," Stone teased.

"Losing" was, as always, a fighting word to Atwater; he knew at that moment that he *had* to get "Straddle" up, and when he had showered and dressed he enlisted Sununu for a final assault on Bush's squeamishness.

Their chance came at the end of a staff meeting early Saturday morning, a run-through of the details of the day's order of battle. As they prepared to scramble to their duty stations, Atwater spoke, his voice low in the room.

"Mr. Vice President, I can't walk out of here without giving you my best advice," he said. The ad needed to run. *Today.*

Sununu backed his play: no one was going to think any less of Bush for toughening up his act.

Bush still seemed uncertain.

"George," his wife said, "I don't think it's so bad."

It was the vote Atwater needed. "Well," Bush said, "you guys know more about the state . . ."

His voice trailed off, and the group broke up.

"What does *that* mean?" Sununu asked Atwater, genuinely baffled.

As far as I'm concerned, Atwater said, it's a green light.

The hawks, as it happened, had already begun moving it out to stations without Bush's consent; the traffic deadlines were on them, and they were taking no chances on a glitch in delivery in the snow. But the shutdown times proved more flexible than they had imagined. With Bush's tacit OK in hand, Ailes's people went to work on the three key Boston stations, placing the ad on two of them, and Sununu was on the phone at 7 A.M. lining up a meeting with David Zamichow, the general manager of WMUR in Manchester. The governor had been courting Zamichow assiduously for two years and in January had brought Bush around in person, to do exclusive live and taped interviews and pose for mantelpiece pictures with the station staff. When Zamichow now agreed to the meeting, the governor took it as a triumph of personal diplomacy.

In fact Zamichow was mainly amused. His small and limber ABC affiliate, operating in the shadow of its larger Boston rivals, was routinely stretching the deadline for any candidate who asked. Kemp did ask, and Al Gore, and Dick Gephardt—everyone, indeed, who needed to make a change except Bob Dole; only Sununu seemed to think he had to make a state visit of it. He appeared at nine with Atwater in tow, natty in a double-breasted camel-hair topcoat and his most ingratiating smile. Atwater's technique for the occasion was to flatter his hosts by flattering their governor; he remarked on how good Sununu looked, for a man pushing fifty, and how bright his future would be in a Bush administration.

"What do you think the governor ought to be, y'know?" he asked. "What Cabinet position?" Bush was going to win, Atwater promised. "This guy right here"—he gestured toward Sununu—"he's going to do it for us."

The show was mostly wasted motion. The ad was already in hand, the station put it on the air and it played all day Saturday, painting Bob Dole as a closet revenuer.

Atwater's outward confidence was mostly manufactured. The dark cloud that had enveloped him coming out of Iowa had not yet parted; the overnight newscasts had been dominated by Haig's endorsement of Dole, and a new survey was circulating, showing Bush ten points behind. Atwater's own review of the polls told him that Dole's bump was over and that Bush's base vote was beginning to reassert itself. But he seemed not to believe the evidence of his eyes or his numbers. He sat up past midnight that night in his room at the Clarion, staring into his own abyss and preparing himself to fall in.

"It don't look good," he told a colleague. "Sununu—I don't know if I should believe him anymore. I don't know where the politics ends and the happy talk begins."

But Atwater was a believer in the big finish, the Churning Effect, he called it, and he was no longer so sunk in gloom that he couldn't stage-manage it. Five hundred volunteers flooded the state for the last days, including the entire Washington headquarters staff. The campaign lost track of whole busloads of them, and Atwater's deputy, Ed Rogers, guessed aloud that some of them would be found in the spring, frozen solid in ponds with their Bush signs still in their hands.

The OVP's ten-hour limit on the vice president's time was forgotten; his last Monday in the state merely began with eight phone-in radio interviews, a sitting on live network TV, and three fast-food breakfasts, the fare including pancakes at Bickford's, an order of Dunkin' Donuts and an Egg McMuffin. The tempo picked up from there, and other Bushes blossomed in out-of-the-way places he couldn't get to. Mailings got mailed, phone calls made and lawn signs posted. You'd put up a Dole sign one night, his man Bob Lighthizer said, and find twenty Bush signs in its place the next morning. It was like rain raising flowers out of the desert, he thought, and it never let up; between midnight and 5 A.M. on primary day, Sununu's volunteers planted five thousand more signs on lawns across southern New Hampshire.

It was a heavy churn indeed, Atwater's men thought with satisfaction, and its crowning touch was the appearance, on Monday, of a mystery guest—an offset, they hoped, to what Al Haig had done for Dole. Atwater and Sununu had booked studio time at WMUR, without saying what for; Roger Ailes simply appeared on schedule, took a look around and, amicably but firmly, started rattling off orders.

"I want that blue curtain," he said. "I want a flag—can you get me a newer flag so it's cleaner? Put this camera here. Put that camera there. Do you have a TelePrompTer?"

The answer was yes.

"How big is the type?"

He was told.

"I'm not sure my guest is going to be able to read from that far away."

Nothing was left to chance, no detail of color or camera angle, not even the look of the on-screen graphics.

"Don't give me a feminine typeface," Ailes said.

Zamichow took him to mean nothing wimpy.

The guest, at Bush's importuning, was Barry Goldwater, and he almost didn't come; he balked on being told that he would have to get up at four in the morning to make it on time, and the vice president was obliged to get on the phone again to beg him onto the plane they had chartered for him. In the end, he showed up, and Ailes taped a five-minute spot of the two men sitting side by side, the old frontiersman of conservative Republicanism conferring his blessing on the somewhat suspect claimant to his mantle.

It wasn't till that day that the cloud really lifted for Lee Atwater. The tracking polls still showed Bush and Dole neck and neck, but as he sat in his room in the Clarion contemplating the numbers, he saw another story hidden in them. The movement was all in the vice president's favor, and even if the polls were even, Atwater's private calculus was that Bush had a built-in seven-point advantage—two points thanks to Sununu's organization, two more courtesy of Dole's accident-prone campaign, and three from his own big churn at the finish.

His math, as it turned out the next night, was conservative. Practically all Bush's lost souls had come back to the fold; his 38 percent of the vote put him ten points ahead of the competition, a landslide in a five-way race. Jack Kemp, twenty-five behind in third place, was grievously wounded.

Pete du Pont, twenty-eight behind, would be back home in Delaware before the week was out. Pat Robertson and his silent army, twenty-nine behind, shrank overnight to human scale; his magic in the caucus halls had deserted him on the more open ground of a primary.

It was down to Bush and Dole, Atwater thought, and the coming showdown, in the South on or about Super Tuesday, seemed to him a foregone conclusion. New Hampshire, he mused, had been like the last scene in the film *Star Wars,* with the attack planes flying into the Death Star; the one and only way to blow up the space station and defeat the Empire was to fly down that groove into the center, and *boom!*—it was all over. Dole had had that chance in New Hampshire, Atwater thought, that one chance to blow us up, but he had crashed instead. The Empire had survived to strike back, and when it did, on Atwater's home field, the race was going to be over.

The Honey Trap

IT WAS ONE OF THOSE DEFINING MOMENTS in a video-age campaign, an electronic epiphany that can make or break a candidacy in the twinkling of a camera eye, and as soon as Dole's media man, Larry McCarthy, saw it he knew its cost. McCarthy was home in Washington, half watching the returns on TV and commiserating over the phone with a colleague, when Dole's dark visage materialized for a live-feed interview with Tom Brokaw on NBC. Brokaw, just finishing up with George Bush, asked whether he had anything he wanted to say to the man he had just beaten.

"No," Bush said, his social graces reinforced by his victory, "just wish him well and meet him in the South."

"And Senator Dole," Brokaw asked, "is there anything you'd like to say to the vice president?"

"Yeah," Dole said, eyes flashing angrily. "Stop lying about my record."

McCarthy's heart sank. A year's cosmetic surgery had been undone in six careless words; the bandages had been peeled back, and the man inside them was still the Bob Dole of stubborn memory and lingering caricature, still the dark prince of American politics. "It's over," McCarthy said into the telephone, and, while no one quite wanted to admit it yet, it was. They had, as a colleague would say later, put a stake into George

269

Bush and missed his heart; it was Dole who had impaled himself instead.

There had been a flicker of hope for Dole's men only the day before, a mini-bump back to a two-point lead in Wirthlin's tracking, but it had evanesced with the early network exit-polling on primary day. It was plain they were going to lose, badly, and Dole's mood was smoky almost from the moment he hit the streets; a du Pont worker needled him outside a polling place, and the senator responded by inviting him, on camera, to get back in his cave. He grumbled all day about Bush's "Straddle" ad and about his campaign's failure to answer it. Calls flew among his message people, warning one another of his displeasure; the shit was going to hit the fan, and everyone needed to get his alibi in order. There were going to be changes, the senator was saying, not caring who heard. The lapse had been inexcusable. "We"—by which he meant they—"dropped the ball."

His upset was visible when he arrived at Tom Rath's law office in Concord for lunch. Rath had arranged to have the best restaurant in town do the catering, as if it were a last meal for a condemned man. But Dole hadn't quit micromanaging his days down to the pettiest detail. A few minutes before his arrival, one of his batmen had called ahead, instructing Rath to forget the fancy spread; the senator would like Kentucky Fried Chicken and soft ice cream.

Dole appeared with Senator Rudman and two of his own senior hands, David Keene and Mari Maseng. They had the subdued look of a ball team that had just blown the World Series on an error in the ninth inning.

"We're going to lose this thing," Dole said. "By five to seven points."

No one argued with him. He and his party ate their chicken in silence, and then went out for a last, futile afternoon's campaigning.

The gloom was thickening when Rath showed up in the Merrimack Hilton lobby at six. With a fixed smile, he told reporters lurking there that it would be a single-digit defeat, worst case, as if they had never even entertained the idea of winning. A couple of drinks with Kim Wells and David Keene in the hotel lounge eased the tension a bit; on his second Stoly on the rocks, Rath did his impression of Senator Simon, intoning, in that sepulchral bass voice, *"It's . . . time . . . we . . . cared . . . again."* But when the news came on television, the group fell silent in the half-light, shushing the piano player so that they could hear.

"It appears that Vice President George Bush has made a remarkable recovery," Brokaw was saying on the outsize screen.

"Oh, come on," Rath pleaded. His cherub face fell. Keene and Wells sat silent, contemplating the void.

A sound bite of Dole's snappish encounter with the du Pont voter came on.

"No, no," Rath moaned.

But the screen kept spewing bad news, and Louis Georgopoulos, a longtime Manchester Republican pol, was looming in the doorway to the lounge, trying to catch Rath's eye. Georgopoulos flashed a thumbs-down sign. Rath knew what it meant. Three bellwether wards, Six, Nine and Eleven, had gone to Bush. It would be hard to catch up.

"I'm ready to hear the piano player again," Rath said.

Upstairs, in a room down the hall from the Dole suite, Dick Wirthlin sat alone and haggard, a man in a bunker, trying to comprehend where his numbers had led him wrong. The tools of his trade were scattered across the bed—charts, printouts, a calculator—and a large binder lay open on his lap. It seemed plain from his last day's polling that the politics of primogeniture had worked for Bush; the president's coattails were the strongest Wirthlin had ever seen. Bush's core support, he thought, had been like a Prussian square in nineteenth-century warfare, a solid block of 22 to 24 percent who held their ground under assault and never moved. Dole's backing, by contrast, had been soft from the beginning, impermanent as breakers on a beach, and Wirthlin, like everyone else, had mistaken it for a tide. The data, he thought, had been trying to tell him something all along, and he hadn't listened closely enough to hear.

He folded up his binder after a time and, without much relish, started down for what was to have been Dole's victory party. It wasn't going to be much fun. He knew he was in for some chivying from the press and his peers in the campaign, and Dole himself was bitter, composing wisecracks in his mind about how the highly paid "Dr. Dick" had begun whistling "Hail to the Chief" before the returns were in. Dole had a bit of Nixon in him, Wirthlin thought, a tendency to expect defeat and to glory in it; the real mistake had been giving him hope and so making his fall harder.

It was quite a game, quite a game, Wirthlin thought, leaving his room. A contact lens had slipped, and his left eye was beginning to water. He thought about a painting in his study, a Charles Russell oil of a hunter who has wounded his prey and lost it; it was called "Meat's Not Meat Till It's in the Pan." He should have remembered that, he thought, starting down the stairs. Sooner or later, everyone learned the meaning of hubris, and he guessed that New Hampshire had been his personal lesson.

The Plane From Hell

Dole slept soundly that night, then snapped bolt upright in bed at four-thirty, wide awake and wired tight; he was in the lobby by seven drinking coffee with his command group, ready to get going again. The campaign was not. Just ahead lay the Lesser Antilles, the trade name for the states between New Hampshire in February and Super Tuesday in March; a couple of them, Minnesota and South Dakota, had a neighborly fondness for the senior senator from Kansas, but Bush had tainted both victories by conceding them without a fight, and the way beyond was as blurry as a hand-drawn road map that had been left out in the rain. Dole's candidacy was sliding into chaos; the only analogues Dick Wirthlin could think of, searching his mental library afterward, were in Dante and Kafka.

They had only spotty resources on the ground for Super Tuesday, and L Street improvised a do-it-with-mirrors strategy to make the most of what there was. Their example was Fritz Mondale, who had won just two out of nine states on Super Tuesday 1984 and yet was perceived to have come back from the dead in his race with Gary Hart. Brock scanned his maps and his readouts for targets of opportunity and singled out Missouri, North Carolina, Oklahoma and Maryland; all four looked tough but doable in Wirthlin's polling.

"But we've got one of our best opportunities in South Carolina," Brock said in the course of the campaign's failed second attempt to recruit John Sears. "If we spend a half-million in media and some of Bob's time, we can win."

"Don't waste your money," Sears said curtly. South Carolina's primary was the Saturday appetizer for the Super Tuesday feast, and Atwater was all over it. It was a loser.

"What if we get Strom?" Brock asked. He meant Senator Strom Thurmond, the preeminent Republican in the state.

"His popularity isn't transferable," Sears said. It took a former senator to believe that a senator could deliver *anything.*

Brock was in fact a great deal less hopeful than he allowed himself to seem. He was losing his stomach for life with Bob, the decisions by whim and the crossed lines of authority; there were days after New Hampshire when he talked nostalgically about the long-ago days down home when politics had really been *fun,* a great, beer-drinking, hell-raising good time. The Dole campaign had stopped being fun maybe the day he arrived, and when the papers started saying that Dole was unhappy with him his best friends started telling him he should resign.

Brock considered it, at a war council with some of them late in February. His decision was to stay, but, he resolved, there were going to be changes, and they were going to begin with Don Devine and David Keene. They were supposed to be advisers, not staffers, and yet they were constantly making decisions and changing schedules without authority. They were undercutting him with their back channel to Dole, and he was going to put an end to it once and for all.

The two men had, in fact, taken over the road show in the days following the defeat in New Hampshire, moved in part by their own reciprocal contempt for Brock. Their loose, raffish manner and their irreverence toward tables of organization made them an impossible match with the chairman; they seemed to him to be ideologues and troublemakers, and he struck them, in Devine's words, as an old Young Republican suffering from arrested development. Keene had reached the limits of his tolerance the Friday after the primary and had walked out of headquarters, too disgusted to hang around any longer. At eleven that night, Dole's scheduler, Judy Harbaugh, called him. The senator had just come home from a Southern swing nursing a heavy chest cold and his smoldering furies, and he would be airborne again for South Dakota and Wyoming at seven the next morning.

"He needs you to come with him," Harbaugh told Keene. "He has no help."

Keene showed up with his bags the next morning and was appalled from the moment he clambered onto Dole's charter jet. The plane itself was a skyworn 737 with sputtery engines that regularly needed the aeronautical equivalent of jump-starting; it was known in the post–New Hampshire campaign as the Plane From Hell. There was no typewriter, no telephone, no fax machine, no way to produce a statement or to communicate with headquarters. The traveling staff consisted of Dole's bag-carrier, Mike Glassner, and his press spokesperson, Mari Maseng, so sick with an ear infection that she could barely drag herself from event to event. Dole's own morale was seabed low, and so was his patience with his new management. Once, popping a cold pill in at a stop in Wyoming, he said, openly, "Maybe I should check with Dr. Dick first."

In his discontent, he reached out to his old crowd and, in the first weekend out of New Hampshire, drew them around—Keene, Devine, Floyd Brown, his Midwest regional director, and Tom Synhorst, the hero of Iowa. Their assembly on the road began with some simple tactical decisions, but it transmuted itself in twenty-four hours into something near a mutiny. The four staff men gathered over beers in Keene's room at the Radisson in Duluth, trading seditious thoughts about the mess on L Street. Synhorst and Brown thought the whole place should be cleaned out, starting with Skip Watts, and they should be put in charge of political operations.

"You ought to send Floyd and me in there for two days," Synhorst said. "They've got to close that headquarters. They've got to fire those people, get rid of them."

Keene and Davis argued for more moderate solutions; the campaign, they said, couldn't afford any more bloodshed. "Just put Watts off in a corner somewhere," Keene said. "Give him a phone that can't dial out."

The meeting broke up after an hour and a half, Synhorst resolving to take his case directly to Dole, Keene retiring to his laptop computer to put his more diplomatic version into a memo. His message was that Brock was a good man and had brought in some good people, but they had little experience of '80s-model presidential politics, and they were doing fatal damage to the campaign. "In fact, all we have accomplished in Washington since the fall," he wrote, "has been to build up a huge institutional bureaucracy that has cost us millions of dollars, hamstrung our field operations and left us unable to make any meaningful decisions. . . . What has been assembled in Washington has not [worked] and will not work." He proposed the nearest thing possible to a bloodless shakeup: easing Brock into a role as principal spokesman, neutralizing Watts as political director, and reconstituting the strategic and political command with the old guard back at the top.

Keene finished the memo, reread it and showed it to Devine. But he never sent it to Dole; there weren't going to be any major changes, he thought, so he and Devine stayed on the plane, kibitzers without portfolio, supporting and even encouraging Dole's tendency to redo his schedules on the fly. The Plane From Hell was ricocheting around the landscape, out of reach of Brock's flight controllers on L Street, and when the senator canceled one stop in Minnesota for two in Springfield, Missouri, and Oklahoma City, Brock blew up.

You can't run a campaign like this, he told Dole long distance when they finally made contact. The people they would be standing up in Minnesota were complaining, there weren't any advance men on the ground in Springfield or Oklahoma City, and as far as Brock was concerned there weren't going to be any.

"When you land," he told Dole, "you can go check in at the Hertz counter."

"We don't need anybody," Dole said. "We're just going to have press conferences. They're important."

"Of course they're important," Brock said. "I agree. It's not the decision that's illogical, it's the timing."

Both timing and logic seemed perfectly in order to Devine and Keene, given that both Missouri and Oklahoma were on the target list for Super Tuesday, but Brock was still sputtering when Devine called in a few minutes later.

"We just want to talk scheduling," Devine said.

"Why you calling *us*?" Brock asked, his irritation showing.

"We wanted to talk to you," Devine said.

"You don't have to talk to me," Brock said. "We've closed the scheduling shop. You're going to do it from the plane, go on and do it. But you're not on the payroll, understand that. You tell the pilot to go anywhere you want to go. If you feel like it, send us a postcard periodically. We'd like to know if you're doing all right and you're healthy."

The mutiny at that point became a skyjacking, the campaign hostage to the insurgents on the plane, and the story was beginning to leak when the Plane From Hell set down in Minneapolis that Tuesday for what would be Dole's last victory party. They checked in with L Street, and Keene found himself on the phone with Brock.

"Hey, Bill," Keene said, "how do you like what's going on?"

"I like the results in Minnesota and South Dakota, and I like nothing else," Brock said. "I intend to come out there and fix you."

He did, catching up with the road company the next night in Charlotte, North Carolina. He didn't speak to Keene or Devine. Instead, he dropped into a seat next to Dole's, and as the Plane From Hell huff-puffed toward Orlando, Florida, he delivered his message: the two had to go.

"They're just trying to help," Dole protested.

"I've had it," Brock said. He had tried to work with them, but they had their own agendas, not necessarily the same as Dole's, and he wasn't comfortable with them; he had to have everybody singing from the same sheet of music. "I'm going to terminate the relationship," he said.

Dole didn't argue the matter; it was plain that Brock would quit if he didn't get his way.

The death warrant accordingly was signed, and while Dole was speaking to a business group at Ronnie's Restaurant in Orlando the next morning Brock sat down with Keene at a table a few yards away. He was starting his lecture about the need for order when a still photographer for *Time* and a camera crew from ABC drifted over, wanting file pictures of two senior Dole operatives talking business. They were busily and obliviously recording the scene when Brock leaned close to Keene, nearly head to head, smiling for the cameras. His voice was pitched low, as if he were making some confidential point about tactics.

"I've decided to cut the string," he said. "You're finished."

"That's fine, Bill," Keene said. "You know I'll always do anything Dole wants."

"Yeah," Brock said, "you get very high marks for loyalty. But you're never going to work on anything for me."

Devine spied them from a distance and, sensing trouble, asked whether he might join them.

"I might as well take both of you on at once," Brock said. "You're fired. You're off the plane in Jacksonville"—the next stop—"if I have to throw you off. You can find your own way home."

The two protested that Brock had no authority to fire them—they had been hired by Dole.

"I tell you what," Brock said. "I sign the checks in my organization. Bob signs the checks in the Senate. You're on his payroll, that's fine. But you're not on mine."

The campaign wandered off to its fittingly surreal next happening, a visit to a movie-production facility going up in Orlando. It was, as Keene would say later, the event of a lifetime, its setting eight hundred windblown acres of dirt, its backdrop a half-finished concrete building, its audience a few chilled civilians, a handful of studio factotums, and four actors dressed up as Charlie Chaplin, Woody Woodpecker, Mae West and the Frankenstein monster. Dole let himself be posed with Chaplin and the monster, a decision he would regret in the morning; the picture ran in the next day's *Washington Post,* close by a headline reading 2 SENIOR CONSULTANTS FIRED FROM SEN. DOLE'S PRESIDENTIAL CAMPAIGN.

The firees had hoped that Dole might reprieve them, but they knew he was in an impossible position. "I'll see you back in Washington," he told Keene when the two were offloaded, as promised, in Jacksonville. "I need your help. I guess that's how it has to be."

"How am I supposed to handle the press?" Keene asked.

"Gingerly," Dole replied.

The Plane From Hell flew on, leaving Devine and Keene to find their way back to their baggage—it had been left behind in Orlando—and their businesses in Washington. It was Bill Brock who remained aboard, his victory and his status nominally secure, but the episode was a public embarrassment for Dole, and the relationship was never more than professionally correct thereafter. Brock receded deeper into the background, alone, passive and depressed, suffering Dole's regular public insults in bruised silence. He likened himself one day to Joe Btfsplk, the luckless character in "L'il Abner" with a permanent black cloud over his head, and he was about as welcome in Dole's presence. "This is a party for my closest friends," the senator would say at a staff gathering late in the campaign. "I understand Bill Brock is out of town."

By then, Brock had made his last and least fortunate contribution to the strategy: urging Dole on in his determination to make a fight for South Carolina. Everyone else in the top echelon opposed the idea. They had already cut their media budget for all of Super Tuesday from an economy-class $2 million to a noncompetitive $800,000, and their low-tech operations on the ground were starving, so straitened that campaign volunteers had to make their own hand-done yard signs. They would be spending money they didn't have on a state they couldn't win. What they needed, in the nearly unanimous view on L Street, was to go back to their short list of Super Tuesday target states, try to cherry-pick a couple of them out of Bush's grasp, hope that Pat Robertson would win a couple more, and carry the fight to the friendlier heartland soil of Illinois.

But the scent of defeat, mingled with the seduction of Thurmond's support, kept drawing Dole and Brock deeper into their own dreamscape. The senior staff met in Dole's rooms at the Atlanta Hilton a week before the primary to look at the arithmetic, a seminar led by one of Brock's men with an easel and a series of charts as visual aids. The picture wasn't a pretty one. Dole would have to hold Bush to something fewer than 600 of the 753 delegates to be chosen on Super Tuesday, and even then he would have to win seven of every ten delegates at stake thereafter. The prospect, as even Brock saw, belonged more in the realm of prayer than of temporal possibility; a megaton-range blowout was already taking form in Wirthlin's polling in the South.

Dole, watching the chalk-talk from behind a desk, seemed to understand how hard it would be to slow Bush's progress. He looked back at Tom Rath, who was leaning on a credenza behind him. "If he gets close to six hundred," Dole said, "it's over."

Yet he seemed impelled to try, and a last, desperate game plan was put together, a $500,000 closing media blitz aimed at stealing some delegates from Bush in his fortress states in the Deep South. Skeptics dubbed the effort Operation Yamamoto, for the Japanese admiral who masterminded Pearl Harbor and went down in flames a year later, and Bill Lacy, among others, argued strenuously against it. "Don't spend it," Lacy said. "You're not going to get a thing out of it. Take your half-million and buy Illinois TV." But the plan went forward, and South Carolina was on the target list.

So Dole plunged on with his hopeless canvass of the state, trying to buy the unattainable with the coin of Thurmond's blessing and his own furious energy; if he and Robertson could somehow scissor Bush there, they would blunt his momentum going into Super Tuesday three days later and survive to the next round.

"We can't get Dole to stop campaigning in South Carolina," his man Bernie Windon told a friend in midpassage. "Something's driving him. He wants to spend all his time there."

Long after the campaign was over, when he and Dole were barely on speaking terms, Bill Brock was reminded of an old Tennessee story that might have served him and his candidate better at the time. It was the tale of a truck-driving instructor asking a trainee what he would do if he were trying to pass a car on a two-lane road and saw another truck barreling straight at him.

"I'd wake up my relief driver," the trainee replied.

The instructor asked why.

" 'Cause," the trainee replied, "he ain't never seen a wreck like this."

Between the Elephant's Toes

What lay ahead for Dole was not so much a head-on collision as a honey trap set for him by Lee Atwater—a temptation he could not resist into a snare he could not escape from alive. South Carolina had been a centerpiece of Atwater's Southern strategy from the beginning, worth, he figured, a five- to eight-point bump on Super Tuesday if Bush won a convincing victory. The papers gave him a bad fright when, a couple of days out of New Hampshire, they reported that Dole had decided to finesse the primary; the trap couldn't be sprung if the senator wasn't there. But Thurmond's fortuitous endorsement had drawn him back in and raised the stakes as well, a perception Atwater cheerfully encouraged. If Bob Dole can't win here, he told reporters in earnest confidence, I don't know where he *can* win. It was, as he knew, a setup, a sucker's game. The state was as wired as a professional wrestling match, which chanced to be his favorite sport. Lee Atwater had come home.

He had spent his months Up North dancing between the elephant's toes, in the vivid phrase of an old associate down home; he had endured the suspicions of the Bush family, the sting of defeat in Iowa, and his own blue funk in New Hampshire, but the elephant couldn't squash you if you were lucky and kept dancing, and Atwater did. Perhaps his strongest single ticket to survival, even when his job had been on the line, had been his knowledge of the South and its seedling Republican Party down to the county-courthouse level. He had persuaded the campaign of its central importance, except they thought of it as a firebreak while he saw it as a kind of secular Armageddon—the decisive last battle for the nomination. It was where they could bury Bob Dole and Pat Robertson, he believed, and in the South, as against Yankee country, he felt utterly sure of his ground.

Its gateway, by happy chance, was South Carolina, where he had come of age and apprenticed in the blade-between-the-ribs school of Southern politics. He cultivated a good-ole-boy style in adulthood, Lee Atwater as one of the Snopeses come drawling out of the pages of Faulkner to euchre the city boys at their own game. His rival David Keene told him once that the Bush crowd would never really accept him, because, Keene teased, "you talk funny." In fact Atwater's Dixified manner was part of his game.

It was not guileless, but little about him was. His real origins were straight-up "Leave It to Beaver"; he was a child of the suburban new South, the son of an insurance adjuster and a high-school Spanish teacher whose pooled incomes put them in the middle of the middle class. He was a jiggly, trembly, nervous boy, his mother, Toddy Atwater, remembered, and until he got serious in college he expended his hyper energies on everything except his studies. He made mischief, led his own rock band— called, prophetically, the Upsetter's Review—and got to be known around A. C. Flora High School in Columbia as Big At. The nickname was his own invention, a denial of his runty size, but he sold it; he was already a master of artifice and illusion in his teens.

He came to professional politics straight out of college and the Young Republicans, a leap he tried to make too high too fast; he was all of twenty-three when he took on his first clients, General William Westmoreland for governor and Carroll A. Campbell Jr. for lieutenant governor, and was mortified when both candidacies crashed. But the connection with Campbell persisted. They were two young men riding the new electoral wave in the South in the early 1970s, the desertion of the white middle class to the Republican Party; each profited by it, and each helped the other up the ladder, until Campbell had wangled a high-up place for Atwater in the Reagan political apparatus and Atwater had advised Campbell in his successful run for the governorship.

On the way up, Atwater acquired his bad-boy reputation, the aura of a man who, a Democratic adversary said, had no moral compass governing his will to win. Even his friends wondered what was in it for Lee; he lived like a disheveled scholarship student, in housing one cut above the slums of Columbia, and drove a battered yellow Datsun with a radio worth more than the hulk around it. A colleague walking the beach with him one day asked him in genuine puzzlement what made Big At run and was struck by his nearly Faustian answer.

"It's not money," Atwater said. "It's not power. It's *knowledge*."

If so, he seemed willing to pay for it, and an anthology of Big At stories grew up in his train, rumors that he had Segrettied one opponent mostly for laughs or sunk another with a seriously dirty trick. Some of the capers ascribed to him were merely prankish, as when a worker in a rival campaign sold a stranger a fifty-dollar ticket to a fund-raising concert and was promptly arrested for scalping. Some were ugly, as when a Jewish candidate running against one of Atwater's clients found himself suddenly under attack from a fringe third-force opponent as a nonbeliever in Jesus Christ; Big At was alleged by a rival to have supplied the ammunition. Atwater denied all the particulars, and most, including the suggestion of anti-Semitism, were unsubstantiated by the available evidence. But the larger air of savagery they gave him became part of his jujitsu, and he did not discourage it. It could be, a friend said, a marvelous distraction in a race; it would get the other side hating him so bad that they would focus on how to fuck Lee instead of on getting their own guy elected.

The further asset he brought to the Bush campaign was his Rolodex, the nearest thing to a comprehensive *Who's Who* in the Republican South. The names were few but precious; there were, by Atwater's reckoning, no more than eighty or ninety people per state who had ever worked full time in a successful Republican campaign, and if you got to them first no one else could get anything going. His strategy from the first had been to lock them down early, and he had stepped up the tempo when, late in 1986, he heard about the Contra half of the Iran-Contra scandal and read its potential in Bush's ashen face. He and his deputy, Ed Rogers, had headed south early in the new year and done a series of statewide meetings, signing up people before there was anything real for them to do. His sales pitch rested less on Bush's locally suspect merits than on their standing by Reagan in a jam. "If you're going to let this attack on the president keep you from doing the right thing and supporting his logical heir," he had said at every stop, "you're not a Reagan party loyalist."

Dole was coming in and entertaining the same people, but his visits, Atwater said, were like Chinese dinners: since there was no one on the ground to follow up, the locals would be hungry again a half hour after he left. Atwater's operatives, by contrast, lived where they worked and saw that there were things for their recruits to do. Much of it was makework— petition drives were one favorite enterprise—but it made people feel involved simply by keeping them busy.

The most important of Atwater's recruits was one of the first, Governor Campbell, a blow-dried, lantern-jawed farmer and fast-food entrepreneur as tough and as hungry as Atwater himself. Their friendship apart, where friendships usually reposed in politics, Campbell fit Atwater's profile of the perfect helpmeet as neatly as John Sununu had in New Hampshire: he was a governor, he had a battle-seasoned organization in place, and he was available at reasonable cost—the chairmanship of Bush's Southern campaign and later, as lagniappe, a token mention as a vice-presidential possibility. His state, moreover, was the indispensable first piece in Atwater's Super Tuesday plan, the cueball, he called it, that would leave the table aligned in their favor if they hit it right.

Neither did he mistake the importance of South Carolina to himself. He liked to say, kiddingly, that the secret of survival was to play dumb and keep moving, but there was always a time and a place where you had to stand and fight, and South Carolina was it for Big At; he needed to win there almost as badly as Bush did, and by payback time in March he had been working at it for three years.

His partner in the enterprise from the first had been Warren Tompkins, then director of the state Republican Party and later Campbell's chief of staff. They set out together in 1985 with a list of the top 250 party people in the state and began their long, patient hunt for support. The currency they traded in was loyalty to Carroll Campbell and Lee Atwater rather than to the vice president; in those days, a rival operative said, no one in the state gave a hoot and a holler for George Bush. By the time one of Atwater's ex-colleagues, Rod Shealy, signed on to do South Carolina for Dole in the late summer of 1987, most of the people in *his* Rolodex were already gone. Just in case, Atwater had worked up a list of twelve or fifteen of Shealy's best contacts—his business partner, his home-county sheriff, even a state legislator who happened also to be Shealy's sister—and delivered it to Bush. On a Sunday afternoon in August, they all got calls from the vice president of the United States, cementing their support, by thanking them personally for it.

L Street seemed oblivious to what was happening, and Shealy thought it best to let them know. "I don't think you guys understand what Atwater's all about," he told Brock not long before the primary. "We're not playing the same game."

It was, by then, too late to start. There were some crazy moments for Atwater in his blue period between Iowa and New Hampshire, days when the bottom seemed to be falling out in South Carolina as it was everywhere else. He kept calling Tompkins, twice a day and more, for reassurance, but the news only aggravated his attack of the williwaws. All hell was breaking loose, Tompkins told him. The numbers were crumbling like crazy. They were doing their phoning every night, trying to shore up their voters, and you could just see them slipping away.

The alarms roused the rebel in Atwater, the side of him that kept a likeness of Stonewall Jackson on his office wall close by the obligatory pictures of Ronald Reagan and Strom Thurmond. His eyes darted, in moments of tension, and his face was as tight and as threatening as a clenched fist.

"Be prepared," he told Tompkins, "for the possibility of do-or-die in South Carolina."

The ship righted itself with Bush's victory in New Hampshire, and his two prime opponents helped, Dole merely by contesting the state and Robertson with the foolish declaration that he was going to win it. Robertson's intent had been in part to re-ignite his believers after his poor finish in New Hampshire, but he seemed to the professionals in his own command to have overread his progress in the polls and his possibilities in what an aide called "God's country" in the South. When he announced on the tarmac at the Greenville-Spartanburg airport that he was throwing down the gauntlet in South Carolina and would be in trouble if he lost it, his manager, Marc Nuttle, appeared to flinch.

Robertson gave it a game shot, grinding through twenty-one towns by bus in two days, but his road show wasn't clicking as it had clicked in Iowa, and by the end he knew it. He didn't have the crowds, he fretted one day, flying in from a side trip to Georgia; he didn't have the time, he didn't have the TV money, he didn't have the organization and he didn't have the feeling that had been so palpable in Iowa. He had, moreover, fallen victim to the amateurism that had once been his prime attraction to his followers; he committed a nearly daily series of gaffes, and when he finally wandered into Lee Atwater's spider web, suggesting without evidence that Atwater had somehow orchestrated the Jimmy Swaggart sex scandal to damage him, he was finished. His rating in his own polls swooned from 19 to 10 percent in a day, and it was all he could do in the time remaining to bring his lost sheep back to the fold. There wasn't any way he was going to get first after that, he mused. He could just sense it in the air.

So, by the close, could Atwater. He had moved into the state, taking rooms at the Radisson in Columbia, nominally to oversee the last ten days of the campaign. In fact he left the heavy organizational lifting to Tompkins, staying largely out of his way and practicing his own mesmeric arts on the press; you could lose an election, a sometime colleague said, and two days later Lee would have everyone believing you had won. They closed, as usual in an Atwater campaign, in full churn, Bush working the soft vote in the mill towns in the northwest, Tompkins loosing bands of fresh-faced kids with yard signs to create the appearance of motion.

The numbers were firming up one night toward the end, not just in South Carolina but across the whole wide terrain of Super Tuesday; Teeter's polls for Bush, like Wirthlin's for Dole, held out the ripening possibility of a seventeen-state shutout. Atwater, his vision affirmed, put in for $750,000 more for TV ads and candidate time in the states where Dole, in his reading, was still within reach—Missouri, Oklahoma and North Carolina. The numbers told him they could win them all.

The idea made some of his more cautious G-6 colleagues nervous, especially Bob Teeter, the polltaker, and Bob Mosbacher, the money man. The two remembered the Mondale precedent; if Dole won even two states, they told Atwater one night, he would still be alive, and they would have busted their budget for nothing.

Atwater heard them out, but he could feel it: he was home. Once South Carolina came in, the rest of the South would follow, and Dole would be mortally wounded.

"We can break his back," he said when the others were finished. "It will finish them."

He was right. The first domino fell, according to plan, on a Saturday night early in March. Bush had won 48 percent of the vote in South Carolina, sweeping all thirty-seven delegates; Dole, at 21 percent, and Robertson, at 19, were lost in the dust. The cueball was rocketing toward Super Tuesday and what would be a sixteen-victory, 577-delegate landslide for the vice president—a rout that left only the Washington State caucuses for Robertson and nothing at all for Dole.

They threw a victory party for Bush at the state fairgrounds in Columbia that night, and Atwater was downstage center with Carroll Campbell when the vice president phoned his congratulations. But he vanished shortly thereafter, and Ed Rogers went looking for him. It was a big fucking moment for Lee, Rogers thought, maybe the biggest in his life; he had been living for weeks with a gun at his head, and he had not just ducked the bullet, he had won big. He had earned his celebration, and he hadn't hung around to savor it. When Rogers found him, after a long search, he was out wandering the parking lot with an old buddy from A. C. Flora High, being Big At again, back in the impish innocence of his youth.

Rogers got him back inside and onstage, and someone put a guitar into his hands, a remembrance of the Upsetter's Review. "Rock me, baby," Big At sang, "like your back ain't got no bone. . . ." There would be bumpy days ahead for him, soul-bruising times when his authority would fall into question again, but he had danced out from under the elephant's toes at least for a season. Even Barbara Bush, who had once mistrusted him, would say that in the weeks to come; Lee, she would say, was the only one who saw that it would be all over on Super Tuesday, and she didn't mind telling the whole country so.

The Final Days

For mind-numbing days, the Plane From Hell had borne Bob Dole through a seventeen-state blur of tarmac scenes, little made-for-television tableaux of the candidate surrounded by beefy state legislators and county commissioners in dark suits and tight smiles. "Looks good," the suits would assure him, or, more guardedly, "It's coming on, Senator." But the senator, in his weariness, was coming to see the futility of the exercise—the aimless, endless flying around looking for crowds and setting down if, say, you saw fifty people in a parking lot in Rhode Island. It was a journey to nowhere, and when he summoned his traveling party to his suite at the Alameda Plaza in Kansas City, Missouri, at eight o'clock on Super Tuesday morning, he seemed to know it.

They found him finishing the laborious daily ritual of tying his own necktie one-handed. He wanted to talk about the delegate numbers, and no one tried to blue-sky it for him. His men had begun thinking of ways to ease him gently, in his own time, toward the exit.

"How tough is it going to be?" he asked Tom Rath.

"We're going to have a tough time, given what's happening today," Rath said. It was going to be a blowout.

There would be compensations, Kim Wells guessed, hoping Dole would get the hint. Bush would surely be defeated in the fall, and Dole would be left standing, the preeminent Republican in a Democratic capital.

The idea plainly had occurred to the senator. Bush couldn't be elected, he said. He would be clobbered with his piece of the Iran-Contra mess and with his dealings as CIA director with General Manuel Antonio Noriega of Panama, who had lately been indicted in a stateside drug-trafficking investigation.

"He'll fold up," Dole said.

He looked down at his tie. It was one of seven given him by a man in New Hampshire who made them by hand.

"It's the only thing I ever got out of New Hampshire," he said. "Seven ties and seven delegates."

But he kept plowing on, driven, some of his people thought, less by any dream of a miracle than by his animus toward the vice president. His passage into the shadow of defeat appeared to his closest friends to have blotted out any last glimmer of tolerance or civility he felt for his rival; he couldn't believe, one of them said, that a man he found so insubstantial was in the process of beating him for the nomination. When Bush ducked an invitation to debate him in Illinois, Dole spoke mordantly of going on alone with a life-size cutout of the veep and a tape recording of his voice squeaking, "I make decisions all the time! I make decisions all the time!"

None of it helped. He had disentangled himself from the knot of dark suits in Peoria and was doing a press conference on the tarmac when Rath called Bill Lacy from a pay phone for the early exit polling. It was worse even than they had imagined—"a wipeout," Lacy said, "of nuclear proportions."

Rath started scribbling numbers on a folded sheet of legal paper: 61–22 Bush in Florida, 68–16 Bush in Kentucky, and on and on. He tucked the paper into his pocket and got back on the plane. We've got a week left, he was thinking.

They were encamped for the night at a suburban Hyatt outside Chicago—our Stalingrad, Mike Murphy, the media consultant, called it—when the final returns revealed the scale of their defeat. Liddy Dole had flown in aboard her charter jet for the vigil, her normally cheerful mien gone pale and morose; she hadn't even brought in her native North Carolina for her husband. It hardly mattered; *none* of Dole's target states had come through for him.

The count and its meaning were plain when Dole encountered Tom Synhorst in the hotel corridor outside his rooms.

"It's almost over," Dole said.

"No, it's not," Synhorst answered gamely, but it was, and everyone knew it.

There was some perfunctory talk at a staff meeting late that night of a last, rearguard attack on Bush as unelectable, a tack plainly made moot by the night's numbers.

"How can we make that argument," Rath wondered, asking the obvious, "when this guy has just carried sixteen states?"

Saturday Night Live

The real business before the Dole command, once they saw the dimensions of his rout, was beginning to prepare the ground for an orderly retreat; in the morning, Wells called L Street to get the legal department working on the details of suspending a campaign. No one, by then, believed Dole should go on much longer. If he lost Illinois, Brock joked aloud, there would be nothing left to do except give him and Liddy a road map and put them on a Greyhound bus—the campaign would be that far gone.

But neither Brock nor anyone else was yet prepared to put the case directly to Dole. When the command group met with him the morning after, nominally to talk about scheduling, the language was carefully indirect.

"Friend," Brock asked, "what do you want to do? We've gone through the numbers—we just can't get them to add up."

Dole wasn't sure; he wanted to wait for one last Wirthlin poll in Illinois. But as he canvassed his people individually during the day, he found little sustenance for his will to carry on.

"We're trying to decide whether to pull the plug," he told Synhorst.

Synhorst, this time, did not bother feigning optimism. He had spent the past several days in Illinois, surveying their operations there with sinking heart; their people on the ground didn't even have a list of phone numbers for their prospective Dole delegates.

"If you're looking for it in Illinois, don't," Synhorst said. "It isn't here."

Dole prided himself on his realism, and was even then in the process of working through his pain toward its inescapable dénouement. He had had a long, bitter acquaintance with adversity, and had always believed that it was useless doing instant replays in your mind; it was best to put it behind you and get on with your life. His wife, in this, was a step behind him. She was a worrier; she had come out of Super Tuesday tormenting herself with what-ifs, till Dole gently told her, "Don't spend any more time than you have to on that project. It doesn't pay off."

But Dole wasn't ready to cry quits yet, certainly not before she was; he chose to stay at the table with his dwindling stack till his last chips were gone. His resolve left his people with no choice but to follow along in his train, groping in the dark for inspiration while they waited for him to come around. One night at midweek, Brock suggested bringing in Jeane Kirkpatrick, the doyenne of the neoconservative right, and Donald Rumsfeld, the former secretary of defense, to blitz the state for Dole.

Kim Wells didn't think it would help.

"You've been taking negative pills again," Brock said, looking nettled.

"No," Dole said, "he's being realistic."

Their course, as usual, was complicated by their slo-mo deliberative processes, about the right media or anything else. A written proposal from Ken Khachigian for a thirty-minute closing TV special had been languishing for weeks, unattended and unanswered. The campaign was still thinking thirty-*second* spots and had a new one in the can, called "Strong Man," trying to transmute Dole's supposed meanness into toughness. In a fit of gallows humor, Dole proposed that they give up and redo it as "Mean Man," with visuals of him kicking a little old lady and pushing a man in a wheelchair over a cliff. His command group was still hemming and hawing over the half-hour show when Wirthlin's new poll came in late Thursday afternoon and showed Dole eighteen points behind. On Friday morning, Dole called in from the road with a command decision: they would do the show Saturday night, live, from Knox College in Galesburg, Illinois.

His media people were horrified; live programming, in politics, was always dicey as against the controlled environment of a studio, and with the National Collegiate Athletic Association basketball tournament in progress, every TV production truck in America appeared to be booked. Liddy Dole was on the phone to Mike Murphy, urging, almost begging him to try harder. "Let's do it for Bob," she said. "He's so tired."

Soon thereafter, Dole himself called in, asking what the problems were. Murphy told him.

Dole was silent for a moment.

"Look," he said finally, "I know it's tough. I'm not asking you to do anything easy. But we're thirty points behind, and if I'm going to go down the tubes, I'd at least rather go down doing something."

It wasn't easy, and the price in what the TV business euphemistically calls production values was only too painfully visible. What amounted to a mobile television station was assembled piece by piece and scrambled to Galesburg, one uplink truck breaking down on the way. Checks for the vendors involved were flown out from Washington; the terms were always cash-and-carry for a dying campaign. The hall was an old one, the site of the fifth Lincoln–Douglas debate in 1858, and the technicians worried about the wiring.

The concern, as it turned out, was well taken. Five minutes into the program, the power abruptly crashed. The on-screen offering showed Dole's face freeze-framed for forty-five seconds. Then the monitors in Galesburg went black. The technicians started ripping up power cords. The station broadcasting the program in Chicago rolled a campaign videotape. "We've got a problem," Dole's voice could be heard saying. He was talking about drugs in America, but he might have been describing the last, terminal throes of his campaign; the next morning, a new poll showed him thirty-four points behind.

A Word from Richard Nixon

The final margin was nineteen, and while he went through the motions of carrying on, his mind was on what he had begun to call the "exit strategy"—a way to get out with as much leverage and as many options as he could preserve. The returns in Illinois were still being counted when Dole called his old friend Bob Ellsworth, in Stuttgart on business, to ask his counsel. Ellsworth had some thoughts on the subject, and he discussed them with Dole, but he knew where to go and whom to see to close the sale. The path of least resistance to advice, with Dole, led to Saddle River.

They met once again over coffee in Richard Nixon's library late in March, Dole and Ellsworth in shirtsleeves, Nixon still buttoned into his suit as if he hadn't been out of it since the last time they had gathered. The mood was forward-looking, and as light as they could make it in the circumstances. At one point, Dole fished up a paper he wanted to show Nixon and extricated it from an envelope with his working left hand.

"For a one-armed guy, he's very ambidextrous, isn't he?" Nixon told Ellsworth.

Dole laughed.

But the subject was serious, and Nixon, whose time was always meticulously planned, got quickly to the point.

"How do you feel," he asked, framing the question as delicately as he could, "about this not working out the way you wanted it to?"

"Oh, you know," Dole said, "there's some pain associated with it, but you've got to move on."

"That's exactly the right attitude to have," Nixon told him, "and I can speak with some authority on how to feel when you've lost a big one. You must never look back."

"Elizabeth worries about it a lot," Dole said; she hadn't yet quit her endless and useless postmortems.

"Tell her to go back and read in the Bible about Lot's wife," Nixon said. "She looked back and was turned into a pillar of salt."

They discussed the tactics of Dole's surrender, not its timing. Dole's first aim should be to keep his options open, Nixon said; the Senate leadership was always there, a kind of security blanket, but there might be something better for him in a Bush administration, if he played his cards right.

"Under no circumstances must you go to Bush," Nixon said. "You can say nice things about Bush, but leave it to occur to Bush to come to you if he wants something."

The question was what Bush might want. There was, Nixon said, the possibility of a place in the Cabinet, though the only job he thought suitable for a man of Dole's talents would be secretary of state.

"I think Jim Baker has that locked up," Dole said.

Nixon agreed, but State wasn't really what he had in mind. Dole, he said, should begin thinking hard about the prospect of being offered the vice-presidential nomination on a Bush ticket, and if it was offered, he should accept. Yes, the former president agreed, it was an improbable pairing, given the bad blood between the two men, but it was irresistible and even imperative that it happen. Without Dole as his running mate, Bush was going to lose in November.

While Dole and Ellsworth listened in absorbed silence, Nixon did what amounted to a state-by-state analysis—a geopolitical profile in which Bush would have problems in the Northeast, the South and the Far West and would need the Midwest to win. The Iowa caucuses had been a foretaste of how the Farm Belt would treat Bush on his own; neither the votes nor the presidency would be there for him without Bob Dole on the ticket.

There was, moreover, no downside risk for Dole in Nixon's scenario. If the ticket won, he would be vice president, vastly more powerful, Nixon thought, than Bush had been in the same job. "And if Bush loses," the former president went on, "you'll be the most important Republican in the country. If he asks, you must accept."

Dole sat quiet, his face impassive.

"I hope you don't have any tough feelings," Nixon said. "You and Bush are nothing compared to the hatred between Eisenhower and Taft."

Dole brushed the notion aside with a wave of his hand. "Yeah," he said, "there's absolutely nothing like that between us."

The sitting ended inconclusively, Dole's cards held close to his shirt-front, but a seed quite evidently had been planted. He called Ellsworth the next day to say he would be pulling out in three or four days—the whole deal in the Senate Caucus Room, he said, with all his colleagues, pro-Dole and pro-Bush, in attendance.

"Call Nixon," he told Ellsworth.

When Ellsworth did, a day later, Nixon sent Dole his regrets along with a last reinforcing bit of advice not to go begging to Bush for anything. He was as sure as ever that his dream match would, or ought to, happen. "If Bush is going to win," he said, "he needs Dole on the ticket."

Three days later, in the bosom of the Senate, Bob Dole finally surrendered his sword. His curtain speech was spare and to the point. "I am a fighter and I don't like to lose," he said in his flat baritone, but the time had come to stand down. He would do all he could to elect Republicans in

November and, he added, as if it hurt a bit to say so, "all I can do for our nominee, George Bush."

He left the crowded room without taking questions, retiring to his office to take a prearranged call from Bush on the road in Wisconsin. "Well, George," he said aloud, waiting for the phone to ring, "you call to apologize for lying about my record?" He was kidding this time, and when the call came through he was gracious, trying not to seem angry or hungry. His interest in the vice-presidency had already begun to show, to the mystification of some of his people; they simply assumed that Bush was going to lose and that, as one of them said that afternoon, Dole would be the early front-runner in '92.

"Yeah, that's how old I'll be," the senator replied dryly.

His friends could see then how hard it would be for him to go back to cloture motions in the Senate, once having soared so near the top. Number two on the ticket had a certain allure as second prize, and Bob Dole, on the best advice, was plainly keeping the way open for Bush to come to him.

Accentuate the Negative

IT WAS A SUNWASHED SPRING FRIDAY in Southern California, a day made for dreaming, but in the shadows in the backseat of his silver Cadillac, George Bush was in an oddly elegiac mode—the manner of a man composing his own political obituary. He wasn't about to let his self-doubt show in public—no way. His nomination was safely in hand, his speeches everywhere were upbeat, and his political reflexes, while still mechanical, appeared to be in working order. He was in midsoliloquy on the subject of his sagging fortunes when he spied a couple of workmen on a street corner, gawking at his motorcade. Gotta get a little eye contact here, he told himself, the candidate as salesman preparing to make a call; you make the eye contact, you get the vote. "Hi, boys," he called out to the workmen with a cheery wave, and when they stared blankly back at him, he seemed not to mind.

What weighed on him instead were the numbers he kept reading, the polls showing him far back of Mike Dukakis and slipping farther. He tried to shrug it all off as something he called "generic overlay," the natural disposition of the voters toward someone new, different and Democratic, at a point when the real line between him and the governor hadn't yet been drawn. Drawing it was his job, he mused, and if he did it well he would win. If not—well, he had learned to live with the consequences. Iowa had taught him that, he said; it hurt having his best friends write him off for dead, but it had made him tougher, less fragile, less uptight. He had discovered, looking inward, that it would not be the worst thing in the world to be gainfully unemployed, free at last to say, "Sorry, I don't want to do the head table." He had sorted it all out philosophically, he told a friend in the car. He had conditioned his psyche to the possibility that he might lose.

The Invisible Man

That Bush could be preparing himself for defeat in the rosy afterglow of victory was a reflection of the gloom endemic in his campaign—a want of faith, at bottom, in the candidate himself. Bush had only just proven himself in combat, wrapping up the race earlier and more decisively than anyone in the history of nomination-by-primary. He had, moreover, been dealt the strongest hand an incumbent might have wished for: the dollar was strong, the Dow was steadying, the economic-misery index was low, and peace was breaking out everywhere from Angola to Afghanistan.

And yet some of his own inner-circle strategists were quoting odds as high as 60–40 that a rank unknown named Dukakis was going to beat the vice president, decisively, in the fall. Their reasons, stripped of the elegant demographic analyses and the raw intramural backbiting, usually came back to George Bush. They liked and admired Bush the man, for the most part, but, as professional managers, they did not really believe in him as a candidate. They were, in fact, moving toward a consensus that he could not win on his own low-watt incandescence and would prevail only by making Mike Dukakis look worse.

His campaign had been adrift since Illinois, a man-of-war cut loose from its moorings with no more battles to be fought; it was as if his success had come too early, John Sununu thought, and no one seemed to know what to do next. Dukakis was dominating the news, putting his clockwork victory of the week on the board against his obliging sparring partner, Jesse Jackson, while Bush roamed the secondary media markets he would not be able to cover in the fall. His backwater itinerary, sensible on paper, played badly in practice and in the press. His name all but disappeared from the headlines except when some fresh bit of bad news attached to it, a new twist in the Noriega scandal or a further dip in the polls. Otherwise, it was as if he and his candidacy had sailed off the edge of the earth.

The nearest thing to a game plan for early spring came out of the internals in Bob Teeter's polling, a vein of public concern about America's competitive slide in commerce and technology. The response was to cart the candidate around from photo op to photo op in high-tech settings—all those fucking chip-makers, Pete Teeley complained, and no red meat. One day, the aspiring leader of the free world found himself at a conference table at Procter & Gamble, being briefed on how superabsorbent polymers had revolutionized the look, fit and efficaciousness of the contemporary diaper. At another stop, at a research center near Fresno, he inspected a state-of-the-art display of irrigation equipment while his Secret Service guards gazed out over the surrounding farm fields, watching, so far as anyone could tell, for the attack of the killer carrots.

His people seemed baffled for a time as to what was happening—why Bush's polls were tumbling when the objective circumstances seemed so favorable to his cause. The simplest argument was that people wanted change for its own sake—that, as Nixon liked to say, paraphrasing de Tocqueville, Americans have always felt a certain restlessness in prosperity and that the in party was likely to pay the dues. Prosperity, indeed, had been crowded back to the business pages after more than five years of sustained economic growth, no matter how hard Bush tried to focus attention on it; there was so much good news that he couldn't leverage it anymore.

"The economy is in great shape," Lee Atwater grumbled over breakfast one day with his fallen adversary, David Keene. "Why aren't we getting any credit for it?"

"Winston Churchill won the war," Keene reminded him, tersely and accurately, "and they threw his ass out."

But when other explanations were exhausted, the biopsies within the campaign kept coming back to Bush himself—to his own stumble-prone deficiencies as a candidate and to his stubborn refusal to disengage himself from his patron, the president. A message might have helped, but as Stu Spencer, a latecomer to his strategy councils, worried aloud, he still didn't have one, after seven years of hoping and three more in active pursuit of the prize. In a largely issueless environment, Spencer thought, the comfort level between the people and the candidate could be decisive, and it wasn't there for the vice president. It was hard for people to get comfortable with a man who seemed so palpably uncomfortable with himself; it seemed to Spencer that Bush, in his middle sixties, still didn't know who he was or where he wanted to go.

His public profile, as a consequence, remained a montage of his vices rather than his virtues; his negatives, against an otherwise blank backdrop, were all the definition he had. The most enduring had to do with his perceived softness, and even his friend Jim Baker worried about the sheer intractability of the problem. Baker had come up against a similar threshold question managing Jerry Ford in 1976, except that with Ford the issue was whether he was *smart* enough to be president; with Bush, it was whether he was *strong* enough. The answer in both cases was yes, Baker believed, but smarts were easier to prove in politics than strength, and a way would have to be found, most likely in hand-to-hand combat with Dukakis. For Bush to win, Dukakis would have to be made to lose.

There was the further matter of Bush's iron handhold on the president's coattails, even when his loyalty had manifestly become dangerous to his health. The separation problem had been seen by his men as a drag on his campaign from the beginning, and with Reagan's fabled luck having suddenly given way to a series of scandals—Iran-Contra, Noriega, Ed Meese—Bush found himself entangled by his own free will in a form of guilt by association.

But it was hard for Bush's own people to budge him from his set-in-concrete solidarity with the president. He was as peevish as ever about being managed—handled, as he put it, like a piece of meat—and they found themselves enlisting surrogates among his key supporters to bear their message for them. He was even persuaded, in April, to receive Richard Nixon, a rendezvous he had hitherto found as welcome as an invitation to a leper colony.

His reluctance had not escaped the former president's notice, and the air was further cooled by a published remark of Nixon's, after Iowa, that Bush did not appear to be up to winning the presidency. His attitude, as intimates knew, had not really changed, about Bush or his prospects, and did not during the course of their evening together; in a privately circulated memo three months later, Nixon would once again express his "grave misgivings" about Bush's prospects in an election that ought on paper to have been his by a landslide. But the two men reached an understanding of sorts over drinks alone in the study, and afterward, at table with the Bushes and Lee Atwater, Nixon offered some home thoughts on the battle ahead.

His advice ranged widely from the geopolitics of autumn—zero in on Ohio, he said—to the choice of a running mate. He did not push his case for Dole directly, thinking it presumptuous to do so, but his specifications seemed tailored to fit the senator. Forget about looking for someone you thought would help you electorally, Nixon said; he had made that mistake choosing Henry Cabot Lodge in 1960. He thought Bush should shop instead for someone experienced, someone, he said, who was up to big-league pitching. Dukakis, in Nixon's view, needed to be painted as a typical Massachusetts liberal and a dewy-eyed dove besides, and Bush was too much the gentleman to do it, too visibly ill-at-ease on the attack. He needed someone strong on the ticket to do it for him, the way Nixon himself had taken on Adlai Stevenson for Eisenhower.

But his bottom-line counsel, drawn again from his own experience, was to step out of Reagan's shadow. "I lost the 1960 election because I was never viewed as my own man," he said. He had wanted, for example, to come out for more defense spending, but Ike had opposed it, and Nixon had had to sit silently by while Kennedy made off with the issue. "You've got to make news," he told Bush, and his loyalty to Reagan was not the way to do it. It was instead, in Nixon's critique, a recipe for invisibility.

More messengers were brought in to underscore the point in a series of meetings with Bush. One such group, a random mix of party leaders from the South, the East and the Midwest, sat down with the vice president one May morning in Washington to urge him to do something to shake loose of Reagan and jump-start his campaign. They had been primed by Atwater, Teeter and Rich Bond over dinner the night before at Joe & Mo's restaurant, a haunt much favored by the die-makers of presidential politics, and when they sat down with the vice president their message had been honed to a sharp edge. Bush was, as one of them put it, digging himself as deep a hole as Jerry Ford had been in twelve years earlier, thirty points behind Jimmy Carter in August. If he didn't do something, and soon, the race would be over.

"I don't agree with you," Bush said. His tone was arctic. He didn't like criticism, and he didn't like doom-crying.

He was no happier at the specifics laid before him, mainly that he disengage from the administration on the Meese mess and on an attempted plea bargain with General Noriega in his Florida drug case. The former particularly troubled one of his guests, a onetime United States attorney from the Midwest.

You can't be associated with it, he told Bush. It's not *you*.

Bush preferred a stealth approach to the case, something quiet and discreet as against loud and vulgar. "Look," he said, "I could go out there today and say Ed Meese ought to go. But what purpose is that going to serve?"

The view in the room was that it might just resurrect his campaign, but the air was turning contentious to no useful end, and the meeting broke up after an hour.

"This is a pretty strong dose of medicine for this early in the morning," Bush said, seeing his guests out empty-handed.

He seemed to have a particularly hard time stepping up to the question of Meese's periodic toe-dancing at the outer edges of the ethical code. The independent prosecutor on the case let it be known early that he didn't mean to recommend criminal charges, but Meese had clearly been reckless of appearances in his off-duty business dealings, and his continuation in office was becoming a major embarrassment to Reagan *and* Bush—the embodiment of what the other side had taken to calling the Sleaze Factor in the Reagan government.

Bush was well aware of the problem, but the president's public support for his old friend Ed left him nearly speechless. For weeks, his strongest words on the subject were that Meese wouldn't be attorney general in *his* administration, a promise so empty as to be just as well left unsaid. His recalcitrance became a kind of litmus test of his courage, for his own people no less than for the press. Maybe Bush would *never* be his own man, some of his handlers brooded over drinks in the late hours one night after work. Maybe he *wasn't* tough enough to be president.

The chief worrier, as it happened, was Jim Baker, then still a gray eminence in the campaign. Baker knew Bush too well and liked him too much to question his intestinal fortitude, but he saw the Meese case as George's millstone. Either he could drag its crippling weight through the rest of the campaign or he could demonstrate his strength convincingly by casting it off.

"It's a freebie to separate yourself from Ed Meese," he told Bush. The attorney general was practically friendless in the government and the press, and not even Reagan would be offended if his vice president broke ranks just this once.

But Bush resisted, and for a troubled passage Baker was in suspense as to the outcome. If George didn't separate himself from Reagan on so easy an issue, he worried to colleagues in the campaign, he would never be able to separate himself on anything.

A window of opportunity finally opened when Baker persuaded Bush to go ask Reagan for leave to speak up; the president, Baker argued, was politically grown-up enough to understand Bush's begging to differ. The sitting was finally arranged, in June, and Reagan was as empathic as Baker had predicted he would be. Meese would be leaving before the election anyway, and if Bush felt he needed to get out from under the problem sooner rather than later, well, Reagan would not stand in his way.

As it worked out, Bush had procrastinated one beat too long. A scenario had been stitched up for him, delicate in weave and design; the White House would alert him in advance when the prosecutor's report on the affair was to be made public, whereupon Bush would sorrowfully tell the world that it was time for Meese to go. The single essential piece of the picture, one of the plotters remarked, was that he be the first to say so. In fact he was the second; it was Meese himself who scooped him, early in July, resigning on his own motion, and Bush was one more voice, dimly heard in the background, saying that Ed had done the right thing. "It's history, baby," a ringleader in the cabal exulted, but a faint tint of disappointment colored the celebration, a sense of opportunity lost.

The Zero-Sum Game

A campaign fallen on hard times is never wanting for advice, and Bush got plenty, much of it the moral equivalent of asking him to empty his closets of his J. Press haberdashery and restock them from Banana Republic. His rich-boy image clung to him, so stubbornly that one adviser suggested that he do a speech actually *declaring* himself to be culturally disadvantaged. His compound in Kennebunkport was a particular symbol of his affluent remove from the rest of America, and his regular retreats there became a point of contention in the campaign, Fuller arguing that they were restorative for the candidate, Atwater fretting over the patrician look of the thing.

Bush cut off the internal debate; he didn't need a lot of advice from image-makers, he said, on where the hell he was going to go for a weekend. But outsiders kept dragging the Kennebunkport Question back into play. One day in July, some of the Bush command gathered in Atwater's office and put together a conference call to some of the viziers of Texas Republican politics. The nominal subject was Lloyd Bentsen, but the state's earthenware governor, William P. Clements, came back again and again to the visuals of Bush as summer person on the coast of Maine.

"Close that goddam house in Kenne*buck*port up," he huffed, his precision gone the way of his patience.

"Governor," Bob Mosbacher answered from the borders of his own frustration, "we've told the vice president that, and we'll continue to tell him that."

The more urgent message, in their view, was that he had to turn things around in the only way left to him, by the systematic dismemberment of Mike Dukakis. The venue for selling this line to the candidate, by wry irony, was Kennebunkport in June. Dukakis by then was beating Bush by eighteen points in Robert Teeter's polls, with no bottom in sight, and Wirthlin's numbers, privately communicated to his friends at Bush Inc., showed him running behind Mikhail Gorbachev in public esteem. The press and the political industry had already begun consigning him to an early grave when he convened a series of meetings in the quiet of his summer place to plan his resuscitation.

His people only lately had been divided along the usual lines, the hawks on Fifteenth Street arguing for a strategy of attack, the doves in the OVP and in Bush's circle of friends countering that they ought to save their bullets for the fall campaign. The unlikely model for the hawks was 1948, when another uncharismatic vice president, named Harry Truman, had run a conscious scare campaign against Thomas E. Dewey and had won against all odds. The analogy had first been put forward by Bush's research director, Jim Pinkerton, a bright, gangly conservative of thirty who had bailed out of Hollywood for politics after two unsold screenplays. Like Bush, he wrote in a prescient early memo, Truman had been maligned and underrated early in his campaign, but he had succeeded in making it sound dangerous to vote Republican, and Pinkerton recommended lifting some variant on his basic message: Don't let them take it away.

But the walk-soft wing then ascendant at Bush Inc. was, or appeared to be, under the spell of Jerry Ford's extraordinary catch-up run against Jimmy Carter in 1976. Even so canny a campaigner as Baker, who had managed Ford, seemed to a friend to have come away with this mental image that you could make up twenty-eight points starting on August 20 if you had to; he had at times to be reminded that the last point or two had been a bridge too far and that Ford had lost the election.

As the meetings in Maine drew near, there were hardly any doves left—none, that is, except Bush himself. The forming consensus was that the vice president had to come out of the August convention no worse than ten to twelve points down to stay in reaching distance, and even then he might not catch Dukakis before mid- to late October. If they just sat still, they would find themselves twenty-five points down, a mountain too steep to climb.

The parallels with Ford were forgotten. The analogy to Truman was inviting. The time-for-a-change factor was working against Bush, as it had been against Truman, and nothing positive seemed to help, not even that golden oldie called peace and prosperity; it was, Stu Spencer guessed, as if the people in their contentment were ready to let the other guy, the little technocrat from Massachusetts, come in and fine-tune what Reagan had wrought. Bush's personal appeal in poll after poll was strongest among brand-name Republican voters, people who would cast ballots for Conan the Barbarian if he were the party's nominee. He was staggering under the weight of his forty-plus negative ratings, a level his own man Atwater had always considered fatal. He had to go bare-knuckle against Dukakis, in the settling view of his command group. If they let Dukakis get away with his Massachusetts Miracle stuff unchallenged, Ailes argued, he would win. Ailes was confident that they could cut into Bush's negatives, but it was a lot easier to raise the other guy's. They had to make the fall campaign a zero-sum game, Bush pumping himself up by tearing Dukakis down.

The last convert to the scorched-earth strategy was Bush himself. He seemed to his men to understand intellectually what he had to do, but politics, for him, had always been a grubby business, distasteful in direct relation to its degree of incivility. Dukakis was a decent man, an able man, he mused in his car one day; he was just coming at things from a different direction, and once people saw how different, the governor wasn't gonna get a free ride anymore. What Bush seemed loath to do was rush into the ring and start swinging. His usual response to the hawks, on the attack strategy as on the separation problem, was that it was too early to be pushing panic buttons. The traditional Labor Day start-up would be soon enough; it was as if he held out some secret hope that if he waited long enough the need to get down and dirty would go away.

His people had to persuade him otherwise. Late in April, Bob Teeter sat down at his home in Ann Arbor with *his* polltaker, Fred Steeper, to start thinking beyond the primaries to the fall campaign. The news in their numbers was unsettling: people were doing well enough economically, but there was an incongruous restlessness out there, Steeper thought, a sense that things were going wrong and that it was time for a change. No one issue drove them; it was instead a worry list of seven or eight things—the environment, the deficit, the homeless—and if Dukakis managed to put them all together, he could win.

He *was* winning, at that point, and the men on Fifteenth Street knew what needed to be done. They had to do what Ailes would call a paint job on Mike Dukakis. The question was how to get Gentleman George fighting mad, and by the time they arrived in Kennebunkport they had the answer.

The Paramus Tapes

The night before the retreat was to begin, five senior hands peeled away from the Bush tour in New Jersey, drove to an office building on Route 17 near the Paramus Park shopping mall, and took seats behind a one-way mirror looking out into a small conference room. On the far side of the glass, a dozen or so residents of the area—all white, all Catholic, all middle-class, all Reagan Democrats leaning to Dukakis—had filed in from a buffet dinner and settled into upholstered chairs around a big, round conference table. A microphone dangled from the ceiling. A camera, out of sight, recorded them on videotape. A moderator was urging them to speak freely; there were no "right" or "wrong" answers. They were that new fountainhead of wisdom in politics, a focus group, and, while they didn't know it at the time, they were about to tell George Bush what to do next.

It was only spring, but the meter was running, and the prospect was bleak. Atwater believed, and would tell Bush straight out a couple of weeks later, that he had no better than a 30 percent chance of winning. The Kennebunkport meetings, in Atwater's view, would be decisive; like the others, he meant to use the retreat to push the vice president into a tougher, more combative mode. The Democratic convention, he reckoned, would be an automatic ten points for Dukakis, blowing his lead out from seventeen points to twenty-seven or twenty-eight. Bush would be in Ford country, so far behind that he could run a perfect campaign and still not catch up.

The focus group in Paramus, along with others like it there and in similar Middletown settings across the country, confirmed to them that they were on the right track. The first lesson was that no one knew either man. The second was that they liked what little they had heard about Dukakis more than what they had seen of Bush. Their impression of the governor was furry but favorable; they found him appealing for his immigrant roots, his plain lifestyle, his seemingly moderate politics, and his look of inner strength—a quality they found wanting in the vice president. It didn't seem to work to tell them that Massachusetts was a hotbed of liberalism, or that a Dukakis administration would be unduly influenced by Jesse Jackson; all that Bush's men got on the latter charge were blank stares.

Bush's image, by contrast, was blank. The good news was that the sample group didn't *dis*like him or believe the business about his being a wimp. The bad news was that they knew nothing at all about him except for the fact that he was vice president; the single person in the room aware that he *had* a past thought, incorrectly, that he had once been a senator. He had neither pedigree nor profile. The words that attached to him were "wishy-washy," even "evasive"; he seemed reluctant, people said, to take a forceful position on anything.

So there were two men to define, and the focus group in Paramus became the taste-testing kitchen. "If you learned the following things about Dukakis," the moderator said, "would it change your mind about him?"

The men behind the mirror leaned forward; it was the point of the exercise. For weeks, Jim Pinkerton had been closeted in his cubicle on Fifteenth Street assembling a dossier of unflattering newspaper cuttings and Nexis files on Dukakis. The euphemism in politics for work like his was "opposition research," which sounded sanitary, almost academic. A more apt analogy might have been dum-dum bullets, and the moderator began firing them. Dukakis had vetoed a bill mandating the Pledge of Allegiance in public schools. He was against the death penalty, even for kingpins in the drug trade. He opposed prayer in the schools. He had stood up for his state's generous program of weekend passes for convicts, even murderers serving life sentences without hope of parole.

No one shot in the volley seemed to draw much blood, but the cumulative effect was dramatic. A palpable unquiet fell over the table. "I didn't realize all these things when I said I was for Dukakis," one woman said. Close to half the people in the room switched to Bush.

Sheltered by the mirror, the vice president's men exchanged glances. Ailes, thinking strategically, was impatient; he regarded focus groups as hand jobs, a new profit center for polltakers, and he had seen enough in the first fifty minutes to confirm what he already knew needed to be done. Atwater, thinking tactically, was ecstatic. They had the means to bring Bush around.

He started the courtship with Bob Teeter the next day, sitting with him at rallies, sharing rides in motorcades, slipping into the chair beside him at a family-style dinner in Kennebunkport that evening. Teeter and Fuller had been slow coming around to the power of negative thinking; until lately, they had thought Atwater a sort of Southern-fried Chicken Little, running around using scare words like "free fall" to describe Bush's situation. But Fuller had seen the Paramus focus group and had got the message. That left Teeter, and while he too was in the picture Atwater devoted the day to stiffening his spine. If Atwater could sell Teeter on the need to move to a war footing, Nick Brady would go along, and once Brady was aboard, Bush would probably follow.

The Kennebunkport meetings became an exercise in persuasion, a united G-6 instructing the vice president that, as Atwater put it, the fat lady had already sung for the Democrats; Dukakis was going to be the nominee, a knight in undented armor, and Bush's abstemious argument that it was too early to start shooting would no longer do. At one session before the fireplace in the family living room, Teeter walked him through the numbers. They were grim, and Fuller reduced them to more graphic terms, sketching a rude chart on the back of a briefing paper. The message in the widening distance between Bush's trend line and Dukakis's was unmistakable: they were in serious danger of losing.

Bush was still hesitant. Teeter got out tapes of two focus groups conducted in Paramus—the one Bush's men had seen and another held the same day.

"I think you should take a look at these," Teeter said.

They regathered the next morning on the back deck of the Bush home, looking out over the rocky Atlantic coastline. The sky was a cloudless spring blue. The buoys marking lobster traps bobbed on the surface of the water. Every twenty minutes or so, a tour boat would chug by with a cargo of sightseers waving at the vice president and his campaign command.

The men on the deck were oblivious to the view. Bush had sat up alone watching the Paramus tapes, and was stunned by what he had seen; some of the participants had actually thought Dukakis was more conservative than he.

"They don't know this guy's record," he said. "They don't know enough about him."

The screening had had its desired effect. Bush still needed more jollying, still wanted assurance that he wouldn't have to get personal or use the hot attack rhetoric known in the trade as red language. But his resistance to the basic strategy melted like butter on a warm biscuit. He never quite said yes. He rarely did, confronting a tough political call. His manner instead was deferential, acquiescing in a decision as if he had no other choice; his virginity, or at least his deniability, was thus preserved. He watched the consensus for action take form around him, passively, more observer than participant. Well, he said finally, you guys are the boss. You all do what you think.

The next day, Atwater flew back to Washington, more hopeful than he had felt for weeks. There was nothing left for him to accomplish in Kennebunkport; the rest of the retreat would be taken up with public-policy discussions—all kinds of eggheads, he thought, talking all kinds of stuff a Bush administration should do once in office. That wasn't Atwater's thing, and he had made quickly for the exit. It's kind of ironical, he thought on the plane down to Washington and his war room on Fifteenth Street. They'll be spending six days up there talking about all these high-blown issues, when it took us six minutes to figure out the only issues we're really going to need.

With Bush's return to the wars, his soul-searching ended, and a season of Dukakis-bashing began. Its first objective, made plain by the Paramus tapes, was to spoil Dukakis's image as a dead-centrist efficiency expert, a perception nourished through the primary season by his Tuesday-night fights with the Reverend Jackson. He had to be driven leftward, Stu Spencer thought, preparing, during the summer, to enlist in the campaign. Spencer had been a bridging figure between the old politics and the new, a salty street fighter who had brought the language and the instincts of the clubhouse to the media age at its dawning in California. His own ideology was elastic, his two all-time favorite clients having been Nelson A. Rockefeller and Ronald Reagan; political belief was a tool for him, not a cause as it seemed to be for some of the kids just coming into the game. His view of his mission was matter-of-fact, almost surgical. Dukakis hadn't had to take any real heat yet, he thought. They had to rattle him, and the way to do it was to bludgeon him with left hooks.

George & Ted & Dan & Willie

The calculated gamble in the strategy was putting Bush out front in the assault. The normal rule in politics is to keep the candidate on the high road and leave the pit-bull campaigning to his ads and his surrogates. But the Bush campaign had come out of California broke, with no more money to spend on advertising until the fall campaign; they would therefore have to rely on what handlers call "free," or sometimes "earned," media—stories in newspapers and magazines and pictures on TV. There was the further necessity of convincing an unpersuaded electorate that Bush cared enough about something—*anything*—to fight for it. He would have to get over his qualms and do the bashing himself; if he was in fact to become the avatar of Harry Truman, a polite give-'em-heck campaign of the sort he had been waging since New Hampshire wouldn't do.

To catch the notice of the boys and girls on the bus, he first had to court them. He was in this like a suitor coming back to an old flame he had once jilted. The national press had been held in a kind of traveling quarantine through much of the spring; only unthreatening local reporters were granted interviews, while the eminences of the Big Media brooded ominously in hotel lobbies and lounges. A key decision of the Kennebunkport retreat was to be cozier with them. Bush had resisted similar suggestions in the past, given his chariness of the press. But this time he acquiesced, and Walker's Point was soon aswarm with reporters eating burgers, pitching horseshoes and taking speedboat rides with the vice president of the United States; it was not hard for a man of his social graces to convey that their company was all he wanted, not their hearts and minds.

The new message was staticky at first. The intent of the paint job was to picture Dukakis as a liberal at odds with the most basic American values. But Bush's early attack speeches were occasionally marred by his tendency to land his left hooks on his own chin; the sound of a Yale man accusing his rival of shopping for foreign-policy ideas at "Harvard Yard's boutique" provoked more amusement than applause.

The dissonance of a campaign run by six colonels without a general added to the noise on the line. It was understood that the G-6 was waiting for the absent seventh man, Jim Baker, to take his place at the head of the table. But he was delaying his arrival as long as he gracefully could, and in his absence the cost in coherence could be almost comically plain. There was, for example, the time in June when Teeter and Fuller booked Bush for an interview on ABC-TV's *Nightline* without troubling to notify Ailes in advance. Operation Paint Job had, by unlucky coincidence, begun only that afternoon in Houston, with a sharp script by Peggy Noonan and a strong performance by Bush himself. The message needed to be clutter-free, and Ailes was furious on being told, just twenty-four hours before airtime, about the late date with Ted Koppel on network TV.

"Are you shitting me?" he roared. "Who dinged me on this?"

The answer was his own colleagues on Fifteenth Street, and when Ailes next confronted them his anger was at a rolling boil. "I only understand friendship or scorched earth," he said, his tone revealing which was his mood of the day. He had a contractual right to be at any senior staff meeting, as he reminded them, and, while he hadn't technically been excluded from the session that settled on the *Nightline* booking, he hadn't been told that they were contemplating throwing Bush into a cage with Koppel on national TV.

"Are you guys nuts?" he bellowed. "You people are crazy. You'd take more time than this to prepare him if he were going to address the PTA."

Fuller explained apologetically that they had treated the interview as a question of scheduling, which was on his watch, and not one of media, which was on Ailes's. Ailes was not appeased. If that was the way they were going to treat him, he said, stalking out of the room, he had better things to do with his time.

Atwater followed him back to his office and sat with him for fifteen minutes or so, trying to calm him. "You're right," he said. "We fucked this one up."

Bush himself seemed bewildered at the booking, coming as it did at the end of a red-eyed, three-time-zone day; too tired to rehearse, he went jogging, took some steam, dragged Ailes off to a joint in the Memorial district for barbecue and a beer, and headed for the studio with a full belly and a numb mind.

"What in the hell are we doing this for?" he asked Ailes.

"Sir," Ailes said, "I'm not sure."

The show was the Dan Rather interview in parodic instant replay, history repeating itself as farce, and the Houston speech was drowned out by the laughter. Koppel, like Rather, had prepared an ambush for the vice president, arming himself with stiletto-tipped questions on both the Iran-Contra and Noriega affairs. This time, Bush walked into it unprepared.

His answers wandered lamely through the briar patch of scandal, which was bad enough. Worse still, he seemed confused as to who exactly was asking the questions at the other end of the live-feed line from Koppel's set in Washington. He had apparently scrambled Koppel with Rather and had called him "Dan" three times when Ailes, in desperation, held up a sign reading TED in his line of sight. It didn't work. "Ted" came out "Dan" yet again. Koppel, obviously miffed, finally reminded Bush who he was, and the vice president wound up apologizing on the air for what must, he said, have been a Freudian slip.

But the attack strategy fell into coherent form in the days and weeks that followed, and Bush's men began assembling a supporting cast around him, the victims and the villains of Dukakis's crypto-liberalism. Their search was made easier by the fact that Dukakis, unlike Bush, had a long, open public record and a train of enemies ready to quote it chapter and verse. There was, for one thing, his affiliation with the American Civil Liberties Union; the governor himself had handed them that one, announcing that he was a "card-carrying member" of the organization. There were those schoolchildren in Massachusetts, denied the daily comfort of saluting the flag. That tip came from Andy Card, a former White House staffer who had been a Massachusetts state legislator at the time; he had joined a majority, some singing "God Bless America," in voting to pass the measure over Dukakis's legalistically framed veto.

And there was, downstage center, Willie Horton, a black convict who had stabbed a white man and raped a white woman in Maryland while on furlough from a life sentence for murder in Massachusetts. Jim Pinkerton— Pink, to his corps of fresh-faced young Duke-busters on Fifteenth Street— had been poring over their findings one day in April when an exchange between Dukakis and Gore caught his eye. Gore had made an issue of the Massachusetts furlough program. Most states had one, and so did the

Federal government, but, as Gore noted, only Massachusetts permitted "weekend passes" for murderers doing life without parole; eleven, he said, had fled, and two had killed again. Dukakis, as it happened, had inherited the program from a Republican predecessor. Still, he had defended it until after the Horton scandal, and his sniffish response to Gore never really addressed the question.

A light had gone off over Pinkerton's head; it was less like a flashbulb than like a neon sign—*weekend passes for first-degree murderers*—and Willie Horton had soon been caught in its lurid glow. Andy Card had remembered the story from a newspaper in the state, *The Lawrence Eagle-Tribune*. So had John Sununu, who despised Dukakis across the distance between their neighboring states and their polar politics; he had clipped and saved it for his own atrocity file early in 1987, meaning to feed it to some Southern candidate to use against the governor in the Democratic primaries. So had Alex Castellanos, a media consultant who remembered a petition campaign against the furlough program; he would commend the Horton story to Ailes's attention later that month, "in case," he wrote, "you need to lob a small, agenda-changing battlefield nuclear weapon against Dukakis in the fall."

Pinkerton had taken his find first to Lee Atwater, who had been his mentor in politics in the Reagan White House and later at Bush's PAC. There would be sales resistance in other quarters on Fifteenth Street at that innocent time, the discomfort of genteel men who questioned the issue's relevance to a presidential election. Atwater had had no such qualms. His single concern had been that Pinkerton be sure of his facts; if the tale was true, Atwater had thought, it was the gold-mine issue of all time.

Its yield, moreover, was greatly magnified when *Reader's Digest* published its own fortuitously timed version of the furlough story. Both the magazine and the author of the piece, an obscure free-lancer named Robert James Bidinotto, denied any intent to do Dukakis harm. Bidinotto had first undertaken his inquest for a small and failing conservative journal in New Jersey, meaning it, he said, as a victims'-rights story and not a political piece at all. The magazine had folded before he finished, whereupon he offered it to the *Digest*. The editors there were similarly insistent that there was nothing personal or political in their decision to run it. It hardly mattered. The *Digest* bought the piece in April, when Dukakis was clearly the Democratic front-runner, and published it to its fifty million readers in mid-June, when Bush had only just begun working the Horton story into his repertoire. The headline was: GETTING AWAY WITH MURDER.

As an issue, the Horton case required delicate handling. Bush's men would insist afterward that there was no racial undertone to the story, no conscious design to inflame white fears of black crime. Their evidence was that the campaign's official advertising never showed Horton's face or alluded to his color; the story, in the official line, was a metaphor for Dukakis's peculiar values, and the race of its protagonist had nothing to do with it. But Horton's mug shot would appear in some independently produced commercials and fliers, and the men on Fifteenth Street sometimes made careless use of his story. When Atwater suggested publicly that Dukakis might just put Horton on the Democratic ticket, it was too much for Bush, even on his new regimen of nasty pills.

I don't like that stuff, he scolded Atwater, and I don't want to hear any more of it.

He would hear more of it, some in his own voice; a strategy had been born at Kennebunkport, a commitment to a campaign aimed less at the elevation of George Bush than at the destruction of Mike Dukakis. It seemed the only recourse at the time; the governor's lead was then still in or near double digits, and, as Atwater told a war council of Western party leaders in Denver in the late spring, Bush might never be ahead in the polls—not till the one that counted on Election Day. The trick was to keep from falling too far behind, and the key to that, Atwater said, his drawl slower and smokier than usual, was to start getting together your compare-and-contrasts—the portrayal of Dukakis as a bona-fide, double-dip, Frost Belt, McGovern-style liberal whose most basic values were alien to most of America.

The neglected problem, in the gloom of summer, was giving people reasons to vote for the vice president, not just against his opponent. The solution kept being postponed, so long as the search-and-destroy mission seemed to be working. Bush's downhill slide in the polls bottomed out between conventions, and there was no great impetus to rush out five-point programs for the public weal or seven-layer confections of visionary prose. The strategy of choice instead was the un-Americanization of Mike Dukakis, and the details fit on a single three-by-five note card in Lee Atwater's pocket, typed edge to edge with the governor's heresies against orthodox middle-class values:

1. High-tax, high spending. Refuses to rule out a tax hike next year. In 1974, said no new taxes, then raised them. Raised taxes in the middle of this campaign. Mass. state spending up 70 percent.
2. To the left of Carter-Mondale in opposing every defense program.

Against MX, Midgetman testing. Monroe Doctrine superseded.
Against all aid to contras and freedom fighters.

3. Social issues. McGovern/Kennedy/Jackson liberal:
   —prison furloughs, 85 convicted felons
   —opposes the death penalty in every case
   —"card-carrying member of the ACLU"
   —supports gun control; "disarm the state"
   —#1 pro-abortion candidate
   —vetoed Pledge of Allegiance

The card could fairly be said to embrace the basic plan of action for the Bush campaign—an accentuate-the-negative strategy aimed at elevating the vice president to the presidency over Dukakis's broken body. The result, as summer faded into fall, would be one of the meanest national campaigns since the McCarthy era—so mean, in its worst moments, as to invite the suspicion that George Bush would say nearly anything to win.

The Unhappy Warrior

On a steamy dog-day Sunday afternoon in August, James A. Baker III found himself applying to Ronald and Nancy Reagan for a job he had never really wanted and wasn't sure he could do: raising his friend George Bush's candidacy from the dead. He had promised Bush a year before that he would be there if and when he was needed and then had retired to his offices at the Treasury Department, hoping that the phone would never ring. He had never been happier in public life than in his years at Treasury, being his own boss for the first time and playing on a global economic stage. But as he watched Bush's backward progress through the spring and the summer, he knew his days there were numbered. Only a shit would say no to a friend in need, Baker believed, and Bush's need was evident. His campaign had the smell of a hospice about it—a scent of defeat to which Baker himself was not immune.

That Bush had to have him was no longer in question; no one else, as Baker was regularly told, had the skills or the stature to keep the vice president's listing ship afloat. Baker had in fact lost two of the three presidential campaigns he had run, but his sheer presence and his record in government had given him a size in the political community larger than his track record might otherwise have bought him; his defeats were commonly blamed on the quality of his clients, not his management. Baker had *aura*, that blend of intelligence, authority and success known in a vogue word of the season as "gravitas." There were those in the vice president's councils, indeed, who believed that Jimmy Baker would make a better president than George Bush.

What was manifest by summer was that the campaign was not in shape to test the proposition by getting Bush elected. Bush's own openly expressed view of his two-track, six-headed table of organization was that it worked, even if it wasn't the kind of tidy wiring diagram they drew at Harvard's School of Business Administration. The private view among Bush's intimates was less sanguine. They regarded his three principal handlers, Atwater, Teeter and Fuller, as exceptionally talented men who couldn't manage anything. To Bush's irritation, things kept disappearing down the cracks between his two competing and often contentious operations, one at campaign headquarters on Fifteenth Street, the other in his vice-presidential shop in the Executive Office Building. In the absence of a true peer—a Baker, say—his people couldn't even decide among themselves who should call him with a problem.

There were, moreover, fault lines appearing among them, craze marks just beneath the polished glaze of unity. Lee Atwater had gone into a slow fade once the race for the nomination was settled; they had to have a bias for *action*, he kept saying, but he was like Patton after V-E Day, a soldier with a chestful of medals and no war to fight. His job was reduced to tending to the minutiae required of a campaign in slow times—deciding, for example, who would get single hotel rooms at the party convention in New Orleans and who would have to double up—and waiting glumly for Baker's arrival to complete his eclipse.

With his decline, Teeter and Fuller rose in influence, two men united in their caution and, Atwater complained, their back channels to the Old Man when they couldn't get their way in open meetings. The spring campaign under their direction had been all photo ops, issue speeches and fundraisers, and Atwater had watched from the wings with a discouragement bordering on contempt; there were days, a friend said, when he felt like closing up headquarters entirely and sending everybody home. Even Roger Ailes, normally a cheerleader, turned cranky in adversity. He was sore at Atwater for his broodiness, sore at the Secret Service for messing up his visuals, sore at the mazy topside bureaucracy for talking too much; there were, he complained, too many fucking people making too few fucking decisions at meetings. Even the highborn Muffies and Buffies wandering around Bush Inc. offended his jaundiced eye; they all looked like refugees from Miss Porter's School.

The net result of the fissuring was, in Stu Spencer's practiced eye and salty tongue, a fucked-up campaign—a candidacy without so much as a strategic plan on paper or a single leader capable of making things happen. The principal voices in the Fifteenth Street Men's Chorus each seemed to be singing from a different score; when six people tried to run a campaign by consensus, a newcomer to their table said, the message was likely to be mush or nothing at all. There was no overall strategic design to the attack on Dukakis, no thought-through line of argument that Bush stood for change of a safe and orderly sort, whereas a Dukakis presidency carried the risk of economic collapse and geopolitical retreat. There wasn't even a clear Bush program in the fourth year of his campaign. One of Baker's outriders, Richard G. Darman, arrived from Treasury with what he called the Matchbook Theory of Political Communication, a notion borrowed from the man who had beaten Dukakis for governor in 1978. Maybe Bush couldn't manage a vision, but, Darman argued, you could lock him in a room for forty-eight hours and tell him to come out with a list of five things he wanted to do, so crisply stated that you could note them all down on the inside face of a matchbook cover.

It never happened. Coherence required discipline, someone with the standing to impose clarity on the candidate and the campaign; they were waiting, that is, for Jim Baker, and the single most positive achievement of the Bush candidacy in the summer of its discontent was coaxing him down from his aerie at Treasury into the full-time management of the enterprise.

The sell wasn't easy. It was no secret in his circle that he didn't want to move to Fifteenth Street, not even for a friend as old and close as Bush. He knew precisely how tough George could be to work with, one close associate said, and he was further aware of what then seemed the formidable odds against winning. His personal stake in Bush's success was high, a nearly certain step up the ladder from Treasury to State, and he had rather more faith in his friend than did others in the campaign; he believed, that is, that Bush *could* be saved from himself. But the smart money in Washington said that he couldn't, and Baker, a man cautious of his own reputation, didn't want to leave Washington a loser. He vastly preferred being remembered for his stewardship of the economy than for having managed one more failed campaign.

He tried, accordingly, to dance free of the call of duty, knowing all along that there was no real hope of escape. He had become a kind of magic talisman in the eyes of the candidate and the party, his size growing as the long wait for his arrival dragged on; he was the one man, Bush himself thought, who could put an end to management by committee and supplant it with clean lines, quick decisions and, as necessary, broken heads. Baker thus found himself in a painful dilemma. If he followed his heart and refused, he would be blamed if Bush lost, and he would never be able to look his friend in the eye again.

The only man who could have reprieved him was Ronald Reagan. It was Baker's own view, expressed to friends, that he could do George at least as much good at Treasury as on Fifteenth Street, keeping the economy perking and advising the campaign by phone. He could not ask openly to be excused from moving over, but his reluctance was not unknown or unwelcome to the president; in fact, Baker's secret hope was that Reagan would say no for him.

For a time, it looked as if he might have his wish. The president had watched Bush's progress from the beginning with odd uninterest, given that his own page in history was on the line with his vice president's fortunes. His public endorsement in May had been long delayed and memorably perfunctory, a postscript paragraph in a speech in which "Bush" came out rhyming with "gush." In the weeks thereafter, Reagan only occasionally asked his aides for situation reports, sometimes wondering aloud at the seeming disarray of the campaign. His attitude toward it otherwise, as to most questions of politics and state in his mauve late period, was one of benign neglect. He cared more, as Baker did, about leaving Washington in glory, and he regarded Baker's continuing reign at Treasury as his insurance policy against economic trouble.

He was therefore resistant to the petitioners, Bush among them, wanting Baker's services for the campaign. The vice president had pleaded his case over lunch one day in June and had come away prematurely glowing with success. "It's gonna happen," he told a friend that afternoon. But, in his deferential way, he had failed to make his case urgently enough, and Reagan had a quite different sense of what they had agreed on: a modified, limited leave of absence, as he understood it, in which Baker would somehow split his time between Treasury and the campaign.

Stu Spencer was propelled forward next, a friend and *consigliere* to the Reagans from their earliest days in politics; he met with them and the president's chief of staff, Ken Duberstein, in the White House family quarters in mid-July to put the request in plainer language. Baker had to be sprung, he said, or Bush was going to go down in flames, carrying the Reagan legacy with him.

But Baker's hand-wringing had sharpened the president's own misgivings. "I don't like the idea," he told Spencer. "I don't want Jimmy to leave, and he doesn't want to leave. He can stay and help George from there.''

"Holy shit," Spencer muttered to Duberstein, a co-conspirator, as they retreated to the West Wing to figure out what to do next. The plan was falling apart, and in their despair they began sorting other names. There was Congressman Richard B. Cheney from Wyoming, once Jerry Ford's chief of staff, but he was scheduled for bypass surgery in August; there was Drew Lewis, a seasoned warhorse retired to the private sector, but he was on Bush's extensive shit list. It *had* to be Jimmy, the two men concluded. There was no one else.

The Reagan entourage was in Toronto next morning on economic business when Duberstein called on Baker in his hotel suite. Baker asked how the meeting had gone.

"Stu ain't talking to you," Duberstein said. "You really screwed this one up good."

Baker paced the floor, his anguish visible. "What am I gonna do?" he said. "You *know* I really don't want to do it."

"You've got to get yourself out of this mess," Duberstein said, and there was only one way out: go to Reagan himself and volunteer his body for what looked at the time like human sacrifice.

And so it was that Baker presented himself unhappily at the White House that muggy August afternoon, lowering his neck for the blade. Bush by then had been back to see the president, making clear, this time, his conviction that he couldn't win without Baker, and Reagan's own adrenaline had at last begun to flow, stirred not so much by any great feeling for his vice president as by his anger at the other side; it had suddenly struck the president that Dukakis was running against *him*.

He was thus in a more pliant mood when he received Baker, with Duberstein and Nancy Reagan in attendance; he had been waiting for Baker to ask.

Bush wanted him, *needed* him, Baker said. There was no choice. "You know I really don't want to do it," he told the president. "I'm absolutely torn. But I think I *ought* to do it."

If that's what you want, Reagan said, I understand.

Baker's formal piping aboard was delayed till the day of Bush's nomination in New Orleans, but his hand was felt in the campaign long before then. New faces appeared at headquarters, men and women Baker knew and trusted. Dick Darman, Charlie Black and Jim Lake were drawn formally into the strategy group. Peggy Noonan and Ken Khachigian signed on to write speeches. Stu Spencer was shriven of the sin of having flirted briefly with the Dole campaign and was engaged as the vice-presidential tour director.

But the most important result of Baker's advent was the sense of command he brought to the bridge of a leaderless campaign—a show of snap-to discipline that began even before he had formally taken charge. The most visible loser, on most scorecards, was Atwater, and the air on Fifteenth Street had been heavy for weeks with his anticipatory gloom. It was like the nights when his rock band opened for the big acts passing through Columbia. He had been the lead guitar as long as the Upsetter's Review had had the stage, but when Percy Sledge had come on, Big At had disappeared to the background, playing rhythm.

For a bruised time, he felt more isolated than ever, alone in a roomful of guys—Baker's guys, for the most part—with club ties and unmussed hair; he had days, he confided in friends, when he felt as if he were about to be gang-raped by men in gray flannel suits. But, as soon became clear, Atwater was not alone in Baker's enveloping shadow. A day or so before his accession, the new boss showed up at a 7 A.M. staff meeting in New Orleans at convention time, steaming at having been left off the routing list for a memo out of Craig Fuller's vice-presidential shop; his courtly boardroom manner gave way, when he was angry, to the toughness and, sometimes, the barracks language of an ex-Marine.

Fuller apologized profusely. It had been, he said, a case of human error, an honest oversight by his staff.

"You tell your people a new day has begun, *starting right now*," Baker said; it was a resurrection they were attempting, and he was going to be in charge. His staff took his meaning. He might have wished, before the day was out, that he had borne the same message to Bush himself.

The Quayle Season

IT WAS DAY ONE of the Age of George Bush, the morning of his arrival in New Orleans to receive his party's nomination and his own manumission from twenty years of servitude to others, and he had a secret: his choice of a running mate and, quite conceivably, a successor to the presidency. He had broken the news to Baker first, a bare ten minutes before the rest of his command group heard it; he had been well forewarned that it would make Jimmy unhappy, and, by sound report, it did. But Baker masked whatever he felt as the others filed into Bush's temporary billet, in the admiral's residence at a Navy supply post stuck in the shabby Algiers section of town. They found the vice president stretched out in the master bedroom in the antebellum mansion, feet up, back against the headboard, taking the ease due a man who, after six weeks' hard labor, had come to his first presidential decision.

"It's Quayle," he told his men. He was proposing to put J. Danforth Quayle, the very blond, very blue-eyed junior senator from Indiana, a pulsebeat away from the Oval Office.

The sound of silence filled the room, a stillness born more of surprise than of disapproval; Bob Teeter would tell friends later that he had nearly fallen out of his chair. Quayle had more support than opposition among

Bush's command group, but most had written him off for dead and placed their bets elsewhere, on Bob Dole or Jack Kemp among others. None had had a clue as to which way the wind was blowing. The vice president had shut them all out—his chairman, his G-6, his own family—and had come to the point of choice *his* way, alone, secretive and reckless of the cost of the consequences.

The Ken Doll

It had been, in a consensus formed in hindsight, a hell of a way to pick a prospective president. Bush had never sat down face to face with the senator, never plumbed the depths of his understanding or asked him a single substantive question about his beliefs. He knew Quayle only casually, as an indistinctly pleasant and right-thinking young man of forty-one who came around to the OVP now and then to say hello and seek a place at table in a national-security advisory group under Bush's purview. The Dan Quayle he put on his ticket was a pastiche of faint impressions and shaky assumptions—that his youth would appeal to baby boomers, his good looks to women, his home address to the Midwest and his conservatism to the ideologues and preachers of the movement right.

The vice president had, in sum, flown blind on his first solo, straight into the side of a mountain. He would, after the crash, be heard muttering that he had been sold a bill of goods about Quayle; people had overstated his standing on the Hill, his skills as a campaigner and his prospects for producing a huge generational bump in the polls. But Bush had himself brushed off contrary advice, from his friend Jimmy Baker among others; the only vote that had mattered had been his own. He had reached across the chessboard, knocking over men of known size and profile, and had snatched up a pawn instead—a back-bench senator of little note, suspect depth and underinvestigated history. The largest visible plus that Quayle brought to the ticket was that he would not overshadow the man at the top. Bush picked his fifth son, Kemp's chairman Ed Rollins said when he heard the news. The more common and less charitable view in New Orleans was that he had chosen his own clone—a man who would be as loyal, as malleable and as invisible as he had been in Reagan's service.

For seventy-two suspenseful hours thereafter, it looked as if he might have spoiled his own coronation party in the bargain. His rite of passage had been artfully choreographed down to the precise moment of his arrival, timed to coincide with Reagan's departure from the city and the center stage of politics. When Air Force One took off at eleven-ten that Tuesday morning bearing the president home, it was, an old Bush hand thought, as if it carried an empty yoke with it—the one the vice president had labored under for seven and a half years. His spirits seemed to his men to rise with his master's departure from his political and emotional airspace. He was his own man at last, ready, in his own mind, to define himself in words and deeds. His choice of Quayle at the outset would be his declaration of independence, a stroke, he believed, that would flatter him by its strength, its daring and its surprise. His acceptance speech at the close would be the credo people had been demanding of him so long, his statement, eloquent in its plainness, of who he was and where he meant to lead the nation.

The speech, happily for Bush, would prove a brilliant success—so glittering as to mitigate, for a time, the damage he had done himself with his selection of an understudy. The choice, as history taught, was one of most serious import; four of America's eight postwar presidents had apprenticed in the vice-presidency, and Bush himself hoped to be the fifth. But the process of selection was flawed from the beginning by his own design for it, a playbook in which appearances seemed to concern him more than results.

He declared, for starters, that he was not going to do driveway interviews with the hopefuls, as Jimmy Carter had done in Plains and Fritz Mondale in St. Paul, or audition them as co-stars at campaign rallies, as Mike Dukakis had only lately done. No, when the story of Bush's talent search was written, it would be said that he had done it with due regard for *dignity*, his own and that of the contenders. There would be no public ''gong show'' in Kennebunkport and no backstairs leakage to the press about who was up, who was down and who had what skeletons rattling in his or her closet. It was going to be a George Bush decision, he resolved, aideless and airtight, a demonstration of the strength and resolve he would bring to the presidency. He could set a plan and stick to it. He was prepared for the loneliness of command.

The road to Quayle thus was paved with good but costly intentions, its dignity purchased at the expense of careful investigation, its secrecy at the price of timely dissent. The normal drill in the selection of a veep was to put someone political in charge; you needed lawyers for the paper chase, but politics was the quicksand, as one seasoned player at the game put it, and you needed someone savvy—a Stu Spencer, say—to look a senator or a governor in the eye and ask him if it was true that he had screwed someone. Bush had other ideas. No one in the campaign was involved in the actual screening process; the start-up list of twenty-five to thirty names was instead turned over to Robert Kimmitt, a Washington lawyer of scant political experience, with instructions that he alone do the interviewing and that he report only to the vice president. Even Spencer, having agreed to manage the vice-presidential road show sight unseen, found himself frozen out with the others, ice-fishing for hints as to who it was he would be handling.

"Pick me a good one," he told Bush near the end of the hunt.

"I will," Bush twitted back. "Clint Eastwood."

The men at the head of the queue for the first casting call were Dole and Kemp, each hungering for the part. Kemp's campaign for it was, at his wish and his express order to his people, low-key; he had been rebuked too many times for talking too much and had begun to worry that Bush might think he couldn't shut up and listen. Dole was more open in his ambition. He had nothing to lose, as he told a friend, so he returned to the road in the late spring and the early summer, making himself visible and useful at party gatherings. "He better say nice things about George Bush," Rich Bond warned Dole's man Bill Lacy early on. The senator hardly needed to be told that, given his aspirations. The only thing he *wouldn't* do, he told the Bush command at a meeting in June, was be their hatchet man; he had played that role for Ford in 1976 and was still trying to live it down. But he was willing to do whatever else he could to help, and if George were to ask him to be on the ticket, he told associates, he wouldn't say no.

The problem was that Bush was never comfortable with either man, in part because of the star qualities that had put them in play in the first place; what one senior adviser called the Overshadow Issue weighed against anyone of independent standing. Each man in fact had much to commend him: Dole his stature and experience in Washington, Kemp his young ideas and his end-of the-rainbow optimism. Dole, moreover, had an influential early advocate in Jim Baker; the chairman refused then and afterward to discuss his advice to Bush, even with colleagues in the campaign, but it was evident to friends that he liked what the senator would bring to the ticket—his size, his skills and his appeal to the battleground Midwest. It was only after a camping trip with Bush in Wyoming in July that Baker's ardor for his choice did seem to cool, or at least his sense of its prospects. The vice president was said to have told him, during their days alone in the big-sky country, that he didn't think he could work with Dole, or with Kemp either.

Still, Dole's name and Kemp's survived a first winnowing-down to a dozen possibles, eight counted serious, the rest merely politic. Most were figures of progressively lower luminosity. There were, besides Dole and Kemp, the senator's wife, Elizabeth; the newly appointed attorney general, Richard Thornburgh and four senators, Alan K. Simpson of Wyoming,

John C. Danforth of Missouri, Pete V. Domenici of New Mexico—and Dan Quayle of Indiana.

Polling, for once in contemporary politics, had proven a blank road map; there was no one compelling candidate, as Atwater said at a staff meeting, no Cincinnatus waiting at the plow for his country's call. The levelness of the playing field made Quayle stand taller, and he had his friends in the Bush command. Bush's chum Nick Brady had met him during his own short tour in the Senate, Fuller remembered him from meetings, and Teeter and Ailes had worked in his Indiana campaigns. All four had been favorably impressed, and Ailes, in a memo to Bush in July, had short-listed Quayle among his three favorites. "We may need several bold strokes between now and the election," he wrote. "One would be a choice of someone unexpected as vice president who symbolizes youth and the future of the party."

The most determined nay-sayer, by authoritative account, was Jim Baker, and he stayed away from open staff discussions of the choice, preferring, in his discretion, to tell his friend the vice president man to man what he thought. His feeling for Dole had shrunk by then to the point where, in some informed postmortems, he administered the final *coup de grace*. His new favorite was his secret—not even his wife knew—but he was less guarded among intimates about his size-up of Danny Quayle. The senator, Baker suggested to friends, was a lightweight, too light to pass the stature test for so high an office, and he told Bush so at their last meeting on the subject. He came away from the conversation, friends said, believing that the nomination would never happen—that only Dole, Domenici and maybe Dick Thornburgh had survived to the final cut. He thought he had driven a stake through Quayle's heart.

He hadn't, and when Bush convened a senior staff meeting at seven-thirty the Friday morning before New Orleans to discuss the choice, Baker wasn't there; his fastidiousness meant that there was no strong voice against Quayle at the table. There were, in fact, a good many more or less enthusiastic votes *for* him when Bush polled the room. The canvass was a kind of pop quiz: name your three favorites along with the pros and cons for each. The cons outweighed the pros for most of the contenders. Kemp had few cheerleaders in the room, and Dole practically none; each was a loose cannon, and both would be seen as safe, boring choices by a candidate who needed above all to look bold. Mrs. Dole, on the other hand, was probably *too* daring a choice for Bush's taste—a view held privately even by those staffers who spoke up for her. Al Simpson did nothing for the ticket geopolitically. Dick Thornburgh was too moderate for the right-meat right. Pete Domenici was vulnerable for having supported tax increases to narrow the deficit and was a bit high-strung besides.

"He's a chain-smoker," someone worried.

"No," someone else said, "he quit."

In the end, Quayle emerged in the Bush poll as a kind of least common denominator—a Ken doll to whom anyone around the table could impute any sort of magic, from sex appeal to sectarian conservatism. His most ardent support came from Roger Ailes and Craig Fuller, two polar personalities caught up in the excitement of going with a young unknown; if the wild man and the cautious man were together, Ailes thought, smiling to himself, maybe Quayle *was* Mr. Right. But they were by no means alone; only Bob Mosbacher among the G-6 left the senator off his ballot. Teeter and Brady short-listed him. So did Lee Atwater, who had a nearly obsessive thing about the dormant political power of the baby-boom generation; the senator, his number-three pick, might tap their still unrealized potential.

Quayle's name thus led all the rest; Teeter, using a simple three-two-one point system, scored him first, Thornburgh second and Mrs. Dole third. Bush by then had already done some of his own pruning; he had, for example, confided in Reagan that Kemp was out of the running. But his intentions stayed veiled in silence and Socratic questions. Suppose it were Dole—would the media drag up all those nasty things he had said during the primaries? Probably. Or Kemp—could he salvage California? Teeter's polling offered no certain guidance.

Or Quayle—what did they know about his personal side?

Well, a couple of voices answered, Danny had quite a nasty temper, and there were those stubborn eight-year-old rumors connecting him with Paula Parkinson, a sometime lobbyist well known for her bedside manner. The suspicion traced to a weekend he had spent in Florida with a couple of fellow congressmen, one of whom brought Parkinson along; she ultimately would say, in *Playboy*, that Quayle had danced with her and spoken suggestively to her. But the whispers of a real liaison had, as Ailes put it, been "overcome" two Senate campaigns ago; people who knew Quayle's nearly religious devotion to his six-handicap game found it easy to believe his story that he had spent *his* time in Florida playing golf. The subject of his family's rich and influential newspaper barony never came up, nor did the matter of his having sat out the Vietnam War as a desk jockey in the Indiana National Guard. The players at the table, having been shut out of the vetting process, knew practically nothing about him beyond the scanty public record.

Bush listened to it all, saying nothing to indicate his leanings. Even his body language was, for once, under control; the only clue it yielded came when Teeter dropped a fragmentation grenade into Dole's diminished hopes. The senator, Teeter said, had sent him a message for Bush's attention: tell George that if he puts Kemp on the ticket, I'm going over the side.

Bush's jaw clenched, a sure sign of his anger. Those at the table who noticed it guessed that Dole had yet again done himself in. They were, as it happened, only prematurely right.

There were no other signals, and as the G-6 dispersed to pack for New Orleans Bush headed north to Kennebunkport for the last time before the election. He had planned an evening off from politics in the bosom of his home and family. It didn't work out. "All right, we're now gonna tell you *our* opinions," one of his sons said, and as they sat around the dinner table over the last of the swordfish and the mounds of denuded corncobs, they did.

Dole was once again the odd man out the first time around the table; several of Bush's children bore him hard feelings for his attacks on their dad. Kemp fared little better. It was Senator Simpson, a warm family friend, who had the loudest cheering section, led by Barbara Bush. No one had mentioned Quayle at all; only on a louder second ballot, a free-for-all in which everybody attacked everybody else's favorite, did George Jr. finally put the senator's name in play. The case for him rested heavily on his youth; the family knew as little about him as did the campaign command.

The Bushes adjourned to bed that night without a clue as to the vice president's intention; they were as surprised as the party elders assembling in New Orleans to read in *The New York Times* next morning that Dan Quayle had made it to the finals. The leak was widely assumed at Bush Inc. to have originated with Jim Baker, though he vigorously denied it; exposing a bad idea to daylight was the classic last recourse in politics for killing it. The early returns, as the story circulated through the lobbies and lounges of the convention hotels, were negative indeed. The first brushfires were already flaring when Jim Lake called Craig Fuller to warn him that Quayle meant trouble.

"I think we're by that," Fuller answered. Neither he nor any of his senior colleagues took the possibility seriously; when he was sent forth to deny all, he did so with a persuasiveness born of the real conviction that Dan Quayle didn't have a chance.

A Squall in New Orleans

In fact Quayle *had* made the finals and had, with rising elation, begun to sense it; he had, as one veteran of past veep-hunts put it, begun his rocket ride from terra firma into the hyperspace of politics at the presidential level, and the resulting state of weightlessness left him floating three feet above the ground. He had begun to suspect what was in store for him when Kimmitt, having interviewed him twice, called him back for eight hours more over the weekend—a series of sittings ranging far beyond the seventy-seven-page written questionnaire he and the other hopefuls had had to endure. The Parkinson matter had been discussed in these sessions and dismissed as empty rumor. The matter of why he had chosen the Guard and how he had got in were, according to one man privy to the talks, only lightly explored.

"Did you pull strings?" Kimmitt asked.

"No," Quayle replied, and that was that. There were no legal problems, no tax delinquencies, no marital crises—nothing, Quayle vowed in response to what had become known as the Tom Eagleton question, that would embarrass the campaign or the candidate. He had passed a lawyer's test, establishing that he was not a felon or a philanderer. What no one ever asked him was what he *was*.

Dole and Kemp followed Quayle to New Orleans afloat on the tides of their own expectations, making the rounds of parties and caucuses and waiting for the phone to ring. Kemp, though he didn't know it, was already out of the running. Bush could, at least on paper, buy the same package in Quayle—the youth, the energy, the movement conservatism—without Kemp's wagging tongue and pushy manner. Only Dole remained even formally in contention, and *his* last tenuous claim on Bush's favor died when, on opening day, he complained on-camera about the way George had kept people hanging out to dry so long. A newsman asked him whether he thought it "demeaning," and he said yes.

Bush, unfortunately for Dole, was watching the show on TV at his residence in Washington and was furious. The way Dole kept calling him "George" or "Bush," never "the vice president," had long rankled him, but insulting the process was like attacking one of his grandchildren; it remained a matter of great pride to him, an edifice built, he thought, to keep from demeaning anyone. *Jesus*, he muttered, shifting irritably in his seat; Dole *was* a loose cannon. A friend in the room guessed, accurately, that Dole was dead.

He was; the next morning, clambering up the ramp onto Air Force Two, Bush made his decision for Quayle. Jim Baker was only the third to hear it, after Barbara Bush and Ronald Reagan, but he knew that it was senseless arguing the call with so stubborn a man as his friend; instead, he started thinking managerially about how to make what he considered a bad decision look good. His first recommendation was that Bush announce the choice that day, instead of saving it as planned for a surprise unveiling the next night; the decision, he said, should be put out as quickly as possible.

Bush agreed, and the calls began going out at one-thirty that afternoon to the dozen people on his long list of finalists. It was one of the toughest decisions he had ever made, he told Dole, but it was going to be someone else; he didn't name names. Ten minutes later, Mrs. Dole got her own call, separate but equal, and equally opaque. Kemp's was rather warmer. "Jack, I just want you to know that . . ." Bush began. Kemp didn't need to hear the rest, the stuff about the great campaign he had run and what a wonderful family he had and how hard a choice it had been; he knew it was over.

"I guess I'll be going to every one of Jimmy's games," he said, setting the phone back in its cradle; his younger son was a high-school quarterback, and Kemp, having decided to give up his seat in Congress, was about to be unemployed.

The last name on the list was Quayle's. By then, the senator sensed that he could be the one; he had gone so far as to call Jim Baker over the weekend before the convention to worry aloud about his support systems. "If it is me," he had said, "I hope to hell you've got a staff or somebody I can use. I'm going to need help."

"Don't worry, I've got that covered," Baker had said. "We've got a whole team." Quayle's distress, indeed, was of only abstract interest to him at the time; he thought Bush was about to choose Dole.

But the straws in the wind had continued blowing Quayle's way, and when Kimmitt called one last time that Tuesday morning to ask whether there was anything else they should know, the senator guessed that the deal was down. He walked his wife, Marilyn, to lunch at Sammy's Seafood in the French Quarter with the bittersweet feeling that their lives were about to change forever. The chatter at the neighboring tables was whether it would be Dole or Kemp. They smiled secret smiles at each other, knowing better.

"This may be our last lunch together," Quayle said.

They had been primed to expect a call that afternoon and had been issued a beeper. Mrs. Quayle had tucked it into her purse, and as they lingered over the last of their meal it sounded.

"Well, there it is," Mrs. Quayle said.

They walked back to their hotel. The message waiting for them was to call Jim Baker. Quayle's heart skipped a beat; candidates tell you yes, he figured, and managers tell you no. But when he got through, surprising himself by dialing the number right the first time, Baker told him to hold for the vice president.

Bush was still propped on the bed in the admiral's residence when Baker handed over the phone. He threw a meaningful glance at George Jr., a look that said, Pay attention, son, this is history.

"Dan," he said, "this is George Bush. I've thought long and hard, and I'd like you to join me as my running mate."

"Yes, sir," Quayle managed, with a thumbs-up sign to Marilyn. There was more, Bush's assurance that the senator had been his choice, his first choice, his *only* choice, but Quayle, entering hyperspace, was barely taking it in.

"This is going to be exciting," Bush was saying. Quayle was too near orbit to guess just how exciting it would turn out to be.

Bush passed the phone back to Baker to describe the splashy rendezvous they had planned, Bush arriving by riverboat for a waterfront rally in Spanish Plaza, Quayle standing up front of the crowd at dockside like a contestant on *The Price Is Right* awaiting the call to come on down. No one at either end of the line knew the site; all the senator knew was that it was somewhere within walking distance of his hotel.

"Listen, Quayle," Baker warned him affably, "don't blow your first assignment. If you do, I want you to know that this decision is revocable."

Quayle found the plaza all right, but had trouble fighting through the crowd; when he told people he was Senator Quayle, they didn't care. He was late getting to the water's edge, and when the good ship *Natchez* first rounded the bend for the landing, with Bush in short shirtsleeves in the wheelhouse, Quayle was nowhere in sight. The *Natchez* swung about for another turn while Ailes, Teeter and Kimmitt climbed onto pylons, anxiously scanning the crowd. An advance man finally found Quayle and propelled him down front; the *Natchez* eased in with whistle blasting and calliope playing "The Stars and Stripes Forever," and the vice president stood eye to eye with *his* number two for the first time since the talent search had begun.

Stu Spencer had watched the docking from his window in the Marriott, but when the ceremony began he retired to his TV; it would be his first introduction to his client. He was as surprised as anyone else when Quayle came bounding onstage, looking, in his excitement, as if he wanted to hug Bush. Holy shit, this is it, Spencer thought; the sum of his knowledge of Quayle at that moment was that he looked a little like Robert Redford and might have some attraction for the ladies. He could tell that the kid was raw, watching his maiden performance on TV, a bit too hot for the medium. But he liked Quayle's looks, and the all-star team of cornermen Spencer had assembled could shape him up for combat. As the idea sank in, he began to laugh.

"Well," he said aloud to an empty room, "this ought to be fun."

His view, in forty-eight hours, would be a lonely one at Bush Inc. Quayle's profile was a nearly total blank, so empty of details that a gathering of Bush's regional directors sent a gofer to the nearest Waldenbooks for a copy of *The Almanac of American Politics 1988* so they would know who in hell it was they were supposed to be out there selling. The book, a desktop standard in politics, was for once not greatly helpful, or cheering either. It described the senator as sunny, articulate and hardworking on his issues, but its account of his legislative record had the sparse look of a farm field in November, and, his entry noted delicately, "he does not seem particularly cerebral."

It was accordingly left to the fifteen thousand journalists assembled in New Orleans to fill in the details, and they did, overnight, with what Bush's managers spoke of with some justice as a feeding frenzy. The main pieces of the picture were his history as an underachiever in school and his service in the Guard rather than the Eighty-second Airborne, say, at the height of the war in Vietnam. Neither was, or should have been, disqualifying; Jimmy Carter had brought home better report cards than Ronald Reagan, and the Guard, as a baby boomer in the Bush command group put it, was at very worst "honorable draft-dodging" as against fleeing to Canada or going underground. But they primed the canvas for a portrait of the senator as a man of indistinction, a playboy coasting through life like a surfer on a wave, and when he floundered through his first public exegeses of his record, the campaign teetered for two days at the edge of panic.

Spencer and Darman had been dispatched to prepare the senator for The Show, the minor leaguers' nickname for the majors. But they found him impervious to coaching; too much had happened to him in too short a time, and he had the slightly dazed look, Spencer thought, of a shellshocked GI. His debut, at a joint press conference with Bush, was a shambles; when he said he hadn't known when he joined the Guard that he would one day be running for vice president, one senior partner in the Bush command wanted to sink into his hotel-room floor.

His handlers decided nevertheless to send him around to the network anchor booths that evening, this time with further prompting from Roger Ailes. Their view at the time was that, with a little touching-up, his version of his Guard service could still repair some of the damage. But Quayle compounded it instead, with his stuttery performance and his scattered recollection of the facts. In one interview, with Tom Brokaw, he conceded that "calls were made" when he first expressed interest in joining the Guard. In another, with Dan Rather, he denied having had sex with Paula Parkinson; Rather, who hadn't asked, had to explain who she was.

The vertigo level in Bush's command rose as word of Quayle's performances spread through the convention hall. None of the talking points they had prepared for him or their own spin patrols were selling, not the material about how patriotic it was to join the Guard or how Dan had, after all, served his country for six years; people on the floor were saying Bush ought to dump him while there was still time.

"Jesus, get an answer on this thing," Deborah Steelman, a campaign-issues adviser, begged speechwriter Bob Grady when they bumped in the aisle. "We're getting *killed*."

But the answers were lost somewhere in the fogbank of Quayle's memory and the gusts of rumor sweeping the arena. Atwater's man Ed Rogers called him away from a celebratory G-6 dinner with a tip: CBS was about to break a story that the Quayles had used influence to get their boy into the Guard. The dinner broke up, and Atwater scrambled for a phone, looking for Baker.

Baker didn't need to be told they had a problem. He had been appalled by Quayle's performance and was angry at himself and his boss, associates said, for the situation he found himself in, sweeping up a mess he had done his best to prevent. Jimmy was *used* to his friend doing stupid things, one chum who saw him soon after the convention said, but not on so epic a scale; he was, in this account, tired, frustrated, aggravated, disgusted with the slipshod screening process and furious with the vice president, who had wrought it.

His duty was nonetheless plain: to defend the choice and control the damage. The kindest words he could bring himself to say for press consumption were that Bush had promised only to pick a qualified running mate, not necessarily the *most* qualified. In private, he got on the blower to Quayle and, with iron civility, warned him of the consequences of further mistakes. It was, he said, a jungle out there, and there were to be no more mess-ups, no errors or lies.

"Make damn sure your recollections are accurate," he said. "If you can't remember something, say you can't. The one thing you *cannot* do is go out there and say something that turns out to be untrue. That would put the vice president—and yourself—in a terribly compromising position."

His tone was brotherly, but his meaning was unmistakable: one more embarrassment and Quayle's place on the ticket was in peril. The drums indeed were beating for his head when Baker convened an emergency command meeting Wednesday at the Marriott, in a thirty-eighth-floor bedroom made over into a workspace. Some of his war council dropped into chairs; some perched on dressers and tables; some stood. Cokes and potato chips sat on a conference table, largely ignored. The only dish on the menu for two and a half insomniac hours was parboiled Quayle.

The possibility of dumping him was not seriously in play, not, anyway, if he could get his act together; the hour was too late, the damage potential too high and the shadow of Thomas F. Eagleton too long. The objective instead was damage control, and, as a first measure, Baker dispatched Darman and Kimmitt to the Westin Canal Place to cross-examine the senator and his father about who had done what to get young Danny into the Guard.

It was half past midnight when the phone rang in Quayle's room, rousing him from his first sound sleep in two nights. Baker was on the line, telling the senator that the two operatives were on the way.

"This is totally ridiculous," Quayle said.

It was a new ball game, Baker told him. They couldn't take any chances.

Quayle, sleep-starved, argued for waiting till morning and calling another news conference. He didn't see what the big deal was. "I'll just go out there and answer the questions," he said.

"How are you going to answer the questions," Baker answered tartly, "when you don't know what happened twenty years ago?"

"I'll give my version of it."

"What if your version is different from somebody else's version?" Baker asked.

"Well, that's life, isn't it?" Quayle answered irritably.

It wasn't life Baker-style, not in a presidential campaign; maybe there was wiggle room in the Senate, but not in high-stakes politics. "We have to know everything before we say anything," he told Quayle. "The one thing you've got to understand is that if you make one misstatement of fact, then your credibility is finished."

Once again, Quayle took his meaning, and when Darman and Kimmitt arrived the fight was out of him; to the extent he could, he told them what they wanted to know.

The clock read one-fifteen when they returned to the command suite, and the suspense in the room was heavy. Darman dispelled it. "There are no surprises," he said. Quayle recalled having phoned home about his decision, and his father in turn had rung up one or the other of two employees who had been senior Guard officers, for information, he insisted, not influence. Their recollections ended there. They weren't concealing any-thing, Darman said. They just didn't remember.

The Bush campaign was no less divided than the nation on the merits of a man's having sat out the war as a weekend soldier, a skirmish fought in part across generational lines. Older hands like Spencer grumbled that no one on Iwo Jima thought much of National Guardsmen. But the boomers in the room, the Atwaters and the Blacks, prevailed with the only argument available to Quayle—that the Guard had been a perfectly respectable alternative to combat duty. It was, as they all knew, a case Quayle would have to make himself, the sooner the better. There was some sentiment for a press conference the next morning. Baker said no. They would be putting a green kid out on the high wire without a net. They had to get their facts in a row first, Baker said, handing out assignments like a city editor. They needed to get out front of the story even if it meant reporting it themselves.

The firefighting operation made some headway through the day, Thurs-day, dousing the uglier rumors. That evening, in the narrow window before the acceptance speeches, they roadblocked the network anchor booths for twenty minutes of prime time with senior Bush operatives expressing their pleasure, pride and confidence in J. Danforth Quayle. The situation seemed to them to be stabilizing, maybe even turning in their favor. "You know, every time that guy's on-camera, it helps us," Spencer said, still smitten with Quayle's cover-boy looks; he would still be worth a couple of points for the ticket if they could just get him through the heavy weather.

Quayle made a good start out of the turbulence when he addressed the convention that night, merely by being adequate. He was nervous waiting to go on, and his stomach was in the second day of a mutiny begun when Bush had tapped him. In the forty-eight hours since, he had been torn from his family, surrounded with wizards and witch doctors—who *were* these guys?—and thrown to the wolf pack lurking in the media workspaces just beyond the convention floor. Stu Spencer, who had once told Jerry Ford to his face that he was a fucked-up campaigner, read the anxiety in Quayle's eyes and was gentle with him. But Quayle's loneliness in the crowd was unabated, and as the time neared for his entrance he asked everyone in the holding room to clear out except Tom Korologos, a prominent lobbyist and a longtime golfing buddy.

"What's up?" Korologos asked, worried.

"I just wanted to be with somebody I've known for more than twenty-four hours," Quayle answered.

They watched the TV monitors for a time. The story of the hour was still

Sergeant Dan Quayle, Indiana National Guard, and it wasn't very flattering to him or his patron.

"Kicking the shit out of me, aren't they?" Quayle said.

Korologos nodded.

"God, I hate to hurt George," Quayle said. "This is *terrible*."

He looked as if he were in pain. For a fleeting moment, Korologos thought he might be preparing to quit the ticket.

"It's too late now," Korologos said.

Yeah, Quayle said, and then he was on. He walked to the podium, squared his shoulders, jutted his jaw, looked straight into the cameras the way Spencer had taught him and, when the crowd quieted, plunged into his speech. He had served in the Guard and was proud of it, he said at one point. He could as well have been announcing a formula for universal peace and prosperity forever. Forget the crowd, they won't even be able to hear you, Spencer had told him, but his defiant answer to the wolf pack brought down the house.

The Instant Hero

In the end, it was Bush who saved the day, the ticket and, very possibly, his candidacy with the single most brilliant speech of his career. It was surely the most important, as people had been telling him for weeks; his man Atwater was saying that if the boss blew this one, they'd go into a tailspin and be counted out of the race. But the text that emerged from Peggy Noonan's word processor, with potshots by Roger Ailes and punch lines by Doug Gamble, a gag writer for Bob Hope, was a masterwork—the creation of an instant mythic persona for a man who had got through two decades of public life without one. His predecessors at the podium had had to be provided with positive words to say about him. His own speech filled in the blanks; at the wave of a wand, or, more accurately, the tap-tap of a keyboard, he had become a man of hitherto unrealized size, strength, wit, grit and compassion.

He even made a grace note of his ineloquence—a quiet man, he said, could hear the voices of need and pain—and a virtue of his want of vision. What he had instead, he said, was a sense of *mission*; the man who had finished his bombing run in a burning plane in World War II and had built a million-dollar business from scratch in West Texas was the man to carry on the work of Ronald Reagan. He too would stand tall against the tax-and-spenders—"read my lips," he said—and he too would defend the old values under siege by the liberals; the line he drew in the dust between himself and Dukakis was ideology, and he would hold it against the pink hordes massing in Harvard Yard. But *his* ideology would be Reaganism with a heart. He dreamed, he said, of a kinder, gentler America, and he would make it the goal of his presidency.

He managed somehow to be heard above the din about Quayle, and, more important, to be appreciated. Another of Teeter's focus groups in Paramus had been wired to electronic response meters, and the results were mostly pleasing, especially for those strategists on Fifteenth Street who favored a meaner-tougher Bush for the fall market. The biggest winner among his software offerings was the tale of his days getting started in Texas—the rich-kid-goes-to-camp story, one campaign official called it. His kinder-gentler thematics got a straight-line response on the readouts, and when he spoke of "a thousand points of light," meaning the volunteered good works of Americans in their daily lives, nobody in the sample group knew what he was talking about. People liked him best when he sounded strongest. His shots at Dukakis for furloughing murderers and vetoing the Pledge of Allegiance drew gushers of blood.

But the whole proved larger and more powerful than the sum of its machine-tooled parts. America met Bush up close and personal for the first time that night, live from New Orleans, and while it was hard to tell precisely which parts of his offering were real and which manufactured, people plainly liked what they saw. He rocketed from ten points down to seven points up in the polls and became the front-runner for the prize he had sought for ten years.

It was possible, in the afterglow, to imagine that they had turned the corner in the matter of Dan Quayle as well. Their technique was a hoary one for a campaign in trouble, a game called beat the press. The senator, in their emerging scenario, was not villain but victim, the innocent quarry of a lynch mob of bloodthirsty reporters. For graphic proof, they sent him home from New Orleans to Huntington, Indiana, on getaway day to meet his tormentors on his ground, not theirs, and under his ground rules. The reporters shagging after him found themselves in a bearpit, conducting their inquisition into the senator's courage and veracity over an open public-address system; around them, a hostile crowd of five thousand of his townsmen hooted, booed and chanted, "Bo-ring! Bo-ring! Bo-ring!" It wasn't a setup, Jim Baker would insist gamely, but it looked like one, and had the desired effect; the tables had turned, and in a matter of days the Quayle hunt subsided into a sullen cold war.

But a certain corroded attitude toward the senator was hardening among the men on Fifteenth Street, a sense that even when the flapping over his Guard duty and his gentleman C's died down, the underlying perception of his unseriousness would remain. He was known around headquarters as Danny or sometimes simply Q, terms of derision more than endearment, and his nearly daily gaffes in the early going were read aloud at staff meetings to hollow gallows laughter. Bush himself was said by a senior aide to be aggravated with the men who had promoted the choice, and as word of his annoyance spread, most of them disowned it. The settling view among them was that the campaign was stuck with the unbearable lightness of Dan Quayle and the not-yet-calculable cost. He was, one of them said sourly, Bush's gift to the next generation of Republican aspirants to the presidency—a guy who, with four or even eight years' apprenticeship, was *never* going to be ready.

PART FOUR

THE FALL CAMPAIGN

Whatever It Takes
—*A SAYING AT AILES*
COMMUNICATIONS INC.,
ROGER AILES, PRESIDENT

Mood Indigo

THROUGH THE LONG, SMOTHERING GREENHOUSE SUMMER OF 1988, Michael Dukakis had wandered the political landscape in one of his funks—a dark mood made darker by the steady disintegration of his candidacy. The seventeen-point lead he had carried out of Atlanta had melted in the heat of Bush's blowtorch campaign, and so had his own carefully drawn self-portrait as a strong, sound, no-nonsense general manager of the American future. He didn't have a strategy or a message. He couldn't even make himself heard. He had lost his confidence in his managers and, so some of them worried, in himself. His spirit had touched bottom when, on a late-August Sunday morning at the Tanglewood Music Festival in Lenox, Massachusetts, he and Kitty breakfasted over the worst news yet: a new poll showing him in a dead heat with Bush in his own home state. He knew then that his dream was dying the death of a thousand sound bites, and that night, in his need, he reached out across a year's separation to the man who had woven it around him. He called John Sasso home from Elba.

The move was a fitting one in what had become the Year of the Handler in our politics, the final triumph of the image-makers, the computer-modelers and the gun-for-hire managers over the process of electing a president. They were, in 1988, like Giotto confronting a bare wall or Joyce a blank page; there were no galvanic issues, no lofty visions, no vivid personalities to get in the way—nothing, that is, to impede their artistic fancies. Their work would be badly reviewed by the press and, finally, the voters for its reduction of politics to made-for-TV mud-wrestling. But it was plain, by the beginning of autumn, whose packagers were the most practiced at their craft, and the cleverer. It could be fairly said that the George Bush and the Michael Dukakis who were presented for public view were articles of manufacture. The problem, from the governor's point of view, was that Bush Inc. had created them both.

Fred MacMurray versus Robert De Niro

The men in Bush's atelier were artists of a sort, but their works were styled for sale, not for museum walls. One was a likeness in a romantic vein, the other brutalist; market values, in the new political portraiture, had little to do with fidelity to life. Dukakis and his insular management team had deluded themselves that Bush was unelectable. They had, as one of Sasso's men put it, this incredible security blanket called Forty-three Negative, the measure, in the polls, of how little America loved the vice president. It was axiomatic in politics that no one with negative ratings that high could get elected anything, let alone president.

They were thus caught off guard by the timing, the ferocity and finally the success of Bush's go-for-the-jugular strategy. By fall, Ed Reilly, the polltaker, warned them, the race had been recast as Fred MacMurray versus Robert De Niro, the safe if slightly goofy nice guy against a figure of dark mien and scary intensity. The governor had become a political E.T. who furloughed murderers, befouled Boston Harbor, spurned the American flag and might just be mentally unstable. "They're throwing the kitchen sink at me," he told Sasso dejectedly the night of their reunion in August—and, worse, it was working.

It worked in part because Dukakis and his people, in their disbelief, let it happen. The candidate and the campaign had fallen into an Alexandrian torpor after the last primaries; there were no new states to conquer, and while they had got up for the convention, no one knew what to do next. Instead, for a dangerous time, they basked in their own radiance; they had built a better spaceship, not realizing that, as Ira Jackson put it, the O-rings were bound to rupture.

It was notorious in Dukakis's circle that he needed a plan—a tight, clear political Baedeker setting out the next stations on his journey, explaining why they were important and telling him how to get there in his methodical left-foot-right-foot way. A friend familiar with the governor's accomplished turkey Tetrazzini asked whether he had any secret ingredients, to which Dukakis said no—the cookbook was good enough for him. His recipes were to his cuisine what Sasso's memos had been to his campaign, a source of direction and confidence. "Give me a target and I'll hit it," he told Sasso's successors in the exasperation of summer. No one did, not, anyway, to his satisfaction, and he was left on his own.

His new team, under Susan Estrich's management, had disappointed him. Estrich was brilliant, everybody conceded that; one of the exiles, Paul Tully, thought her smarter than the campaign turned out to be. She had successfully overseen the war of attrition for the nomination; that it was a triumph of money and organization more than of her political genius mattered less than the fact that they had won.

But Dukakis could be a maddeningly slow learner at presidential politics, and, as Tully would put it in retrospect, Estrich never had the standing to get him to do things he didn't want to do. In some ways, they were opposites, Dukakis cool and contained, Estrich volatile and profane. In others, they were almost too much alike—two stubborn souls who did not listen or tolerate argument well. Her relationship with Dukakis had never approached his nearly brotherly trust in Sasso, and by summer it was next to nonexistent. The strain of trying to deal with him showed in her sleepless eyes and her unwonted silences. She was, or felt, unwelcome in Dukakis's hotel suite at the convention, and she quit speaking up much at meetings; she made her points instead through surrogates and through memos bearing other people's signatures.

Her relations with some of the Chauncy Street staff were almost as strained. Estrich seemed to colleagues to be jealous of her authority and her reputation. One by one, men who thought themselves friends found themselves in Coventry for infractions of her code; even her deputy Jack Corrigan had bailed out on her, seeing the downward drift of the campaign, and had petitioned Dukakis in writing to bring Sasso back. She resisted drawing in outsiders as well, until the governor's situation had deteriorated from bad to desperate. Michael doesn't want to see people, she would say. The others were never sure whether his insulation was really his wish or hers.

As the doors swung shut, résumés and strategy memos gathered dust on Estrich's desk and Corrigan's, unattended and often unanswered. The preferred ideas on Chauncy Street were homegrown, which meant lawyerly, liberal, cerebral and, for the most part, risk-averse. The response to anything new, one outside friend of some of the principals thought, was to look for what was wrong with it. There would almost always be something, if a tableful of lawyers looked hard enough. Those ideas that survived their scrutiny did not add up to a strategy, or so Dukakis regularly complained. Estrich thought they did, if only she could have got his ear.

There was no message, either, beyond the pale promise of good jobs and effective government that had got Dukakis through the primaries. He was, as one of his theme doctors put it, incapable of seeing expansively, and when his people dunned him for his vision, his reason for wanting to be president, his response, typically, was, "Give me the lines." His reaction, when they tried, made them wish they hadn't. Tubby Harrison made the effort early in the summer, arguing, as he had done many times, for a tough, populist stand on trade and going on at length as to why it would work.

"No, no," Dukakis told him. "You're giving me *analysis*. That's not my long suit—give me the *message*."

What he seemed to be demanding was the language—the bumper sticker down to the precise words. Harrison, fed up, retreated to his hole-in-the-wall offices in Cambridge, announcing to Estrich that he wasn't coming to any more of those fucking meetings; he would send in his ideas in writing. Jack Corrigan tried to coax him out of hiding and put him on the Dukakis tour, hoping he could somehow get things thematically on track. Corrigan was his best friend, but Harrison said no; he wasn't going out on the plane, he said, so Dukakis could play Mister Governor with him again.

No one else fared much better. Sasso had always been the narrow end of the funnel, the single channel for ideas and information. The flow had stopped with his departure; Dukakis quit accepting advice, from outside experts on the issues, even from his own staff. The campaign was a litter of unused themes and unproduced scripts that had offended his unpredictable tastes. Even ideas that would find their way into his rhetoric months later came back from his first viewing encased in ice. Someone once proposed the phrase "Strong Leadership to Revitalize America" as a thematic.

" 'Revitalize?' " Dukakis snapped. "Sounds like a building to me."

Another memo offered "The Best Is Yet to Come." It was returned to its author ink-stained with grammatical corrections and a scrawled "Lousy writing. MSD." Only later would the words be resurrected, as a signature of his candidacy.

The result was a void at the center of the campaign, in the heart and mind of the governor; he could neither reveal himself nor define what he wanted, and Bush's imagists had an empty screen for their lantern slides of Dukakis as a wet, dangerous and arguably unpatriotic liberal. It did not take a brain surgeon, one of the governor's people said, to have seen what was coming; Kirk O'Donnell, a senior strategist in the campaign, had heard Atwater outline it openly at a panel discussion in June, and Tubby Harrison's memos were a serial warning as to the consequences "if Bush is able to paint MSD as a liberal."

It was June when Harrison first sounded that alarm. But Dukakis was caught off guard when, at the end of a successful "theme week" on crime and drugs that month, Bush smacked him between the eyes with the case of Willie Horton and his felonies on furlough. Two subsequent theme weeks were canceled, and Dukakis retreated under fire to Nantucket for a few days, stunned and wounded. Michael the Good, as he was unlovingly known around the statehouse, had not expected the mud to start flying before Labor Day and believed that even then it would splash back on Bush. He was wrong on both counts and was left floundering for answers; by Labor Day, Harrison's bad dream would be reality.

The charges kept coming, thick and fast as jabs in a bantam-weight title fight, and Dukakis was pinned down all summer trying lamely to ward them off. His posture reminded Hank Morris, a New York consultant, of Muhammad Ali's old rope-a-dope strategy, hanging on the ropes and letting the other guy punch himself out. The problem, as Morris warned in a memo to Chauncy Street, was that what worked in a prize ring did not necessarily travel well in politics, and Bush's body blows were taking a devastating toll. The Pledge, for example: Bush led mass recitations at his convention and at most of his rallies afterward, wondering all the while whether the governor had some, well, *problem* with it. Or the ACLU: its name became a four-letter word in Bush's hands, and Dukakis a friend of atheists, criminals and pornographers. Or the raw sewage and chemical effluents in Boston Harbor, graphically depicted in one of Bush's strongest attack ads; the fact that Dukakis's belated clean-up effort had been impeded by the Reagan administration got lost somewhere on the cutting-room floor.

There was even the rumor, wholly unsubstantiated, that Dukakis had twice been treated for depression, after the death of his brother in 1973 and after his loss of the governorship in 1978. The story was never successfully tracked to Bush Inc., though Atwater was reflexively numbered among the suspects; the first people to circulate it openly were, rather, the followers of the fringe candidate Lyndon LaRouche Jr. But the vice president's men did not conceal their happiness, and no less a surrogate than Ronald Reagan made sure the point got made, referring to Dukakis, in a bad joke, as an "invalid."

The story by then had been allowed to fester for days while Dukakis stood, as was his wont, on principle—a course as fruitful in politics as preaching the Eighth Commandment to a mugger in a dark alley. Only after the president piled on was Dukakis's doctor, Gerald Plotkin, scrambled before the press to attest to his client's good health. His file on the governor was so thin, indeed, that the campaign press secretariat made him bulk it up with Latin words, urinalysis results and accounts of a couple of colds and a stubborn splinter just to make it look comprehensive. There had been no clinical depressions, Plotkin said, and no psychiatric treatment. The record didn't matter, nor did Reagan's apologies; as Dukakis's resident Cassandra, Tubby Harrison watched morosely while eight more points fell away overnight.

Neither Dukakis nor his people seemed able to frame a coherent response to the attacks or, better still, launch their own counteroffensive. The governor reminded his New York political-advertising consultant Scott Miller of a prizefighter dazzled by an opponent's speed and skill; you stand there taking hits and thinking *Wow!*, and only when you get back to your corner do you realize that you're bleeding from both eyes. He seemed so paralyzed that another of his operatives quite seriously proposed putting his peppery cousin Olympia on TV to do his fighting for him.

When he did swing back, his aim was imperfect. His single attempt at a gut punch came when, speaking of corruption in the Reagan administration, he quoted an old Greek proverb to the effect that a fish rots from the head down.

"Jesus, Tommy," Sasso asked Kiley, by phone from his seat on the sidelines, "where'd he come up with the fish-head line?"

It was his own, Kiley said unhappily. Attacking Reagan, as both men knew, was borrowing trouble. De Niro against MacMurray was bad enough. The Raging Bull against the Gipper was a self-administered one-punch kayo.

The governor's script came more often from his own bionic heart; he no longer had enough confidence in his strategists to follow their instincts, and his own were built for a Kennedy School seminar, not a Pier Six brawl of a campaign. He was badly bloodied by the Pledge issue, but his response through the summer was, as one of his people put it, as dry as a first-year recitation in law school. Democratic politicians around the country were beefing about it, as Alice Travis, a veteran field staffer, complained to Estrich one day; for ordinary folks, as against constitutional scholars, it was a bit abstract.

"I know," Estrich said wanly. "That's Michael." But, in fact, it was

Estrich too. Weeks earlier, Ken Swope, the media man, had warned her about the Pledge issue. "They're not going to get anywhere with that," Estrich told him. "Because we've got the Supreme Court answer."

Even when the governor wanted to fight back, his people were slow providing ammunition. All summer Estrich had shrugged off her men's worries about the Willie Horton story. It would spatter back on the Republicans, she claimed. She was wrong. At Dukakis's order, the staff hunted for a comparable horror tale from the Federal prison-furlough program; by the time they found one, in late autumn, it was too late to do any good. They were tipped five days in advance that Bush planned a show visit to Boston Harbor to tut-tut over its filthiness, but they were still war-gaming responses the night before. Should they fly a plane overhead with a banner? How many letters would it hold? What should it say? Should Dukakis himself show up and offer to lead the tour? Much of it was silly, and none of it got done; Bush had the harbor, the sound bites and the issue to himself.

It was a bruising season, and as it progressed, Dukakis seemed to his people to recede deeper and deeper into himself, away from them and the voters. One campaign adviser tracked the beginnings of his summer slump to his June getaway in Nantucket between the primaries and the convention. His people had meant the down time as a mercy to him, a hedge against combat fatigue and the sorts of gaffes that are its symptom; some of them who had soldiered with Jimmy Carter recalled how he had pushed himself past exhaustion, to a point where he had to be propped up between Secret Service agents just to get to and from a podium. Dukakis seemed near that point, getting by on five hours' sleep a night. Even his flying time was work time, the governor sitting pale and pouchy-eyed in his forward section, hunched over a backlog of statehouse business.

But his holiday on the beach gave him brooding time as well, a passage, one of his cannier aides said, when the adrenaline quit flowing and all the downside stuff came washing in—his concerns about the price his family was paying for his candidacy; his sense that he was flying without a pilot or a flight plan; his upset at Bush's bully-boy campaigning; his wholly human doubts about himself. I don't want to hear about it, Kitty would tell him impatiently, but veterans of past campaigns thought they recognized the syndrome. Saying over and over that you were going to be president gave you a kind of runner's high; but when the cheering stopped, a certain hollow feeling set in, a sudden vertigo of the soul.

His public performances turned sluggish thereafter, a rote repetition of his only-in-America-and-especially-in-Massachusetts road speech. His private mood grew sullen, snappish and closed to advice. By the end of the summer, people inside the campaign and out were hammering at him to come out swinging—to fire back at Bush and open up his own second-front offensive addressing the economic anxieties of the middle class. "I know, I know," he would say, brushing them off.

Dukakis in turn felt ill-served by his people. He complained regularly that he was all alone out there, with no help from surrogates and precious little from his relays of high-powered ad-makers. It was as if nothing got done unless he willed it to happen, and he seemed reinforced in his suicidal resolve to manage his own campaign. His days on the road took on an unremitting sameness. "Why am I doing this?" he would explode between events. He usually meant the next stop on the day's schedule, but it sometimes sounded as if he regretted running at all. His bookings were gradually whittled down from three a day to two and finally one, and Chauncy Street saw to it that Kitty or one of his daughters traveled with him as often as possible, to lift his chapfallen spirits and restore a sense of grounding to his life.

He had always been a creature of routine, and in his summer-long brown study he clung to them harder than ever. He had done most of the campaign on a slow and homely jet known among his entourage as the Sky Pig, actually Bob Dole's Plane From Hell under a new and similarly unaffectionate name. Its look was a good deal less than presidential, but when his people replaced it with a bigger, faster plane early in August he was manifestly not pleased.

"Where are Jennifer and Gloria?" he asked, looking around for his accustomed flight attendants.

They had gone the way of the Sky Pig, and he missed them.

"Where's my divider?"

There was no curtain separating him from the press, and he wanted one.

"Where's my Raisin Bran?"

The new plane stocked a different brand, and he was furious. The next day, the Sky Pig was back on the tarmac waiting for him.

Dukakis, as one aide said, had only two emotions, mad and madder, and as his spirits eddied downward his temper rose. He was booked to do a speech and collect an endorsement at an AFL-CIO meeting in Washington in August, but his one-man ghostwriting team was late getting him a script, and he wakened a staffer at home in Boston at seven-thirty the morning he was to give it.

"It's mush," he said. "Rip it up."

He was to go on in five hours. The text was redone in two, but it had to be faxed to the road company and then put on a TelePrompTer, devouring what time was left. The clock showed twelve-fifteen when Dukakis's patience broke.

"What the hell is going on?" he flared. He wasn't waiting any longer, not even till his scheduled hour. Instead, he stalked out to the podium ten minutes early and started reading the first page, angrily, while his people were frantically feeding the twelfth into the fax machine on Chauncy Street. His best sound bites got lost in the transmission, and the speech was a dud on the news.

Dukakis's state of mind was nothing like his past reactions to death and defeat; its arc, according to one aide tracking it, led not so much downward as inward, and by August it drew him back to the familiar soil of his home state. His time there was another of his rituals, a "regional tour" he had taken to doing every August. His people argued that the other forty-nine states needed his attention more. He tuned them out and clung to his stay-at-home travels as tightly as he did to the outworn Filene's suits and the down-at-heel wingtips in his closet, because he felt more comfortable in them. He was, in Tom Kiley's gently put words, an extremely unhappy man.

His people, with no other choice, told the world bravely that there was method in the governor's retreat: he was showing off the Massachusetts Miracle to the rest of America. In fact it wasn't even playing at home; Harrison's latest numbers, and *The Boston Herald*'s, showed him in danger of losing the state. His budget was a shambles, and Dukakis buried himself in it, to the dismay of his people on Chauncy Street. His candidacy for president was unraveling, but when Estrich tried to get his ear he shut her out; she grumbled he was too busy with his paper-pushing and his photo ops at some tollbooth somewhere in his own little world, the principality he knew as against the kingdom he sought. The campaign would have to wait; he had always insisted on spending more than half his days in the statehouse, and by August the number he was prepared to sacrifice to the campaign was down from three to two a week.

"Look," Estrich would tell him, almost begging, "we'd better get together for a half hour. We've got some things to go over."

"I can't," he would reply; any attention he gave to her problems would have to come out of what he called *her* time, by which he meant that dwindling ration of days he had allotted to his own quest for the presidency.

Estrich by then was near despair. There were days when she felt sorry for Dukakis in his obvious unhappiness and days when she thought him merely pigheaded. She understood that he had long since lost whatever pleasure there had been for him in the campaign; he was, as he told her sadly and accurately, getting the shit kicked out of him every day. Her impatient view, though she kept it to herself, was, So what?—that was life if you really wanted to be president. Whatever else you might say about George Bush, she thought, he was willing to wade through mud for three months to get where he wanted to go. Dukakis plainly was not.

"This is not the kind of campaigning I like," he told her. "This isn't as much fun as the primaries."

"You've got to fight back," she said. "That's all you can do. This is not going to stop happening because you'd like it to."

But he retreated into his misery, and Estrich retired to the deepening despond on Chauncy Street, no longer troubling to hide her feelings even from outsiders. The Friday before Labor Day, Estrich finally asked three Washington professionals, Bob Beckel, Bill Carrick and Tom Donilon, to come by with advice. As it happened, they had plenty. The campaign seemed to them to be rudderless and to have gone limp under Bush's broadside attack. Dukakis needed to hit back and to put forward a positive economic message of his own. With Beckel leading the chorus, the visitors spent three hours urging what Dukakis's own advisers had been pushing for a year: a new thematic line positioning himself as the champion of the middle class.

The problem was how to get any advice through to Dukakis; he seemed, in Estrich's private view, to be in hiding from his own campaign. Her decision to look outside for help was the child of desperation, and it showed in her demeanor and in her agenda; her session with the three Washingtonians spent more time on Dukakis than on Bush. She looked terrible, they thought, tired, tense and frustrated with her candidate. Dukakis wasn't listening, she told them. His anger was showing. He was more than any campaign could handle. They couldn't get him down from the high road into the trenches with Bush. They could hardly even get him out of Massachusetts.

That weekend, indeed, he abandoned campaigning altogether and adjourned with Kitty to her father's place in the Berkshires for two days of music and meditation. What the hell was Dukakis doing in *Tanglewood,* Paul Maslin, the polltaker, asked a friend on Chauncy Street, when he needed to be out telling the country who he was and what he stood for?

The answer, had either of them known it, might have pleased them: Dukakis, for a rare time that summer, was listening to advice from his friends, his strategists, his outside admirers, and, finally and decisively, his wife. The net of it was that he needed John Sasso, and its urgency had grown as his polls sank. Dukakis had resisted till then, fearing that it would look bad for a man of his own Mr. Clean image; there was, besides, the prospect of civil war on Chauncy Street if Sasso returned, Estrich and her crowd against Sasso and his. But with the end of summer, the pressures were irresistible, as Kitty Dukakis made plain to him. Her vote, a campaign hand said, was delivered as usual with the subtlety of a two-by-four in the face.

Bring Sasso back, she told Dukakis. If you don't, you'll lose.

Return of the Exile

The call went out that Monday night, the governor tracking his lost alter ego to his own vacation retreat on Martha's Vineyard. A year of enforced exile yawned between them, and, some mutual friends thought, neither man had got over the sense of having been betrayed by the other. It had taken Sasso six or eight weeks to get over the shock of his forced resignation, and his store of grievance had deepened, some friends said, with each failed attempt at restoration. In fact, he had never *entirely* left the campaign. He had stayed regularly in telephone contact, through friends like Corrigan and Mitropoulos, not the governor; in the summer doldrums, his shadow presence began to be openly felt in meetings, in sentences that began "John thinks" or "John says." But he was enjoying his new job at Hill, Holliday, the high-powered Boston ad agency where he had been sitting out the past eight months of his lost year, and he had not fully reengaged until the governor called. By Tuesday night, twenty-four hours after their first gingerly contact, he found himself in the Dukakises' kitchen talking about what could still be done.

John, Dukakis said, the campaign is in terrible shape. We're directionless. It's an organization without a captain. Will you come back and run it?

Sasso hesitated, caught between his bitterness and the lure of finishing what he had begun years before.

Governor, he said, I've got my own life now. We've been there together already, and we've had some great times. But you got through the campaign and the convention yourself, and I'm happy now. I've got a career. I can spend time with my family. I don't know if I want to give that up.

We really need you, Dukakis said. His tone was sad, almost beseeching.

I need to talk to Francine, Sasso said.

As his wife, Fran Sasso was less than pleased; their lives *had* been good since his departure from Chauncy Street, and when she had dropped him off at the tiny Vineyard airport for the flight to Boston that morning she told him, "I hope you're coming back."

By no means everyone at 105 Chauncy welcomed him back home. They were a family reunited, Estrich said, smiling bravely for the cameras in a staged tableau of unity, but she had exacted a price for peace; she kept the title of manager—Sasso would be "vice chairman"—and she remained, at her adamant insistence, the chief public spokesperson for the campaign. Sasso, in turn, was careful of her feelings, polite, some friends thought, to a fault; he hung in the background at her morning meetings, ceding her the head of the table and speaking only when called on. But Estrich, having resisted his return all summer, was upset—by several accounts to the point of tears—when it happened. During Sasso's first weeks back, she disappeared from her office for days at a time.

The returning exiles found themselves embroiled in what would become a guerrilla war for control of the campaign. Their first staff meeting was a kind of one-woman show, Estrich in her talky I'm-in-charge-here mode. She wasn't really, but Sasso deferred, and even some of the Chauncy Street regulars were confused as to the new chain of command. In the weeks that followed, parallel meetings sprang up, Estrich chairing hers at headquarters, Sasso running his an hour earlier. By the second week, more people were at his meetings than at hers.

It hadn't taken Sasso long to size up how difficult the task was going to be. He spent a week collecting ideas—he made Hank Morris, the New York consultant, read him a twenty-seven-page memo over the phone—and sizing up the rickety state of the campaign. It was a mess, and his own authority was compromised by the year he had been out of the rhythm and by the lateness of his return. The disarray on Chauncy Street was advanced, probably beyond repair. Even the Idea of Michael Dukakis, the paradigm of good, clean, efficient postliberal government Sasso had spun the campaign around, was dying in the marketplace.

It was disheartening. Sasso found himself aboard the shuttle to New York one day soon after his return, with an old friend and comrade-in-arms, Paul Bograd, in the cramped seat beside him. He was the architect visiting his masterwork in the aftermath of an earthquake, his eyes sad, his voice strained.

"It's really broken," he said.

The field organization, he could see, was strong; some people were saying it was *too* strong, given the higher importance of television advertising in a fall campaign. The rest was chaos. There was no strategy, no rationale behind the governor's scheduling, no definition to his campaign. Jesse was feeling left out and pissed off. The debates were up in the air. The negative-research file on Bush was virtually empty. The candidate was tired, battered and discouraged. Sasso's own last memo to Dukakis, more than a year earlier, had warned him that his message urgently needed work, but nothing had happened; the Dukakis he had come back to was the same stubborn and self-important man he had left. The man never grew, Sasso would tell friends afterward, when the consequences of not growing had become plain. He campaigned for a year and a half and he didn't grow one bit.

A new course for the campaign was set on Sasso's first Sunday back in business, when he and five of the men he had recalled from purgatory met in the deserted headquarters building. Their welcome, intended or not, was literally chilly. Estrich had left the air-conditioning on high; the controls were in her office, and so was the conference table, but she had locked up when she went home for the weekend, and Sasso's men crowded into a smaller and messier room, sweatered and shivering in the cold.

Sasso got quickly down to business, ticking off everything wrong with the campaign. "It's worse than I thought," he said grimly. "If I had known last week what I know now, I'm not sure I'd have done this. This has *got* to get straightened out."

He knew there were things that couldn't be fixed, systemic flaws that he would have to layer over or work around. The most urgent business, he said, was to look ahead to what they wanted the voters thinking about on Election Day and work back from there—develop a systematic eight-week game plan, subdivided into three-day thematic blocks, and not let Bush drive them off it. Scheduling had to be made to fit it; anyone who changed the itinerary unbidden, Sasso promised, would be punished under what some staffers called the Orange Juice Rule—a glass of cold juice in the face at the next morning's staff morning.

The message, distilled from the memos Sasso had been reading, was going to be economics, in two interlocking parts. The plight of the poor would not be one of them; in a campaign representing itself as having moved beyond ideology, anything that smelled of Old Deal liberalism was a nonstarter. Sasso's point one, targeted to women, was instead the middle-class squeeze—the struggle that even two-income families were having to find affordable housing, educate their kids or just make ends meet from day to day. Point two, tailored to men, was the nation's loss of jobs, business and a once unchallenged high-tech supremacy to Japan Inc. The connective tissue between them was the diminution of the American

Dream—the expectation, Sasso said, that you would live better than your parents and that your children would live better than you.

They had just two months to get people thinking their way. "If the issues on voters' minds are America's place in the world and the family squeeze," Sasso said, "we win. If it's peace and prosperity, we lose."

The loudest sound in the room when he finished, one participant remembered, was the clock ticking; there was too much to do in too little time. The subtext of their discussions was that they had a demoralized candidate on their hands, and it wasn't going to be enough to cut back his schedule or surround him with family. They had to give him back his confidence, and the only way to do it was to provide him a new strategy paper, something he could follow from A to B to C with the sense he was going somewhere. If you gave the governor a plan, Sasso said, he would lock in on it and do it.

Three days after their rump session, Sasso and his people tried out a working draft on Estrich and *her* crowd. Sasso as usual deferred to her feelings; all they wanted to do, he said, was put some thoughts on the table for discussion, and he called on another of the ex-*desaparecidos,* Peter Jacobs, to do the show-and-tell. Jacobs spoke a bit about how they were getting badly beaten at the politics of symbolism; Bush was on TV regularly with cops and honor guards, while Michael was usually in front of some blue curtain on some badly lit stage somewhere, unadorned except for, say, an AFL-CIO logo. They had to think visuals, Jacobs said, and he ticked off some ideas for the coming week.

"Well, this is nice," Estrich said, "but we've already got next week taken care of."

"Then why the fuck didn't you say so an hour ago," Corrigan demanded, turning on her, "instead of having us waste the last hour?"

"That's OK," Sasso said, trying to keep the peace. "Let's not start."

But he had to skip a further meeting on scheduling that night to treat with Jesse Jackson, and in his absence Estrich made his sidekick Jacobs a surrogate target for her pent-up anger. Jacobs was a stolid Maine lawyer who had started working in Dukakis's campaigns as a high-school boy and had subsequently helped arrange the match between him and Sasso. He counted both men friends, but when Sasso left he had followed, thinking the punishment larger than the crime. He had called the governor several times thereafter, urging him to bring John back. Dukakis didn't want to hear it; some old hands in his service were complaining by then that he no longer seemed to regard them as intellectual equals worthy of his time and attention. Jacobs succeeded only in getting himself identified on Chauncy

Street with the Sasso cabal, and in Sasso's absence he became the bogey in Estrich's sights.

His offense was telling the gathering what "we" had decided about what to do next.

"Listen, buster," Estrich said, "I will not put up with hearing you people use the word 'we' anymore. You're making a mistake if you're going to make this we–they, my team against your team, because *my* team is stronger than *your* team. Who the hell do you think you are, telling us what to do?"

She stormed on for ten minutes, and when she finished, her protégé Leslie Dach followed, in, as he himself said, less tactful terms than hers. Jacobs was stunned. He guessed that Estrich wanted a confrontation, and he chose not to respond; instead, he sat in silence, scribbling it all down on a legal pad until they finished with him.

They didn't finish, not that night. The next week, Estrich interrupted a senior-staff meeting to order Jacobs to get his desk out of the office he shared with Sasso in the third-floor executive suite and move it down to the basement.

The room was silent. Jacobs stared at her. The future of the country, maybe the world, was riding on what they were doing, he thought, and they were squabbling about who sits where.

"No, Susan," he said finally. "I won't."

From that moment, she seemed to surrender. She sat quiet and deflated for the rest of the meeting, and she was often absent in the days thereafter, until someone chided her for her truancies; it didn't look right for the manager of a presidential campaign to be away from her desk in September.

The Producers

Soon after Sasso's return, a group of his people found themselves in a richly appointed glass aerie in the John Hancock tower, fifty-nine stories above the grainy realities of the campaign. The setting was heady, even awesome, a quiet display of corporate money and power. Invisible hands had set out cold cuts and sodas for their arrival. The nightscape of Boston twinkled below them, like diamonds in a coffer exposed to light. The visitors felt somehow empowered by their surroundings, charged with adrenaline and capable of anything, even the revival of their faltering campaign.

The numbers were grim, as Tubby Harrison reminded them, reading from his latest returns as if they were the Book of the Not Quite Dead. The governor's early lead by then was long gone; he didn't seem to voters to stand for anything very much except a certain gauzy promise of leadership, and a new George Bush had erased that fragile last advantage. But the problems seemed smaller, seen from the sky, and when their host, David D'Alessandro, showed them his proposed solutions, they were like the managers of a faltering business, ready to be sold.

Their ad campaign till then had been a shambles, the victim of too many *sous-chefs* preparing scripts and too many cooks on Chauncy Street finding fault with them. Their rose-tinted plan going in had been to steal a page from the Republican campaign manual, assembling an all-star team of professional admen of the sort that had made four years of Ronald Reagan's amiable gerontocracy look like "Morning in America." The lineup seemed strong on paper, a mix of savvy political pros like Scott Miller and Madison Avenue hucksters like Ed McCabe, the man who had made a star of the chicken prince Frank Perdue. But their "Future Group," as it was too optimistically christened at launch, was never told precisely who was running things or what was expected of them. The future, as a result, looked as hopelessly vague to them as to everyone else trying to explain Michael Dukakis. There was no consistent guidance as to message or style; the single marching order, as Dan Payne would remember it afterward, was, "Just do a good ad."

The result was an anarchic tumble of ideas, some better than others; the slogan "Little Big Man!" was mercifully buried and forgotten, an example of the deleterious effect of a vacuum on the creative faculties. By the time Sasso took over, no more than two or three ads were on the air, the best among them a leftover from the convention. A thousand others had been rejected, many of them by Dukakis, who insisted on reading every script and rarely liked any. Once, Gary Susnjara, then nominally head of the ad team, showed Dukakis and Estrich an eloquently simple Reagan spot from 1980, the candidate speaking straight into the camera about how he would beat inflation. Susnjara wanted to try something similar, something framing Dukakis as a tough little sonofabitch who could get things done, but they heard only Reagan's words, not the underlying music. Reagan was bad; therefore the commercial was bad.

Not many survived the gauntlet of ten or a dozen people with a vote. Some spots had been produced but had never run. A few had got on the air, seemed to click, and then unaccountably disappeared. One that nobody liked had run anyway, before it could be recalled. The budget was badly overspent. What remained of the Future Group was thinned out, burned out and rebellious; its luckier members had returned to their respective pasts in commercial advertising, where the products—a tube of toothpaste, say, or a station wagon—had certain identifiable purposes and didn't talk back.

If images are the costumes in the teleplay of modern politics, the governor was naked, and Sasso, as an early order of business, reached out to D'Alessandro for help. D'Alessandro, then thirty-seven, was the John Hancock executive behind a prizewinning ad campaign, a series of riveting black-and-white mini-dramas of Real People having angst attacks over money problems soluble only by Hancock or a referee in bankruptcy. The ads had been produced by Hill, Holliday, which had subsequently become Sasso's haven; the two men had met on business there and had become friends.

D'Alessandro had been approached by the campaign once before, in its Fat City period following the primaries, and had been invited to submit ideas for the autumn. He had responded with a dense, nine-page memo, counseling, among other things, clarity, consistency and discipline as the essentials of any successful ad strategy. None of these attributes was in long supply on Chauncy Street at the time, nor was reliance on the kindness of strangers, particularly those strangers who chanced to be identified with Sasso. "Gee, I really liked your memo," Tom Kiley, who had solicited it, told D'Alessandro at the time. It was the last D'Alessandro heard from the campaign until Sasso piped him urgently aboard.

His first visit to the Future Group's tenth-floor office at 99 Chauncy, a few doors down from headquarters, made him wonder why he had said yes. It was, he thought, like walking into a Devil's Island prison scene from the movie *Papillon*. The place was teeming, creative people bumping into traffic people sharing the same cramped quarters. The management was crosswired among three men, each of whom thought he was or should be in charge; one of them, Susnjara, was in despair and would shortly return to his real job at Saatchi & Saatchi. A half-dozen writers were laboring over scripts, with the haunted look of the permanently unpublished awaiting their next rejection slips. Tapes were piled up, interred in their cans and cassettes. What few ads were available tested badly with focus groups. D'Alessandro faulted their *auteurs* less than he did the campaign management, which had never provided a coherent strategy; still, he saw little recourse but to junk the entire inventory and start again from scratch.

There was no time to reconstruct the team and develop the sort of orderly, getting-to-know-you campaign that ought to have been launched in the spring. The single compelling fact before them, D'Alessandro thought, was that Bush's low blows were landing; a guy who had gone into the election year as Don Knotts had come out like John Wayne. The governor's affirmative message would accordingly have to wait. He had to throw something up fast to stop the bleeding, and the way to do it was to strip off the vice president's new clothes; they had to reveal him as an artifact, the product not of his past but of his packagers. That, D'Alessandro wrote in a memo, was the "silver bullet"; once it hit, they could go after the *real* Bush directly, followed by a big positive sell at the close.

While eight or ten separate groups worked on scripts and storyboards, some in competition with one another, D'Alessandro walked the senior staff and the governor through his overall design; his visual aids were done up with colors and arrows, which, in his experience, always helped make the close. The very orderliness of it seemed to please Dukakis and embarrass his command team; his expression, looking around the room, seemed to one man to be asking his own people where the fuck they had been for the past two months. He had his usual compunctions about going negative, but he bought the basic concept of doing ads on Bush's packaging.

"It's right," he said. "The guy *is* packaged."

By the time Sasso's men trooped into D'Alessandro's offices in the Hancock tower, a demonstration tape was ready for showing. The group talked for a while in a spacious conference area, dolefully trading numbers over their sandwiches and Cokes. Then D'Alessandro led them to his screening room. They took seats on a leather couch, an object, like everything in the suite, of understated luxury. D'Alessandro opened a cabinet, revealing a television monitor. The lights dimmed. The first ad rolled.

The scene was a room meant to resemble an advertising-agency office. Four or five men were sitting around a table. They were talking about their client, George Bush, as if he were a blob of soft plastic to be molded and styled to the demands of fashion.

"He'll do *anything*," one of the men in the ad assured the others.

The scene faded to a black screen with the words "The Making of a President."

"They'd like to sell you a package," the voice-over said. "Wouldn't you rather choose a president?"

There were more ads like it in the works. Dukakis's people chortled. It was payback time; the spots might just remind people of the Old George Bush of a thousand columns and cartoons, the soft-centered patrician with no core or compass of his own.

The room was still when the lights came up.

"Is it too subtle?" someone asked.

The consensus was no. It was kind of like *Hill Street Blues,* Sasso's man Tom Glynn was thinking; maybe you didn't quite get it the first time, but if you kept watching you'd get addicted.

He and the others dashed back to Chauncy Street to tell Sasso.

"This could be a breakthrough," Glynn said.

"Sounds interesting," Sasso said. For a rare time since his return, he was smiling.

The euphorics were premature. A first flight of five packaging ads was flung together by the Sawyer/Miller Group, Scott Miller's firm in mid-Manhattan; Dukakis approved them at a screening between flights at the Newark, New Jersey, airport, with Robert Redford for company, and they were on the air by the end of September. The response was a dull thud. The strongest claim any of their advocates would make for them was that they froze the polls where they were, buying time for Dukakis, had he been able, to recover his footing. But the general reaction was that they were too cute by half, too cerebral an answer to Bush's visceral campaign and not a very persuasive answer at that; in a time of widespread cynicism about both candidates, they required the belief that only Bush had handlers, while Dukakis had sprung unadorned from the brow of Zeus.

They were quickly orphaned on Chauncy Street, after the fact; they had an elitist, even an arty look about them, and some state Dukakis organizations substituted their own simpler ads. The reaction among Bush's *real* handlers to being thus targeted was rather more benign. Ailes, for one, professed to find them aesthetically OK, but you couldn't run them long or often enough; you'd have to keep them on for a *year* for anybody to understand what they were about. However flattering to him, it was, he thought, a dumb-ass idea. The other guys were running Michael Dukakis against Roger Ailes.

"When Is He Going to Get Angry?"

"It's ours to lose," people on Chauncy Street had told one another in the afterglow of the last primaries and the seductive light of the first national polls. By fall, it was plain they had been right, in ways they had not then imagined. They *were* losing, and the Sasso party at headquarters felt like Sisyphus at the foot of the hill, their spirits fluctuating between determination and despair. Not even the governor seemed to think Sasso's return would help; when his press secretary, Dayton Duncan, congratulated him on it, Dukakis answered sadly, "It's too late."

Sasso was a scenarist, not a poet; he could not himself bring eloquence to a messageless campaign, nor could he induce his obdurate candidate to be larger than he was in life. He was instead a mechanic, and where he could make things happen, he did. He tried to reassert a sense of discipline on Chauncy Street, and offenders against it were swiftly punished; the advance men responsible for a disastrous Labor Day trip to Philadelphia were banished from the campaign, and Mike Berman, an old Mondale hand, was brought in to put things in order. New faces and fresh ideas were suddenly welcome, though with no guarantee Dukakis would listen to them. Sasso would; where the old crowd had resisted advice, he devoured it.

A further consequence of Sasso's return was a belated access of concern for Jesse Jackson's feelings; the wounded relationship between him and the campaign, if not entirely healed, was at least bandaged tightly enough to keep him productively involved in the campaign. The reverend had always been unfond of the governor, considering him a cold fish; when Gary Hart reentered the primary campaign in December, Jackson had taken him aside before a debate and warned him to watch out for Dukakis—he was *mean*. Chauncy Street in turn had been careless of Jackson's sensibilities and, to a great degree, black America's. By Labor Day, discussions as to what, if anything, Jackson would do for Dukakis in the fall had reached an impasse, caught between his bruised pride and Jack Corrigan's fixation on recapturing the white middle class.

It didn't take a genius to put things back together, as Donna Brazile, a class of '84 Jackson alumna, would say afterward from her desk in what she called the Colored Girls' Room at 105 Chauncy; it just took a politician, and Sasso, filling the bill, flew to New York on his third day back to see what he could do. His opening to the reverend was brilliant in its simplicity: he asked Jackson what he thought of Michael Dukakis.

"He's steady, he's bright, he's well-prepared," Jackson said, obviously pleased to have been asked. "But he's the most unspontaneous guy I've ever met. You've got to tell him to just get up there and *let it go!*"

His critique and his ideas were borne back to the governor, one more powerful voice against the antisepsis of his campaign, and his complaints about his role in the fall were patched over. Four days later, Jackson came out vigorously for Dukakis in a speech, sounding for the first time as if his heart were in it; by mid-September, Dukakis's lead over Bush among blacks, in Harrison's polling, had boomed from fifty-one to eighty-one points. When the campaign hit a low ebb between debates, Jackson was the one who made the rounds at 105 Chauncy bucking people up. Dukakis had never so much as paid a visit.

Sasso, though good, was not in fact a genius, or a magician either. He could not, for example, get Dukakis's misbegotten ad campaign on track, nor could he force the candidate himself to address the serious lack of inspiration in the campaign. It had been easier spelling out the elements of the new message than getting the governor to run with it. The twin themes Sasso outlined at his first meeting had been lying around headquarters unused for a year or more; Dukakis was particularly mulish about using the trade issue, which sounded too much like Japan-bashing to him.

"Give me more time," Sasso said when Tubby Harrison got impatient. "You know Michael."

Sasso, in fact, knew him too well: you just couldn't convince him that he needed to find the language to move people to his cause.

But as the restoration took hold, a sense of something like coherence returned to the campaign for the first time since the primaries. Within a week of his arrival, Sasso had a day-by-day playbook in the governor's hands, listing the date, the place, the theme and the message in tabular form for easy reading. They would stress national-security issues in the first weeks—Dukakis was hemorrhaging on that subject—and follow on with the economic squeeze. It was all there, in orderly columns and assimilable prose. If Sasso could not effect a soul transplant, he could at least produce a credible user's manual, and once Dukakis had it, his own zest for battle seemed to rise. "When is he going to get *angry*?" Ira Jackson had raged at one meeting. By the end of Sasso's first week, he did, with a speech in Commerce, Texas, defending his patriotism and his values against Bush's red-white-and-bluer-than-thou assault. It was like McCarthyism, Dukakis said, and the people could smell the garbage.

The cloud lingering over the campaign, by then, was whether the revival of Dukakis's spirits and the formulation of a comeback strategy were too little too late. Harrison's early-September numbers showed Dukakis nine points down and swimming against a rising tide of optimism about the state of the economy. Some people hearing his presentation argued against telling Dukakis the returns, given his mood. "They could *destroy* him," one worried. But Harrison and later Sasso thought they ought to inform him—throw a match on him to fire him up.

The debates lay ahead, a theater, his people hoped, for his own rehabilitation and for his too-long-delayed counterattack on George Bush. But after a summer's largely unanswered bashing, Dukakis's unfavorable rating in some polls had surged into the forties, where the vice president's had lodged before his successful dewimpification. Bush Inc.'s assault on the governor was to politics what the introduction of the wrecking ball had been to the demolition business: it looked ugly, and its single purpose was destruction, but it was working.

Waving the Bloody Shirt

STU SPENCER WAS ONE OF THE FIRST of the modern political consultants, the men who made a rich business of telemarketing candidates like Tums or Isuzus. But he was uneasy in the fancified language of his trade—a euphemistic newspeak in which getting your guy on Rather or Brokaw was called "earned media" and having him sling mud when he got there was "comparative campaigning." Spencer's speech, like his politics, was as subtle as a blackjack, and the counsel he brought to Bush Inc. when he joined up formally in New Orleans had less to do with the marketability of their own product than with the weaknesses of the competition. Mike Dukakis was a mean little prick from Harvard, in Spencer's view, a wise-ass rookie who didn't know what it was like flying around with a hundred Sam Donaldsons baying in the back of the plane. You had to get to him, show him up for what he was. You had to put a knife to his throat and hold it there for sixty days. If he breaks, Spencer mused, you win. If he doesn't, you lose—it was as simple as that.

Spencer's formula, more elegantly framed, had already become the core strategy for Bush's fall campaign—a strategy whose subtext was that the vice president would have to savage Dukakis because he was not good enough at the game to win on his own. Bush knew he was underestimated on Fifteenth Street, though he liked to think, or say, that the hand-wringing was mostly at the lower levels. In fact it was endemic even in his command group and was the motive force behind what would become a campaign memorable mostly for nothing so much as its unbridled nastiness.

The candidate was retrofitted by his managers with a new set of ''values'' and with an array of powerful symbols to give them force—a black rapist, a befouled harbor, an empty electric chair, a revolving-door prison, and the American flag. Few of the issues or the metaphors had figured prominently in his past as a public man; in none of his changing shadings of ideology had he been known, for example, as a flag-waver, a crime-buster or a battler for the environment. But he slipped willingly into his new character and was further blessed with an opponent who seemed not to know how to respond. Dukakis, Roger Ailes guessed, would on the whole rather talk about auto insurance; he seemed to Bush's men not to understand that politics is an emotional, not an intellectual, pursuit and that, absent hard times or unpopular wars, emotions are most easily stirred by waving the bloody shirt at one's rival.

Bush's transformation from pragmatist to ideologue was brilliantly conceived and greatly aided by the governor's tongue-tied reaction to it; the vice president became the strong man in the field and Dukakis the wimp, soft on taxes, criminals, polluters, pornographers and the Red menace. The blunt-instrument approach to what Bush Inc. chose to call the Mondale-izing of Mike Dukakis was raw, and his handlers were defensive about it; by late fall, engulfed in bad notices and souring polls, Baker would produce a list of 207 affirmative policy proposals advanced by the vice president in the course of his campaign.

But the politics of incivility remained the dominant tone of his candidacy, and Bush's men had too little faith in him to tone it down, even when his lead over Dukakis was flirting with double digits. You still needed the negative stuff, one of its architects said, to make people afraid of Mike Dukakis; if your own candidate was weak, too much of the kinder-gentler persona he had assumed in New Orleans would only re-create the wimp image and drag him back down again.

The stronger case for the strategy, in the winning-is-everything world of the professional managers, was that it worked so well. As John Sununu, one of its earliest advocates, put it, no sensible campaign repeats a line if it doesn't play the first time, and most of Bush's passed the first-use test. His militance was cynical in a match between two ideologically nondescript men, Mr. Résumé, as one nonaligned Democratic operative put it, against Mr. Position Paper; it required that Bush run against the fugitive murderer Willie Horton as Dukakis's surrogate and that he make the Pledge of

Allegiance the leitmotif of his campaign when he himself couldn't dependably remember the words.

The justification, for Bush Inc., was in the marketplace. Aesthetically, one conceded, the flag-and-furlough business was terrible stuff, but it stuck as metaphor because it touched real chords in the electorate—a vein of doubt as to who the governor was and what he did stand for. It was a given, in this view, that the election was about change; the next president would not be Ronald Reagan. The only recourse was to make change look safe in Bush's hands and scary in Dukakis's; they had to use whatever symbols were at hand to make life with the Duke sound dangerous.

The vice president's men had by then spent three months sowing and nurturing those doubts, with the care and attention to detail of the gardeners who planted Versailles. They would argue afterward that the Democrats were to blame for the shabbiness of the politics of 1988, having started the name-calling at their own clamorously partisan convention in July. But Bush's attack strategy had been set in place more than a month earlier, at his spring retreat in Kennebunkport, and the festival of insult in Atlanta was in one sense Dukakis's gift to the vice president's men—a useful tool for keeping him pumped up for battle.

Bush's game was horseshoes, not alley fighting; it was easier to get him down-and-dirty if you persuaded him that he had been wronged and that the manly thing was to fight back. When he came home from his convention-week camping trip, Ailes, Atwater and Barbara Bush were waiting with the news that the Democrats had just spent four nights punching his lights out on prime-time TV, chorusing, "Where was George?" and hooting that he had been born with a silver foot in his mouth. Politics, in Ailes's combative view, was like a six-month hockey game. It all seemed gentlemanly enough until you got bounced off the boards a few times and took a couple of sticks in the teeth, whereupon even a George Bush would come up fighting; all his people had to do then was pass the ammunition.

Their arsenal was already well stocked and market-tested. The first-wave assault in June was followed by a second in late summer, even more violent. Willie Horton and the flag became the centerpieces of what Bush Inc. chose to call a values agenda, the whole cluster of hot-button issues designed to call Dukakis's sense, his will, his record and even his patriotism into question. The racist and nativist undertones in some of the rhetoric lay in the ear of the listener, so far as Bush's managers were concerned, and were of secondary concern in any case; in a war, only throw-weights counted. The Pledge issue alone, one senior strategist guessed, would be worth a hundred and fifty electoral votes, mainly in the South, but the agenda as a whole had the potential to *destroy* Dukakis.

Gampy Goes Ballistic

The case for going ballistic was further reinforced by the continuing difficulty on Fifteenth Street of finding anything very positive for Bush to say in his own behalf. In the normal course of politics, Teeter's man Fred Steeper mused, you couldn't just give voters a reason to vote against the other guy—you had to give them a reason to vote for *you*. They had a lot of reasons for voting against Dukakis, however removed from the real concerns of the presidency. But as they cranked up in the summer, Bush still hadn't answered the why-me? question that had dogged his campaign from the beginning, and his handlers were still searching for meanings in his candidacy, as if it were a Rubik's Cube with one color missing. With the fall campaign almost upon them, they knew only that Bush had to take some kind of strong stand. They didn't know, and would never quite figure out, what he should stand *for*.

The search was not greatly advanced by a second, more elaborate series of focus groups in Paramus and elsewhere, sessions in which gatherings of Reagan Democrats were wired with electronic-response meters and shown a series of dummied "news" videos detailing the candidates' positions on various issues. In preparation, David Sparks, another of Teeter's men, had set down the likely point-counterpoint of the campaign in parallel columns, one listing possible affirmative claims for the Republicans, the other the potential Democratic responses:

REPUBLICAN	DEMOCRATIC
USA is prosperous.	The poor are poorer and the rich are richer.
USA is at peace.	No response.
Democrats are big spenders.	USA gone from creditor to debtor nation since 1980.
USA trade deficit is declining.	USA competitive position in the world has declined since 1980.
Tons of illegal drugs have been seized since 1980.	USA drug problem is out of control.
Reagan punished Qaddafi and other terrorists.	Reagan and Bush traded arms for hostages with the Ayatollah.
Bush has foreign policy experience.	Bush only attended funerals.
Democrats pander to special-interest groups.	Republicans don't care about the little person.

For the focus groups, Steeper and Sparks commissioned a series of two-to-four-minute scripts in newscast style, each based on one of the pairings of issues. A Las Vegas actor was hired to read them, and the participants were asked to respond by twisting a dial on a scale of zero to one hundred; a stylus recorded their reactions. None of the vice president's positives moved the needle much in his favor; his scores were strongest when he was at his most reactive, coming out against what Dukakis was, or was perceived to be, for. Pro-Bush issues that ought to have been salient weren't. Prosperity, the classic winner for in parties in good times, was a surprising dud. The Reagan Democrats simply didn't recognize it as a description of their own lives, and the P word was whited out of the Republican lexicon, in both ads and fliers. More modest boasts were preferred; Bush's slogan for the fall would be "Experienced Leadership for a Changing World."

What did work were the so-called wedge social issues, the us-against-them hammering on who hated rape and murder most and who loved the flag best. There was in fact little difference between Bush's core values and Dukakis's, both being patriotic and rectitudinous men; Dukakis, in fact, had more to brag about in the falling crime rate on his watch as governor than Bush did in impeding the flood of cocaine on his as Reagan's drug-buster. There were, moreover, strong anti-Bush entries on Sparks's ledger, things Dukakis could have used if he had had the skill and imagination; it was considered a wonder on Fifteenth Street that, for only one ripe example, they never saw a Dukakis ad with the Ayatollah's picture in it.

But Dukakis had a way of fighting fire with paper, volumes of it, drawn from casebooks in constitutional law rather than from hornbooks on rudimentary political strategy. When he answered at all, his response time was too slow and his cast of mind too legalistic to stand up to what Sparks called, in an August report on his focus groups, "the litany of criticism"—the whole bill of goods about how Dukakis was for everything liberal from abortion to taxes and against everything wholesome from handguns to school prayer to saluting the flag.

The results were sent forward to Bush's propagandists with EKG-style readouts attached—user-friendly guides to what buttons to push to rouse what emotions among voters. The first reactions were sour, the reflexive response of people who thought themselves artists at politics standing against men who thought they could reduce it to a binary science; it was, Sparks thought, like trying to sell a paint-by-numbers kit to people lying on their backs getting ready to do the Sistine Chapel ceiling. But when the initial grumbling had subsided, some of the core findings found their way into the ad campaign; several spots used the Litany Effect, cramming three of Dukakis's heresies instead of one into thirty seconds, and the governor's negatives began their steady uphill climb.

The issues involved had little to do with the business of the presidency, but they made effective politics, the beginning of the promised paint job on Dukakis in shadings of liberal pink rather than his preferred managerial gray. "By the time this election is over, Willie Horton will be a household name," Atwater boasted to a meeting of party operatives early in the summer. They were skeptical; one man in his audience wondered whether Lee meant the same Willie Horton who played outfield for the Detroit Tigers. But by fall, Willie the Bad was indeed a national celebrity, his story the stuff of campaign speeches and *Reader's Digest* reprints, his crimes told and retold by his white victims and by Bush's surrogates. In one excess of enthusiasm, a Bush operative said Dukakis had put a hundred million people at risk along the path Horton traveled from Boston to Maryland in his flight from the law.

There was at least arguably an ugly underside to the Horton issue, a play, intended or not, on white fears and prejudices about blacks; even George Wallace in his prime as a national politician had been more fastidious about his choice of symbols. The men at Bush Inc. insisted that crime was the issue, not color; they never produced an ad targeting Horton alone, and none of their spots on law and order showed his likeness or mentioned his race. But a committee called Americans for Bush, a right-wing hawks' nest not traceably connected to the campaign, produced its own commercial featuring Horton's baleful face over the words KIDNAPPING, STABBING and RAPING. There were protests from Fifteenth Street, with the faintly hollow ring of Casanova lamenting the decline of chastity in the world. When the committee announced plans in early September to put the ad on the air for twenty-eight days, it wrote Jim Baker a letter offering to withdraw it if he wished. Baker responded on day twenty-five—three days before the ad was due to go off anyway.

No single "issue" was quite so devastating to Dukakis. It seemed not to matter that more than forty other states had home-leave programs, too, or that Massachusetts's generous version started under a Republican governor, or that there had been similar horror stories involving furloughed Federal prisoners in the Reagan-Bush years. What counted for the men on Fifteenth Street was that Dukakis was wounded and doing nothing visible to stop the bleeding; the end, in knife-at-the-throat politics, justified the mean. Bush ranged the countryside like a candidate for district attorney, posing, in Dukakis's Boston among other ports of call, with ranks of officers in police blues and khakis. The message was that the governor cared more for criminals than for their victims or for the policemen charged with stopping them; his word to felons, Bush said, was not "Make my day" but "Have a nice weekend."

What Bush couldn't say, Roger Ailes did, eagerly and well, in his advertising campaign. Ailes was in his warrior mode, psyched for battle against an opponent he referred to variously as Shorty for his size, Grape-leaf for his origins, and That Heartless Little Robot for his demeanor. He had gone so far as to consult a psychologist about what made Dukakis tick and had been advised that the governor had the symptoms of a classic narcissist: he was self-absorbed, a guy who believed that only he was right and everyone else was wrong. Smugness in an opponent can be disabling, even paralytic, and the expert opinion only reinforced Ailes's feeling that Shorty could be had.

The means, moreover, were at hand; the attack ad had become to the modern political handler what Flavour-aide had been to Jonestown, a harmless-looking medium for the mass administration of deadly toxins. Both parties had experimented with the form in more primitive times; Lyndon Johnson's spot suggesting that small girls would be vaporized by nuclear weapons in a Barry Goldwater administration was only the worst of a memorably *ad hominem* campaign. But the real killer potential of negative ads had only been fully realized in state and local races over the past ten or twelve years, most notoriously with the far-right purge of several liberal Democrats from the Senate in 1980. The *idea* of savaging an opponent on TV was not new when Bush and his men embraced it; what distinguished their attack campaign was its central place in their strategy, its coded appeal to racial and ethnic prejudices and its irrelevance to the real business of the presidency.

It was sometimes forgotten, except by Ailes, that only fourteen of the campaign's thirty-seven spots could be construed as direct attacks on Dukakis. The others were more or less positive, and some were artworks of the "Morning in America" school, soft-focus mini-films splicing bits of kinder-gentler rhetoric with shots of "Gampy" Bush at home hoisting one of his granddaughters joyously into the air. But the negative com-mercials Ailes made or commissioned, if less numerous and less stylish, were the more potent and more clearly the hallmark of the campaign. The morning-in-Kennebunkport promos became complements to the attack ads; they presented Bush for the most part not as a bold, heroic or even particularly leaderly man but as a candidate for First Uncle, a safe alternative to the swarthy little guy with the ACLU card and the get-out-of-jail-free tickets in his hip pocket.

The negative spots aimed at the jugular rather than the heart, and their superior punch was obvious in the polls; Bush's favorable ratings stayed flat through the fall, the Gampy Tapes notwithstanding, but the picture of Dukakis as a taxer, a polluter and a coddler of criminals was beginning to stick.

There were, of course, limits, though they lay at the far horizons of taste. Ailes's eyes lit at the news that Shorty had long ago allowed his name to go on a bill to clear an old law forbidding "unnatural" sexual acts from the Massachusetts statute books. The measure had not, in fact, been his idea; it came from a constituent, and Dukakis, then a legislator, was obliged by a quirk in the state law to present it for consideration. But it became the subject of some serious discussion and much ribald laughter on Fifteenth Street. "Hey, don't worry, I got the big one in the drawer," Ailes would tell the others on a particularly rough day in the campaign. It opened, he would say, with white letters crawling silently up a black screen: "In 1970, Governor Michael Dukakis introduced legislation in Massachusetts to repeal the ban on sodomy and bestiality." As the last words faded to black, you'd hear a din of moos, baas and other barnyard noises.

That ad—"Bestiality," Ailes called it—never got made. But the jokes continued, and Bush himself joined in one day when his pet dog wandered in on a meeting.

"You're the reason I'm running," the vice president said. "We've got to keep those people away from you."

The Ads That Ate Dukakis

If bestiality was out of bounds, the ethics of negative advertising were otherwise expansively roomy. Its canon for Ailes, as for others of its practitioners in both parties, appeared on inquiry to come down on two cardinal rules. The first was that it work, which usually meant that it had to play on some preexisting feeling about its target; you couldn't make Dukakis into an odd duck if people didn't already suspect he might be one. The second was that it be at least technically accurate. The latter rule was accepted in the business not so much out of respect for truth as out of fear of getting caught; Ailes, for one, was a frank advocate of working right up to that line where fact ends and fiction begins. But he was a bear for documentation, even if it were no more than an ambiguous quote in some newspaper somewhere, and he would, in his own phrase, go completely batshit about demanding it of his subordinates. If you couldn't back your claims with *something*, the press would blow them up on you. Your ad would set off a backlash, and you'd lose the election.

He enforced Ailes's Rules of Order with an iron hand, in sharp contrast to the indiscipline in Dukakis's ad factory. He had begun by ignoring the high-priced Ad Alley talents who had staffed past Republican campaigns, and did deals instead with smaller agencies around the country, who would, among other virtues, have unformed attitudes about national politics and would be obedient to him. One of his star finds, Dennis Frankenberry, had worked on precisely one political campaign before Bush's, a race for district attorney in Oshkosh, Wisconsin; the candidate was the wife of one of his former commercial clients. He was happily selling Leinenkugel Beer and Sentry Insurance at his agency in Milwaukee when Fifteenth Street called. Frankenberry had never heard of Ailes, but he signed on, and, in the year of the hit man in presidential politics, he became the hired gun's hired gun.

The recruits met Bush, Ailes and one another for the first time in June, at a day of briefings in Washington. The vice president wondered, in his time with them, why people were surprised that he was tall and why the media thought he was faking when he said he liked country music; maybe those were things they could fix. His real problems, as his handlers said once he had departed the meetings, were a good deal more nettlesome. There were no big peace-and-prosperity issues out there, Teeter said, only a wide unease about the unraveling social fabric of the country. People questioned Bush's strength, his resolve and his trustworthiness; in fact, they didn't know him at all. The job of the admen, Teeter said, was to change the calculus. They had to reduce the election to a single question: whether Michael Dukakis's values were in sync with the average American's.

The preferred answer, it went without saying, was no, and the media men dispersed to see what they could do to encourage it. "We don't like to do any negative advertising," Ailes told them. "We call it 'comparative.' " It was a difference without a distinction. Comparative advertising, in the politics of 1988, was like putting the two candidates into a room, rolling a live grenade in after them, and then comparing the quick to the dead; the one still breathing would be president.

One of Dennis Frankenberry's first and strongest offerings toward that end was his Boston Harbor spot, taped from a hired whaler on a suitably gray and drizzly day; the weather gave the polluted waters an even sicklier pallor. Some touches were heightened by editing tricks; an open pipe dribbling wastes into the harbor looked even worse in a slowed-down, stop-frame treatment, with background music of the sort normally associated with the invasion of the killer mutants in sci-fi movies. Some embellishments were dropped; Frankenberry thought better of showing a Dukakis poster floating face up among the flotsam and jetsam, and Ailes vetoed a closing shot of an oil-soaked bird, thinking it rather too much of a bad thing.

But standards of accuracy were less rigorously applied than aesthetics. The ad, at a climactic moment, showed a sign reading DANGER/RADIATION HAZARD/NO SWIMMING. No one on Fifteenth Street questioned it, not until complaints were raised in public that the sign was a leftover from a long-closed Navy submarine facility. Ailes called the producers in.

"You guys didn't fuck around here, did you?" he demanded. "Put something in there that was not in Boston Harbor?"

"I swear to God, Rog," one of them answered, "it's right there. You can see it."

"Are you guys sure?" Ailes pressed. "This is the workhorse right now. We got it on the air. I don't want to have to pull it. I don't want to have to apologize. Get the sonofabitch right."

Right, by Ailes's definition, meant only that such a sign existed in Boston Harbor, not that it necessarily referred to a clear and present danger. It wasn't his job to go find out who put it up when and why; it was enough that the sign was there, and once Ailes was satisfied on that score he relaxed. The ad would stay on-screen, the lapping yellowed waters of the harbor corroding the very foundations of the Massachusetts Miracle; Mr. Competent couldn't even clean up his own state. If any more reporters came around complaining, Ailes said, he'd offer to go catch a fish in the harbor if they would agree to eat it; at that point, they'd back off, and there wouldn't be any more crap about the sign.

Frankenberry's further and deadlier contribution to the First Quadrennial George Bush *Film Noir* Festival was a prison picture, arguably the strongest, frame for frame, since *Cool Hand Luke*. His firm had been assigned one of the litany ads, a three-fer roughing up Dukakis for furloughing murderers, opposing the death penalty and vetoing mandatory sentences for drug dealers. An inspiration struck Frankenberry as he and his two partners sat up brainstorming one evening: the sum of the governor's policies was like installing a revolving door in prison. Great idea, his colleagues said, and Frankenberry ran it up the flagpole to see if anyone on Fifteenth Street saluted. Everyone did, and two days later Frankenberry found himself in

Salt Lake City, recruiting extras and scouting the Utah State Prison as a location.

He felt disappointed with the site at first, looking over its clean lines and cyclone fencing; he had hoped for a more *Late Show* look, something with thick walls, high parapets and stir-crazy cons banging the bars with tin cups. But there was not a wide range of choices on the rent-a-joint market, and Frankenberry made do. A revolving door was custom-made at what had once been Donny and Marie Osmond's studio in Provo, and was trucked in for the shoot. A cast of seventy was assembled, some scrubbed-up Mormon youths from Republican headquarters, some homeless men rousted out of the parks in town; they were dressed in prison fatigues and taped in deathly silence, filing in and out through the built-to-order revolving door.

The raw footage alone was powerful, the blank faces of the "convicts" edged with menace. Its passage through the editing room made it even scarier. The work, for once in contemporary television, was *de*colorized, and slowed down, besides, to give it a grainy documentary feel. Doomsday music pulsed in the background. A voice-over said that Dukakis "gave weekend furloughs to first-degree murderers not eligible for parole." The accompanying graphics reported that 268 ESCAPED and MANY ARE STILL AT LARGE. The claims taken singly passed the Ailes test for truth, which could fairly be defined as useful fact. The ad did not find it necessary to explain that the 268 "escapes" had occurred over ten years; that just three of the AWOLs were still at large, as against one-third to one-half who merely had come in late on the day they were due—and that only four of the escapees over that period had in fact been murderers doing life with no parole.

It would pain Ailes, in the aftermath, to be held up to scolding in the media as the assassin of the 1988 campaign. No one, in his view, seemed to notice that his ad mix was on balance pro-Bush rather than anti-Dukakis or that he would afterward be honored by his industry with an award for his positive ads; no one seemed to notice *anything* he did unless it was negative. He argued with considerable justice that handlers in search of attention and reporters in quest of stories inhabit the same bubble, feeding one another's needs. When Bush himself began catching heat from his tonier friends about the warlike cast of his campaign, his managers, Ailes among them, said, OK—let's ignore Dukakis and give them straight issues and position papers for a week. The turn to the new leaf lasted for roughly four days, by the end of which Bush had all but disappeared from public view; on the evidence of the evening news, it might have been a one-man race.

For Ailes, the outcome confirmed what he had suspected all along, that the media on the one hand were tut-tutting about trash politics and on the other were willing accomplices at it. One sure way to make the newscasts, as anyone in the trade could tell you, was to put up a negative ad and deliver copies to the networks; they'd give you a free hit by running it as news. The only things they were interested in, Ailes told his G-6 comrades, were pictures, attacks and mistakes, and since mistakes were a no-no for Bush, they had only two choices left. If pretty visuals and harsh words were the only thing the media would publish, screw 'em. Give it to 'em every night, Ailes said. We ought to run all the way to Election Day with that.

There were no longer any vocal dissenters on Fifteenth Street. At the start of the summer offensive, Bush's unfavorable ratings in the polls had seemed stuck in the middle forties, roughly double Dukakis's at the time. In the settled wisdom of politics, as Atwater reminded Ailes early on, the patient's condition was inoperable.

You'll never get his negatives below thirty-five, Atwater said. No way. Nobody's ever gotten negatives down more than five or six points.

Ailes bet that he could; he would, he said, move Bush's negatives into the manageable low thirties and drive Dukakis's up ten points or more in the process. By fall, it was plain that he had won his bet. "Keep watching those focus groups," he twitted Teeter as the lines crossed. "Let me know how to do this." In fact, thanks in important measure to the magic of attack advertising, it was already done: they had succeeded in making George Bush look better by making Michael Dukakis look worse.

Good George, Bad George

In normal circumstances, Ailes might have led the charge in company with Dan Quayle; the low road, in presidential politics, was what admen and running mates were for. But the second objective of the attack strategy, after the dismemberment of Michael Dukakis, was the reconstruction of George Bush into a figure of strong will and fighting faith. He had to be seen doing battle for his values; his road persona accordingly passed through daily and even hourly swings from Mr. Smith going to Washington to Dirty Harry packing a .44 mag.

It was possible, as his handlers discovered, to do too much of a good thing, even swaddling the candidate in the Stars and Stripes. Flags in ever-larger sizes and numbers became the standard decor at his rallies through the summer and the early fall, and so did the ritual recitation of the

Pledge, often losing something in Bush's translation; even with practice, he seemed not to know it as well as his audiences did.

Fidelity to the text didn't count. The message did; it was nationalist and nativist, a thinly coded way of suggesting that Dukakis was less than a hundred percent American. But the men on Fifteenth Street ignored its retro-fifties aroma as long as it kept putting points on the scoreboard. It wasn't till the day late in September when Bush carried his campaign to a flag factory in New Jersey that he crossed some invisible threshold of tolerance and taste. "Why do we have to go there?" he had asked at the time. Even he seemed to realize that, as one aide put it, they had gone a flag too far; their reward was a three-network scolding on the news that night for the abject emptiness of their campaign.

But with the passage from summer to fall, the ledgers at Bush Inc. showed all profit for the vice president at small cost, even for his excesses; in the absence of any coherent response from Dukakis, there was no one to call him on them. The flaccidity of the opposition was the source of enduring amazement among Bush's men. Ailes had sat in front of his TV set during the Democratic convention with a yellow pad in his lap, listening to the whole repertoire of attack lines—Iran, Noriega, where was George?—and composing instant anti-Bush commercials he might some-day have to answer. In the event, hardly any materialized in the early going, and none that did stayed on long enough to trouble Ailes greatly. He presumed, accurately enough, that Dukakis's campaign was no purer of heart than Bush's—that its silence was a consequence of bad implemen-tation rather than good intentions. But its failure to pursue its own offensive after Atlanta was, in his eyes, like punching someone in the mouth and then saying you didn't want to fight; it was, by then, a bit late for nonviolence.

In the vacuum, even Bush's blurry political profile suddenly became a blessing, a clean slate on which he could credibly write anything he chose, and so did the soft-edged personality once called wimpy. Dukakis looked cold and mean, as likable, Ailes gloated, as the kid who puts up his hand in school on Friday afternoon and says, "You forgot to give us our homework." Bush by contrast radiated a kind of awkward amiability, and Peggy Noonan had packaged it for sale in a series of luminous Good George speeches, hymns to compassion and clean water and those thousand mysterious points of light brightening the lives of the afflicted. The man once derided as the Velcro candidate had grown his own coating of Teflon; so long as he spoke softly, it seemed not to matter what he said.

Just in case, his road-company stagehands kept him layered in batting against the reemergence of what one of them called the Silly Factor—the vice president's propensity for tripping over his own tongue. He still got into trouble on those rare occasions when he strayed from his script, as when he declared himself to be "for anti-bigotry, anti-Semitism, anti-racism" or when he misplaced Pearl Harbor Day in September instead of December. The gaffes caused only minor flutters, to the relief of his men, but he was otherwise insulated from the national press and discouraged from ad-libbing; he was, in their view, better in Noonan's sentimentalized rendering than in his own unpredictable words.

His public appearances were choreographed as carefully as Ronald Reagan's, by some of the same dance masters. His settings were chosen to flatter him on television, usually in sunshine, sometimes in shirtsleeves. His performances were stage-managed down to the last spontaneous gesture; an advance man down front would signal him when to flash a thumbs-up sign, when to fling his arms aloft and when to start speaking. His texts were reduced to five-by-seven index cards, periodically modified in form to break his habit of tromping on his own material. Whatever Bush was, an aide said, he was not Reagan; he could actually correct lines to ensure that they *wouldn't* get applause. His card-makers first tried putting his best shots at the ends of paragraphs, hoping he would get the hint and pause a moment before plunging on. He didn't, not till his people, in desperation, redid his cards with the punch lines at the bottom; he *had* to stop at least long enough to flip to the next card.

There was a schizoid quality to his days on tour, a personality split between the Good George with "a heart that does not bleed but feels" and the Bad George re-creating Dukakis as the Brothers Grimm might have invented an ogre or a troll. But in contrast to the staticky sounds emitting from Chauncy Street, Bush's message, positive or negative, was driven home with a rigorous singleness of purpose and tone. You had to have that kind of discipline, a senior strategist warned, joining Bush's team in the summer, if you wanted to win—especially, he added with *this* guy.

Spontaneity was accordingly out on Fifteenth Street, and orderliness was in, a politics of meticulous programming. Bush's campaign, like Dukakis's, was often inhospitable to outsiders come late to the train; the difference, as one Republican consultant put it, was that when the doors to Bush Inc. were closed and bolted, the people inside knew from experience how to win presidential elections. They began the campaign with a calendar of "issues of the day" pre-chosen through election eve, and they met daily to coin the line-of-the-day as well, the sound bite they hoped would dominate the nightly news and the morning front pages.

Dukakis's surrogate operation was a shambles. Bush's was as star-spangled and as miked-up as a charity rock concert. Dan Quayle, to be sure, was hidden away in tertiary media markets. Even Toledo and Hartford seemed to his schedulers on Fifteenth Street to be too big-time for Danny's chancy talents, and a trip to New York, for him, meant *upstate* New York; he would be allowed in the city, one of his schedulers said, when he was vice president. But a squadron of speakers of higher-watt luminescence, led, once or twice a week, by the president, played the major-league circuit. For a thousand dollars, the campaign could buy enough satellite time to serve up live interviews to eight local newscasts a night.

There was a time in late September when a certain lassitude set in at Bush Inc.—a slump of the sort induced by doing the same thing too well for too long. Dukakis seemed finally to be getting his act together, playing to the pinched middle class with programs for college loans, health insurance and prenatal care, while Bush was still out speaking the dread L word and deriding the "Massachusetts Mirage." The vice president's lead melted down literally to nothing in Bob Teeter's polling, and one national survey actually put Dukakis three points ahead. "We are beginning to lose the war of themes and ideas," a young Bush speechwriter, Bob Grady, worried in a memo to the command group. They had, in fact, been "absolutely themeless" since Labor Day, he wrote, and were overworking the flag-and-country business to the point of muddying everything else. "If we do not address this situation quickly," Grady went on, "we are going to lose the election. . . . The charge that we are a party that has 'run out of ideas' is sticking."

The memo landed three days before the first debate in Winston-Salem, North Carolina, a matter of some suspense among Bush's men. The prospect had reawakened all their bad dreams of what the vice president might do if left to his own devices; a Bush victory, in their eyes, meant his surviving ninety minutes without a major howler. That he might somehow do so was not counted a safe bet on Fifteenth Street; his people had, in fact, seriously considered not putting him into the ring at all. They could not flatly refuse without looking cowardly; their ploy instead was to get a quick proposal on the table for two debates and then walk away, blaming Dukakis, if he demanded more.

To their regret, he didn't, and Bush was stuck with a fight that his own corner men doubted he could win. When they played the traditional game of lowering expectations, their hearts were wholly in it; they saw, among other protective measures, that his speeches were salted with bits of self-deprecating humor—a way, one of them said, of putting the voters on notice that some deep doo-doo would be coming in Winston-Salem and should not be taken too seriously.

The disquiet they felt only redoubled their resolve to shrink Mike Dukakis—to make Bush look big by making the governor look small. Grady's memo stirred some thought at Fifteenth Street, and a few fresh programmatic ideas, most notably a son-of-VISTA youth corps to work among the poor, began appearing in Bush's Good George rhetoric. But the sound of 1988 for most of America was the boom-boom of artillery rounds raining down on Chauncy Street and the answering pop-pop of small-arms fire in the rough direction of George Bush. "Tell George to start talking about the issues," Barry Goldwater chided Dan Quayle in public one day. Bush Inc., in its unconfidence, was too fearful to stop the name-calling, and Bush in his ambition was too malleable to object. He had got where he was by blackguarding his opponent. The question neither he nor his men had addressed was what he was doing to himself.

Three Nights in
Tension City

THE SETTING WAS A COLLEGE CHAPEL in Winston-Salem, but the blood lust was as acrid in the air as at ringside in a heavyweight title fight, and George Bush was battling down a bad case of the butterflies. He had been told too often that his two debates with Michael Dukakis were do-or-die time for him, and he knew what the hand-wringers in his own organization were thinking: that he was a better-than-fair bet to foul up, massively, by saying something foolish. His days of cramming facts and rehearsing lines had dissolved into that blurry state familiar to undergraduates during exam week. When he encountered two young aides in a corridor a bare hour before the opening bell, he startled them by asking what *they* thought he ought to say out there; it was, one of them felt, as if he were going out to wing a speech at some Lincoln Day dinner somewhere. Bush was back in Tension City, his jumpiness increasing as the clock ran down, and his managers, seeing his uncomfort, tried to buck him up.

"Go out there and have some fun," his friend and field marshal Jim Baker told him.

"*You* go out there and have some fun in front of a hundred million people," Bush answered, with as game a smile as he could muster.

Roger Ailes, recognizing the syndrome, shooed the others out. He had let himself lose control of the holding room for the first time all year; there were too many people wandering around, too many distractions. Ailes wanted a last word alone with his pupil. He *always* did; it was part of his job to absorb some of the tension for a client, and, given the stakes, Bush needed bracing more than most. The guy could go inside on you, Ailes thought. He had looked off his feed all day.

"Stay in focus," Ailes told him. "Listen. Don't get distracted and don't let your mind wander."

Bush nodded. The time was gone.

"Hey, pal," Ailes said as the vice president started to walk onstage. "This isn't about your reputation—it's about mine. Don't screw it up out there."

The Shadow War

The season's two encounters between Bush and Dukakis, and a third between Bentsen and Quayle, were indeed partly about the reputations of their coaches; none of them was thought good enough at telepolitics to win on his own. That so much was made of the outcome was itself a measure of the degree to which the medium had devoured the process of choosing a president. What headline writers persisted in calling the Great Debates were more nearly politics as game show, ninety minutes of trivia-tease questions, pre-packaged answers and media-hyped suspense. Their pop-quiz format discouraged the serious discussion of issues—a grin, a gesture, a joke or a flub was vastly more likely to be decisive than the dull business of public policy—and their promise was further reduced in 1988 by the quality of the campaign, a cranky quarrel between two men of low allure as to which was the least worse. And yet they had taken on a nearly mythic force in politics and political journalism since Kennedy's smile beat Nixon's beard in 1960. They became important because the industry believed they were, and candidacies had been made or broken by them.

Both camps accordingly approached the facedown at Wake Forest University in late September as anxiously as if it were Waterloo or Vicksburg, a battleground on which the fate of nations would be decided. Even the dickering over ground rules took on a kind of sweaty, hyperinflated importance, as if the distance between lecterns or the color of the backdrop really mattered. Each side wheeled out its big guns—Jim Baker, Roger Ailes and a Washington lawyer, Robert Goodwin, for Bush; Paul Brountas, Susan Estrich and later Tom Donilon for Dukakis. The cast thus consisted of five attorneys huffing and bluffing like litigators over the pettiest details and one political propagandist stewing over appearances; the negotiation at moments invited the view that the election was not about ideology *or* competence—it was about cosmetics.

There was, for one example, the Bush team's demand that their man be positioned stage right, which would favor his good side and hide his receding hairline. There was, for another, the question of whether he and Dukakis should sit or stand, an issue so weighty as to divide the vice president's own men into opposing camps. Dukakis's people wanted a stand-up debate, and Goodwin was disposed to agree; he argued in a memo that Bush would look stronger standing, and standing tall at that—six inches taller than the governor. But the antivertical party at Bush Inc. worried that Dukakis's outsized head made him seem bigger than he actually was, neutralizing Bush's height advantage. Ailes, for one, preferred that the two men be seated, which would make the whole thing look less important; it was a way of offsetting Dukakis's edge in debating experience and Bush's tendency toward goofiness under pressure.

In the event, standing won, though Baker added the proviso that there be no artificiality—no lift to make Dukakis look taller.

"Just a little riser," Brountas said.

"What are you gonna do, have your guy carry a little ramp around with him when Gorbachev's in town?" Baker twitted, but it was all gamesmanship, making the other guy sweat. The bicker dragged on until five o'clock the day before the first debate, whereupon the Bush team magnanimously allowed the governor his riser and his presidentialized size.

The men from Fifteenth Street had by then won everything they really wanted anyway. Brountas had opened with a proposal for four presidential debates. For effect, Baker offered one. In fact he wanted no more than two, with the second at least three weeks before Election Day; he and his unconfident colleagues preferred that the airwaves be dominated at the end by Ailes's commercials, not by commentators picking over how badly Bush had done.

"We really aren't very close to an agreement," Brountas said toward the end of the first session in Washington.

"We're quite prepared to take the heat," Baker answered evenly. Reagan and Mondale had agreed on a three-debate package, two presidential and one vice-presidential, in 1984; precedent, as Baker reminded Dukakis's team, was on his side. Of course, he added, tongue in cheek, we might agree to a third presidential debate and no vice-presidential debate.

"No, no!" Brountas and Estrich protested, almost leaping the table in their agitation; a Bentsen–Quayle debate was their ace in the hole, and losing it was no joking matter.

The talks dragged on through a second sitting, by conference call between the two campaign offices, and a third, face to face, back in Washington. Dukakis's seconds gave in to the two-debate formula; the sticking point remained the timing of the second encounter. Brountas wanted October 25. Baker offered October 14, twenty-four days before the election.

"There haven't been any negotiations yet," Brountas complained. "It's been all give on our part."

He sounded like a player holding a losing hand, and Baker sensed it. "We have come toward you," Baker said. "We stated we would be content with one debate."

"You've been ready to accept only two debates from the beginning, and you know it," Brountas said.

"We think we've made a very forthcoming offer," Baker said.

"Your position is getting to the edge of unreasonableness," Brountas protested. "You're dictating terms to us. You're making a big mistake."

"We don't want to be unreasonable," Baker said, but he wasn't giving up a day of Bush's postdebate recuperation time.

"We've got to have that date," Brountas said.

Baker didn't budge.

"I've got to get off October 25 because I'm not going to be successful, right?" Brountas said finally.

"Right," Baker replied.

The shadow war was over, on terms that portended badly for Dukakis. His seconds had been outmatched by Bush's. The calendar favored the vice president, and the first debate was seventeen days away.

The Ice Man versus the Nice Man

The countdown was dangerously low when Dukakis's handlers finally got down to the real labor confronting them: preparing their moody gladiator to fight for his life with the whole world at ringside. The governor's natural demeanor was chilly even for a cool medium, and, with Bush's handlers framing the match as the Ice Man versus the Nice Man, neither Dukakis nor his management team had the time or the resources to turn it around.

They hadn't even begun thinking seriously about the debates until it was nearly too late. Dukakis's Bostonians were as provincial in their way as Jimmy Carter's Georgians had been in 1976, at once too proud and too insecure to open up to the party pros volunteering to help out; the Chauncy Street crowd was, as one discouraged outsider put it, a hard bunch to help. It had been late summer before Estrich had finally begun inviting ideas on debate strategy, and even then they had piled up unattended and unused.

The governor's preparations for battle were further undermined by what one strategist called the balkanization of his campaign, an old problem exacerbated by Sasso's return and Estrich's rearguard resistance to it. There was no consensus plan among the senior staff, only a series of two-minute speeches that, stretched end to end, reached nowhere. It was nearly Labor Day when the campaign finally reached out to Tom Donilon, a young veteran of the Carter and Mondale campaigns, for help. Donilon was hesitant, but the situation sounded desperate, and he said yes. He drove up from the beach in Rhode Island, the sand still clinging to his knees, and took on his impossible commission: overseeing everything having to do with the debates from issues to tickets. Mondale's men had spent five weeks prepping him for his first debate with Ronald Reagan. Donilon would have less than a week.

He brought a sizable reputation to his task, and an almost equally sizable concern for preserving it undamaged. Within days of his arrival on Chauncy Street, he was openly prophesying his own ruin. The situation, he told people, was horrible; it was like falling into a hole, an utter void of leadership, strategy and message, and the splat at the bottom was going to be the sound of him crash-landing. There was no advance team scouting the debate site, no pool of writers composing mini-speeches, not even a briefing book worthy of the name. The logical person to have compiled one was Vicki Rideout, a bright, blond M.A. in history who had helped prep the governor for roughly fifty debates over the past three years and could produce the kind of how-to paper he liked. But she was out on the road tour with the candidate, and while she had implored Estrich in a memo to get moving on preparations, not much had been done.

The book had been farmed out to a group of seven or eight junior staffers in the issues shop, some of them brand-new hires, few of them acquainted firsthand with Dukakis. Rideout was called home to spend a half hour or so walking them through the mechanics of their task. What they really needed was guidance on goals and objectives, but Paul Tully, who had been arguably the best strategic thinker on Chauncy Street, was long gone, and the senior issues people were too caught up in their own Byzantine intriguing to attend the meeting. When Rideout went back to the Sky Pig, the junior staffers were left on their own.

Their work, unsurprisingly, was a compendium of speechlets with no connecting thread. Even the luckless people who produced it knew it was inadequate; it was the management Donilon blamed, not them. Rideout was recalled from the road. Donilon handed the book over to her. He looked pale, even frightened.

"It's worthless," he said. "I don't know what to do."

Rideout leafed through the ring-bound pages, imposing in bulk, light in weight.

"This is shit," she said. It would have to be redone from scratch.

Rideout's task was complicated by her inability to get anyone at the command level to focus on strategy, which was their game, as against substance, which was hers. Estrich, in her estrangement, seemed uninterested when you could find her at all, and Sasso, in his preoccupation, was no more helpful. Both pleaded fatigue; in fact, Donilon thought, there never *had* been a Dukakis message, a coherent theme to build a battle plan around. The briefing book was accordingly finished on autopilot, and was, in Donilon's carefully chosen word, usable. By the time Dukakis got it, his oral exam for the presidency was only a week away.

He had himself approached the debates at first with a nonchalance born of his own experience in the form—he had done forty in the past year or so—and of his low regard for Bush both as a man and as a performer. It was mid-September before he got seriously down to his homework, and even then he tolerated the open squabbling between the Sasso and Estrich parties over first premises—whether, for example, it was more important to get out his own message or go after the vice president for having distorted it. He didn't want to do a mock debate at all, and when he finally did, four days before the real thing, it was, in the view of the people, as if he had walked into an ambush untrained and unarmed.

The result was a rout; if his opponent had been Bush instead of a Washington lawyer named Bob Barnett, one man in the room thought, you would have walked away and said the race was over. Dukakis had breezed into the sealed-off presidential suite at the Lafayette Hotel thinking it would be easy, and his people had taken pains to keep his mood light; a squash racquet had been left poking out from under a bed, and a copy of *Town & Country* lay on a coffee table, two visual puns on the fact that George Bush had slept there. Twenty people were scattered around the room, chattering happily in anticipation. The real business of the evening seemed less important that what Dukakis should wear; for an hour, he tested his chosen suit and a series of ties under the TV lights, fussing over which made the most presidential fashion statement.

But the smiles faded when Barnett laid into Dukakis, repeating a role he had mastered as Geraldine Ferraro's sparring partner in 1984 and had updated assiduously since. He had come with a three-inch-thick looseleaf album of the Best of George Bush; at the drop of a question, he would flip to the appropriate page and do Bush's answers in Bush's language with

Bush's odd cadences. It was raining L words on the governor's head, the whole Bad George repertoire from flags to furloughs, and he was caught without an umbrella. Dukakis never liked being shown up in front of others; it was said on Chauncy Street that he never lost an argument with more than two people in the room, and here was Barnett tattooing him in front of his entire senior staff. His tone turned pettish, his manner defensive; a debate is theater, and he was doing rote news-conference answers instead.

When it was over, Dukakis stepped from behind his lectern, the scowl lines creasing his face and knotting his brow.

"We've got a lot of work to do, don't we," he said.

Someone asked whether he wanted to review the tape.

"No," he said. "I know what went on."

So did everyone else; the sense of the room, as one senior hand put it, was that Barnett had cleaned Michael's clock. Sasso found Tubby Harrison in the back, slumped in a corner, looking, typically, as if he wished he could disappear.

"What did you think?" Sasso asked.

"There was no message," Harrison said.

Sasso nodded. They did have work to do, more than they had time for and more than Dukakis would be able to absorb.

The candidate and his people sat up late that evening, too deflated to enjoy an elaborate room-service dinner; everyone in the room feared that the race was over. The table talk was cacophonous, everyone volunteering magical solutions except Sasso, who found the one-on-one approach more useful, and Donilon, who was dismayed by the babel. Fritz Mondale would never have put up with this, he grumbled aloud; Mondale hated what he called strategy rallies. Dukakis seemed to want them. At moments, the governor seemed to become one more clinician at the patient's bedside, talking about himself in the third person. "What should Dukakis's main attack be?" he wondered from his out-of-body distance. "How can Dukakis make it different next time?"

Kim Shafer, a young lawyer on the prep team, found herself worried for him; she had read Roger Ailes's published account of how Reagan's handlers had destroyed his confidence going into his first debate with Mondale, and it looked to her as if history might be repeating itself.

"Somebody's *got* to tell him tonight that one-third of his answers were terrific," she whispered to Nick Mitropoulos.

Mitropoulos nodded, and when he drove the governor home that night he tried to sound cheerful. You didn't do so badly, he said. You'll be all right.

Dukakis hit the books hard after that, with a resolve born of fear; the witnesses to his humiliation were ordered not to talk about it, and the loop actively involved in preparations was tightened. Donilon pulled together a strategy memo reducing the cross-talk to three tasks Dukakis could assimilate and follow: first, to take the offensive and crowd Bush; second, to do his own paint job on the vice president as a weakling and an underachiever; third, to get out his case for economic change. A second mock debate went better. But the cockiness on Chauncy Street had oozed away after the first; they were attempting a seventy-two-hour personality transplant with a team of surgeons at odds with one another.

Bush's training camp was just as anxious, given its want of faith in him, but his people were more single-minded about what needed doing at Wake Forest and how to get it done. The vice president's briefing books were right from the start, and so were his Q&A sessions with his prep team and his warmups with *his* sparring partner, Dick Darman; in the course of his drills, they anticipated every topic put to him, and nearly every question. They prepared him for combat as well. Dukakis had to come out swinging, Ailes told him; he was a forty-mile-an-hour guy, a governor with a governor on his soul, but he was smart enough to figure out he was in a fight.

"If you get hit," Ailes said, "take the little guy out. Go right back at him and ram it down his throat."

While the vice president was in the room, his men swallowed their fears that he would do something malapropos; in fact, they considered having him make a self-deprecating joke of his gaffery. The matchup with Dukakis was scheduled for September 25, and since Bush had already declared September 7 to be Pearl Harbor Day, Ailes suggested that he ask Dukakis why they were debating on Christmas. A joke in Bush's hands was an endangered species, and he kept butchering it, beyond its author's recognition. "Jesus, don't do Christmas," Ailes begged. *"No Christmas! Forget it!"*

In private, Bush's men had sweaty palms, as they always did sending him into an unstructured setting; it comforted Ailes knowing he had the "Revolving Door" ad in the can and ready to roll the day after the debate if they were in trouble. As a further precaution, he sent an assistant around to Bush's house the day before their departure for Winston-Salem with some last briefing material for him to read. The next morning, Ailes came by in person to check on his pupil's progress.

"Did he read the stuff I sent over last night?" he asked Mrs. Bush.

"No," she said. "He was out looking for Spikey."

"He *what*?" Ailes demanded, jaw dropping.

Spikey, it turned out, was a stuffed animal dear to one of Bush's granddaughters. She had mislaid it somewhere during the day, and when he had gone upstairs to tuck her in for the night he found her in tears—she couldn't sleep without Spikey. Barbara was out for the evening, so the vice president of the United States had put on his raincoat, gone out into the night chill and, with his mystified Secret Service bodyguards holding flashlights, rooted around in the shrubbery looking for a lost toy. He was, as it happened, searching in the wrong place; Spikey would turn up the next morning behind a sofa. So he had rustled up another animal, concocted a story about how Spikey had gone to someone else's place for the night, and somehow restored peace to the household.

But the search had left him exhausted and a bit coldish besides, and he confessed to Ailes, "I didn't read anything."

In the event, it didn't seem to matter that he was underprepared, or that he was feeling off his game, or even that, once onstage, he would mangle his little Christmas joke beyond recognition. He had caught himself in an error, got flustered and suddenly exclaimed, "It's Christmas, it's Christmas! . . . Wouldn't it be nice to be the Ice Man so you never make a mistake?" Hardly anyone knew what he was talking about, or cared. The botched gag was quickly forgotten. The Ice Man label was not. The Force was with the Nice Man that night, an intangible called likability; in the new videopolitics, it was less important to be sound of thought and syntax than to look agreeable on-screen.

Dukakis's coaches were aware of the game and had belabored the governor to lighten up a little—to skewer Bush with a smile, as the polltaker Paul Maslin put it in a memo. Mario Cuomo had dropped in on one practice session to advise him to be warm and tell stories. Bill Clinton, the governor of Arkansas, had urged him at another to get angry; they had called him everything but a mongrel dog, Clinton said, and America wanted him to do *something* human, like fight back. Scott Miller, the adman, had even sent him a set of three Frank Capra films on videotape, *Mr. Smith Goes to Washington* among them, as study guides in how to be serious and smile at the same time.

If Dukakis had seen the tapes or heard the advice, it didn't show in his performance. He came at Bush like a fancified boxer, jab-jabbing to make points with the judges when he needed to win by a knockout. His worse moment came when, in response to a direct question, he insisted in his abstract way that he did so have passion. His best was when he actually showed some, accusing the vice president at last of having impugned his patriotism and saying, with flashing eyes, "I resent it." But he was more often merely relentless. His lines sounded as if they had been written in a law library, his smiles were what his people called the shark-tooth model, and his tone was taunting, even snide. Some of his people, reviewing the tapes afterward, wished he had called Bush "George" a time or two less often.

The consensus in both holding rooms was that, if the debate had been a trial, Mr. District Attorney Dukakis had won. The governor's people were on their feet, whooping and punching the air with their fists. Bush's were more restrained. Their man scored once with a shot at the ACLU, the moral equivalent of a free kick in the game as his men had framed it; Lee Atwater came up out of his chair with a rebel yell at the exchange, and one of Teeter's focus groups in Paramus was only slightly less restrained. But even Ailes thought that Bush had called Dukakis a liberal a bit too frequently—four times in one answer—and that his performance was otherwise off stride. He had seemed undecided when asked whether women should be put in jail for having abortions; it was one question his handlers had missed in the prep sessions, and they knew they had a problem, one that Jim Baker at his persuasive best would be hard put to explain away the next day.

The forming consensus was shared by the vice president, retiring to his holding room. He slumped into a chair, drained, dejected and rheumy with his settling cold. His shirt was soaked through with sweat.

"I didn't do very well," he said.

"You did very well," Ailes replied, his heart only half in it. In his relentlessly affirmative view, the vice president had achieved the two prime strategic objectives they had set for him: a week or ten days out, all that people would remember was that Dukakis was pretty far left and that they sort of liked Bush. But the first notices were going to be tough; everybody was going to score it 55–45 Dukakis, and, in tactical terms, Ailes did not disagree.

"This guy's not that good," Bush said. "I can take him." But he knew he hadn't done it, not that night. He had been too hesitant. He felt he had let his people down.

"I missed some opportunities," he said.

Ailes liked the little flash of competitive spirit and tried to nurture it. "You did real well," he said again. "You won the debate."

"Let's see what the experts have to say," Bush answered.

The governor, as it happened, needed almost as much reassuring. Debates, Dukakis thought, were like final exams that way—you didn't know whether you had scored until you got your grade—and his first question to his crowd was, "How'd I do?"

Sasso smothered him in a hug. "Don't you *know*?" he said. "You did great."

In the bosom of his staff, warm and cheering, Dukakis began to believe it. He had done pretty well, he thought. Bush in the flesh had been the Bush of their packaging ads, the creation of his handlers. He had seemed so manipulated, so *programmed*. He had looked lost out there with no one telling him what to say or do, Dukakis said. It was, the more the governor thought about it, no contest; he had met the enemy, taken his measure and pounded him.

Intellectually, as even Jim Baker would concede privately, he had a case; if a debate were a forensic event, Dukakis had indeed won. But Sasso's mood, in the midnight hours afterward, was a great deal less celebratory than he had let on backstage, to Dukakis or the others; knowing the governor's fragile mood, he had hidden his misgivings behind a masker's smile. It was only when he got back to his hotel room that the worry lines formed across his forehead and the lost chances flashed in endless instant replay through his mind.

Dukakis, he thought, hadn't done what he most needed to do—give people some reason to vote for him. He had been primed, as he had been through the campaign, to address what his inside and outside advisers saw as a longing for something new, something more than just the managerial competence he had offered at the convention; he had been urged to frame the debates and the election as a choice between change and the status quo. He had been all ready to talk about change, or so Sasso thought. But he hadn't done it; the message hadn't got out.

The room was jammed with younger staffers, eating sandwiches and chirping gleefully at how the governor had kept knocking them out of the park. Sasso, encased in his unhappiness, might have been alone in the crowd. He lay exhausted on his bed, tie flung aside and shirt collar open, absently sipping at a beer.

"Michael did not hit the passion question well," he said; for all the drilling and all the stories they had armed him with, he had simply declared passion and walked away. It was Bush who had seized the moment, bending that question and a number of others into an indictment of Dukakis's supposed liberalism. People had actually *laughed* when Dukakis said he was tough on crime, and you couldn't tell on television that the merriment was mostly on the Republican side of the house. Bush had painted a big L on the governor's forehead like a scarlet letter, and absent some positive credo of Dukakis's own, it was likely to stick.

"The positioning was not good," Sasso said.

The first flash polling brought some small comfort; the verdict of the voters was that Dukakis had won the battle of Winston-Salem, and for a day or two thereafter Bush's traveling party gave the vice president a wide berth, leaving it to his pal Baker to nurse him through his postforensic *tristesse*. But within seventy-two hours, the tide of sentiment seemed to change; Bush's lead opened out to what it had been before the debate. It was as if the numbers were clicking into the Bush column by default, Paul Maslin thought, pondering some state polling he had done for Chauncy Street. The governor was trying to light a fire without matches; people were looking for reasons to like him, and he hadn't yet offered them anything except risk.

Dukakis's "victory" was thus an empty one, the triumph, one Bush adviser said, of the smartest kid in the class; he had got A's for his answers, in the growing second-wave consensus, and D's in popularity. He had, as one of his own people said, looked more like a candidate for chief policy adviser than for president. Within a week after Dukakis won the battle of Winston-Salem, his unfavorable rating in the polls broke 40 percent for the first time, a level that, if history taught anything, made him all but unelectable. It would take a second Massachusetts Miracle for him to win, and if he did, his people knew then, it would certainly not be with the slogan "I Like Mike."

A Quayle Roast

His Secret Service code name was "Supervisor," but in the year of the handler J. Danforth Quayle was the preeminent handlee—the most supervised candidate in modern times after Ronald Reagan. He was held in thinly veiled disdain on Fifteenth Street and, with the notable exception of Stu Spencer, among some of his own corps of managers as well; asked if he was qualified to be president, one of them replied, curtly and quickly, "Of course not." His high-powered road team took it as its job to make him look the part, at least, and they fell to like Dr. Frankenstein's lab technicians, assembling a second humanoid with rather more attractive body parts than had been available for the first. What they left out of their creation was the life. The senator had submitted unhappily to them, knowing with some precision what they were doing and why, and by the time he walked onstage at the Omaha Civic Auditorium for his debate with Lloyd Bentsen early in October, his deconstruction was complete. He had become the Stepford Candidate, a talking mannequin programmed, as it turned out, for disaster.

He was up against a formidable opponent in Bentsen, his senior in age, service and standing in the politics and society of Washington. The Texan's sixty-seven years showed plainly in his dewlapped face and his funereal mien, and he dressed, as a member of his entourage said, as fashionably as a Calvinist minister might. But he more than anyone on either ticket conveyed that aura thought to be "presidential." He was better prepared for Quayle, moreover, than Dukakis had been for Bush, though the Chauncy Street crowd made it harder by regularly reminding him how much was riding on his performance and as regularly rewriting his lines. Bentsen spent one sleepless night in his bathrobe pondering the last of their briefing books, studying its tinned answers until he finally gagged on them. "This two-minute-speech stuff is driving me *crazy*!" he told his people finally. He was going to be his own man in his own words, a course that made him the opposite—and, finally, the master—of Senator Quayle.

Quayle's words were mostly spooned out to him, in a series of prep sessions so unsparing as to drain what confidence he had left. The premise of his crash course was the widespread perception, shared by some of his handlers, that he was a bit of a twit—some kind of gaffomatic candidate, as he himself brooded, who couldn't open his mouth without making some kind of mistake. The first objective of his training camp in an office building in Georgetown was to stuff him with the facts he had somehow missed on his passage through the Senate; the second was to correct for his tendency to overheat on the cool medium of TV. The hammering was heavy, and when his managers let up, his wife waded in, a constant presence kibitzing on issues, strategy and style; not even so formidable a figure as Ailes could get in his usual last words alone with the client.

They were prepping Quayle to survive, not to win, and the fruits of their low estimate of him showed in his performances in his two dress rehearsals. The basic game plan handed to him was, Speak slowly, look into the camera and don't fuck up, a set of orders that succeeded mainly in scaring all his coltish energy out of him. He looked stiff as a board, Lee Atwater thought, watching one warmup from a sideline seat; maybe they had slowed him down *too* much. A saving thought, or wish, was that the real Lloyd Bentsen wouldn't be as tough on him as Robert W. Packwood, the senator from Oregon, had been in playing Bentsen in the run-throughs. "I know Lloyd Bentsen," Packwood told Quayle. "He won't attack you like I did—that's just not his personality. He's a gentleman."

Quayle was thus overtrained and underprepared when, an hour into the debate, Gentleman Lloyd hit him in the teeth with a velvet-wrapped tire iron. The opening came when Quayle was asked, for the third time, what he would do if he suddenly found himself president. His handlers had not anticipated that particular spin on the issue of his readiness to occupy the

Oval Office and had not primed him for it; all he had managed on his own, up to that point, was that he would say a prayer and talk to Bush's Cabinet and staff. Otherwise, he had done as he had been rehearsed to do, reciting his résumé each time the panel of inquisitors pushed the button. The first two times, he looked and sounded merely robotic. The third time, he strayed from his script into the mythical kingdom of Camelot and found Bentsen waiting for him like a game warden gunning for poachers.

His misstep was innocent enough, an attempted further display of his credentials for the job he was running for. "I have far more experience than many others that have sought the office of vice president of this country," Quayle said. "I have as much experience in the Congress as Jack Kennedy did when he sought the presidency."

"Senator," Bentsen replied, fixing Quayle with a look of sad reproof, "I served with Jack Kennedy. Jack Kennedy was a friend of mine. Senator, you're no Jack Kennedy."

Dukakis's admirers cheered. Others in the hall fell still for a moment, the silence of witnesses to a hanging. Quayle flushed visibly. His Adam's apple jumped.

"That was really uncalled for, Senator." he said.

"You're the one that was making the comparison, *Senator*." Bentsen retorted.

Quayle's own trainers had in fact warned him against it. They had liked his invoking Kennedy's name on his tour of the boonies, as a way of quieting concerns about his tenderness of age and experience. At one point, they had considered an even more presumptuous stunt, posing him in front of the likenesses of Washington, Jefferson, Lincoln and Teddy Roosevelt on Mount Rushmore to show that he wasn't all that much younger than they had been; in fact their average age on assuming the presidency had been fifty-two, and the idea was quickly burn-bagged. The Kennedy analogy stayed in Quayle's repertoire, but the road show, in the view of his handlers, was one thing and network television quite another; you didn't match yourself with an authentic American folk hero with the whole country watching. But Danny did, and Bentsen had the moment his team had prepped him for, a chance, one of them said, to roll up a newspaper and smack Quayle in the nose as if he were a mischievous puppy.

"Well, there's the bite," Bentsen's debate coach, Michael Sheehan, said, watching in a room offstage. Sheehan had figured from the beginning that they would lose if Quayle came off as Robert Redford and win if he looked more like Archie Andrews. The camera had just freeze-framed him pitilessly as Archie, straight out of the funny papers, and he never recovered his stride. He had, as he would concede afterward, led with his chin, and had lost the point and the bout by a standing TKO.

"How'd I do?" he asked Spencer afterward.

"You did fine," Spencer told him, veiling his feelings. He liked Danny—Spencer hadn't cracked a book in *his* schooldays either—and had defended him against the sniper fire from Fifteenth Street. Maybe the kid ain't Sam Nunn, he said, but he's more substantive than people think. He just can't catch a break in the press; some of these goddam reporters have come to Omaha with their stories all written, just waiting to fill in Danny's mistakes. The problem, as Spencer knew in his heart, was that Quayle had given them something to fill the blanks with. He figured the kid had just blown two points in the polls.

Quayle had guessed as much. His mood was down as he left the auditorium, and when he was finally reunited with his wife, his disappointment in himself boiled over into mutinous anger. The spark was struck, as often happened, by Marilyn Quayle; the book on her among the mercenaries running the senator's campaign was that she was smarter, stronger and more ambitious than her husband, and they were generally happier when she was not around. The two had lingered at the auditorium watching Jim Baker practice that black art called spin control on TV, telling the world how mature Dan had been and what an excellent performance he had put on. But when Baker referred to Bentsen as "my good friend and fellow Texan" and allowed that *both* men had done a good job, Mrs. Quayle was livid. She and the senator exchanged glances, his icy, hers smoky hot.

"The damn spinners aren't spinning it right," she muttered.

A hollow "victory" rally afterward did little to cheer her, and when she and the senator were alone in their rooms at the Marriott her rage fueled his. He had been a most unhappy fellow anyway, between the hammering he had taken in the media and the pummeling he had endured from his management. He could hardly pick up a paper without reading what a featherweight he was, and the dirty allegations about him and Paula Parkinson had got back to his nine-year-old daughter. His lowest moment in the campaign, he had told an aide, was when she asked him, "Did you dance with the *Playboy* Bunny?"

"How long does this last?" he had asked Spencer one day on the plane. "When's it gonna stop?"

"It'll go away when one of the other three guys screws up," Spencer had said. "You just gotta hang in there."

But the pounding continued, and it didn't help, in Quayle's view, that his own guys seemed more interested in protecting themselves than him. They kept crowding him, telling him what he could and couldn't do; they wouldn't even let him shuck his jacket, a trademark of his past campaigns, or come out from behind his lectern to make a point. The stage-frightened senator who had implored Jim Baker in New Orleans for adequate staffing had turned mutinous at the degree and the condescension of their help. He had put on a one-day insurgency, bagging a prepared text for a speech in Chicago and doing it his own errant way. His guys had let him do it, *hoping* he'd make a sap of himself as an object lesson, and he had obliged them.

Ailes had been sent out afterward to hose him down. "Stay on the script," he told Quayle. "You're in a different league here."

Quayle had complied, but he remained as ripe for revolution as Boston before the Tea Party, and when Marilyn kept him up half the night of the debate complaining that his own spin doctors had let him down, it was like tossing a lighted match into a bucket of kerosene. If that's the best protection they can give you, she told him, you might as well start calling the shots yourself. He agreed, and the next morning he put his people on notice that he was thinking of doing just that.

Talk him down, the men on Fifteenth Street instructed his tour directors; it was OK to be sympathetic, so long as they kept Q on the reservation. But Quayle kept taking a tattooing from the media in the first days out of Omaha, some of it emanating, unattributed, from Bush headquarters; guys there were saying for *print* that he had come off like a wounded fawn and that he could cost Bush the election, and Baker's crowd wasn't out front defending him. They had cut and run when they should have stayed in the batter's box slugging away, Quayle thought, and he was fuming.

"I've had it," he told his road company. He had listened to all the crap he was prepared to take, and that was it, folks; he was going to go back there to the press section on the plane and do his own spinning.

"Be careful," Spencer warned him. "I've never seen them so surly. You don't know what you're getting into."

"I may not know what I'm getting into," Quayle said, "but I know what I've been through. *I'm* spinning this from now on."

"Fine," Spencer said. "Just don't step on it."

Quayle's notices didn't improve, on the road or on Fifteenth Street, and he appealed to a higher court, Jim Baker, tracking him to his home on Foxhall Road in Washington on a Sunday night. He was being screwed by the staff, he said bitterly, and Baker wasn't doing enough to shut them down.

"Let me explain to you how it works," Baker shot back. He and Bush were just as mad as Quayle was about the in-house sniping; the vice president, in fact, was telling people he was sick and tired of these guys running with the antelopes, away from Danny, and if he caught any of them talking they'd be fired. But a presidential campaign wasn't a Senate office, Baker told Quayle. You couldn't shut down three hundred people, even under the threat of capital punishment.

Quayle was unappeased. The campaign, he said, should be touching up Bentsen.

"Well," Baker said, "we wanted to get the focus back on George."

"Fine," Quayle said, "but it doesn't help George to take this beating out here, and it doesn't help when your people are perceived as running away from me."

"We're not," Baker said.

"Well, I'm just telling you how I feel," Quayle said, and how he felt was rebellious. When Baker called back two days later for a temperature check, the senator said he was going public, declaring his independence of his handlers. From now on, as he would shortly tell the boys and girls in the bus, *he* was Dr. Spin.

Baker smiled to himself. The kid was naive, a rookie showing the stress of moving up from double-A ball to the Show; he didn't understand yet that vice-presidential candidates are *supposed* to be dull, that the very essence of their job is to stay out of the limelight and not embarrass the ticket. But Baker's own sense of the race was comfortable, and he did not tell Quayle no.

"Dan, you be careful," he said instead. "They're laying for you."

They were, though the free-range Quayle proved considerably more engaging than the cast-in-plastic look-alike who had earlier claimed to be running—or, more accurately, standing—for vice president. His reviews got only marginally better, in the media and among his own and his boss's handlers. Even under the new save-the-Quayles dispensation, the kindest words his men seemed able to find for him were that he was "potentially smart" or that he might be ready for the presidency "someday."

The star born onstage in Omaha instead was Lloyd Bentsen, his own gray solidity made luminescent by the pallor of the other three men in the lists. He had been the forgotten man of 1988 till then, spending much of his time in Texas trying to win it for the ticket or, failing that, to secure his own reelection to the Senate. Before the debate, his name was barely mentioned in Dukakis's ads; afterward, it was, in the words of an outside adviser to the campaign, as if the governor's first name were Dukakis and his last name Bentsen.

"Did I look too mean?" the senator had asked coming offstage. But his wide smile revealed his and the campaign's answer: in a single sound bite, he had accomplished what Dukakis had not managed, making Quayle an issue. Chauncy Street put up two new spots attacking the choice, one of them the last and strongest of the series of handler ads; in it, the men playing Bush's packagers wondered wistfully whether it was too late to dump Quayle and put Dole on the ticket instead. Bush's margin in the polls shriveled from a landslide ten points to a bridgeable six in less than a week, and Dukakis's men began thinking the unthinkable. Maybe, one senior hand on Chauncy Street told a friend, only half in jest, we ought to switch the ticket. Maybe they had got the wrong guy at the top.

Rape and Murder in Los Angeles

Governor Dukakis sat stony-faced with his managers in a high-rise hotel suite in Los Angeles the day before the last debate, in mid-October, warming up with the doom-haunted air of Michael Spinks training for Mike Tyson. He felt and looked lousy, his road-weariness made worse by a flu bug, a sore throat, a 101-degree fever and an acutely painful bad back. His head rang with an anvil chorus of advice, begun in Boston, continued cross-country and still in progress. Everyone agreed, for a change, on the basic strategy, which was to get aggressive with Bush. The problem was that they wanted him to look voter-friendly at the same time, to smile big and gesture broadly, as Michael Sheehan had put it. He seemed at an impasse in his own mind. Even he conceded dryly that he had a warm-and-fuzzy problem, but when his people tried out some jokes they had scrambled up at his order, he was not amused. Everyone else in the suite was laughing, and there was the governor, impervious as Plymouth Rock, saying, I don't get it.

His war party had arrived in California in a down-but-not-out mood; the Wake Forest debate had at least helped arrest Dukakis's slide in the polls, and Bentsen's one-sided win over Quayle had given them a fresh hit of adrenaline, a sense of opportunity waiting to be seized in the rematch with Bush at the University of California at Los Angeles. Dukakis had practiced harder for the rematch and, up to the last forty-eight hours, had done better. He had even seemed to give in to the cosmetic necessities, the requirement that a candidate for president be at least as ingratiating as the better sort of maître d.' Look, he had told Sheehan, I know we've got challenges, and I want to beat them.

The first challenge was his layering, his inability to open his emotions to strangers or even, some thought, to himself. The public Dukakis was as bright and as cold as a suit of burnished armor, and Sheehan's task was to draw him out of it. If he was to crowd the vice president, as his strategists wanted, he still had to look sympathetic doing it.

"You and Bush were like two boxers head to head," Sheehan had told him, critiquing the first debate. "You got in all these little jabs, but I ended up feeling roughed up by you."

The patient had seemed responsive at first. He replayed his Wake Forest tapes and was surprised at how deadly serious he looked. As the replay went on, he murmured stage directions to his image on the screen: "Come on, Michael, *smile*! . . . Keep those hands up!"

But he could not create a new persona overnight, nor could he seem to fuse the need to look nicer and act tougher into a single whole. As the pressure rose and the poll numbers fell, he appeared to his people instead to be turning inward, perhaps even losing his heart, or his nerve, for the whole undertaking. The morning before the debate, he told his astonished entourage that he didn't buy either the inflated weight they appeared to be giving the event or the get-tough strategy they were recommending for it. He had been castigated for his clinical manner the last time, and he had decided to show a softer side. He might even challenge Bush to a ban on all negative campaigning.

"You can do that," Bob Squier, a Washington media consultant lately added to the campaign, told him, "but if you do, you'll lose."

"This is not a make-or-break thing," Dukakis said. "And I'm not inclined to be negative on Bush."

But, Governor, someone said, it was accepted as given that he had to win the debate to turn the polls around. David Broder had said as much in *The Washington Post* that very morning; he was one of the grand gurus of political journalism, and his writings were often quoted by handlers as received wisdom, at least when his views chanced to agree with their own.

Dukakis was unmoved. "The polls are all over the place," he said.

Tom Donilon was stunned by the governor's intransigence. Donilon was not normally among the hand-wringers on Chauncy Street complaining about the governor's refusal to listen to advice; sometimes, indeed, Dukakis seemed to Donilon to tolerate too many voices talking in too many directions at once. But this time he was closing down on them, and Donilon's heart sank.

"This is a make-or-break event," he told Dukakis; it wasn't just one more leg in the marathon.

"I disagree," Dukakis answered, signaling, by his peevish tone, that the subject was closed.

A shudder of anxiety coursed through the room, and Estrich convened an emergency meeting over lunch to talk about it. The fractures within the campaign had seemed temporarily less important; they *had* to get Dukakis to get serious about the debate, to go after Bush hard. Estrich, in her gloom, had been pessimistic about their prospects of getting through to him. She had seen him like that in the primaries, she said. He meant what he had told them. He was going to stay passive.

Sasso, Donilon and Nick Mitropoulos tried anyway, cornering Dukakis that afternoon and spelling out the consequences of his behavior in vivid terms. He assented to the practice session, and, to the relief of his seconds, he seemed finally to have received and digested the core strategy. But hope faded again like a jug-wine high when, in midsession, *ABC News* came on a television set at the far end of the room. The business of the evening, prepping Dukakis for a mock debate, was momentarily forgotten; half his team peeled away to watch, and the anxious cross-chat among them interrupted the drills.

"Keep it quiet back there!" Sasso yelled.

No one heard him. The network had a new poll showing Bush's lead at only six points, but his lock on the Electoral College was hardening into certainty. The guys were awarding state after state to Bush, putting them up like occupied zones on a battle map. It went on and on. They were all but declaring the race over.

"Six minutes," Kirk O'Donnell said, looking at his watch. His face darkened. "Jesus, that's devastating. They gave it six minutes."

The pall in the room was palpable, the gray presence of defeat.

"I don't want to do any more," Dukakis said. He was scrubbing his dress rehearsal.

"How about a ninety-minute mock?" someone pleaded.

"I don't need one," Dukakis replied, an edge of finality in his tone.

"Well, how about sixty?"

"I'm afraid I'll get stale," Dukakis said.

The meeting thereupon adjourned; it was, his people thought afterward, as if he were saying "Screw it" to the debate and maybe the whole campaign. He seemed to be bridling at their do-or-die attitude and at the yin–yang paradoxes he thought he divined in their strategy—be tough/be nice, be substantive/be emotional, be aggressive/be messagey. They had long since lost his confidence, anyway, and when he dismissed them from his presence it was his signal that he had had it with their counsel. He fell back instead on what one called his residuals, the mini-speeches and the moot-court arguments that had got him that far, and when he did he walked into a one-punch knockout.

Bush, in contrast, was up for the fight this time, though he too was tired and fluish; his head coach, Ailes, had looked at the vice president's eyes ten minutes into the first debate and had seen blood in them, the inner resolve that round two would be payback time. The spark lingered and was reinforced by Bush's growing sense that he hadn't done all *that* badly in Winston-Salem—that he had maybe come out a little bit better than even. He studied harder for the rematch, but, in his confidence, he set the rules. There would be no more cramming facts and figures, only general answers; in a duel of statistics, he told Ailes, the Ice Man was going to win.

Bush's training camp accordingly had a relaxed air, given the stakes. His homework was cooked down from a thick, tab-divided ring binder to fifty tight pages, plain-spoken enough to be accessible and thin enough to be held together by a single clip at the top; there was less to read, but, as he would sheepishly let on to Ailes long after, he gave it more time.

His dining room was once again converted into a sound stage for two mock debates, authentic down to the lecterns and the blue backdrop, and Darman was waiting to play Dukakis, better, some thought, than the real thing. Bush showed up feeling offish and grumpy for the first run-through, cutting it short before the closing statements to go do a campaign event. But his performance was sharp and self-assured, ready, Atwater thought, for prime time; it was as if *both* candidates had said "Screw it," Bush in his belief that he was going to win, Dukakis in his depressive doubt that it really mattered.

When the vice president dismissed *his* prep team the day before the debate, it was an act of cockiness, not despair; as Jim Baker had told him, their team had already lost two debates in the press and was still moving up in the polls, so there wasn't a whole lot for him to worry about. Bush had agreed, and when he had pitched camp at the Four Seasons in Beverly Hills he told his tutors that school was out for the day.

"To hell with this," he said. "I can't do any more of this stuff. I'm going to the ball game."

The issues people had a collective anxiety attack. Ailes quieted them; if the guy was loose enough to go out to the ball park and have a couple of beers, he would be OK.

That night, Bush and Baker watched another underrated enterprise, the Los Angeles Dodgers, win the National League playoffs. None of his senior staff really minded his cutting classes. His seconds had accurately figured the contradiction at the core of Dukakis's only available strategy for the debate, the need to be good guy and bad guy at the same time; he was thus up against a challenge that had defeated Bob Dole in the primaries. I don't underestimate the little fucker, Atwater said, but he's got to be an asshole to do what he has to do.

The next day, Bush ran on cruise control, touring the theater of battle in the morning, lunching on pasta and politics with Atwater and Fuller at midday, sitting still for one last pepper drill in the afternoon. Ailes's objective in the latter exercise was to test his reflexes with a few quick and dirty questions. Bush's responses were good, and Ailes cut the drill short. If a guy's on his game, he figured, you don't start messing with it; you might hit him with something he *really* doesn't know and screw him up.

As showtime approached, he and Bush went back to Pauley Pavilion for a walk around the stage. Across the way, they saw Dukakis on a similar tour with two of his coaches, Donilon and Bob Squier. The mere sight roused the brawler resident in Ailes's ample breast; Bush liked to say that every American should have the right to bear arms except Roger.

"Let's yuk it up and unnerve them," Ailes said *sotto voce.*

To put Bush in the mood, Ailes reminded him of a new negative spot they had previewed that day, using new clips of Dukakis riding around in a tank in a silly helmet; the guy, Ailes said, looked just like Snoopy on top of his doghouse. Bush laughed. Ailes flung a clownish wave in the governor's direction. Dukakis, to his delight, saw them giggling. He folded his arms and glowered back.

The governor was in no mood to be teased; the past twenty-four hours had not been his best. The sense spreading through his entourage was that the new polling had set the bar almost impossibly high—higher than he could get over without totally demolishing Bush that night. Whatever fighting spirit he had brought to Los Angeles seemed to drain away. He was retiring into what one staff man worriedly called his capsule of moody introspection, and his advisers found themselves shut outside looking in.

When Donilon visited him at the Westin Bonaventure during the morning, the governor barely spoke. He looked bedraggled, his tie off, his collar open. He was very sick, he said. His throat was raw. He was throwing up. His voice was gone.

For a time, his team panicked, fearful that he might have to cancel out of the debate entirely. Nick Mitropoulos called Chauncy Street, his voice thick with worry. He's feeling like shit, Mitropoulos told the scheduling director, Mindy Lubber. Something's wrong. On his orders, an advance man, John Blackshaw, was dispatched to a nearby hospital to pick up a couple of doctors. The marching orders were that it was a secret mission, and as they approached the governor's hotel Blackshaw had the doctors take off their white lab coats so that they could slip past the media pack unseen.

They checked Dukakis, worked on his throat, gave him some medication, then emerged looking unconcerned. There was, they said, nothing to worry about—just a virus attack brought on by fatigue and stress; they prescribed that the patient rest and refrain from talking. Dukakis dragged himself through a preliminary reconaissance trip to the arena, but the day's practice had to be scrubbed. Instead, he checked into another hotel closer by and took to his bed, sucking lozenges. Belowstairs, his staff fretted. Politics and sports shared a common macho ethic; in the championships, you played hurt, but Dukakis seemed to be surrendering to his illness.

The debate was less than an hour off when Sasso, Donilon and Mitropoulos rousted him out of his suite and got him to the arena, staying close as if to prop up his fevered body and his battered ego with their presence. As airtime approached, he submitted unhappily to the makeup artist who had been added to his road company, letting her hide his five-o'clock shadow under layers of Pan-Cake. There were troubling signs, some anecdotal, some buried in the campaign's polling, that the flag-waving nativism of the Bush campaign had made Dukakis's Mediterranean roots a liability, and his dark stubble, in the view from Chauncy Street, only made him look more alien, more *foreign*.

Then he headed out onstage, his seconds still at his side pumping him up. They glimpsed Bush, twenty yards away. Sasso gestured toward him.

"Jesus, Michael," he said, "you can't let that guy be president. You've got to be *aggressive!*"

But Dukakis wasn't up, and it showed from the opening question—a hypothetical from Bernard Shaw of Cable News Network as to whether the governor would still oppose capital punishment if his wife were to be raped and murdered. It was a fat pitch disguised as a beanball, a chance for Dukakis to show some core of human emotion; he might, for example, have talked about the rage anyone would feel in such circumstances, or about how his own father had been mugged in his office at age seventy-seven, or about his brother having been cut down by a hit-and-run driver. But Dukakis, as his media man Dan Payne put it, responded to a caveman question with a lawyer's answer; he made his academic case against the death penalty and went on to tout his antidrug position without so much as mentioning Kitty's name.

The should-have-saids were flying from Pauley Pavilion to Chauncy Street. Charlie Baker, the field director, giggled and twirled a forefinger at his temple. In their holding room, Sasso and Estrich stared at the TV, bound together for once by their despond and by a sudden, enveloping silence. In the conference room of his New York consulting firm, Scott Miller and his staff sat around a handsome marble conference table littered with Cokes, beers and carryout pizza. Miller had come in from a shoot in his work clothes, corduroys, a sweater and a blue baseball cap, and had set out a yellow pad to note down moments he might make into ads. The Kitty question wasn't one of them. You had to show some outrage, he thought, slumping deeper into his chair; the guy's wife has just been killed, and he's talking about his crime program.

Dukakis never regained his footing. He seemed to lock onto the two-minute set pieces from his briefing books, reciting them as grimly as a schoolboy eating broccoli. His tone was uninflected, as if, in the effort to make him likable, all the emotion had been leached out of him, even the indignation at the core of his politics. When his script failed him, he floundered. A blind-side question about who he considered his heroes elicited one name—Dr. Jonas Salk. Otherwise, he listed public-spirited occupations, policemen and schoolteachers and the like; given a minute more, one of his people thought, he probably would have thrown in chemists.

Bush's performance was hardly Hall of Fame material, but, once Dukakis had blown the first question, all the vice president had to do was shadow-box for the last eighty-eight minutes. He seemed steady, commanding and, measured against the governor, an appealingly mortal man. The floor was littered with lost opportunities, most of them Dukakis's, and the governor knew it; he understood, as he would say a day or so later, that he *should* have stuck it in Bush's ear more if only he were a stick-it-in-your-ear kind of guy. When his torment was over, he tarried onstage long enough to hug Kitty, then turned on his heel and stalked away scowling; nothing so defined the debate as his leaving of it.

"I fucked up the first question," he told his seconds. Their glum faces said eloquently that they agreed.

"Truly it's over," Scott Miller said, turning his dejected gaze from the screen to his nearly blank legal pad, "Something had to happen. People were ready to listen to Dukakis. But it didn't happen. The rest of this campaign is going to be like watching a basketball team sit on a three-point lead."

"He had to throw a bomb," a colleague, Mandy Grunwald, agreed. "The Quayle debate set it up. He could have clinched it tonight."

"Dukakis hasn't given them anything to vote for," Miller said. With less than four weeks to go, he *still* hadn't defined himself.

"Remember liquor?" Grunwald asked. She was contemplating getting very drunk.

She would not be drinking alone; pessimism was endemic among Dukakis's people, some to the point of wondering yet again whether he really wanted to be president at all. His forty-eight hours in Los Angeles had reaffirmed their fears. He had had bad patches like that before, blue periods and black humors. Sometimes they came at high moments, as when he had first decided to seek the office and again after he wrapped up the nomination, sometimes at low tides, as when Sasso left and when Bush had first taken a chainsaw to him.

His candidacy had gone flaccid through the summer, the consequence, some thought, of the campaign's crossed wires and his own irresolution, and had never fully recovered. When he insisted on a town meeting in Brookline as his last stop before Los Angeles, his people exchanged knowing glances. He wants to be governor, not president, a man present at the birth of his candidacy guessed, and the tug between the comfort of home and the goal that had been handed him had helped pull him apart in front of sixty-two million people. His failure to respond to the rape-and-murder question had seemed, in the sinking hearts of his managers, a window into the emptiness of his candidacy—the want of heart, of feeling, even of the will to win.

As he fled the stage, his handlers descended dutifully into Spin Valley, the corner of the arena set apart for propagandizing the press, and did their best to look as if they meant it when they said how wonderfully the Duke had done. One knot formed around Susan Estrich, bravely claiming that Bush's won–lost record was zero-and-three.

"Who's that?" a local reporter wondered aloud, gesturing in her direction.

"Susan Estrich," someone said.

"What does she do?" the reporter asked.

Dick Darman, wandering by, overheard the exchange. Estrich was held in some contempt on Fifteenth Street—her nickname in the boys'-club atmosphere there was Susan Estrogen—and Darman could not resist the opening for a slap shot.

"She runs the losing campaign," he said.

The confidence of Bush's men was largely ex post facto. A debate involving the vice president was always a high-wire walk without a net, and Ailes had sweated it out in an agony of suspense, a spent, wrung-out ruin before the night was out. He had prowled the holding room like a caged animal, his shirttails flapping, his necktie knot dragged down to his sternum. At one point he had knocked over a lamp in his anxiety, smashing it on the floor.

Well, that makes it nine hundred ninety-nine points of light, Stu Spencer had said.

Everyone had laughed except Ailes; he had kept pacing, barely able to look at the screen. "Is he doing all right? Is he doing all right?" he had asked. Everyone had told him Bush was doing just fine, but when Ailes permitted himself a glance in the early going he hadn't liked what he was seeing. Bush was too animated, too *hot*. They had to get a message to him, put someone down front to do hand signals telling him to tamp it down. Baker had shrugged, and Ailes had finally surrendered to the obvious; when Bush left the stage, his coach was waiting, arms wide.

"I'm proud of you," Ailes told him. "You hit it out of the park."

The verdict was as nearly unanimous as so partisan a sport as politics permits. George Bush closed the sale, Charlie Black, a migrant from Kemp's campaign to the vice president's, said when the show was over, and John Sununu proposed heading for Spin Valley with signs that said NSR—no spin required. None was. The polls would stay static for a few days, then break sharply to the vice president; it was, as one of the governor's outside advisers said, as if America had decided halfway through the debate that it was all right for Bush to be president.

For several days thereafter, Dukakis's war counselors were furious with him, and he, for once, seemed apologetic; the debate, he understood, had been a break point in the campaign after all. But his appreciation of its cost came too late. Gloom settled over his road company like a miasmic fog; reporters on the Sky Pig were wearing black armbands, and the tour, as one staffer put it privately, took on the aspect of the Bataan Death March. "The debate was a clear loss for us," Tubby Harrison wrote in one of his communiqués to Chauncy Street; within the week, Bush's lead in Harrison's polling had blown open to fifteen points. Tom Kiley went home and told his wife, "It's over."

The mood was leaden when Kitty Dukakis called her father, Harry Ellis Dickson, a Boston Pops conductor, in the first days out of Los Angeles. She found him, too, low in spirit, upset by the debate and the mudslinging and by the downhill side of the campaign.

"Daddy, if you're pessimistic, don't talk to Michael," Kitty said. He had three weeks more to drag himself through, and the last thing he needed to hear from his loved ones—from *anyone*—was that he was going to lose.

President Bush

In the last weeks of his long-distance run for the presidency, Michael Dukakis finally became the candidate he might have been—a sleeves-up, back-to-basics Democrat who actually looked as if he wanted to win and sounded as if he knew why. He was still stained by the toxic-waste dumping that had passed for a campaign; his moods and his speeches were still governed by some invisible toggle switch, ON one day, OFF the next; his headquarters on Chauncy Street was still a Great Dismal Swamp of personal jealousies and professional miscalculations. There were bleak passages when a member of his advance team thought he looked dead— moments when even Sasso feared that the candidate and the campaign were on the verge of falling apart.

But on his good days, Dukakis and his audiences seemed to take fire from one another in the twilight of the long campaign, the man and the party coming together in their common need. He seemed toward the end to be surging, and if his ignition began as sleight of hand, an illusion spun by John Sasso out of three aberrant state polls, it came to look like the real thing. Over one angst-ridden weekend in late October, George Bush's command was frightened enough to lower its sights, from its will-o'-the-wisp pursuit of a mandate to the suddenly suspenseful work of getting their man elected.

That a candidate as damaged as Dukakis could still rattle teacups on Fifteenth Street was a further measure of the weakness of the field and the squalor of the campaign. A presidential election, as the polltaker Ed Reilly mused in ashy late autumn, has never been a game for the squeamish; the stakes are power, privilege and wealth, and what other societies have settled with knives in the night Americans do to one another with "comparative" ads on prime-time television. But 1988 seemed likely to be remembered as a benchmark election for its relentless *ad hominem* attacks, and in its closing days the public blame seemed finally to have attached to Bush and his merchandisers for having set its low tone. It had become by then the year of voting negatively, whether against Dukakis or Bush, Willie Horton or Danny Quayle, muddy harbors or dirty ads; a great majority of Americans, on the evidence of the polls, found neither a man nor a public agenda they very much wanted to vote *for*.

It was only toward the end, when Dukakis made an issue of his wounds, that Bush's men got nervous about the politics of slander. "We need to be very careful," Jim Baker would warn his senior staff at a meeting six days before the election, with the governor's footfalls audible behind them. "This [negative] thing has been pushed right to the limit." But no one even then had confidence enough to let go of the tiger's tail; the last recourse of a salesman who doubted his own product was to talk about why Brand X was worse.

The Invasion of the L People

The case for going positive was never seriously in play, not even in the first flush of victory after Los Angeles. Bush's men had left Pauley Pavilion bathed in euphoria, their cheer over his victory in the debate made more delicious by their surprise that he had managed it. Their single worst enemy then was overconfidence, as no less keen an observer than Richard Nixon warned in one of his privately circulated memos four days later. Dukakis, in his view, had "set a record for incompetence as a candidate"; his campaign had been so "pathetically amateurish" that Bush and his men would have to be geniuses to blow the election.

The Bush command, in those sunny autumn days, was disposed to agree. On Lee Atwater's scorecard, after Los Angeles, they seemed close to a lock on 410 electoral votes—you needed only 270—and no one was thinking win–lose anymore; they were afloat on their dreams of winning big, of empowering a Bush presidency with a landslide vote and maybe even a

Republican majority in the Senate. Defeat seemed impossible; when one senior hand was asked what it would take for Bush to lose, he replied, "Sodomy."

What never changed was the core strategy of attack; in the afterglow of the last debate, the subject never came up except as a joke.

"Well," Baker had said that night, celebrating with his team at his hotel in Beverly Hills, "this debate's gone so good, I guess we can pull all the negatives."

He winked broadly when he said it, but Lee Atwater, sitting behind him, couldn't see it, and his face froze in something near horror.

"Don't be shakin' your knee," Baker said quickly, knowing Atwater's whole bag of tics. He was just having fun, yanking Lee's chain. It was a rule in politics that you danced with the one that brung you. The assault on Dukakis's bloodied person would go on; it had made Bush the front-runner, and to let up, in Baker's view, would be a dangerous show of overconfidence, a signal that they were sitting on their lead.

So the beat went on, fine-tuned but otherwise unabated. A sign on the men's-room mirror at headquarters exhorted DON'T LET UP, and no one did. The plan coming out of Los Angeles was to repaint the vice president in softer hues, leaving the negatives to his ads and his surrogates while he did uplifting theme weeks on peace, prosperity and what his strategists called the Combination Plate, blending both into a grand finale. It was important, in their eyes, that he not be seen as having won solely by picking on Dukakis.

Bush's stay on the high road, in the event, lasted less than thirty-six hours. One day out of Los Angeles, on his own motion, he moderated a Duke-bashing speech on the environment, substituting his kinder-gentler tone of voice and a cleaner-bluer vision of the sea and the sky. Two days out, he was back in full battle gear, boarding a bus nicknamed Asphalt Two and coursing California like a horror-flick hero warning against the Invasion of the L People; his Good George/Bad George personae would run on alternating current to the eve of the election.

He was, to be sure, more squeamish than ever in his warrior role, his qualms rising as the tarnish began to show on his breastplate. In the waning days of October, he called Roger Ailes to lament what he had to do to win.

"I want to get back on the issues," he said, "and quit talking about *him*."

"We plan to do that November ninth," Ailes told him; the morning after his election would be soon enough to start talking about what it was he actually planned to do as president.

Ailes, as it happened, had grown his own case of self-consciousness at having his signature on so nasty a campaign. He was tired of all the dark-prince horseshit he kept reading about himself, an evolving portrait of the artist as a crazy killer; he ordered up a survey by his New York office demonstrating that 80 percent of the political ads he had made in his twenty-year career had been positive, and in the counsels of Bush Inc. he found himself arguing for infusing more kinder-gentler material into the media mix than the fifty-fifty balance they had planned for the closeout of the campaign.

But he was a lone and unlikely pacifist in a roomful of warmongers, and his own lust for battle was not easily repressed in any case. As their notices got worse, his ad team got more obsessive about security, as if there were indeed something to hide; a last, five-minute attack ad was edited in the black, the trade word for a sealed and shuttered room, and its air dates were kept secret even from the men who made it.

Otherwise, the Duke-busting went on, with Ailes in full war paint leading the charge. He churned through his days, brooding, bellowing, flogging, dictating scripts into a microcassette recorder. His rest at night was fitful; one of his strongest contributions to the campaign came to him, in fact, in his sleep. He had thought a lot about the news clips he had seen of Dukakis on his tank ride, a media event of the sort that schedulers wish in retrospect they could undo; he had even alluded to it in speeches, unfailingly getting a laugh. But the elements didn't click together until the night he stirred awake, sort of, and scribbled something on the pad he kept beside his bed. "Tank," it said when he looked at it the next morning. It took him half a day to figure out what he had been thinking of; once he cracked the code, his memory jogged by a photo in a newsmagazine, he had an ad in production in twenty-four hours.

Unlike some of his works, the spot at least had to do with issues of direct presidential concern. The voice-over attacked the governor as soft on defense, ticking off a list of weapons systems he was alleged, more or less accurately, to have opposed; the visuals fastened on his head poking out of a turret, wearing a Mickey Mouse helmet and a schoolboy-at-Disneyland grin. The ad went up six days after the last debate, and it plainly touched an exposed nerve in Dukakis, who took ridicule as happily as an ordinary citizen might take a tax audit, say, or a punch in the mouth.

His complaints as to the ad's accuracy were at least arguably well taken; there were *some* weapons he had actually come out for. But complaints to Ailes were like blood in the water to a piranha, and he cranked out "Tank II," an even tougher sixty-second sequel using the same footage; what the governor and the literal-minded lawyers advising him seemed not to get was that one picture had vastly more kill power than a thousand words.

That's what Dukakis got for bitching; attack one ad, Ailes said, and I'll stick another, meaner one in your ear.

Any further impulse to lighten up died two weeks before Election Day, in that panic-button passage when Dukakis seemed to be rising from the early grave they had consigned him to. Bush's lead in Bob Teeter's private polling, while never in the double-digit latitudes recorded in several national surveys, had stayed within a comfort zone of five to eight points all fall; the margin, coupled with the vice president's secure hold on his electoral-fortress states in the South and the West, made his victory look bankable and a landslide at least possible.

But as October faded, Dukakis seemed suddenly recharged, lighting up his rallies, sharpening his own attack rhetoric and appearing on any TV show that would have him short of *The Home Shopping Club*. He *out-presenced* us, a senior official at Bush headquarters said. The numbers in Teeter's tracking polls, mostly straight as a clothesline till then, turned abruptly south. The lead Bush had held for much of the fall melted from seven to four to zero in the space of forty-eight hours, and his margins were crumbling in the big battleground states he needed to fill out his hand.

For two days more, code-blue alarms had rung on Fifteenth Street, sometimes to the bewilderment of the vice-presidential party on Air Force Two. Like any presidential campaign, Bush's was caught between two distorted perceptions of reality; the alarums and excursions at headquarters at every new twitch in the polls were in constant tension with the contented smiles on the plane at every big crowd at a rally. Craig Fuller, traveling with the combat-weary candidate, thought the people on the ground were overreacting; it did not greatly spook him, for example, when Darman lowered the odds against Dukakis from an impossible hundred-to-one to a merely improbable ten-to-one. He tried accordingly to shelter Bush from the angst-of-the-day in Washington. *Please*, Fuller implored the ground crew, don't start the vice president's day by telling him the overnight tracking numbers were down three points or something; it was—um— disquieting to him.

Fuller tried, in fact, to keep the daily numbers from him entirely, without success; Bush would start each morning agreeing that they were bad for him, but his resolve not to ask would typically break down by, say, 8 A.M. "What did Teeter tell you?" he would ask urgently. "Have you heard from Teeter?" Fuller usually had, but his reports to Bush tended to iron out the day-to-day wrinkles. We've got a six-to-ten-point lead, he would say reassuringly, his soft face a Buddhaic mask. His real guess, privately held, was that it would be closer to four.

Teeter himself would come to wonder whether the slide had been real or just a nightmare; one day in its aftermath, he sat cooling his brow with an empty Evian bottle and pored over his data like a scholiast at his studies, hunting for evidence that, as he had come to suspect, it had resulted from some glitch in his sampling. But the storm, while it lasted, had been a scary one. For one rare time, the entire Bush command reported to its battle stations over the weekend. Baker called Bush on the road and got him to scrub a scheduled Sunday off; rest for the weary was no longer a luxury they could afford. Ronald Reagan was drafted for an extra visit to California, where the vice president's margin had melted to three percentage points.

The mere idea of easing up on Dukakis fell prey to the vertigo attack. Bush was getting balkier about doing the necessary dirty work himself, preferring to close out his campaign on the high road, as one unhappy staffer put it, saying nice things; when a Boston newspaper did a story on the Massachusetts budget crisis, with the screamer headline WHAT A MESS, the vice president had to be bludgeoned into displaying it, once, at a campaign rally.

But his periodically expressed preference for softening the attack no longer had many friends on Fifteenth Street, not after the October scare. A headquarters directive to the Bush and Quayle planes to be kinder and gentler the rest of the way was rescinded less than a week after its issue; Dukakis was out there doing a Bob Dole, accusing Bush of lying about his record, and the walk-soft approach looked rather too much like a plea of guilty. Eight days before the end of the campaign, the Bush command signed off on yet another attack ad. Its taunting last visual was Mount Rushmore as the Democrats of the seventies and eighties might have redone it, with likenesses of George McGovern, Jimmy Carter, Fritz Mondale—and Michael Dukakis.

"Nobody's Listening"

Dukakis's surge was in fact part real and part chimera. As Sasso confided to a couple of friends late one night in a hotel room in San Jose, it had begun when he took some mildly heartening poll returns from Ohio, Wisconsin and California and persuaded the media that they were looking at a national trend; he had simply fed them the numbers, he said, and the reporters had run with them. But they would be back for more, he knew that, and he was going to have to have something for them, something *real*.

He sat gray with fatigue in the corner of a couch, dragging at a cigarette and flicking the ashes into a room-service glass. Maybe the national polls *would* start closing, the men in the room told one another; maybe they *could* still do it. None of them believed it. Sasso was out of tricks, out of strategies. All he could do was put Michael behind a podium and tell him to open fire, the straight-shooting underdog up against the Great Bush Packaging Machine, and see where it led.

Sasso and his friends weren't talking about winning anymore, not at that point. They knew that the party was furious at them, for having won the nomination in the first place with big bucks and bland talk and then having shut out the pros who might have helped them. They were seen as having kicked away a chance—maybe the last chance in this century—for a Democratic revival. Apart from salvaging Michael's pride, they had to do what they could to keep his party from being buried alive.

Sasso had understood for weeks that he had come back too late to fix a badly broken candidacy. The "surge" he had pumped up had helped, masking the real deterioration of the campaign from the candidate and from the media. In fact, no one outside knew how bad things were, how perilously near the point of collapse; in the vertiginous days after Los Angeles, Dukakis tumbled seventeen points behind in the campaign's confidential polling and some of Sasso's boys believed that they were looking at a 60–40 landslide.

Sasso had done what he could, but it was like trying to turn the *QE2*, as one of his admirers on Chauncy Street said, and it was more than even John could manage. John was no savior, just one fallible man up against the broodiness and the stubbornness of the candidate and the hostility of the management he had displaced. He carried his own store of bitterness, at Dukakis for having disowned him for so long and at Estrich and Brountas for having resisted his return even after it had happened. It was not until after the disastrous second debate that they surrendered control to him; there was little left for him then except to go out on the plane and try to keep Dukakis moving through the fog of his exhaustion and his gloom. Sasso was, by the end, as much hand-holder as manager. After an especially bad time, he would disengage the governor from his retinue and speak with him alone for twenty minutes or so; the two men would sit, eyes locked, Sasso doing most of the talking, Dukakis listening, for once, and nodding. Afterward, he was usually better.

The message of his last weeks was a series of daily improvisations; the want of a rationale for his candidacy was by then beyond repair by anything but fresh Band-Aids. A plan to ride out the last weeks on a positive note was forgotten after Los Angeles; the governor's people returned to economics and trade, the populist issues they had urged on him all along. But he seemed to his managers as fixed in his old politics as a fly in amber. He wasn't reaching people with his themes or his language, his people said, and you couldn't make him work on it; his learning curve, as senior campaign officials traced it, was a flat line. He wanted to run *his* way, to make his campaign as rational and as pacific as a graduate seminar when he was really involved in a war.

"What's the matter?" his son, John, asked Tubby Harrison one day when things were plainly unraveling.

"All of us have beliefs when we are young that we tend to change," Harrison said out of his own despond. "Your father is a man in his fifties, and yet he doesn't realize that he can't be president on his own terms."

For a time, little changed. The campaign was still groping for ideas when, with just three weeks left, the newly reconstituted issues command convened a secret meeting at the Lafayette to figure out some way of explaining why the governor wanted to be president. The scene was politics as Dada art, Surrealism carried to its comedic extreme. The room was swept for bugs. A guard was posted at the door. A dozen people sat around a conference table; the campaign pros felt surrounded by state-government employees, *kids*, some of them, with little experience of presidential politics. A Georgetown professor stood at an easel, leading a Jesuitical debate on what Michael really meant when he spoke of "the best America" in his speeches. A strong America? A powerful America? Lunch was served. America the tough? America as number one? The professor scribbled answers on his easel, ripping off pages one by one and sticking them to the wall. Eyes were glazing. Old-timers excused themselves at intervals, mainly to escape.

A stripling from the parks department was doing *his* presentation when, at one o'clock, Sasso walked in. The room fell silent. He looked around, then sat down, only his deepening color betraying his feelings. He listened while the kid from parks finished his recitation. Then he rose.

"This meeting is adjourned," he said, "and I don't want one word of it to ever leave this room."

He started out, then turned back toward the professor's sheets of graffiti. *"And take those things off the wall!"* he said.

The candidate's spirits were no better. He had come out of Los Angeles in a down mood, pissed off at himself, an aide said, for his performance and discouraged at his prospects. The fight seemed to drain from him like an ebbing tide, and as he sat in a hotel suite in Denver one night nearly two weeks later, preparing to carry his desperate free-media blitz onto Ted Koppel's *Nightline*, it seemed perilously near gone. His collar was open and his tie askew. His cosmetician was Pan-Caking his stubble and the bags under his eyes. The day had been a bad one, made worse by a new poll showing him eleven points down in California. He seemed to his people to be tired and ineffably sad, the prisoner of his manufactured candidacy.

"Governor," someone said, trying to cheer him, "Kitty and the girls were wonderful on David Frost."

"Yeah," Dukakis said, "I have a great family." He paused. "Maybe," he said, almost inaudibly, "they should be the candidate."

"Michael, they loved you on the Larry King show," someone else said.

"Well, they sure don't in California," he said.

His mood showed on Koppel that night. He sat through a tough opening pounding on the state of his polls and a long interrogation on the details of his foreign policy. His answers were tired and mechanical. During commercial breaks, Tom Donilon tried to reflate the governor, yelling at him to smile, get mad—do *something*. The pep-talking didn't work; as the show dragged on, he sank deeper and deeper into a hunch. He was asking America for one more chance, a second look before they made up their minds, and there he sat, getting smaller and smaller, shrinking into himself. His people applauded him when it was finally over, but they were only trying to buoy him up, and he knew it. He shrugged at them, palms up, and when Sasso apologized for having overloaded his schedule he said, "No, no"—he should have done better.

His response, this time, was not depressive but angry, with himself and his opposition; it was, an aide said, as if he had kicked himself in the butt and got himself back in the ring. His people knew he was back when he started bracketing Bush with Ed King, the man who had run him out of the statehouse in 1978 with a similarly ugly campaign; he had waited then too for a backlash that never happened, and he wasn't going to let history repeat itself. He despised King, and when the two faces fused in his mind the chemistry of his campaign changed almost literally overnight; he was sore enough, finally, to fight back, and on those days when he was up to it, his access of passion transformed his road show into something nearer a crusade.

The governor slipped into the shirtsleeve, damn-mad populism his people had long since tailored for him, telling his audiences of blue- and new-collar Democrats that he was "on your side" against the champion of the powerful and the privileged. His new clothes were not an easy fit; he thought of himself as a consensus-builder, not a class warrior, and he cut some of the tougher rhetoric out of his early speeches in the new vein. But as he began connecting with his crowds, he seemed to warm to the role and even to enjoy it. "Yes, I am a liberal," he declared nine days before the election, hastening to add that he meant a liberal in the Roosevelt-Truman-

Kennedy tradition. Only Kitty was said to have known of his confessional in advance. It was the product, his people guessed afterward, less of design than of that psychic process known in the consulting trade as internalizing the strategy; what they meant, translated into English, was that he had come to believe what he had been told to say.

Some of his schismatic command team were horrified at hearing him confess the creed that dared not speak its name, not, anyway, in the fetid political climate of 1988. He had waved a red flag in the faces of the Reagan Democrats they had been chasing from the start, and Sasso, who hadn't seen the change of signals coming, yelled at Dukakis, ''Are you *crazy*?'' Others were angry that, once having come out of the closet, he didn't stay out; Estrich wept in frustration when the I-am-a-liberal line disappeared from his repertoire after a single day. But his crowds seemed by their growing size and decibel level to love his new act, L word and all, and even, *mirabile dictu*, to like Mike. The din at his speeches and the visuals on the news created the appearance of movement, and, in the mirror world of media politics, the appearance of movement created real movement in the polls.

The rallies were party affairs, of course, the faithful returning to the fold at the end as they had returned with similar exuberance to Fritz Mondale in 1984. They had nowhere else to go, and neither, by then, did Dukakis. The genius of the Republican campaign, Paul Tully thought, was that it had painted the governor out of the mainstream not merely in ideology but in competence as well, the very ground on which he had planted his flag from the beginning. It was, Tully grumbled to a friend, a race the Democrats should have won. Bush? Quayle? Nothing! Empty! All you needed was 51 percent of the vote against the weakest Republican you could have found. But Dukakis hadn't stepped up to it, hadn't cracked down on his team, hadn't even defended himself. After a summer-long siege, the questions about his beliefs and his skills had fused into one—whether he knew what he was doing—and his candidacy was undone.

In the twilight of his campaign, old-line Democrats embraced him, welcoming him home. The effects could be intoxicating on the road, in what Dukakis thought of as the airless silver cylinder encapsulating a modern campaign, but the cannier of his strategists did not delude themselves as to what the crowd noise meant. They had a paper strategy for winning, a list of eighteen target states with enough electoral votes, barely, for a majority. They seemed, in fact, to be competitive in most of them, as close as two or three points at the peak of Dukakis's closing rush. The problem was that they had to win them all, the political equivalent, as Lee Atwater liked to say, of drawing to an inside straight. The realists in the campaign held out no more than the faintest hope that it was going to happen; not even Dukakis seemed persuaded, at least till his heady last days.

"You'll keep it as close as you can out here, won't you?" the governor asked his man in one of the must states on his list; his fight, at the end, was for pride and party, not for victory.

"I'll do the best I can, Governor," the operative answered. But the victory that had seemed so palpably within reach in July had all but evanesced. The campaign came down at the end to an exercise in cutting losses, trying for what the governor's men called a "decent showing" for himself and the candidates below him on the Democratic ticket. The Dukakis "surge" was still gathering force when Chauncy Street quietly began back-channeling money into state Democratic campaigns as survival insurance for the party; they were, an adviser to the campaign said, playing for history, not for themselves.

Still, they gave it a game try, keeping the governor airborne as if he could win by sheer motion and applying psychic CPR when he fell into one of his defeatist moods. There were days when he was just going through the motions, John Blackshaw thought, days when he wasn't really *there*. "Why the fuck am I doing this?" he would demand between events; the answer was not always clear even to his handlers, given the jangled circuitry of the campaign. He arrived for a speech in Milwaukee eight days before the end, limp with fatigue and visibly demoralized by the latest poll numbers. His frightened advance people arranged for Kitty to call him, and, in the minutes before he was to go on, Sasso and Mitropoulos whispered into his ears like seconds in a prizefight: "Go, Governor, go! You can do it! *Go!*" He forced himself onstage, and, as he spoke, Mitropoulos stood down front, thumping the podium as if Dukakis might somehow take life from the beat. His people, on these occasions, would ritually tell him afterward that he had been great.

"Yeah," he answered once. "But nobody's listening."

Kitty was put on the plane with him by conscious strategic decision, for her buoying effect on his spirits, and Sasso became a kind of traveling cheerleader, rallying the candidate and the staff alike with the cry, borrowed from a Bob Marley song, "Stir it up! Stir it up!" Toward the end, with Dukakis's *esprit* sagging, Sasso told him, "Get tough!"

"Get tough on what?" Dukakis asked.

"*Get tough!*" Sasso repeated, pounding a radiator for emphasis.

"Get tough on the *radiator*?" Dukakis asked.

Somehow, he summoned up the energy for his last, desperate red-eye marathon, fueled less by hope than by prayer. Chauncy Street's own final national poll showed them a dispiriting eight points down with five days left, but there were glimmers of hope in their tracking, and the undecideds appeared to be breaking their way, driven in part by revulsion at the quality of the Bush campaign.

The governor was accordingly put back on the Sky Pig and sent ricocheting across the country and back, again and yet again. For one stretch of fifty hours, he never saw the inside of a hotel room, instead catnapping in his forward compartment. His scheduling, always ragged, became totally improvisational, his stops dictated by a bump up or down in the polls or by the direction and speed of the jet stream. His eyes were pouchy, his hands tremulous, and his voice was a hoarse rasp; he wound up the campaign on steroids, not for his musculature but for his throat. And yet he went out with a show of fire his own people had thought wanting in him. He was campaigning with freedom as the singer-songwriter Kris Kristofferson once defined it—another word for nothing left to lose.

The Party's Over

The anxieties on the governor's side were very nearly matched on the vice president's. A glance at the map reminded the Bush people of the electoral fortress favoring *any* Republican candidate, a two-hundred-plus head start centered in the South and the West. But their own polls took another turn down in the last days; they felt, one senior hand said, like a basketball team that couldn't score that last big hoop, the three-pointer that breaks the other side's heart. The big states were looking particularly soft; Illinois was gone, Atwater decided four or five days out, and some of the others were in danger of going.

In their shakiness, the strategic command split into two camps, Fundamentalists against Opportunists. The former, led by men like Atwater and Teeter who made their livings wining elections, argued for a simple go-for-270 strategy, the fortress states plus New Jersey and Ohio. The latter, centered around men like Baker and Darman who would be following Bush into the government, were still in a modified, limited shoot-for-a-mandate mode and favored contesting the iffier states to run up the score. Each side won some scheduling squabble, at various points in the vice president's own frenetic dash through the end game; the Fundamentalists got extra stops in Ohio and New Jersey, the Opportunists in Pennsylvania and Connecticut. But both schools were governed nearly to the end by a certain feeling that Dukakis was in fact gathering steam—that he had, as one of Atwater's men put it, finally become a *candidate* in the waning hours of his campaign and had turned their strategy of calumny against them.

The needle was still fluttering when, three days before the election, Fuller called Baker to beg for mercy. The vice president was worn out, and, as his exhaustion grew, the Chucklehead Factor was beginning to reassert itself; he bragged at Notre Dame, for one of numerous examples, about how the Reagan-Bush administration had stopped the slide show, when all he had meant to say was the slide. But Fifteenth Street kept piling new events onto the schedule with every new squiggle in the polls. It was, Fuller protested, more important that Bush do three or four good shows a day than try six and screw up.

Baker quite agreed, but when he, Atwater and Margaret Tutwiler, Baker's longtime deputy, joined the tour in St. Louis on election eve, they all seemed victim to the williwaws. Dukakis was putting on his big finish, rocketing across the country live and by satellite. Maybe, the crowd from headquarters thought, they should respond with their own last-minute sideshow. Maybe, instead of shutting the tour down in Houston as scheduled, they should add a zig-out to New Orleans, say, or Baton Rouge.

"Make your case," Fuller told them, "but I'm telling you, it won't happen. He's driving to the goal line, and the last play of the game is in Houston. He's not going anywhere else after that."

Fuller and common sense prevailed; the campaign ended where it had begun, in Houston, the last stop in a journey of ten years. By the time Bush and his family sat down to an election-eve dinner at the Houstonian Hotel, he could barely believe it was over—that America's judgment on him was only hours away. His daughter, Doro, tried to tease him out of his worrying, dubbing him "P. E. Herman." P. E. stood for president-elect, she explained, and everybody laughed. But the vice president slid back into a contemplative silence.

"You've run a great campaign," George Jr. said, raising a glass to him.

"Well," Bush said, "we haven't won yet."

The first reports from the field on Election Day were not comforting; Bush's lead in Teeter's tracking had fallen back to four points, its low since his two-day dive in late October, and even that was inflated by his massive margins in the South.

"It's really tightening up," Atwater fretted, encountering his deputy, Ed Rogers, in a corridor at the Houstonian at six forty-five that morning.

"What's the bottom line?" Rogers asked.

"We win," Atwater said, "but it's just going to be a longer night than we thought."

Not long after, Teeter, Fuller and George Jr. brought Bush the scary numbers.

"Let's go through the states," he said.

Only his son sounded upbeat, though the Southern and Western base was strong and some of the big states, the Fundamentalists' two favorites among them, were firming up. Dukakis would have to win every close state to be elected and probably couldn't. The tone, even so, was tentative. Teeter spun out a worst-case scenario for Bush, a 275- or 280-vote squeaker.

"I hope you're right," Bush said.

No one thought they were looking at a blowout anymore. They would settle, happily, for a victory, and when the exit polls later placed their probable score closer to 350 than to 270 electoral votes, the mood was more subdued than celebratory. Grins flashed, and a couple of fists thumped the table, but no one was popping the champagne just yet.

There had been a last frisson of hope on Chauncy Street that morning, a feeling that Dukakis might actually win; it was as if the low drone of bad tidings on television had to do with some other candidate in some other country. Victory scenarios flew from office to office. Tubby Harrison was filling a blank page with numbers, totting up 280 electoral votes for the governor. Leslie Dach grinned into a phone, rattling off the swing states they were sure to win. "I better start writing my transition memo," Chris Edley, the issues director, told his number two, Tom Herman.

But as the day dragged on, their hopes faded into a threnody of what-ifs and might-have-beens—a sense that a rare opportunity for the restoration of the Democracy to power had indeed slipped through their error-prone fingers. They briefly contemplated sending the governor on one last kamikaze flight to Detroit and maybe St. Louis, where he might catch the drive-time radio crowd coming home from work and tip a couple of closely contested must states into his column. The plan was abandoned, but Dukakis was hustled to a radio station for satellite-feed interviews, fourteen of them in an hour and a half, beamed at his target states.

Otherwise, he stayed close to home, gazing into his future and seeing nothing. Ted Kennedy and his nephew Joe, the congressman, dropped by during the day and found the governor at his kitchen table, beginning to compose his curtain speech. They tried to cheer him with praise and small talk, but he cut them short.

"This is no time for levity," he said.

It wasn't. His eighteen-state strategy was, in the words of a consultant to the campaign, the equivalent of threading a needle. Their target list left them no margin for error, and when first Missouri and then Connecticut went up on the network maps in Bush red that evening, the fat lady sang for Michael Dukakis. They had, as Sasso said, run out of time.

"It looks bad," Ed Reilly said into a phone. "The party's over."

It was not much past 9 P.M. when Rather came on, declaring Bush the winner.

"Jesus!" Tom Herman said, watching the returns with some Chauncy Street pals at his loft on Beacon Hill. The remains of a carryout Thai dinner lay around. Everyone was drinking. "He doesn't know what he's talking about," Herman said, staring at Rather through wire-rim glasses. "Bullshit!"

But it was true; the fact and the scale of the rout were becoming clear when Sasso, Kirk O'Donnell and Tom Donilon headed out from headquarters to the governor's house in Brookline. They found him looking dazed and depressed. He had been watching the returns with his family in their living room, thinking nearly to the end that he still had a chance. When the networks had begun calling it for Bush instead he had disappeared upstairs for a time. Kitty had followed him, then had come back down and told the children that he needed a little time alone; they would all have to be at their strongest for him. When his men appeared, he greeted them, enfolding Sasso in an embrace. He put in a call to Bentsen; then he sat down at the kitchen table, where they had planned his candidacy, and began work on the speech conceding its failure. He told the others what he wanted: Bush up front, he said; the obligatory thank-yous; a reprise of what they had been fighting for. He would improvise the coda on his own.

His mood was bleak and getting bleaker. When he met backstage with his staff for the last time as a candidate that evening, moments before his concession speech, they tried to cheer him. You did great, it was a great effort, they said. "When you win only forty-six percent it's not great," Dukakis replied. "And I didn't do great."

The outcome had still looked uncertain when the Bushes and their senior staff set out for an old friend's house for a victory buffet; for a scary passage in the late afternoon, three of their Western fortress states had seemed to be slipping away.

"We're not out of the woods yet," Baker told George Jr., walking in. They had designated Michigan and Ohio as insurance states in their electoral strategy, figuring Dukakis couldn't win without them, and had worked them as intensively as if Bush were running for governor. Ohio was looking solid, but Michigan was still up for grabs. They needed Michigan, Baker said, before they started lighting any victory cigars.

The guests were scattered around the house, perched in front of TV sets with plates of food on their knees, when one of the networks awarded the state to Bush. A war whoop went up in the living room, where three sets were going at once.

"Why are y'all cheering?" Bush asked.

"They've given you Michigan," his son Jeb said, hugging him tight. "Congratulations, Mr. President-elect."

"Great going, Dad," George Jr. echoed.

"Thanks, son," Bush said, grinning.

It was a while longer before the suspense really ended for him. He had returned to his rooms at the Houstonian and sat waiting for the networks to declare him the winner. They wouldn't, not for hours. People were drinking and partying all around him, and he was staring at the screen, muttering, Jesus, is this over or isn't it over? It *looks* over. Why doesn't somebody *call* it over?

It *was* over; George Herbert Walker Bush had been chosen the forty-first president of the United States. His forty-state, seven-million-vote victory was in one sense a brilliant achievement, its scale magnified by the distance he had run to get there; one of the least esteemed political campaigners of his time had come from seventeen points down in July to win by nearly eight in November, a split hair short of a landslide.

What was less becoming to him was the manner of his triumph. He owed it in important part to his paid handlers, the cosmeticians who had made a mild man look hard and the armorers who had made a genteel man sound like a back-street brawler. No recent president had been, or been presented as, so completely an artifact of packaging and promotion; even Ronald Reagan, after a working lifetime as an actor and an after-dinner speaker, had brought a core of real and deeply held beliefs to politics and had required that his costumers and makeup men work around them. Bush had not. His most distinguishing mark, on the evidence of his campaign, was not his platform or his ideology but his pliancy in the hands of his managers.

The long, often irrational process of choosing a president has been defended as a means of revealing the character of the contenders, throwing their strengths and weaknesses into high relief over a year and more of almost unremitting pressure. But the quest for the presidency in 1988 had been an opaque window into the soul of the winner; it would be January 1989 before the nation would really begin to know President Bush and his design for the American future.

The Triumph
of the Body Snatchers

What do we do now?
—BILL McKAY to his chief
handler, on being elected
senator, in *The Candidate*,
1972

IN THE WINTER OF 1988–89, the real George Bush finally stood up and turned out to be the man Washington had known for two decades: a well-bred, well-mannered chap of sound intelligence, solid experience, agreeable nature, cautious instincts and only modest flair for the public arts of leadership. He claimed the office on a crisp morning in January, offering a prayer, neglecting the Pledge, extending a hand of friendship to the opposition and otherwise presenting himself in Peggy Noonan's kinder, gentler colorization. "A new breeze is blowing," he proclaimed from the Capitol steps, and, to the degree that the means of his election had already receded in memory, so it was. Once installed, he was no longer obliged to play George Wallace reincarnated in chinos by L. L. Bean and values by Atwater & Ailes. He could be himself again, and his countrymen appeared to like him better than they once had thought they would.

It seemed not to matter that, in the first months of his presidency, his administration sailed adrift on the tides. Having brought neither vision nor agenda to the White House with him, he was slow imposing any clear direction on the government. His stewardship of the economy was a suspenseful watch for the day of reckoning after six years of borrowed prosperity; his domestic policies were prisoner to his pledge not to raise taxes, which had a powerful chilling effect on new initiatives; his foreign policy seemed unsure, even timorous, in the early going, his first steps fashioned in reaction to Mikhail Gorbachev's brilliant theatrics in the center ring. But he had made a life's work of being ingratiating, and it served him well both with the public and with his partners in government. Only the press, in the spring of 1989, appeared to be asking when something was going to happen.

The cynicism of his campaign appeared by then to have been largely forgotten, mercifully for the president and for the country. His candidacy had been designed by men with the usual mix of motives in their trade, among them money, position and genuine admiration for their client as a public and private man. What was wanting was any central *idea,* any large sense of public purpose, since Bush himself had brought none to the table beyond his abstract Roman notion of service. His people were accordingly obliged to weave a tapestry around him, using whatever threads they could find. That so many of them had to do with the vices of Michael Dukakis as against the paler virtues of George Bush was, however regrettably, a necessity; the object of politics, and of political management, is not to illuminate but to win.

Bush's stylists achieved this end masterfully, having a clean page to draw on and a candidate willing to be redrawn; next to a referendum campaign, the Republican consultant David Keene mused dryly, the handler's ideal client is the candidate who *understands* that he is a necessary pain in the ass and does as he is told. Bush did, once persuaded he was in trouble, and his stage managers were, for the most part, well rewarded. Jim Baker, who chaired a singularly noisome campaign, got his wish to be secretary of state. John Sununu, a charter advocate of the attack strategy, became White House chief of staff; Lee Atwater, its ramrod, was seated as Republican national chairman; Roger Ailes, its propagandist-in-chief, went back to his New York offices tired and bruised but a good deal richer; Dick Darman, its most elegant apologist, took his keen intellect and his gift for public policy to more suitable work as director of the Federal budget.

It was easy in the aftermath, perhaps too easy, for the Democrats to attack them for their dirty work and blame Dukakis even more for his enfeebled response to it. The governor, a lovelorn figure in the winter of his humiliation, returned to his statehouse with his Miracle crumbling around him. His senior people, Sasso and Estrich among them, came around the day after the election to help rehearse him for a farewell press conference. He greeted them without seeming to look any one of them in the eye, and his attention wandered during the run-through.

I'm sorry it couldn't have ended differently, he told them. It wasn't for lack of trying.

They pressed on with the rehearsal, but there were more Q's than A's; the governor seemed out of focus.

"Why didn't we find the on-your-side message earlier?" he asked suddenly.

The group was silent. Their unspoken response was equivalent to Louis Armstrong's on being asked to define the blues: if they had to tell him, they couldn't.

The view within Dukakis's party of his and his management's work was poisonous, born as it was of a need to blame *someone* for having squandered so rare a chance for the Restoration. The talk was not unknown to Dukakis, and visitors to his office in the new year found him distracted and depressed, almost, one said, a zombie. He had no spoils to distribute to his handlers, no White House offices or weekends at Camp David, and most of them had abandoned him, Estrich for her professorship at Harvard Law, Sasso for his six-figure salary and his company BMW at Hill, Holliday. For them and most of their colleagues on Chauncy Street, the campaign had become a bad dream best forgotten.

Dukakis had decided against seeking a fourth term as governor in 1990, inviting speculation that he meant to try for president again. In fact, he wanted to and might have begun planning for it, if he had not been deserted by his troops and his fighting spirit. His thoughts seemed to callers to be fixed less on the future than on his doleful immediate past. "They tell me that everybody in Yugoslavia liked me," he said apropos of nothing in the middle of one purely social chat in his office. "I would have won there."

His party had deeper systemic problems, and while the Dukakis campaign brought its own set of debilities to the game, none of those problems had gone away. The Democrats remained by one measure the natural majority party in America, having won 52 percent of the votes for Senate seats and 51 percent in contested House races; against the grain of Bush's victory, they achieved net gains in Congress, in governorships and in the state legislatures. But their record as a presidential party consisted of one fluke victory in the past six elections, and the experience of 1988, as golden as the opportunity had seemed at the beginning, had brought them only marginally closer to finding a path out of the wilderness. Each of the magical remedies prominently in play had, in fact, already been tried at least once: the party had nominated two old-time Washington liberals, one prairie progressive, one Southern moderate and finally one post-ideological technocrat, and each had come swiftly or slowly to grief.

A wing of the party, or rather two mutually exclusive wings, continued to look southward for salvation. Its Washington establishment, older and more Southern, continued pressing the case for a Sam Nunn or a Chuck Robb to bring the renegade Democrats back home; its progressive left, younger and blacker, saw riper possibilities somewhere at the end of Jesse Jackson's rainbow. The record of the past six elections was not encouraging to either group—only Jimmy Carter in pristine condition had prospered in the South since 1964—nor were the geopolitics of 1988. Bush and his adopted Southern values beat Dukakis and his homegrown Southern running mate by eighteen points in the eleven states of the Old Confederacy. His margin in the rest of America was six.

The spreading view among more liberal Democratic professionals was to go north and west instead, and there was evidence in the 1988 returns to support them. Dukakis had done well in the upper-tier industrial states of the East and the Midwest, though not nearly so well as he had to in order to fill his inside straight, and he was the first Democrat since 1968 to win anything at all in the Far West. He bit deeply into Reagan's margins, indeed, in every region *except* the South and in almost every demographic group except Southern white men. A good many of the party's Wednesday-morning quarterbacks believed, indeed, that the Sasso-Corrigan Southern strategy had been a major blunder, leading as it did to the denaturing of Dukakis's message and the selection of a running mate from a state he had no hope of winning. The dominant new word in the trade was, Forget the South, or at least deemphasize it; the Republicans, as the historian Arthur M. Schlesinger Jr. noted, had won every presidential election but two from 1864 to 1912 without it.

The more difficult question than where to go was what to say when you got there. Nothing the Democrats had offered for twenty years had sold except Jimmy Carter's smile, which had seemed to offer probity in the ashes of Watergate and peace in the aftermath of Vietnam. The combatants for the party's soul were divided not only on a North–South but on a left–center axis. The former camp argued for a return to the liberal core values and the traditional base voters of the party's glory days; the latter, notwithstanding the 1988 returns, was still mesmerized by its dreams of recapturing the white middle-class Democrats who had got away in the two decades since the high times ended in the 1960s.

There was even an emerging school in favor of letting Jesse Jackson have the nomination, should he choose to run again. It sprouted not among those true believers who thought he could win but among discouraged liberals who, while they held him in genuine admiration, saw him as a useful human sacrifice—a kamikaze candidate likely to lose everything except the District of Columbia and bring the whole edifice of Democratic power down with him. It was politics in the Götterdämmerung Zone, but, as one of its advocates, the polltaker Paul Maslin, argued, a mass immolation beat wasting slowly away for want of any beliefs at all. Jackson, in his view, could be the Democrats' Barry Goldwater; at least he stood for something, and if it took the party sixteen years to recover, as it had taken the Republicans after the Goldwater debacle, they would crawl out of the ruins stronger and purer of heart.

The further task for the party was catching up with the Republicans at the art and the vocabulary of politics as it was played in 1988: a game come almost wholly under the dominion of professionals at the art of political manipulation. Handlers are by no means new in American politics. Until William Jennings Bryan and Theodore Roosevelt, indeed, handlers *were* the campaign; it was thought unseemly for the candidates to go out begging money and votes in person, and for the first century of our history few ventured much farther afield than their own front porches. Managers went with the territory, whether party leaders or personal friends. William McKinley had his Mark Hanna, Woodrow Wilson his Colonel House, FDR his Felix Frankfurter and Sam Rosenman; even George Washington was rather heavily dependent on Alexander Hamilton to tell *him* what to do now.

Neither were the basic arts, crafts and motives of the trade much different in 1788 or 1888 than now; the object has always been to win, and the means, in a refreshingly blunt corridor saying at Ailes Communications, has usually been whatever it takes. The reductionism of politics to bumper-strip size began long before bumpers, as in "Tippecanoe and Tyler Too," and reached full flower while the Lee Atwaters and John Sassos were in swaddling clothes. "I Like Ike," as the New York consultant David Garth acidly noted, didn't come from the Bible—it came from some smart guy in a room who knew how to crunch words into the most powerful slogan in postwar history. Image-making wasn't born yesterday, either; William Henry Harrison, the log-cabin candidate, owned a mansion, and Honest Abe the Rail Splitter hadn't taken an ax to a rail for years. Negative campaigning has always been a further arrow in the quiver, as Thomas Jefferson could testify from bitter experience. Having already been vilified as a cheat, a thief, a half-breed, a deist and a Jacobin, he was subjected in 1800 to the ultimate low blow: the rumor, briskly traded by John Adams's handlers, that he was dead. He wasn't, and he won.

But the election of 1988 crossed some invisible threshold of pain, a revulsion at the dependence on artifice in both camps and at the resort to the low road in Bush's. The new breed of handlers had been around for a generation and more, their influence growing with the decline of the political parties and the rise of the new technologies of television, polling and direct mail. Douglas Bailey, an early practitioner of the new telepolitics, hung out his shingle in partnership with John Deardourff two decades ago and set out to help people they found worthy—moderate Republicans, for the most part—achieve public office. By the middle 1980s, Bailey was losing his taste for the game. Life, by then, had begun imitating art; the candidates presenting themselves to his and Deardourff's attention were too often into their polls and too seldom concerned with the real business of leadership once they got in office.

The artists who painted ''George Bush'' and ''Mike Dukakis'' were less fastidious; they saw the featurelessness of their clients as an opportunity, a pair of empty canvases inviting court portraits in heightened colors and heroic attitudes. Each studio did its work well in the primary season, one presenting Dukakis as the Massachusetts Miracle Worker, the other displaying Bush as a man of hitherto unappreciated strength and leaderliness. Each camp suspected otherwise, having little confidence in its candidate, but handlers are paid for winning, nor for pleasing their critics or soft-selling their wares. If you're working for George Bush, as Ailes would say afterward, you don't say, ''Ready on day one hundred to be an OK president''—you say, ''Ready on day one to be a *great* president.''

The vice of the spring campaign was fabulism, an old and accepted practice in politics. The hallmarks of the general election were its violence of spirit on one side and its bankruptcy of direction on the other; until Dukakis recostumed himself as a populist for the finale, the match had the raw look of a schoolyard bully punching the class nerd senseless. Professionals in both parties—those, anyway, who were not resident on Chauncy Street—took a rather tolerant view of the proceedings, blaming the punchee for his weakness more than the puncher for his aggression. Handlers tend to have ideals, contrary to their image in the media, but are not so burdened by them as to lose sight of their main purpose in life. Agendas are worthless paper unless you win first, and the wonder of 1988, in their all's-fair view, was not that Bush threw low blows to get where he wanted to go; it was that Dukakis did not answer in kind.

There was little sentiment in the trade for renouncing negative campaigning; the 1988 returns, on the contrary, were taken as confirmation of just how brutally efficient it could be. Its attractions were heightened, in Ed Reilly's ironic view, by the spending limits imposed in the wave of reform after Watergate. If the two rival camps started with finite and roughly equal pots of money, they *had* to look for the most cost-effective ways to move public opinion, and attack advertising, till lately a secondary weapon in most presidential campaigns, had proven its worth; it was, Reilly said, a hell of a lot easier to just start off beating the hell out of the other guy than trying to tell some soft, warm, fuzzy story about yourself.

The public was less forgiving than the tradesmen of politics. Toward the end of the campaign, Reilly's New York firm, Kennan Research & Consulting, did a series of focus groups on contract to the Dukakis campaign and found what its final report called "an extremely high level of frustration" with the palpably low level of the campaign. The alienation of the voters involved in the discussions, mostly swing Democrats, flowed from a sense that neither candidate was addressing the issues that most concerned them. The message, if either man had one, had got drowned out by the mudslinging; the panelists mainly blamed Bush for that, but they regarded *both* contenders as having been " 'managed' and 'handled' to such an extreme degree that they . . . have lost any sense of authenticity."

The campaign was thus finally demeaning to both men, victor and vanquished alike. The day's big winner was None of the Above, since two-thirds of the electorate wished there had been someone better to vote for and half stayed home; the turnout was the lowest since Calvin Coolidge beat John W. Davis in 1924. Bush's charter to govern was conferred on him unlovingly by 27 percent of adult America, the fraction persuaded, on the evidence of the exit polls, that he was the competent man in the field and Dukakis the dangerous liberal. Each candidate thus became the image created for him by Bush's packagers. Bush wore his willingly for a season, then cast it off like old clothing. In the year of the handler, it could fairly be said that the most malleable man won.

Appendix:
The Anatomy of a Victory

The polling appendix: data in the table below chart the progress of the 1988 campaign from Michael Dukakis's crest in the spring and summer to his fall and George Bush's victory in November. The data through August are drawn from surveys by the Gallup Organization. The day-by-day tracking poll in the fall was the work of KRC Hotline.

DATES AND EVENTS	THE RACE BUSH–DUKAKIS	FAVORABLE/UNFAVORABLE BUSH	DUKAKIS
March			
10–12	52–40		
15: Bush wins Illinois primary, cinches nomination.			
April			
19: Dukakis wins New York primary, eliminates Gore.			
21–23	45–43		
26: Dukakis wins Pennsylvania primary.			
May			
3: Dukakis wins Ohio primary.			
10: Dukakis wins West Virginia, Nebraska primaries.			
11: Reagan endorses Bush.			
13–15	38–54	52/41	71/15
18: Bush opposes deal with Noriega.			
27–June 2: The Kennebunkport meetings plan Bush attack strategy.			

DATES AND EVENTS	THE RACE BUSH–DUKAKIS	FAVORABLE/UNFAVORABLE BUSH	DUKAKIS
June			
7: Dukakis wins last primaries, cinches nomination.			
9: Bush launches attack strategy in Houston.			
10–12	38–52	53/40	70/20
18–24: Bush steps up attack on crime, prison furloughs.			
24–26	41–46		
July			
5: Edwin Meese III says he will resign as attorney general.			
8–10	41–47	52/40	57/31
12: Dukakis chooses Bentsen for vice president.			
18–21: The Democratic convention in Atlanta.			
22–24	37–54		
29: Dukakis campaign denies he's had clinical depressions.			
August			
3: Dukakis's doctor gives him clean bill of health.			
5–7	42–49	51/42	61/30
15–18: The Republican convention; Bush chooses Quayle.			
19–21	48–44		
September			
2: Dukakis rehires Sasso.			
5	46–43	53/33	48/34
6	44–43	52/34	48/34
7	44–42	50/34	48/34
8	45–41	50/33	45/36
9	47–39	51/34	44/38
10	48–39	52/32	44/37
11	46–39	51/34	46/36
12	44–42	50/34	46/34
13: Bush's Boston Harbor ad starts.	45–42	49/35	45/35

DATES AND EVENTS	THE RACE	FAVORABLE/UNFAVORABLE	
	BUSH–DUKAKIS	BUSH	DUKAKIS
14	46–42	49/34	43/37
15	48–39	53/32	41/38
16	49–38	55/29	40/38
17	49–38	55/30	42/37
18	48–39	52/32	44/35
19	46–40	50/33	45/34
20: Bush's flag-factory visit—"a flag too far."	46–40	51/34	45/35
21	44–40	51/33	44/35
22	45–39	51/34	43/37
23	46–40	51/33	44/36
24	48–39	50/32	42/37
25: Bush and Dukakis debate in Winston-Salem.	50–38	50/31	40/35
26	50–38	48/31	40/34
27	48–41	48/32	44/32
28	47–42	49/32	45/34
29	46–41	52/33	45/37
30: The first Dukakis packaging ads start.	47–41	53/33	43/40
October			
1	47–40	52/34	42/41
2	48–40	52/33	40/40
3: Bush's Revolving-Door prison ad starts.	48–40	50/33	41/38
4	48–40	52/33	41/37
5: Bentsen and Quayle debate in Omaha.	49–39	52/32	42/37
6	48–39	54/30	41/39
7	48–39	53/30	42/39
8	48–40	53/32	42/38
9	48–42	52/35	43/38
10	48–41	51/35	41/39
11	48–40	52/34	41/41
12	48–39	51/33	40/42
13: Bush and Dukakis debate in Los Angeles.	47–41	53/33	42/42
14	48–40	52/34	40/42
15	47–39	52/32	40/40
16	48–39	51/32	40/41

DATES AND EVENTS	THE RACE	FAVORABLE/UNFAVORABLE	
	BUSH—DUKAKIS	BUSH	DUKAKIS
17	47–40	53/32	41/41
18	49–39	54/32	41/43
19: Bush's Tank ad starts.	49–39	55/32	41/43
20	50–39	55/32	42/43
21	51–38	55/32	42/42
22	52–39	55/33	42/42
23	51–38	54/33	41/42
24: Dukakis starts his talk-show blitz and his ''On Your Side'' counterattack.	50–40	53/34	41/42
25	51–40	53/35	41/44
26	50–39	55/33	41/43
27	49–37	53/33	40/41
28	49–36	53/32	38/43
29	49–37	50/35	39/42
30: Dukakis says, ''Yes, I am a liberal.''	50–36	51/35	38/45
31	49–38	49/37	40/44
November			
1	48–39	49/37	40/45
2	48–40	49/38	42/44
3	47–39	51/36	41/43
4	48–40	52/35	42/43
5	48–39	54/34	43/44
6	49–40	54/36	43/45
7	49–40	55/36	45/45
8: Election Day.	48–42	53/37	45/44

Index

Abbott, Will, 259, 263
Ackerman, Annie, 147
Ailes, Roger, 184, 190–96, 197–99, 200,
   256, 263, 264, 299, 301, 304, 305,
   309, 318, 319, 323, 324, 328, 331,
   351, 355, 356, 360, 361–62, 363,
   364–65, 366, 370–71, 376, 377–78,
   379, 390, 395, 398–99, 400, 417
Anderson, John B., 46, 79–80
Arafat, Yasir, 162
Arendt, Hannah, 207–8
Armandt, Lynn, 83, 90
Atwater, Lee, 182–83, 185, 187, 188,
   191–92, 198, 201, 223, 225, 228–29,
   230, 231, 236, 237, 251–52, 258–59,
   260, 263, 264, 265, 266, 267, 268,
   278, 279–82, 283, 284, 293, 295, 299,
   300, 301, 304, 306, 307, 309, 313,
   318, 319, 325, 337, 356, 359, 365,
   379, 382, 391, 397, 398, 407, 408,
   409, 413, 416
Atwater, Toddy, 279
Axelrod, David, 119, 122, 129

Babbitt, Bruce, 43, 48, 55, 59, 77, 98,
   101–5, 144, 178
Babbitt, Hattie, 102
Baker, Howard, Jr., 37, 215–16
Baker, James A., III, 182, 205, 263,
   289, 294, 296, 304, 308–9, 311–12,
   313, 315, 317, 318, 320, 321–23,
   322–23, 325, 326, 327, 329, 355, 359,
   370, 371, 372, 373, 379, 380, 381,
   384, 385–86, 390, 397, 401, 407,
   410, 411, 413
Barnett, Bob, 375, 376
Beatty, Warren, 85, 95
Beckel, Bob, 168, 342
Bendixen, Sergio, 101, 102, 103, 104
Bentsen, Lloyd, 170, 171, 172, 178,
   297, 371, 372, 381–87
Biden, Joseph R., Jr., 42, 43, 46, 82,
   96, 105–10, 112, 118, 119, 123
Bidinotto, Robert James, 306
Black, Charlie, 183, 205, 206, 312, 395
Blackshaw, John, 391–92, 406
Bograd, Paul, 161, 344